Why Managers and Companies Take Risks

Contributions to Management Science

Les Coleman

Why Managers and Companies Take Risks

With 24 Figures
and 46 Tables

Physica-Verlag

A Springer Company

658.155
C 69 w

Series Editors
Werner A. Müller
Martina Bihn

Author
Dr. Les Coleman
Department of Finance
The University of Melbourne
Parkville. Victoria 3010
Australia
les.coleman@unimelb.edu.au

Publication of this work was assisted by a publication grant from the University of Melbourne.

ISSN 1431-1941
ISBN-10   3-7980-1695-7   Physica-Verlag Heidelberg New York
ISBN-13   978-3-7908-1695-2   Physica-Verlag Heidelberg New York

Physica-Verlag is a part of Springer Science+Business Media
springer.com

© Physica-Verlag Heidelberg 2006
Printed in Germany

The use of general descriptive names, registered names, trademarks, etc. in this publication does not imply, even in the absence of a specific statement, that such names are exempt from the relevant protective laws and regulations and therefore free for general use.

Typesetting: Camera ready by author
Cover Design: Erich Kirchner, Heidelberg
Production: LE-TEX, Jelonek, Schmidt & Vöckler GbR, Leipzig

SPIN 11668084   Printed on acid-free paper – 88/3100 – 5 4 3 2 1 0

Preface

This book uses risk in its dictionary meaning as the probability of an undesirable outcome, and has two research questions: when managers make decisions, what leads them to choose a risky alternative? and: what determines whether the decision proves correct? Answers to these questions form a model of decision making that explains the process and results of managers' risk-taking in the real world.

There is an extensive literature on risk and decision making because the topic has been of interest in many disciplines since at least the 18th century. Thus insights on the research questions are available from studies of animals, humans and organisations; and have been drawn by scholars in biology, psychology, finance and management. Even so, there is a large gap as most studies are conducted away from corporate settings and use subjects with limited decision experience. The few studies set in real-world conditions tend to concentrate on just a single aspect of decision makers' attributes, setting and behaviour, and on either decision choices or outcomes. The empirical work in this book is designed to fill part of this gap.

My specific purpose is to integrate a wide spectrum of decision features and provide a seamless link between decision maker, environment and outcomes in relation to non-diversifiable risks associated with the decisions of individual managers. A model is developed from the literature which indicates that the main determinants of individuals' risk-taking are personality, decision making style and expectations in regard to the outcome. This theoretical model is then quantified using a hypothetical business decision which records decision maker attributes and examines why they take a risky alternative or not. A second survey records the attributes of executives and their organisations, and uses this material to explain financial results and crisis frequencies in terms of decision maker attributes, industry and organisation characteristics, and organisational environment and risk practices. Thus conclusions are drawn from representative real-world data through surveys of experienced managers.

The materials address the organisation-level topic of risk-taking by managers, and point to strategies for organisations to dial up the right level of risk. Conclusions from the research are presented as an extended explanation of the causes and consequences of risk-taking; a new model of decision making called Risk Budget Theory; and a manager oriented guide to developing risk-based strategy. This extends the scope of risk management which – in Australia, at least – has largely addressed workplace hazards or provided defences for Boards against potential litigation. Apart from the book's contribution to management theory, the holistic description of managers' real-world decision making has applicability to practising managers, and the explanation of corporate results will interest investors.

This book had its origins in a casual remark by a colleague who suggested that many people would be interested in whether risk was rising or falling. In my ignorance of risk, the answer seemed obvious. However, it proved anything but; and launched me into a decade of fascination with a topic that has engaged researchers for centuries.

Since Murray Cliffe's observation, many people have generously helped with insights, ideas, comments and feedback. Professor Danny Samson, who supervised my research for the PhD thesis which formed the basis of this book, has been generous with his time and expertise: this book has greatly benefited from his input. Professor Ira Horowitz also made valuable comments. Professor Rob Brown and other Finance faculty at the University of Melbourne have provided great assistance and encouragement. Other academic colleagues – particularly Mitch Casselman, Victor del Rio, and Dayna Simpson – provided rich support, as have friends at ExxonMobil and other organisations who kept my research relevant to management.

I appreciate the assistance of Springer in progressing this work, and acknowledge a grant from the University of Melbourne that facilitated its publication.

I am particularly grateful to Sue, Lou, Georgie and Robbie who were interested and supportive of this research, as were a wide circle of family and friends who provided continuous help and encouragement. Naturally all errors and omissions are mine.

January 2006   Les Coleman

Contents

CHAPTER 1   Introduction

"To avoid all mistakes in the conduct of great enterprises is beyond man's powers"
Plutarch, *Lives: Fabius*

Management can be reduced to the task of serial decision making, frequently in unfamiliar areas. When risk is defined as the possibility of a significant, adverse outcome, successful management requires correct choices in the face of uncertainty. Thus management skill is a function of analysis, foresight and risk evaluation.

This book focuses on the last competency and seeks to answer two simple questions: when individual decision makers – particularly managers – face choices, what makes them prefer a risky alternative? And: what determines whether the decision proves correct? To take concrete examples: why do some managers conduct in-house research and development, whilst others purchase developed technologies? when decisions are post-audited, what leads a few mergers and acquisitions to succeed, whilst most fail? why are some firms crisis-prone, whilst others prove trouble-free?

This book's focus is on the top level of organisations, particularly on the causes and consequences of risk-taking by managers, and on the strategies that organisations can employ to dial up the right level of risk.

This chapter sets the scene for the book as a whole and proceeds in four parts. The first amplifies the questions above to describe the `research problems' which are tackled, and the next section outlines the strategy followed. The third section describes the contribution of the book; whilst the chapter closes with an outline of general strands in the literature to put the book in the context of existing thought.

Research Problems Tackled by this Book

Bewley (2002: 343) wrote that "the most fundamental elements of economic life are the decisions made by its participants" and then observed that explanatory models are "inappropriate". According to Huber and

Kühberger (1996: 329): "most of the experimental results on the risky behavior of individuals have been in reference to simple gambles... [But] behavior in the gambling tasks differed systematically from that in the natural-decision tasks."

It is hard to envisage a larger research target than an important discipline whose fundamental elements lack an appropriate explanatory model. And it is hard to envisage a larger research void than an important behaviour that is being incorrectly investigated. This book uses real-world data to tackle part of the research target, specifically the mechanisms which lead managers to select risky alternatives and the financial and risk implications of these decisions.

Two common threads link materials in this book: consideration of risk in its dictionary meaning as the probability of an undesirable outcome; and behavioural economics (especially natural decision making)[1].

Behavioural economics (BE), which incorporated psychology into economics, emerged in the 1950s through the efforts of scholars including Richard Cyert, Herbert Simon and James March [Augier and March (2002)]. They encouraged wholesale rejection of the normative economic assumption that individuals operate rationally to ensure their behaviour is optimised. The eclectic discipline sought to explain real-world economic behaviour, rather than advancing proscriptive solutions, and the term behavioural economics came into common use after 1980 [Gilad et al. (1984)]. The state of thinking of this fascinating discipline is well described by Kahneman (2003) and Camerer and Loewenstein (2004).

A study of individuals' risk-taking behaviour (such as set out here) would not be important so long as the dominant normative assumption of expected utility (EU) held true. Under expected utility, decision makers choose the best probability-weighted outcome from all available choices. Markets ensure that equilibrium prices are derived for the present value of the expected outcomes. To the extent that decisions (including market prices) do not maximise expected utility, there is an opportunity for a utility-optimiser to generate profit.

---

[1] *Behavioural Economics* lacks an agreed definition, but a good example is provided by Mullainathan and Thaler (2000: 1): "the combination of psychology and economics that investigates what happens in markets in which some of the agents display human limitations and complications." *Natural Decision Making* involves experienced decision makers in field settings where decisions are not routine. These are investors and managers, airline pilots and fire chiefs whose decisions involve a struggle with complexity, lack of data and poorly known risks. Their decisions have urgency, immediacy and serious consequences. According to Meso et al. (2002: 64) natural decision making is "how people use their experience to make decisions in complex, dynamic real-time environments."

The self-correcting features of this process were clear to Evans (1997) who found that individuals' anomalous behaviour was reduced when they are placed in a market setting, presumably because markets are sufficiently large to eliminate any irrational biases, either by smoothing them or applying the error-correcting power of rational participants.

Under assumptions of EU, no matter how interesting it might be to understand individual decision making, the knowledge is of little economic relevance. This view dates to at least the 1980 opinion of Schumpeter [Machlup (1978: 465)]:

"It is methodologically mistaken for economics to deal with ... the motives of human conduct ... A relationship between the value functions which the economist must assume and certain psychological or physiological facts may well exist, but this relationship is only of philosophical interest. For the economic results it is irrelevant and can never be the task of the economist to go into these matters."

This explains how the results of behavioural studies can be dismissed by macro-economists as merely pointing up the mechanics of individual decisions, rather than displaying revealed preferences which are critical, especially to market valuations. It also explains why behavioural economics is outside the mainstream of the discipline[2], and has not yet been widely taken up in the management literature.

Despite patchy coverage elsewhere, behavioural economics has found considerable application in finance. This is because of its measurable impact on markets, the availability of good data to conduct tests, and strong incentives to find explanations. For instance, De Bondt and Thaler (1990: 57) point to extremes in market swings and analysts' forecasts and conclude there is no alternative but "to take seriously the behavioural explanations of anomalous financial market outcomes." Another motivation is the growth in retirement savings and savers' preference for mutual funds which is increasing the dominance of markets by professional investors: in theory, this should make individual biases less important. However, the evidence shows that investment professionals are subject to behavioural biases [Shapira and Venezia (2001)], and so their garnering of market power may exacerbate anomalies. The evidence is clear that decisions of individuals contribute to biases which are able to distort markets (even quite significantly, for instance through formation of bubbles). And, of course, biases are important in corporate finance when individuals make major decisions such as in takeovers. Thus it has become impossible to

---

[2] A still tentative alternative view comes from Berg (2003: 412) who argues that "major themes in behavioural economics ... now fit comfortably into most major journals in economics...[although] it has not been accompanied by a new normative framework for analysing policy."

sustain the comfortable assumption that individuals' behavioural biases are irrelevant to finance and management.

A second justification for dismissing individuals' behavioural biases is that they only affect the demand side of markets. Supply side impacts, however, are increasingly evident. For instance, investors are more willing to sell assets (such as stocks and houses) which have been profitable than they are to sell equivalent assets which have returned a loss [Odean (1998)]; evidence also shows that transactions depend on their assets' price path [Heath et al. (1999)].

Decision making is clearly far more than a clinical calculation using rational methodology. Thus an important question raised by this book is the extent to which risk and systematic deviations from profit maximisation should be incorporated into formal decision making models. Some authors believe it is necessary to correct irrational decision making, and they advocate more intensive teaching of normative decision models such as expected utility.

The opposite view is advanced by Raiffa (1961: 692) who pointed to the "need to teach people how to cope with uncertainty in a purposive and reflective manner." In addition there are valid reasons why stakeholders would prefer managers to actively control operational risk. And – as discussed by Berg (2003) – there are situations in markets where non-optimising decisions ('anomalies') can have positive consequences. Moreover context can be critical to risk: what is an appropriate decision for a hedge fund may not be appropriate for a charity.

This book assumes that decision makers act rationally when facing risks; that their approach has behavioural, economic and social elements; and that the results of their decisions are economically important at the level of individuals, firms and markets. The book also finds significant shortcomings in the considerable body of work published on risk and decision making. In particular there is not a satisfactory model of how people make decisions which is both predictive and consistent with evolutionary pressures to accumulate knowledge and optimise outcomes[3].

The significance and breadth of the influences of risk on decision making offer major challenges in the recognition, analysis and consummation

---

[3] There is a longstanding association between finance and biology. Malthus (1798, reprinted 1973) linked the biology of population growth to the economics of natural resource supply; Schumpeter (1939) adopted a Darwinian view of business cycles with his description of capitalist development as an evolutionary process incorporating natural selection and punctuated equilibria. Nelson and Winter (1982) arguably popularised the modern association between evolution and economics, and encouraged Hodgson (1995) to collect 30 key papers charting the post-1950 emergence of biological analogies in economics.

of a decision. So for this book to have a manageable topic, the focus has been reduced to two simple research questions.

The first research question is: when individual decision makers – particularly managers – face multiple choices, what makes them adopt a risky alternative? In specific terms:

- what elements of behavioural economics help to explain decision making by individuals in real-world settings?
- how applicabile are published theories to managers' decision making, especially Prospect Theory?
- what are the relative influences of the decision facts, the personality and other attributes of managers, institutional setting and culture, and risk environment?
- which models are best able to explain managers' decisions?
- what is the role of experts in decision making under risk?

The second research question is: what determines whether managers' choice of a risky alternative proves successful? Again this can be broken into specifics:

- what features of decision makers and organisations explain the occurrence of crises and serious incidents?
- is there a linear relationship between firm risk and return?
- which of published models explain the relationship between risk and financial performance of companies?
- what are the relative influences on firm returns of managers' characteristics, corporate structure, industry parameters, and risk environment?

This book seeks a solution to these research questions by developing a decision making model to explain the behaviour of individuals under risk; and then examining its implications. The strategic objectives of the approach are to:

- Take a real-world view of risk by using its common, dictionary meaning as the chance of bad consequences or loss (*Oxford Dictionary* defines risk as "hazard, chance of or of bad consequences, loss, etc, exposure to mischance").
- Focus on risky decisions without assuming that decision makers treat gains and losses symmetrically, nor that they place them on a continuum
- Separate the process of decision making followed by individuals (especially managers) from that used by organisations. Previous work commingled the two, and ran into difficulties over risk preferences which can be determined *ex ante* for individuals (by interviews and questionnaires at the time of decision), but not for organisations

(where risk attitude is usually measured *ex post* by a proxy related to variation in accounting or market measures)

- Replicate real-world decision making by heterogeneous individuals rather than measuring less representative responses of homogenous, naive subjects.
- Include a large number of independent variables in an initial screen of the drivers of decision making under risk, and so guard against the hypothesis myopia that has plagued a number of models
- Be multidisciplinary and draw the best contributions from a variety of studies by researchers in the natural and social sciences. Lopes (1994: 198) warned against a uni-disciplinary approach: "just as psychologists construe the world in ways to fit it to the lab, economists construe the world in ways to make it mathematically tractable." Although risky decision making by investors and managers should notionally be the preserve of economic theory, the issue and its consequences are "much too serious to be left to economists" [McClelland (1961: 12)].

The analysis owes a large intellectual debt to six pioneering works[4]:

1. `Timid Choices and Bold Forecasts: A cognitive perspective on risk taking' by Kahneman and Lovallo (1993) which explains how managers can misjudge decision outcomes
2. `Characteristics of Risk Taking Executives' by MacCrimmon and Wehrung (1990) which used a survey of 509 senior business executives to examine differences in the socio-economic characteristics of those who take risks and those who avoid them.
3. `Managerial Perspectives on Risk and Risk Taking' by March and Shapira (1987) which was published in *Management Science*
4. `The Expected Utility Model: Its variants, purposes, evidence and limitations' by Schoemaker (1982) which provides an illuminating evaluation of one of decision making's most important tools
5. `Performance, Slack and Risk Taking in Organisational Decision Making' by Singh (1986) which was published in the *Academy of Management Journal*.
6. `Determinants of Risky Decision-making Behaviour: A test of the mediating role of risk perceptions and propensity' by Sitkin and Weingart (1995) which was published in the *Academy of Management Journal*.

---

[4] In mid 2003, the ICI Web of Science citation database listed 132, 43, 210, 349, 148 and 44 citations, respectively, for these papers.

The Analytical Strategy of this Book

Economics has four principal techniques to describe the way people reach decisions when facing risk or uncertainty. The first is a normative depiction of what should happen, and is typified by the subject-free thought experiments of Bernoulli (1738, translated 1954) and Ellsberg (1961). The second technique uses mathematics to codify the outcome. Good examples are provided in finance by the Capital Asset Pricing Model (CAPM) and Black-Scholes option pricing model. The third – and arguably most topical – approach uses laboratory experiments to develop descriptive models such as those of Kahneman and Tversky (1979). The fourth technique studies the act of natural decision making and builds models that describe real-world behaviours and outcomes.

This book follows the last technique and proceeds through two broad stages. The first is to describe what is known about how individuals make decisions when facing risk. Given my intent to develop a unified model of the influence of risk on decision making, the literature search covered numerous disciplines: human and animal behaviour, financial markets data, and management and social sciences. The resulting 'material' includes experimental studies and field evaluations; old theories, and new concepts such as enterprise risk management; and studies from psychology, engineering and mathematics as well as economics and management.

The first figure summarises my approach.

The literature survey provides lessons from: studies of human behaviour and its interpretation by biologists and psychologists; animal behavioural studies; and analyses of human decisions at the individual level (e.g. merger transactions) and aggregated in equity and other financial markets. Decision models are drawn from traditional disciplines of economics and psychology, and use is made of advances in other disciplines such as engineering, mathematics and law. The disparate literature and existing models are combined to develop a revised model of risk and decision making which is then validated using tailored surveys of executives. The result gives the ability to project the outcome of risk-sensitive decisions and so form expectations of future risk.

The first part of the literature survey identified the process by which a decision is reached. As noted by Schoemaker (1982), this includes how the facts of a decision are understood and processed; what information is incorporated in the decision process, and the way it is sought and analysed; and how conflicts are resolved. This goes beyond a description of the ideal process where decision makers are well informed, understand their situation and alternatives, target economic optimisation and are purposively rational. Alchian (1950: 211) pointed out that even though such "unrealistic postulates" typify post-War economic methodology, they cannot be assumed for real-world decisions which are characterised by incomplete information and less than robust analysis.

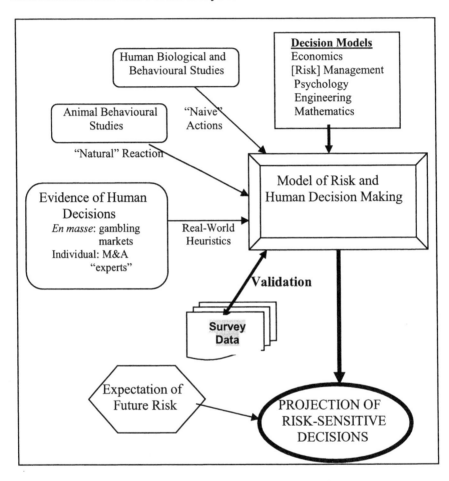

Fig. 1.1. Constructing a Risk and Decision Making Model

The second element of the literature search is to actively seek out evidence to support the mechanisms identified. My aim is to collect a representative sample of materials which describe the process surrounding decision making by individuals when facing decisions with risky alternatives in the real world.

Unfortunately most empirical studies examining decision making deal with known probabilities, or what Knight (1921) called probabilistic risk.

Data are derived from experiments in unreal settings such as laboratories using unrepresentative decisions such as fair gambles with dice and the like. Experiments are qualitatively different to all real-world decisions (bar those in games of pure chance) which involve uncertain outcomes whose statistical distribution is not known. According to Fox and Tversky (1998: 881), "there is ample evidence that people's intuitive probability judgements are often inconsistent with the laws of chance." Allais (1988: 274) was similarly critical of what he termed a 'fundamental gap' in research and asked rhetorically: "how can the validity of axioms and their implications be tested without referring to observed facts?" Without belabouring the point, there is room to doubt the extent to which traditional risk-based experimental studies can be generalised to real-world behaviours.

A further concern about many research materials is the homogeneity of their subjects: a surprisingly high proportion of studies rely upon responses solely from undergraduate students. Perhaps because the use of these homogenous, naïf subjects is so experimentally convenient, researchers rarely discuss the inevitable bias to results. Only a handful of studies have compared large enough samples of students and more representative subjects to give a statistically meaningful comparison. A good example is provided by Frederick (2003) who tested intergenerational time preferences using 158 Pittsburgh jurors and 243 undergraduates at the University of Arizona and Carnegie Mellon University. He found consistent differences between the two groups in all measures, and one third were statistically significant ($p<0.05$). A similar conclusion was reached by Potters and van Winden (2000) who compared the responses of 142 students and 30 public affairs professionals. They concluded that there were significant differences ($p<0.1$) in the decisions of the two groups. Schoemaker and Kunreuther (1979) studied the insurance decisions of 201 undergraduates and 101 insurance buyers and found significant differences in risk attitudes (students were more risk prone), and in decision making style.

The need to obtain representative, preferably real-world, evidence also recognises the arguments of Friedman (1953) and Machlup (1978) that economic theories are only valid if they are able to accurately predict (or at least explain) behaviour which has not been used in constructing the model. This avoids data-mining of the type which *ex post* rationalises observed experimental behaviour; and it eschews normative descriptions which explain away any inconsistencies or violations as anomalies, or due to confounding data. The latter approaches mean that no 'law' can ever be disproven: each is merely tautological; and prediction is impossible.

A good example of the way that anomalies are rationalised away is the concept of satisficing which Simon (1955) advanced to explain how humans are prevented from optimising their decisions because of a shortage of time, data, computational capacity and so on. Decision makers are boundedly rational and abandon further effort when the cost of obtaining information exceeds a threshold. Another example is the extensive catalogue of evidence that decision makers do not make sensible decisions [e.g. Rabin (1998)]: most are dismissed as decision shortcuts that induce cognitive illusions in people (and animals), rather than analysed for evidence of purposeful decision intent.

The approach here assumes that real-world decisions have a logical basis, and collects empirical data to develop a comprehensive decision making model. Two types of dataset are available. The first is obtained by examining individuals' hypothetical or actual decisions, and collects data by intensive study such as surveys of subjects' *ex ante* characteristics and expectations. The second method considers the aggregated outcomes of many similar decisions which have been made at the enterprise or market level such as in market trading[5].

Despite the superficial attractiveness of real-world settings, these approaches still suffer from several deficiencies. First they address only a single decision in isolation: what should I do in this particular case? This ignores the editing process which preceded or even triggered the decision (that is, not everyone gambles, invests, or holidays overseas). In addition, analyses can be only ever be partially alert to all situational parameters, which means the impact of some salient forces may not be recognised. A third deficiency is that the approaches cannot control the decision context and stimuli: thus they have difficulty in precisely calibrating risks, probabilities and outcomes.

Perhaps most importantly, it is not always easy to precisely titrate what is the 'real world' and what is not. A laboratory experiment involving students in a hypothetical gamble is not; and examining the actual performance of companies in light of their characteristics is. However, this does not imply that all laboratory experiments should be dismissed as artificial; nor that the results of all field experiments be accepted uncritically. As Schoemaker (1982) points out, a valid decision making model will be used successfully in experimental settings. Distinctions are even more complicated in the grey area of hypothetical decisions. Tsevat et al. (1995), for instance, evaluated the health values of seriously ill, hospitalised patients using the following question: 'would you prefer living one year in your

---

[5] A further extension is possible where firms are driven in accordance with the assumptions of rational principal-actor models. This compiles *ex post* outcomes, typically financial results, and analyses them in the light of managers' attributes and firm characteristics (e.g. size, market, governance).

current state of health or 11 months in excellent health?' Is this realistic? What if the patient's physician or family are asked about their preference?

For simplicity, my view is that real-world studies must involve subjects who are experienced decision makers and present decisions in a natural manner using material that is relevant to subjects' experience. Moreover, evidence which is most valued will come from settings which approximate real-world circumstances. Because it can be challenging to lay down hard guidelines on what is 'real-world' and what is 'artificial', the merit of evidence is determined by its representativeness, rather than its context.

The complex issues surrounding risk and decision making make it tempting to concentrate the literature survey around a single discipline. But cursory reading shows that a fragmented approach will not adequately address such a complex topic where the individual and market, process and mathematical model, risk and reward circle each other like sets of twin suns. It is not possible to understand decision making without using multiple disciplines to examine both the decision stimuli and the decision makers' personal attributes.

It proved a significant challenge to synthesise knowledge from a variety of disparate paradigms and intellectual traditions. The result incorporates assumptions, conclusions and methodologies which often conflict, and have rarely been integrated. As a stark example, psychologists studying decision making focus on the person and process; whereas economists focus on the aggregate outcomes; and engineers and lawyers look at specific outcomes, particularly failures. Thus psychologists' models of decision making look like road maps or how-to guides, whilst economists compile pages of complex formulae. In epistemological terms, this is the conflict between anti-positivists and positivists who, respectively, see the world as comprehensible only from an individual's unique position, or as subject to depiction by causal relationships [Burrell and Morgan (1985)].

The goal of the literature search is to develop a model of decision making which can be empirically validated, and used to make at least qualitative predictions. The model is required to be testable, and provide guidance on how behaviours – particularly in management – change under shifting risks.

The second stage of the book's analysis is to validate the model and use real-world data to examine the implications of risk-taking behaviour by managers. The empirical analysis is largely intensive in the form of surveys as this gives sufficient granularity in responses to examine the influence on decision making of individual differences.

Such intensive methods suffer from a number of deficiencies. One is the *Hawthorne Effect* where simply observing behaviour can possibly change it [Mayo (1933)]. Intensive studies must also recognise the Soros (1994)

Theory of Reflexivity in which systems with thinking participants are shaped by decision makers' actions. These concerns are exacerbated by the ethical research requirement for informed consent: describing the research proposal effectively frames the subjects' responses. Moreover surveys merely recognise patterns in subjects' reports and their validity relies upon the goodwill of participants. In a socially sensitive area such as risk and decisions, there is no guarantee that subjects' responses will reflect their true preferences.

Another deficiency is that – although the surveys are wide-ranging – they are not designed to evaluate the processes of making a decision, and hence are blind to the quality of risk-taking. In addition, the surveys do not consider operational risks such as workplace hazards and similar safety issues which are clearly important given the report by Studdert (2004) that a quarter of workplace accidents are associated with drugs or alcohol.

To counter possible biases in the preferred data collection strategy, two surveys are used so that hypotheses can be confirmed by independent datasets. This protects against the concern discussed above that some economic theories merely explain the data which have been used in constructing the model: the conclusions are tautological in developing *ex post* rationalisations of observed experimental behaviour.

Despite some limitations, the strategy followed by this book ensures that its findings have important strengths, especially: strong grounding in the literature, including results of empirical studies; linkage between the various research tools to ensure internal consistency of findings; explicit tie-ins to independent, published statistics; strong emphasis on real-world decisions so that decision makers are operating in a familiar environment without artificial distortions; and use of heterogeneous samples of experienced decision makers. This should develop and test hypotheses in a realistic environment.

Whilst this approach appears logical, developing the model involved a fragmented approach of gathering data from numerous sources. To facilitate the reader's monitoring of the research process, figure 1.2 uses an approach suggested by Holloway (1979) to show the overall framework of the book.

Essentially risk and decision making are each analysed in parallel by means of a literature survey and empirical research. The results lead to the three contributions shown in heavy boxes – an update of Applied Behavioural Economics, Risk Budget Theory, and Enterprise Level Risk Strategy – which are discussed in the following section.

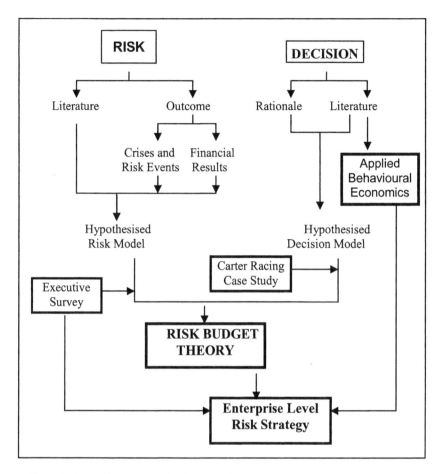

Fig. 1.2. Overall Framework of the Book

Chapters three and four cover the literature on risk and decision making by individuals, while chapter five covers the influence of risk taking by organisations on their performance. Chapter six reviews published models on risk and decision making to develop the hypothesised model discussed in chapter seven. The basis of the two surveys is discussed in chapter seven and results are provided in chapter eight. Chapter nine synthesises material from the literature survey and empirical analyses. Chapter ten reviews Risk Budget Theory whilst chapter eleven covers applied behavioural economics and enterprise level risk strategy.

The Contribution of this Book

The contribution of this book is to improve our understanding of the mechanisms and consequences of risky decision making by individuals, especially managers. This is relevant for two reasons. First risk is topical. A recent cover story in the magazine *Business Review Weekly* [17 April 2003] was subtitled: "Obsessed with corporate governance, company boards are afraid to take risks." And Chair of CSIRO, the Australian government funded research body, Catherine Livingstone has pointed to the 'risk paradox' where voters are becoming more risk averse just when greater risk is required to tap increasingly beneficial new technologies [Livingstone (2002)].

The second reason to address risk is its centrality to microeconomics and its importance in management theory. Risk-taking by individuals (and by all but the largest organisations) is not diversifiable in the manner assumed in modern capital markets theory: decisions frequently result in a single risk:reward trade-off and lack a clear probability distribution. As a result, risky decisions hold the potential for financial catastrophe. Given that most of the individuals examined in the research here are managers, the principal-agent interaction means their decisions impact on the risk: reward trade-offs of their employer. The research strategy specifically addresses this topic, and determines the importance to firm success of good risk-taking (as opposed to the importance of strategy and structure as depicted in, for instance, the Porter (1980) competitive model).

A further contribution of the book is to unify knowledge from a variety of disciplines which – because it has been developed virtually independently – remains fragmented. Relevant literature is spread across animal behaviour, economics (accounting, finance and management), engineering, and psychology. There are also useful concepts and applications in fields as far apart as anthropology, politics, law and sociology. Although there have been some sporadic attempts to unify parts of this knowledge (e.g. economics and psychology by economists Simon (1955) and Rabin (1998), and by psychologists Edwards (1954) and Lopes (1994)), the disciplines have generally not communicated their understanding and unique insights.

This book has the generic goals of linking disparate literatures on risk and decision making, and providing useful guidance on the topic for managers who might wish to strategically influence their level of risk. Its specific goal is to contribute to improved knowledge through: summarising and extending empirical data, particularly on the population of risky decisions, the outcomes of risky decisions, and risk management practices; evaluating the influence of demographic and personality measures on risk propensity, and explaining their action; using heterogeneous subjects in representative settings to examine the motivations, goals and results of risky decision making by individuals and organisations; and developing an improved model of decision making that is able to accommodate influences on individuals such as differences in personality, assets, and overall portfolio of risks.

These contributions are drawn together in the final chapters under three themes: Risk Budget Theory of Decision Making; Applied Behavioural Economics; and Enterprise-Level Risk Strategy. A brief summary follows of each so that their development can be traced through the literature review and empirical studies.

Key to the Risk Budget Theory of Decision Making (RBT) are conclusions that decision makers: are subject to bounded rationality; make decisions in stages; use reference levels to divide outcomes into losses and gains; feel a loss more than the equivalent gain; treat separate decisions as a sequence and mentally account for net moves above and below the reference level; and are loss-averse in that they avoid a net losing outcome. In addition, they pay minimal attention to outcome probabilities and do not follow a logical process of comparing alternatives; nor do they have stable risk attitudes, but rank alternatives by their utility (which is efficiently described by an exponential function).

RBT proposes that decision makers simplify their task by using a risk budget, ρ, which is a function of the sum they are prepared to lose at any point in time. The budget is a unique function of the decision maker's personality, endowment and context. As decisions proceed through a sequence, decision makers accumulate their net change in endowment, and – when further decisions are offered – deduct potential losses from the accumulated position: if this revised outcome produces a loss greater than the risk budget, it is rejected; if the worst outcome does not blow the risk budget, then the decision is assessed on its merits. Decision makers whose net loss position exceeds the risk budget will either take no action, or – if strongly loss averse – will select an alternative whose outcome will wipe out accumulated losses, irrespective of the risks involved. The theory is applicable to all forms of endowment ranging from wealth to health and prestige.

The book also provides a partial update of *Applied Behavioural Economics* (ABE), which is a term coined by Maital (1988) in his introduction to a volume of conference proceedings that provided empirical results of relevance to managers and policy makers, and addressed issues as diverse as productivity, labour relations, and tax evasion. Although not widely studied as a formal discipline, ABE sits astride the real-world interface between psychology and markets where minds meet dollars, and its knowledge base has expanded rapidly following developments in animal behaviour, psychology and economics; and through derivative models from fields including law, medicine, and politics. This book seeks to draw together many relevant studies of ABE to provide representative evidence to support decision theories.

Enterprise-Level Risk Strategy uses recent findings from behavioural research to update previous concepts of corporate risk strategy, and provides empirical support through field research into executives' attitudes towards risk. The result is a comprehensive approach to corporate risk strategy which covers manager selection, risk philosophy, measures of organisation risk, and financial consequences. The Strategy should allow organisations to better educate their managers about influences on risk-taking, involve appropriate staff in risky decision making, and evaluate exposures to potential crises.

This Book in Context of the Literature

Because decision making underpins our whole commercial structure and is driven in large measure by perceptions, risky decision making is an important behaviour which has long attracted interest from many research fields. Milestones in building its truly vast scope are well reviewed by Simon (1959), Yates (1990) and Svenson (1996).

Today it is possible to discern eight important themes in the literature related to managerial risk and decision making:

1. Decision theory is made most relevant by drawing on a variety of disciplines and by learning from observations in natural settings. Those relevant to risk are typified in the paper 'Prospect Theory in the Wild: Evidence from the field' by Camerer (1998). Other learnings from a useful natural risk laboratory – racetrack betting markets – have been captured by Schnytzer et al. (2002) and Vaughan Williams (1999).
2. Psychologists have developed an extensive literature on risk. Kogan and Wallach (1964) established the yardstick with their book *Risk Taking – A study in cognition and personality*, whilst modern treatments include Trimpop (1994) *The Psychology of Risk Taking Behavior* and Lopes (1994) 'Psychology and Economics – Perspectives on risk, cooperation and the marketplace'.
3. The last few decades have seen emergence of a catalogue of examples which show that people do not follow normative economic assumptions, particularly maximisation of their utility. The key issues are brought out by Barberis and Thaler (2002) in 'A Survey of Behavio-

ral Finance'. These ideas have begun to cross into the management literature with a good example provided by Lovallo and Kahneman (2003).

4. Because risk and decision making defies `rational logic', its long history has attracted innovative and free-thinking contributions. Contemporary examples include `Psychology and Economics' by Rabin (1998) and `The three Ps of total risk management' by Lo (1999).

5. Decision makers handle risk in a complex fashion which is related to their history, interpretation of the problem, personal attributes and judgements. Guidance on untangling these processes can be found in the paper `Reconceptualising the determinants of risk behaviour' by Sitkin and Pablo (1992) which won the Academy of Management's Best Paper of the year in 1992.

6. Risk has exploded as a topic of public interest after gaining a compelling immediacy for its impacts on boards, social policy and technology. Work first merely identified sources of risk, but is now beginning to struggle with what risks might look like in the future. An insightful example is *Reckoning with Risk* by Gigerenzer (2002).

7. Deployment of new technologies and synergistic breakthroughs from their integration have brought what Beck (1992: 12-13) called the *Risk Society*. He believes that today's global society and technologies have made risk a key trait of modern life:

   "The productive forces [of modern industrial society] have lost their innocence in the reflexivity of modernisation processes. The gain in power from techno-economic `progress' is being increasingly overshadowed by the production of risks."

8. Interest in enterprise level risk management has been revived by a number of high profile crises and governance failures in Australia, Europe and the United States. Consulting firms have quickly responded with a number of recent books including Deloach (2000) and McCarthy and Flynn (2004).

Finally, the topic is so broad and so important to survival, or at least success, that it constantly encourages evolutionary thinking. Lo (1999: 20), for instance, proposed decision making as risk management in:

"a broadened view of economic science, one based on the principles of ecology and evolutionary biology [as] ... the messy empirical history of markets and economic interactions suggests a more organic interpretation... If we are to understand the roots of risk preferences, it must be in the context of the survival instinct and how that has shaped economic institutions."

This owes much to the thinking of polymath biologist Wilson (1975: 4) who neatly codified his thoughts as *sociobiology* which he defined as "the systematic study of the biological basis of all social behaviour." He sees decisions as driven by a sort of behavioural software, with built-in contingencies and risk as one of the key inputs. Winterhalder and Smith (2000) suggested that human decisions are driven by 'specialised cognitive modules' which have evolved over aeons.

Despite considerable progression on a number of fronts, gaps remain in our knowledge of risk and decision making. Those of particular importance to management research comprise the following:

1. There is no agreement on the definition of risk, nor is there a good understanding of the empirical relationship between various definitions and the latent risk variables that they measure. The literature similarly lacks consensus on what empirical measures are appropriate to describe levels of risk and the risk propensity of individuals and organisations; and it is imprecise in the meaning attached to many terms used to describe decision making anomalies.

2. There is little information on changes in different measures of risk over time; nor on changes in risk propensity for both individuals and populations.

3. The frequency of risky decisions is unknown, although Howard (1988) suggests that it might impact less than ten percent of business decisions. Similarly there is a dearth of empirical data describing other populations such as corporate crises (i.e. realisation of a risk), and the proportion of successful outcomes of risky decisions.

4. Although a number of personality measures have been proposed as indicators of attitudes towards risk, it is not clear how much confidence can be attached to their reliability. In addition, consensus is lacking on the effects of key demographic variables including age, gender and nationality. Without precision in how demographic and personality measures drive risk propensity, models of decision making have difficulty in accommodating basic differences between individuals and decisions.

5. Most studies of risky decision making have used small, homogeneous samples in artificial settings, and assumed that decision makers' aim is to maximise value. There have been few studies which encompass individuals' circumstances, real-world behaviours and decision outcomes. Thus the motivations, goals and results of risky decision making are not linked; and the normative assumptions of decision models are not verified.

6. Few experimental studies have examined the hypothesis that human decision making is risk sensitive, nor examined the transition between risk aversion and risk embrace.

7. Few studies have examined natural, or real-world, decision making across animals, humans and organisations using comparable metho-

dologies. There would be intriguing conceptual implications from qualitatively similar behaviours by qualitatively dissimilar organisms.

8. Analysis of risk-taking by organisations has not fully detailed the influence of organisation parameters and structures, and the impact of risk on organisation performance.

9. There is no template or guidance available to organisations which might wish to strategically influence their level of risk and propensity for new risk.

This book concentrates on items 3 to 5, 7 and 9, and seeks to make its contribution by compiling real-world evidence, linking circumstances to risk outcomes, and developing an holistic model of decision making. Generic goals are to link disparate literatures and provide useful guidance for managers on the organisation-level topics of the causes and consequences of risk-taking by managers, and strategies for organisations to dial up the right level of risk.

With this background, let us turn to the evidence on risk and decision making, particularly as it relates to managers.

CHAPTER 2   Theory of Risk and Decision Making in Management

Decision making and risk are important topics for managers. For instance, Peter Drucker (1992: 374), often proposed as the `father of modern management', wrote: "Executives do many things in addition to making decisions. But only executives make decisions. The first managerial skill is, therefore, the making of effective decisions." According to Hammond et al. (1998: 47): "making decisions is the most important job of any executive. It's also the toughest and the riskiest." Emphasising the risk inherent in decision making, US heart surgeon Robert Jarvik (2003: 1) said: "Leaders are visionaries with a poorly developed sense of fear and no concept of the odds against them. They make the impossible happen." Nutt (1999) highlighted the fate of most decisions with his observation that half are wrong.

This chapter discusses the role of risk in decision making, principally from the perspective of management science. That is not to ignore other rich literatures on risk, especially in finance. However, most of these look at risk from a market perspective, assuming it is diversifiable, whereas real-world decisions by managers are not usually diversifiable.

The balance of this chapter starts with a discussion of the various meanings of risk, and is followed by an analysis of its role in decision making. The third section examines techniques developed in economics and operations research to quantify managers' risk preferences, and the final section foreshadows the risk-related contributions of this book.

Definitions of Risk

Any discussion of risk quickly reveals it is not a shared concept. A good example came in questions posed by Professor Bernd Rohrmann [personal communication, 7 March 2003]: "what risk? who's risk? [is it] risk perception, risk attitudes, risk behavior?" As my scope is all this and more, it is appropriate to clarify the meaning of significant words in this analysis, particularly `risk', `uncertainty', and `risk aversion'.

In the discussion that follows I propose to use risk with the meaning given by the *Concise Oxford Dictionary*: "hazard, chance of or of bad consequences, loss, etc, exposure to mischance ..." Similarly a decision is defined as a "...conclusion, formal judgement, making up one's mind, resolve..." Thus a risky decision involves a conclusion or action with at least one possible outcome that could have a loss or bad consequence. Such decisions range from near automatic responses driven by routine or habit (e.g. daily travel routes, menu selections) to complex choices with conflicting objectives and highly uncertain outcomes [Svenson (1996)]. Conversely, the result of a `non risky' action is known relatively precisely in advance, or is unlikely to prove adverse[6].

Despite the dictionary, risk has different meanings depending on context: in finance it means statistical uncertainty arising from the variability of a known population of returns; engineers worry about risks from lack of accurate data; and consumers and voters think of risk as the possibility of failure. As risk is a perceptual construct, it means different things to different people according to their emphasis on quantitative and qualitative features (such as historical and potential consequences, respectively). This imprecision in risk's meaning leaves it open to expropriation: Beck (1992: 3), for instance, gives risk a philosophical meaning as "an intellectual and political web across which thread many strands of discourse relating to the slow crisis of modernity and industrial society."

Another complication of risk is that decision makers' attitudes towards it are not directly measurable. Even its mathematical construct is a proxy and relies on accurate measurement of other variables (such as corporate income and share prices) which themselves may not be directly measurable. Equating any measure to the variable `risk' is fraught with difficulty.

Thus most analysts implicitly treat risk as a latent variable which is related to one or more quantifiable variables. A common approach to measuring risk is surveys which collate self-reported perceptions and behaviours; another is to estimate risk attitudes from hypothetical decisions. Although these follow the advice of West and Berthon (1997: 28) that "the measurement of risk is best left to the participants in the process rather than the observers of the outcomes", they introduce sources of error such as failure by the measure to actually record `risk', misleading or incorrect responses, survey and sample bias, noise and so on. This points to a third

---

[6] No attempt is made to develop a taxonomy of risks in terms of environment, timing, knowledge, controllability and so on. Baird and Thomas (1985) produced a management version where firm risk is the sum of six measures: strategic risk taking; general environmental risk; industry risk; organisational risk; risks specific to a problem (e.g. outcomes, probabilities, and framing); and decision maker risk.

technique to quantify risk attitudes which uses actual behaviour. Each technique, though, only provides point in time measures that may not be stable, and probably vary across risk domains.

It is hardly surprising, then, that the literature has struggled with 'risk'. Since at least Knight (1921), economists have made the distinction between strong or fundamental uncertainty, and probabilistic risk or weak uncertainty. Probabilistic risk can be defined by a reliable distribution and hence is amenable to confident modelling using historical data: this type of risk involves known consequences and is most often used by risk managers and financial economists. Bromiley (1991: 38), for instance, had a clear position: "I defined risk as the uncertainty of a company's income stream." A good example of how probabilistic risk leads to narrow outlooks on decision making is given by Sprent (1988) in a book entitled *Taking Risks* which ignores every non numerical factor such as lack of control and novelty which can personalise risk, and coldly dismisses fear of flying as irrational by pointing out that it is eight times safer than driving. Similarly financial planners use models and history to confidently predict their clients' long-term returns to a decimal place without the need to consider that the future might be different.

Another example of probabilistic risk was given by Miller and Bromiley (1990) who took nine different measures of a firm's risk and used factor analysis to derive three groups which they termed: (i) income stream risk - variation in return on equity and return on assets, and raw and normalised forecasts by analysts of earnings per share; (ii) stock returns risk - systematic risk (beta or market risk) and unsystematic risk (uniquely related to a firm); and (iii) strategic risk - debt to equity (risk of bankruptcy), capital intensity (ratio of total assets to sales), and the inverse of R&D intensity (ratio of R&D expenditure to sales). Correlations between the principal component variables of these risk factors lay between 0.11 and 0.23 and are statistically significant ($p < 0.05$).

This study is one of a number which suggest that – despite significant differences in definition - the various risk parameters used across economics, finance and management are measuring similar latent variables. That is not to say that the risk measures are each equivalent: for instance, no study has shown that any measure using returns risk is able to meaningfully explain any measure of managerial risk [e.g. Palmer and Wiseman (1999)]. Even so, the apparent likelihood that different risk constructs are measuring similar latent variables is an intriguing research topic.

Despite statistical links between different risk types, managers (and by implication investors) do not see risk in the same way as economists. March and Shapira (1987) documented managers' perspectives on risk, in particular typical beliefs that: risk is a negative outcome; risk and return are not necessarily positively correlated; risk attitude is dependent upon situation and perception; and risk can be reduced by managers who have appropriate skill sets. In particular, managers and investors do not have a symmetrical view of performance variation and make clear distinctions between gains and losses, or variations above and below a reference level.

The popularly broad view of risk was put succinctly by Payne et al. (1980) who asked CFOs of Fortune 500 companies to define a risky investment. The most common reply was that it was one with a significant 'probability of not achieving a target rate of return.' Another neat summary comes from Byrnes et al. (1999: 367): "Risk taking involves the implementation of options that could lead to negative consequences."

Miller and Reuer (1996: 671) were critical of imprecision in the definition of risk: "despite the widespread incorporation of risk in empirical strategy research, there is little consensus regarding the meaning of the concept and its measurement." Equally critical were Das and Teng (2001: 517) for whom "risk appears to be one of the most commonly abused concepts in the social sciences."

The dichotomy between risk as perceived by different groups of academic researchers and by managers has potentially serious consequences. Ruefli et al. (1999: 167-168) were so concerned at lack of agreement on the definition of risk and at the failure to develop appropriate measures that they suggested it had become a "fundamental methodological challenge." In their view, risk is defined too narrowly, and measured too simply using derivative (rather than primary) data and relying on metrics from other disciplines:

"The corpus of strategic management research has been dominated by a few easy-to-calculate, borrowed measures of risk, and, as a result, our theorising has been focussed narrowly on variance avoidance while central concerns of managers and strategists have been neglected."

Perhaps reflecting deficiencies in risk measures and inconsistent findings about the influence of risk, few studies from economics, strategy and management even mention risk, although it is central to most important decisions[7].

The different views of risk as an *ex post* measure of variance or *ex ante* expectation of adverse outcome have recently begun to encourage alternative risk measures, particularly downside risk which Reuer and Leiblein

---

[7] Howard (1988: 689) suggests, though, that risk preferences are "matter[s] of real practical concern in only five to ten percent of business decision analyses." This opens up an unresolved debate (see, for instance, Wally and Baum (1994)) over the relative importance of risks associated with high volume, routine decisions and lower volume, strategic decisions. Few firms fail because of poorly judged strategic initiatives, but equally few firms prove successful without them.

(2000: 203) defined as "a probability-weighted function of below target performance outcomes ... [which] explicitly incorporates the notion of reference levels."

Miller and Reuer (1996) derived 13 measures of downside risk from analysts' forecasts of earnings (which are available *ex ante* but do introduce subjective judgement), traditional CAPM beta, and historical accounting returns; and then tested their measures against conventional risk proxies such as earnings volatility and Altman's Z (which is a measure of credit default risk[8]). These measures of risk proved to be closely related: only 20 out of 78 reported correlations were not statistically significant (p>0.10), and half the correlations were highly significant (p<0.001). Even though the authors seemed disappointed (page 684) that "many of the downside risk measures proposed in this research have measurement properties similar to those of existing risk measures", they reached an important conclusion which supports my proposition that superficially different risk measures respond to common latent risk variables.

A different outlook on risk proposed by Zaleskiewicz (2001) is its motivation. He describes instrumental risk taking as goal oriented in seeking future profit, and - as a deliberate, cerebral process following expected utility type analysis - is directed at achievement. Examples are education and investment in retirement savings. Stimulating risk taking is arousal oriented, with a desire for immediate excitement which is independent of the outcome. It is non-cognitive, almost reflexive, in nature and driven by sensation seeking such as seen in adventure sports.

When the definition of risk is broadened, there is a need to recognise uncertainty. This allows for structural change in the decision framework and points to the indeterminacy of a future which cannot be known because it is not yet determined: uncertainty implies the possibility that making a decision can actually influence the future, and points to the difficulties of precisely evaluating consequences and probabilities. The key feature of uncertainty is that at least some aspects of a decision are beyond the control and/or knowledge of the decision maker: it cannot be measured, only estimated. Thus an uncertain risk is evaluated by perception and judgement: it invites debate and controversy.

Although it is possible to argue that we cannot know anything about the future and that uncertain decisions are simply random gambles, my assumption is quite the opposite. Looking ahead is practicable over short time horizons because institutions, trends and broad linkages hold true for

---

[8] Altman's Z is defined by Miller and Reuer (1996) as: [1.2*Working Capital + 1.4*Retained earnings + 3.3*EBIT + Sales]/Total Assets + 0.6* [Market Capitalisation/Book Liabilities]

varying periods, and so can be relied upon by decision makers. Whilst the concept of forecasting is beyond my scope, some people have this skill, especially what has been called *strategic foresight*. This is a function of creativity and experience, intelligence and communication skills, and a willingness to tolerate uncertainty and move outside conventional wisdom.

Although risks in the real world involve uncertainty, they are amenable to influence and control by decision makers. A particularly powerful tool is risk management which involves extrapolating current events and taking actions which avoid exposure to an outcome that will be regretted. It incorporates decision maker options to control risk consequences, and accepts opportunity costs to avoid the risk of loss.

At this point it is useful to introduce the concept of utility which dates to Bernoulli (1738, translated 1954) and his contemporaries. Decision makers facing a series of monetary choices do not necessarily choose between them based on the outcomes expected, but on their utility which is assumed to be proportional to the value of the outcome and inversely proportional to the decision maker's assets. Thus the utility of any choice, or prospect, rises with its value, but less slowly as assets accumulate [Munier (1988)].

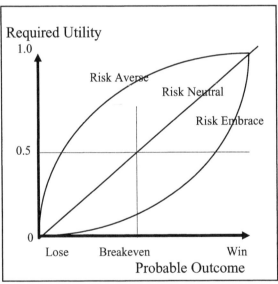

Fig. 2.1. Attitudes Toward Risk

By definition, a risk neutral person "attaches equal utility to each increment in wealth" [Peirson et al. (2002: 203)] or "judges prospects solely by their expected rates of return [so that] risk is irrelevant" [Bodie et al. (2005: 170)]. Other people are risk sensitive as wealth rises or falls. As wealth increases, a risk averse person attaches less utility to each increment, whilst a risk embracing person places increasing utility on each increment in wealth.

The figure above is a simple depiction of how utility influences individuals' attitudes towards risk. When faced with two choices which have an equivalent expected outcome, a risk neutral person accepts breakeven: thus the utility which they place on any proposal is equal to its expected value. Conversely a risk averse person requires greater than 50 percent probability of breakeven and so places a lower utility on an uncertain outcome than its expected value. For any outcome, the risk averse person will require a greater utility than a risk neutral person: the risk averse decision maker's utility curve is concave (∩ shaped). Normative economic theory assumes that individuals are risk averse because money has decreasing utility, and so any given gain is of less utility than a smaller previous gain (or a corresponding loss). This makes risk preferences non-linear, and defined by a utility curve which is concave with a positive, but decreasing, slope (if u(x) is the utility of x, $u' > 0$, and $u'' < 0$).

The diagram shows that attitudes towards risk are based around subjective expectations of the utility of alternative choices, and vary between different quanta of risk. Thus risk preference has a significant influence on decision making; and risk sensitivity is key to understanding human behaviour.

Putting this in specifics, consider the choice between two outcomes with the same expected return: a certain $1,000 and an equal chance of $2,000 or zero. This is close to many everyday decisions ranging from commuting route (a usually fast arterial road which is occasionally gridlocked) to investments (equities vs. bonds). In our simple decision, a risk neutral person is indifferent between the choices. A risk averse person would need more than a 50 percent chance of $2,000 to give up a certain $1,000; and a risk-embracing person welcomes the chance of securing the higher outcome. Risk averse people will sell a fair gamble at less than its expected value rather than take the gamble. Thus they can become `money pumps' when they buy an uncertain outcome at its fair price, and then sell it at a lower price. In colloquial terms, a risk averse person will buy high and sell low; whereas a risk embracing person may be countercyclical.

In summary, risk in the real world is measured both by the possibility of an adverse outcome, and by the scale of possible loss. Risk acts as a lens through which decision makers evaluate the elements of a decision, particularly its consequences and the merits of alternative solutions; and risk becomes a planning tool by shaping the strategy which is followed to implement a decision. This last is an important theme in the book; and one of the conclusions is that organisational strategy suffers unless it explicitly recognizes the role of risk.

Incorporation of Risk into Decision Making Theory

The mechanics of decision making have fascinated psychologists and other researchers since pioneering consideration by Bernoulli, Leibniz, and Pascal in the 18th century. But the topic lay dormant until narrowed with an analysis of game theory by Von Neuman and Morgenstern (1953), and contributions from Friedman and Savage (1948), and Arrow (1971). Although it quickly ran into trouble with doubts cast by the Allais (1952) paradoxes which exploded into a catalogue of violations [compiled by Machina (1987) and updated in McFadden (1999)], decision making theory was seemingly brought back on track by Prospect Theory [Kahneman and Tversky (1979)]. These developments are reviewed by Starmer (2000), while Camerer (1999) helped pull together much of the multi-disciplinary evidence.

An authoritative survey of the state of decision making theory was provided by Machina (1987: 121) who adopted a Dickensian opening:

> "Fifteen years ago, the theory of choice under uncertainty could be considered one of the 'success stories' of economic analysis: it rested on solid axiomatic foundations, it had seen important breakthroughs in the analytics of risk, risk aversion and their applications to economic issues, and it stood ready to provide the theoretical underpinnings for the newly emerging 'information revolution' in economics. Today choice under uncertainty is a field in flux ..."

Two decades later the position seems little changed. The leading explanations of risk and decision making continue to be normative models which assume that people make decisions to maximise their benefit using the key levers of probability and payoff. It is taken as axiomatic that decision making processes are a function of analytical and cognitive inputs, and so should be derived mathematically. Despite this, there is widespread dissatisfaction with theory because it is such a poor match to reality. Even though decision research has incorporated economic and behavioural concepts, most resulting explanations are merely variations on expected utility or updates of Prospect Theory, particularly Rank Dependent Expected Utility and Cumulative Prospect Theory. Unfortunately no model offering a parsimonious quantitative solution has been developed to satisfactorily explain decision making under risk in the real world.

Modern theories of choice or decision making under risk and uncertainty fall into three broad categories:

1. Expected utility
2. Non-linear utility functions
3. Behavioural models and process descriptions.

Within this broad classification, decision making explanations are divided into those which hold the situation constant and assume that unique personality traits drive the decision; and those that hold personal traits as irrelevant and put all the explanation on the stimulus [Lopes (1987)].

In brief, Expected Utility Theory (EUT) – which was first proposed by Bernoulli (1738, translated 1954) - considers that a decision is the acceptance of an uncertain proposition which delivers a probable benefit (termed 'expected utility') equal to the sum of each of the possible results multiplied by their individual probability of occurrence:

$$E(U) = \sum_{i=1}^{n} P_i * \pi_i \qquad (2.1)$$

where P_i is the utility from possible outcome i, and π_i is its population-based statistical probability of occurrence (naturally $\sum_{i=1}^{n} \pi_i = 1$).

This mathematical treatment and the normative assumption of rationality have a number of attractive properties, and so utility models are used in most analyses involving choice[9]. Unfortunately, it has become clear that behaviour violates simple expected utility theory: decisions are not made in isolation but are contingent on other factors, including alternatives; and decision makers are not adequately equipped to correctly evaluate utility, which is made most obvious by different choices when the same data are presented differently ('reframed').

The fundamental defect of utility theory is that it does not take risk into account in the way it is generally perceived by decision makers, particularly the outcomes of earlier decisions and their immediate circumstances. Almost as serious is that identical data will stimulate quite different responses in people. It is this difference of opinion that makes horses race [Twain (1894, reprinted 1996)], and is responsible for every trade, whether in shares or consumables[10]. The literature is now replete with examples of

---

[9] Expected utility spilled over into what might be called Benthamite Utility concepts which postulate that optimum policy aims to deliver the greatest good to the greatest number.

[10] Utility Theory is normative, mathematical and parsimonious, which - like CAPM – gives it desired research attributes. Perhaps that is why these two theories retain currency long after experimental and revealed evidence made it clear that they have limited applicability.

serious violations of Expected Utility Theory in financial markets, management and consumer behaviour[11].

Given people's consistent failure to maximise utility, researchers have developed a dozen or more non-expected utility models [Starmer (2000)]. Typical versions describe decision processes in the form:

$$E(U) = \sum_{i=1}^{n} w_i * u(x_i) \qquad (2.2)$$

where w_i is a decision weight and $u(x_i)$ is the utility of outcome x_i.

This recognises that people assign different weights to different events (for example by overweighting dramatic occurrences; and preferring gains to losses). These weights can be related to both the event and to its outcome, particularly when ambiguity is involved.

The best-known rejection of expected utility theory was by Tversky and Kahneman (1992: 297): "there is now general agreement that [Expected Utility] theory does not provide an adequate description of individuals' choice." They proposed Prospect Theory which is discussed at length in chapter six.

The third broad category of theory of choice under uncertainty is behaviourally based and describes the mental processes which are involved, rather than projecting the expected result: these are the how of decision making, instead of the what. Such models recognise that decision makers will only prefer a risky alternative if there is some benefit to it, and this benefit can come in many forms, not just financial optimisation[12].

These models are well recognised in psychology where feelings and emotions have a significant role in human decisions [Damasio (1994)]. Cognitive psychology makes room for individual behavioural styles; and assumes decisions involve non-linear (even non-mathematical) processing of information. It examines how decision makers actually reach decisions [McFadden (1999: 75)]:

> "The primary focus of psychologists is to understand the nature of these decision elements, how they are established and modified by experience, and how they determine values. The prime focus of economists is on the mapping of information inputs to choice. Preferences, or values, can be treated for most economic applications as primitives of the analysis, and the decision as a black box."

---

[11] This does not mean that all experiments and studies show violation of EU. For instance, Hey and Orme (1994: 1321) offered 80 subjects a series of paired risky prospects and concluded: "expected utility theory ... emerges from this analysis fairly intact." Thus – in many quarters - expected utility (arguably with some modifications) remains a good approximation to decision making.

[12] See the special issue of *Organisational Behaviour and Human Decision Processes* on 'Perspectives of Behavioural Decision Making' (1996) **65** (3) 169-304.

Behavioural models allow for multiple outcomes and eschew rigid mathematical treatments as they see – with Klein et al. (1993: vii) – that decisions are characterised by: "dynamic and continually changing conditions, real-time reactions to these changes, ill-defined goals and ill-structured tasks, and knowledgeable people." Most models adopt the managerial view of risk, and see decisions as an outcome of the interplay between decision makers and their situation which involves: individual appraisal of the situation which is determined by personal traits unique to the decision maker; and the stimuli on the decision maker which are triggered by the decision and its circumstances. Examples, respectively, are personality driven explanations such as sensation seeking or risk aversion, and reliance upon framing as a decision determinant.

Specifying Managerial Risk Preference

Normative theory proposes that managers handle risk through diversification because modern capital markets ensure a risk-neutral outcome. Individual investment decisions are then optimised by choosing alternatives with the greatest value, a process which is typified by discounted cash flow (DCF) techniques. This is the school of thought termed Decision Analysis which grew out of operations research and the scientific approach to management [Taylor (1967)] and secured wide support during the 1970s. It provided a formal language and clarified the basic assumptions behind any decision, and so brought transparency to an otherwise complex process. Dearlove (1998) and Samson (1988) provide comprehensive depictions of the discipline, and it is well summarised at the height of its influence in the collection compiled by Howard and Matheson (ca 1989).

Exponents of decision analysis fall into two distinct camps. The first might be thought of as objectivists who believe that decisions should be based on objective reality, best estimates and expected values. Decisions for them follow a logical process of data collection, analysis and synthesis to rigorously present alternatives for consideration. They see little room for subjectivity in decision making, save to warn that it can confound results.

The second group are described by Raiffa (1968: xx) as "Bayesians or subjectivists [who] wish to introduce intuitive judgments and feelings directly into the formal analysis of a decision problem". For them, decision analysis is a standardised process to incorporate "a decision maker's preferences for consequences, attitudes towards risk, and judgments about uncertain events."

The approach in this book is sympathetic to the Bayesians. Numerous studies have convinced managers that capital markets do not ensure risk neutral outcomes. Bowman (1980) was the first to point out that high risk firms have poor returns; then Fama and French (1992) confirmed that the capital asset pricing model (CAPM) has trivial ability to explain market behaviours. And many firms suffer poor financial results even after decades of approving only those investments whose returns exceed a tough hurdle rate. The clearest evidence of managers' rejection of normative economic theory is that risk management is a major concern of executives.

Given the Bayesian recognition that real-world decision makers incorporate their own biases and risk propensity into the evaluation process, it is incumbent on decision analysts to measure the effect. The most effective approach is to assume that decision makers think in terms of the utility of any risk-weighted value.

To describe the process of quantifying risk using a utility function, first consider the Allais Paradox which is one of the most commonly cited examples of a decision making anomaly. This was named for the French Nobel Prize winner who showed that sane decision makers typically prefer to receive $1 million for certain, rather than accept a gamble which has a 10 percent probability of paying $5 million, 89 percent of $1 million and one percent chance of paying nothing. As the latter alternative has an expected value of $1.39 million, it should be preferred; but most decision makers will choose the smaller, certain amount rather than accept the risk of loss associated with the higher expected value.

This can be generalised to the proposal that a decision maker is indifferent between accepting $A for certain and accepting a gamble which has a probability π of paying $B and a probability $(1-\pi)$ of paying nothing. $A is the certainty equivalent (CE) of the uncertain outcome which has an expected value of $\pi*B [Raiffa (1968)].

The difference between the CE and expected value of the gamble is the decision maker's risk premium. Thought of in a different way, it is an opportunity cost (or insurance payment) equal to the amount that the decision maker is willing to forego to obtain the CE. The existence of this risk premium means that the decision maker places a utility on the monetary outcome which is different to its expected value. The question then becomes how to relate utility and expected value.

The most common approach is to ignore the difference. Corner and Corner (1995) surveyed 86 decision analysis models published between 1970 and 1989, and found that 67 percent of them used expected value as the decision criterion and did not incorporate any measure of risk aversion.

Of the models that incorporated risk, virtually all did so by means of a function which transforms a monetary value, x, into a utility, u(x). Consider a decision maker whose utility preferences are described by u(x), and who is faced with two outcomes which pay x_1 and x_2 with respective probabilities of π_1 and π_2. She will prefer the greater of $\pi_1{}^* u(x_1)$ and $\pi_2{}^* u(x_2)$.

To determine the shape of u(x), most analyses use some variant of the exponential utility function which was first proposed by Pratt (1964)[13]. In calculating the exponential utility function, it is generally assumed that risk preferences are captured by an expression of the form:

$$u(x) = x \cdot e^{-\frac{x}{\rho}} \qquad (2.3)$$

where u(x) is the utility to the decision maker of \$x and ρ is the decision maker's risk tolerance.

An example is shown in the figure below.

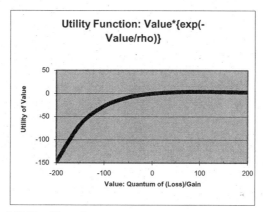

Fig. 2.2. Typical Utility Function

This type of utility function has the property:

$$\rho = -\frac{x \cdot}{\ln[\frac{u(x)}{x}]} \qquad (2.4)$$

The exponential utility function has the advantage that it is a simple expression with only one varying parameter that can be elicited consistently with minimal effort from a single observation of any pair of u(x) and x.

---

[13] Pratt used $u(x) = - e^{-xc}$ for c>0; and $u(x) = e^{-xc}$ for c<0; where u(x) is the utility of a monetary value x, and c is the *risk aversion coefficient*

Also it incorporates increasing risk aversion so that risk looms larger as its quantum rises.

Finally the exponential function is mathematically practical. Thus, for instance, Raiffa (1968: 211) took the common situation where an uncertain payoff is normally distributed with expected value (EV) or mean μ, and standard deviation σ, and showed that:

$$CE = \mu - \frac{\sigma^2}{2\rho} \tag{2.5}$$

This allows calculation of risk tolerance:

$$\rho = \frac{\sigma^2}{2 * (EV - CE)} \tag{2.6}$$

In words, risk tolerance is equal to half the variance per unit of risk premium, and risk aversion grows (i.e. ρ falls) with the decision maker's discount for avoiding the uncertain outcome.

Apart from the commonly used exponential function, utility has been captured in a number of other formats such as the following [Hartog et al. (2000)]:

$$\rho = \frac{2 * (\alpha.Z - \lambda)}{\lambda^2 - 2 * \alpha.\lambda.Z + \alpha.Z^2} \tag{2.7}$$

where: ρ is the Arrow-Pratt measure of absolute risk aversion,
   Z is the expected outcome
       α is the probability of achieving outcome Z
   λ is the utility or valuation of the choice
The value of ρ is zero at risk neutrality (i.e. λ = α.Z), negative for risk embrace (i.e. λ > α.Z), and positive for risk aversion [Mehra and Prescott (1985) found it was between zero and 10 for US equities in the preceding century].

Tversky and Kahneman (1992) proposed that people transform actual probability, p, to subjective probability, π, through a non-linear expression of the following form:

$$\pi = w(p) = \frac{p^\gamma}{\left[p^\gamma + (1-p)^\gamma\right]^{-\gamma}} \tag{2.8}$$

Although it is possible to consider numerous possible utility curves, there is little benefit after Kirkwood (2002) examined candidate functions and concluded that the exponential function generally performs as well as any alternative.

Individuals' utility functions have a counterpart in corporate utility functions, which have been estimated using three approaches which assume an exponential shape and are quantified using lottery-style questions. The first is described by Spetzler (1968) and obtains the certainty equivalent of several pairs of alternatives from which ρ is calculated. The second approach was followed by Howard (1988) and proposes that the value of ρ is the sum of money where executives are indifferent between an equal risk of doubling the sum and losing half the amount[14]. The third approach is to specify the values of each outcome and obtain minimum acceptable probabilities from which ρ is calculated[15].

An alternative to intensive, survey style assessment of risk propensity is to derive estimates of ρ from published data. For instance, Walls et al. (1995) examined actual investment decisions in large oil exploration firms (annual revenues of around $US3 billion) and calculated that ρ was equal to $US16 million for Phillips Petroleum Company; they also reported a value of $US30 million for BP Exploration Inc.

Another approach is to assume that loss aversion is related to wealth or endowment, and derive utility from accounting data. Charreton and Bourdaire (1988) suggested that the maximum allowable loss is around 30 percent of total equity for large international companies. Howard (1988) proposed a somewhat lower value of ρ at around 15 percent of equity, 120 percent of net income and six percent of sales. Kirkwood (2002) recommended using a value of ρ that is equal to ten percent of the value of assets under the decision maker's direct control. Applying this to several Australian companies gives values of ρ in the range $430-700 million for Amcor Limited; $580-720 million for Mobil Oil Australia Limited; and $410-790 million for Qantas Limited. These values, however, seem very high (and are an order of magnitude greater than the value calculated by field research reported in chapter eight).

---

[14] If losses are weighted twice as much as gains: u(2*amount) + u(-0.5*amount) = 0. Using the exponential utility function: $2*amount.e^{-2*amount/\rho} = 0.5.amount.e^{-0.5.amount/\rho}$. Thus $\rho = (-1.5.amount)/(\ln 4) = amount$.

[15] Schoemaker (1982) reports that the three different approaches, respectively, provide decreasing values of risk aversion. Herschey et al. (1982) warn that these assessments of utility tend to produce responses which are more risk-averse than the decision makers' inherent attitudes, presumably because they explicitly highlight loss possibilities

Once risk and utility have been determined, how might they be incorporated into decision making? According to Samson (1987: 107): "the risk philosophy of a company can be formally established and represented as a utility function, enabling coordination of risk management decisions with the more general risk policies of the organization." The aim is to determine the utility of each set of decision alternatives, and – in an approach similar to DCF analysis – rank them. This can be expressed mathematically by choosing that strategic alternative with the highest utility calculated as:

$$u(\text{Strategy}) = \sum_{i=1}^{n} \pi_i . u(\text{Expected Outcome}_i) \qquad (2.9)$$

For example, assume that a company has an exponential utility function in the form $u(x) = x * e^{-x/100}$, and its manager faces a choice between the four alternative investments. Each investment has equal probability of success or failure, so that utility is calculated as:

u (investment)   =   0.5 * u(success) + 0.5 * u(failure).

Table 2.1.   Project Evaluation Using Corporate Utility where $u(x) = x * e^{-x/100}$

Investment	Result		Expected Value	Expected Utility
	Success	Failure		
1	40	-20	10.0	1.2
2	50	-25	12.5	-0.9
3	60	-30	15.0	-3.8
4	70	-35	17.5	-7.5

Ranking the alternative investments by their expected value - which applies risk-free analysis – concludes that investment number 4, the alternative in the bottom row, is preferred. Using expected utility reverses the preferences and investment number 1 is most preferred.

The reason for the *preference reversal* is that the exponential function gives proportionately greater weight to losses: a loss of 30 has the same utility as a gain of 70. Thus as the level of potential loss rises, decision makers become increasingly loss averse and avoid choices which embody greater risk.

In terms proposed by Kahneman and Tversky (1979), utility-based investment analysis may be thought of as determining preferences from risk appetite rather than calculating expected value from probabilistic returns. Because conventional economic analysis only incorporates a portion of the data available to decision makers, adding utility significantly broadens the nature of decision making. Introducing a personalised decision making component (in this case incorporated in the value of ρ) re-orders the expected value of decision alternates to take account of the decision maker's risk attitude and thus can change decision makers' preferences between uncertain outcomes. Because different decision makers have different utility functions, their unique perception of risk induces different treatment of identical decisions (e.g. buy and sell, invest or forego).

As an aside, choice of the utility function can introduce some anomalies such as the counter-intuitive result described by Clyman et al. (1999) in which decision makers are less likely to increase their exposure to an opportunity even though its expected value is increased. This, of course, is exactly the outcome shown in table 2.1. Thus Kirkwood (2002) advises running sensitivities using different values of ρ and different specifications of the utility function.

The explicit use of risk estimates was of considerable academic interest in the 1970s as the field of operations research burgeoned. But interest waned, and Samson (1987) was one of the last significant papers. By the end of the 1980s, utility and risk evaluation techniques had fallen into abeyance.

Although it is not exactly clear what led to this decline, five reasons seem likely. First, as Samson (1987) pointed out, expected utility theory did not serve management's needs. Confidence was lost in scientific management methods in the late 1980s as a variety of strategy tools went out of fashion (e.g. scenario planning), and – under pressure to cut costs - companies scaled back their Planning Departments. Second was doubt that the technique had any real application given the view advanced by Howard (1988) that risk is relatively unimportant to decisions. Third was the emergence of behavioural emphases in decision making, best evidenced by growing acceptance of Prospect Theory. Fourth, the emergence of CAPM as a dominant finance paradigm saw economists shift their focus away from corporate-level risks and towards the implications of risk from markets; thus estimating corporate risk came to mean calculating the variance in one or more of a firm's accounting measures. Students of risk in economics during the 1990s looked at markets rather than smaller units.

There are other, more speculative, reasons. One is that consideration of risk was abandoned to the practitioner literature. As just one example, searching *American Banker* for articles containing the words 'risk' and 'decision' found no papers between 1980 and 1986, but an average of 45 articles per year for the next decade. Another possible reason is that the spread of personal computers and powerful decision software [e.g. Samson (1988)] facilitated ready treatment of complexity and reduced interest in more basic techniques.

In any event, little material was published on risk and decision making in the academic literature after 1989. For instance, in their comprehensive text entitled *Making Hard Decisions*, Clemen and Reilly (2001) allocated only two of their 17 chapters to risk and behavioural aspects of decision making. Modern management textbooks on decision making frequently omit any mention of risk [e.g. Dearlove (1998)], and the only significant applications of utility analyses today are seen in oil exploration [for instance: Walls and Dyer (1996) and Walls et al. (1995)].

Summary and Conclusions

The literature does not have a clear position on risk. One perspective is that risk is a behavioural aberration that can be ignored because it is an inappropriate consideration in objective analyses, or because it will be offset by arbitrage and market efficiency. Thus depictions of modern decision analyses – such as investment in new projects – focus on techniques to establish the distribution and most likely outcomes of key variables; and then recommend proceeding if the expected value exceeds a return threshold. Because the latter builds in systemic risk, any risks specific to individual decisions are irrelevant and analytical techniques are independent of the decision maker's risk preferences. As Kahneman (1991: 145) put it: "the field [of judgement and decision making] treats irrationality as a failure of reasoning."

The other perspective on risk – which is clear in the level of interest by companies in risk management – is that it needs to be specifically comprehended in analyses. One motive is that the outcomes of risky decisions can often be significant for individual decision makers but are not diversifiable; this is why so much attention is paid to managing risks associated with individual projects or investments. Second is that the characteristics of decision makers inevitably shape the level of risk or loss that they can accept: an investment or financial commitment which is attractive to a large, prosperous firm might be quite inappropriate to a smaller firm or a charity. Thus risk attitudes are specifically factored into organisation decision making. The third reason is that risk is such a significant feature of individuals' decisions that behavioural anomalies are impacting markets: thus risk cannot be ignored.

The division between these two perspectives is a classic example of the split between normative and descriptive theories: is it the role of analysts to proscribe or describe behaviour? In the case of decision making, should models help eliminate outcomes which are non-optimising (irrespective of the definition of 'optimum'), or specifically incorporate real-world behaviours?

This book adopts the second perspective, and the following chapters examine the role of risk in the behaviour and decision making of animals, humans and organisations. The explicit assumption is that decision making cannot be explained, much less predicted, without a comprehensive understanding of the processes that people use to incorporate risk into their decisions [Schoemaker (1982)]. Thus risk is a critical component of strategy and management, and we cannot expect to understand firm performance without specifically incorporating it into managerial decision making.

This chapter also reveals a number of gaps in our knowledge. The first surrounds the definition of risk. It would be useful to have a taxonomy of risk, perhaps achieved through a meta survey of the topic. A good pointer to the potential of such an effort is Campbell-Hunt (2000) who surveyed the literature examining the real-world applicability of the Porter (1980, 1985) model of competitive strategy. A related gap is in the measures of risk, and in rationalising differences between them.

A second gap in our knowledge is an appreciation of the actual importance of risk in decision making. Beyond a few broad guesses [e.g. Howard (1988)], there is no information on the frequency and significance of risk in decisions. Intuitively one would expect most decisions involve an element of risk, and that risk is commonly important. But the proportions are not well documented.

A third gap that gains attention in the following chapters is how to estimate risk. Measures include individuals' risk propensity and the risk environment and risk propensity of organisations. Without an understanding of the normal levels of risk parameters, their role is indeterminate.

The fourth gap – and an important outcome of this book – is the absence of guidance to organisations that wish to strategically shape their risk taking.

The following chapters use the literature to build theoretical foundations of each of these approaches and the final chapters develop their principles and implications.

CHAPTER 3   Behavioural Evidence on Risk and Decision Making

This chapter summarises evidence from laboratory experiments which used human and animal subjects to study decision making under risk. It first describes the principal studies, and then details their summary findings with key conclusions.

Principal Studies

There is a copious literature reporting experiments on animal and human behaviour, and this section merely reviews a representative selection of those which examine the role of risk in decision making.

Animal Studies of Risk and Decision Making

Since the 1980s, a number of studies have been conducted to examine risk taking by animals, chiefly birds, rats and butterflies. Using animals to study risky decision making has the significant benefit that the payoffs can be real and significant, whereas most human studies involve trivial or hypothetical payoffs. This is important because – despite conceptual doubt about the generalisability of animal decision making to humans - the discussion below shows that different species make common choices in qualitatively similar situations.

A good summary of animal cognition is given by Vauclair (1996), with results of behavioural studies in Kamil and Roitblat (1985), Kacelnik and Bateson (1996) and Waite (2001)[16]. These studies conclude that animals are risk-sensitive in their behaviour, and conform to a mechanism which is

---

[16] Kacelnik and Bateson's paper is one of an interesting series in *American Zoologist* (volume 36, pages 389-531) which reached the cautionary conclusion (page 530) that "most empirical tests of risk sensitivity are necessarily qualitative".

best explained using the accompanying diagram suggested by Smallwood (1996). The proposal is that an animal can choose between two foraging strategies, which – for simplicity – have the same expected outcome, but sharply differing variances. The first option (the distribution shown as a solid line) has low variance and means the animal is relatively certain of the result, irrespective of any endogenous skill or exogenous influences. The second option (the distribution with a dashed line) has much higher variance and a wider range of possible outcomes.

Risk-sensitive foraging assumes that animals choose strategy in light of their food needs. Consider, for instance, that the solid vertical line in figure 3.1 is the minimum acceptable outcome or required result: the animal is best served by a risk averse strategy as there is scant probability of not meeting its needs. However, as the animal's food needs rise and the vertical line moves to the right, the acceptability of a risk averse strategy declines until the only choice for survival is to embrace the risky, highly variable strategy.

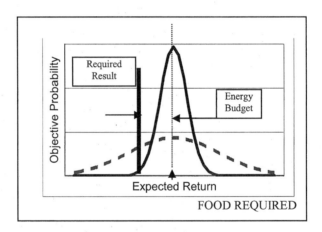

Fig. 3.1. Risk Sensitive Foraging

The rationale for this can be shown mathematically, such that the probability of a poor result is minimised by selecting the highest value of z, where:

$$z = \frac{\text{Expected Return - Required Result}}{\text{Standard Deviation}}$$

When the required result is below the expected return, the latter is acceptable and so low variance, risk aversion is selected; conversely when the required result is greater than the mean, the only chance of achieving an acceptable outcome is a course with high variance. This has been termed the energy budget rule, where the energy budget is the value of 'Expected Result (i.e. mean) - Required Result'. The rule postulates that risk embrace only occurs when the energy budget is negative, and vice versa.

Amplification of animals' risk sentience is provided in two types of experimental studies. The first is in equilibrium environmental conditions where researchers hold the expected outcome of alternative choices constant (and usually positive). A typical example [e.g. Real (1991)] gives bees or birds the choice of feeding from one of two coloured flowers: each colour has the same expected quantity of nectar, but one colour has constant amounts and the other has varying amounts, sometimes quite disparate. The animals learn to identify the difference between the flowers, and behave in a risk averse fashion by preferring the constant reward. A similar experiment was conducted by Battalio et al. (1985) using rats. Invariably such studies conclude that risk aversion is common in the absence of any threat, and is animals' preferred choice in fair gambles (as it is with humans [Hartog et al. (2000)]).

Risk aversion appears to be most true of animals that live in colonies. Real (1991) found that bees are consistently risk averse, whilst the experiments of Perez and Waddington (1996) using carpenter bees confirmed that they are not risk sensitive. The collectivist lives of colony dwellers means that they have no individual influence over the outcome, and so risk sensitivity makes little biological sense as they achieve the same result whether they are prone, averse or indifferent to risk.

However, it is clear that animals with control over their destiny do not behave in a myopically risk-averse fashion. Even the studies above which concluded that animals are risk averse found that – after the 'learning phase' is completed – animals still take a risky choice between 14 and 54 percent of the time. This is consistent with maximising survival prospects, as occasional greenfields foraging tests alternative patches, and is alert to recovery of previously inferior areas. Houston and McNamara (1982) developed a mathematical model of risk-sensitive foraging and showed that when alternatives are highly variable, the logic of diversification makes it prudent to occasionally sample less preferred areas. Risk taking promotes fitness.

This reinforces a consistent feature of animals' behaviour in risky decisions which is their application of judgement. A good example comes from a study of one of the few types of spider that uses venom, not webs, to capture its prey. In a series of macabre experiments, Malli et al. (1999) found that spiders inject venom in proportion to the level and duration of their prey's struggles, without regard to a target dose or the size of the prey. They clearly apply judgement in the risky business of killing.

The second relevant type of animal behavioural study varies the environment to show that attitudes towards risk are not stable. Here risk embrace becomes predominant in the face of a negative expected outcome and confirms the energy budget rule. In a breakthrough experimental procedure, Caraco et al. (1990) established birds in a laboratory habitat, and then threatened their survival by reducing the temperature. The birds proved to be risk sensitive as their state changed: risk averse when food was adequate and temperatures warm, and risk embracing as the temperature dropped and food supplies became more critical.

Another study by Smallwood (1996) of birds preparing to migrate for the winter found they were risk-embracing until they reached maximum body weight and then became risk averse. Despite evidence that normally risk-averse animals will accept risk to reach a challenging target, few data exist on when they cross over from risk aversion to risk embrace.

Marsh and Kacelnik (2002) experimented on 14 starlings using a methodology that eliminated risk sensitivity. The birds were trained to peck on keys to obtain food and recognise which key delivered a fixed (risk averse) or variable (risk seeking) reward. The reward size was then manipulated to randomly dispense one pellet every 45 seconds, or a single serve of seven pellets every 320 seconds. The outcomes were designated 'gains' and 'losses', respectively. The birds revealed different decision preferences: 86 percent were risk prone after losses, but only 57 percent were risk averse after gains (the latter was not significantly different from a random 50:50 selection)[17].

Risk featured in a long running study by Gasser et al. (2000) who established two isolated, but genetically identical, populations of fruit flies. They were housed under the same conditions, but subjected to different mortality rates such that the probability of surviving one week as an adult was either 0.01 or 0.6-0.8. The greater stress in the high mortality population saw its females mature earlier (seven percent shorter development time), lay more eggs (eight percent), and – probably as a consequence of faster development - have lower body weight (13 percent). Risk clearly influenced reproduction.

An interesting segue to the next section is another link between behaviour of animals and humans which was found by Gray and Lowery (1998)

---

[17] This matches findings from qualitatively similar human studies such as Forlani (2002) and Laughhunn et al. (1980)

in their study of US political lobbyists. Like animals, lobbyists go hungry unless their foraging (for food and friendly policy, respectively) is success-ful. They face strategic choices over the techniques employed, including formation of alliances. The latter is influenced by policy competition, dis-tribution of resources and challenges, and organisational priorities. Gray and Lowery (1998) found that the biological interpretation provided a sta-tistically significant explanation for lobbyists' behaviour[18]. This strength-ens the relevance of similarities in the behaviour of animals which led Vauclair (1996: 172) to conclude: "further study of animal cognition should continue to help us understand our own intelligence and its evolu-tion."

Human Studies of Risk and Decision Making

Moving on to humans, a good summary of findings from behavioural stud-ies is given by Camerer (1998), with a different perspective offered by Winterhalder and Smith (2000).

Although it is relatively easy to alter the risk environment with animals, it is obviously more difficult to achieve with humans. So, unfortunately for our aim of identifying the behavioural impacts of risk, the large majority of human studies involving risky decisions rely on fair gambles as their event. Thus Cubitt and Sugden (2001: 104) confess:

"Almost all the existing literature on choice under uncertainty in experimental eco-nomics and experimental psychology uses some version of the following standard de-sign. Each subject is presented with a choice between a pair of single stage lotteries, or with a series of such choices."

This 'lottery paradigm' deliberately simplifies decisions and isolates them from all factors other than probability to give the experimenter full control over inputs and outcomes. Unfortunately artificial experiments tell us only about how people respond to random chance or probabilistic risk, and thus owe much to conventional utility theory[19]. Not surprisingly they

---

[18] An important feature of risk attitudes discussed here is that they are a cross-species truth: both animals and humans are risk-sentient and assign probabilities in a non linear fashion. This extends to organisations after Singh (1986) used a diagram similar to Smallwood's in his study of corporate returns. He argued that risk-taking only occurs when profits drop below a satisficing level: in the context of the diagram, the expected result is less than the required result.

[19] Such findings have applicability only to real-world decisions which rely on the performance of essentially unpredictable systems such as weather (consider the deci-sion processes and expected returns of fishermen, farmers and ski resort operators), fashion and exchange rates.

have low explanatory power, and – for the few papers that indicate any measure of confidence - typical values of R^2 lie in the range 0.05-0.2.

Given the limited value of laboratory experiments using probabilistic gambles, the following discussion covers only the classic learnings, and gives more room to the relatively few studies which use decisions that are more representative of real-world situations.

The hypothesis of economically rational behaviour seems unconstrained in lottery experiments, and March and Shapira (1992: 172) neatly summarise the key implication:

"Theories of decision making under uncertainty most commonly assume that the returns to decisions are drawn from a probabilistic distribution that is conditional on the choice made."

Thus it was puzzling when behavioural anomalies began to appear in psychology laboratories during the 1960s[20]. For decades, the typical research response was to validate the finding using a different sample of poorly paid students from another university. The consistency of results finally led to the blindingly obvious conclusion [e.g. Barrett and Fiddick (1999: 251)]: "people routinely deviate from the standard norms of probability theory and expected utility theory ... [and psychologists] view people as susceptible to an extensive catalog of deficits and biases."

Despite the proliferation of anomalies, surprisingly little attempt was made to develop causal justifications. Thus after their survey of the field, Barrett and Fiddick (1999: 252) concluded that the various paradoxes thrown up by behavioural studies are yet to be explained by any unifying theory of choice under risk: "the question of the proper domain of the mechanism or mechanisms generating risk-sensitivity remains open."

The first of the decision making anomalies which have been well-established by behavioural studies is the *Allais Paradox* where subjects are offered the choice between either: a certain one million francs; or a ten percent chance of five million francs, 89 percent chance of one million francs, and one percent chance of nothing. The latter alternative has an expected value of 1.39 million francs and should be chosen because it clearly has the higher value; however, repeated studies have shown that it is not the preferred choice [e.g. Neilson and Stowe (2002) and Rabin (1996)]. They also found that loss aversion becomes more pronounced as a positive

---

[20] I acknowledge the argument that the extensive catalogue of biases could arise from procedural shortcomings. Also interesting is the explanation by Kahneman (1991: 144) for why there might be "too many biases: ... standard features of psychological methodology [are to study normal behaviour] ... by inducing failure ... [and the] objective of most psychological research is the rejection of a plausible or otherwise respectable null hypothesis."

outcome becomes more certain: decision makers are less willing to take a risk when they have a choice that yields gains.

A second anomaly is *preference reversal* in which people put a different value on a choice when it is presented in an alternate form. Tversky et al. (1990) ran a series of experiments where people were offered the choice between cash, a larger delayed payment, and a larger distant payout; and between cash, a low probability bet, and a high probability bet with similar expected outcomes. The respondents preferred a payout that is short term (74 percent) and high probability (74 percent). They were then asked the smallest amount of cash that they would accept to give up their bet: in each case about two thirds of respondents valued their preferred bet at a lower price than their non-preferred bet.

Tversky et al. (1990: 214) attributed the finding to "overpricing of low-probability high-payoff bets" (which can also be thought of as a longshot bias). Their explanation is that people making a decision mis-price probabilities by giving greatest weight to that characteristic of the object involved in the decision which is most compatible with the response: in a choice between alternative gambles, probabilities are most important; if the decision involves a payoff, then price is most important. According to this *compatibility principle*, when choosing between bets, subjects emphasise probability; but when selling their preferred bet they emphasise the potential price: because the payoff in low probability bets is higher than in high probability bets, the low probability bets are overvalued.

A measure of the subtlety of biases was given in experiments by Loewenstein and Adler (1995) who showed students a university mug and asked the hypothetical price they would trade it; subjects were then presented with the mug and given a real life chance to sell. Students underestimated their selling price by about 30 percent. Arguably a clear example of preference reversal, this was termed the *endowment effect* and attributed to the tendency for people who own an object to value it more highly than they would if they did not own it.

As an aside, Tversky et al. (1990) found the exact opposite of an endowment effect in their study discussed above. This points to an interesting feature of many behavioural studies which is that seemingly identical patterns of decision making can be assigned different causes: in these examples, the endowment bias is caused by ownership, whereas the compatibility principle is caused by categorising the decision type. Examples of competing causal explanations are common because of the narrow scope of experiments that are essentially qualitative tests.

Yet another paradox is that context is important to decision making. A simple, well-known example is shown in the figure below: the two middle circles are the same diameter, but the eye misinterprets this fact due to the way the data are presented. Tversky and Simonson (1993) showed that choices alter when decision makers are offered fewer or more selections. Also framing means that choices shift when a question is repackaged. Thus under the *event-splitting effect* an outcome is seen as being more probable when it is presented as two sub-events even though its overall probability and consequences are unchanged (Humphrey (2001) discusses the experimental evidence).

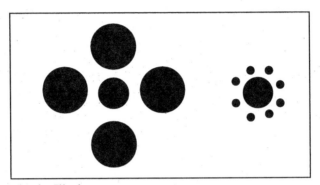

Fig. 3.2. Framing by Illusion

Changing the frame of a decision can alter the choice through operation of the *affect heuristic* by which people mentally tag objects and events with their affects (in the psychological meaning of the associated feeling or emotion). Finucane et al. (2000) argue that decision makers refer to a mental database of images and feelings that generate favourable and unfavourable affects. This explains why people intuitively perceive an inverse relationship between risk and benefit or reward: as the perceived benefit of an event rises, it is increasingly liked or preferred and the associated risk is perceived as falling. It also explains why staunch advocates can be so wrong: they subjectively assign a higher probability to preferred outcomes, irrespective of the evidence.

An important decision making behaviour is risk preference, or the instinctively preferred level of risk. Normative economic theory holds that any normal good (such as money) has decreasing utility and so the utility of any gain is less than the utility of an equivalent previous gain and less than the decline in utility from a corresponding loss. Thus people are loss averse and require a positive expected outcome from an uncertain decision. An example comes from Hartog et al. (2000) who analysed three independent datasets containing the following question (or a slight variant): among ten people, 1000 guilders are disposed of by lottery; what is the most that you would be willing to pay for a ticket in this lottery? They found that risk aversion is typical of their Dutch subjects, with between 54 and 96 percent behaving in a risk averse fashion, with most of the balance risk neutral.

Conversely a significant portion of the population can be risk-loving. Another study in Holland by Donkers et al. (2001) analysed data from 2,780 households and estimated that between 21 and 56 percent of the adult Dutch population is risk loving[21].

An important aspect of risk is loss aversion. An illuminating study by Schneider and Lopes (1986) reports the results of a survey of 1,382 University of Wisconsin psychology students who were asked to choose between pairs shown in the table below which have equal expected value, but different possible outcomes. Even though the values of the gamble and certain amount are economically identical, subjects increasingly preferred the certain amount as the size of the loss – in terms of the opportunity cost of the certain amount that is foregone – rises. Similar findings are reported by other authors, including Benartzi and Thaler (1999). These results show that subjects are loss averse: irrespective of the size of the gain or the expected outcome, decision makers avoid alternatives that could produce a loss.

Table 3.1. Loss Aversion

Choice pairs	Percent of subjects choosing gamble
0.8 of $4,000 vs. $3,200 for sure	9
0.2 of $15,000 vs. $3,000 for sure	12
0.5 of $5,000 vs. $2,500 for sure	25
0.9 of $2,000 vs. $1,800 for sure	42
0.1 of $16,000 vs. $1,600 for sure	16

When the data are regressed, they yield an expression of the following form:

Proportion preferring certain amount (CE) over gamble with same expected value $= 0.54 \, e^{CE/6480}$ ($R^2 = 0.36$).

Thus a large proportion (36 percent) of the variance in students' preference between a gamble and its expected value is explained by the opportunity cost or potential loss of the gamble. As the value of the sure bet rises (along with the opportunity cost from losing the amount in a gamble), the proportion of students preferring the gamble declines exponentially.

---

[21] This conflicting evidence is a stark warning to researchers that behaviour is inherently variable, and the instruments used to measure risk exert considerable influence over the result.

Whilst the students are clearly loss averse, that is not the whole picture as multiple regression shows that they pay no heed to probabilities and are virtually blind to win possibilities $(p>0.75)$[22]. The predictability of responses suggests that decision makers suffer from what Benartzi and Thaler (1995) called 'myopic loss aversion.'

People not only avoid risk and the possibility of loss, but also avoid regret. In the words that Ozzens (1942) put in Judge Coates' mouth: "When we think of the past we regret and when we think of the future we fear." An attribute close to risk aversion is ambiguity aversion (also termed the *Ellsberg Paradox* since 1961) which impacts on decision makers who are facing an uncertain outcome: subjects cannot select their preferred risk from unknown probabilities, and so avoid them. Raiffa (1961: 690) put it succinctly: "most people can be shown to be inconsistent in their manifest choice behavior". Kahneman (2003: 1450) was more critical: "people are not accustomed to thinking hard."

Fox and Tversky (1995) found a *competency effect* where decision makers' sense of their ability is undermined by comparison between events. In their study, most subjects were prepared to place a bet on the maximum temperature one week from today in their home town, but many were daunted when offered the choice between betting on the temperature in Istanbul and their home town; or when they are told the bet is simultaneously – but independently – being offered to weather professionals. Heath and Tversky (1991) found a similar attitude where people are willing to bet on uncertain questions (results of elections or sports events) involving topics where they have knowledge; otherwise they trust to chance. It seems that people prefer a choice that they know most about (thus avoiding ambiguity), irrespective of its objective merits.

An intuitively significant feature of risk embracing behaviour is the decision maker's personal attributes, including personality. However, only a decade ago Dahlbäck (1990) was able to write:

"Many experts on decision-making believe that there is no individual inclination of high generality to take risks of a certain magnitude. Reported research on the relationships between different kinds of risk-taking measures has been interpreted as supporting this view."

Because measures of personality had only a weak link with traits they sought to measure, psychologists studying risk lost interest in the influence of personality and turned to modelling decision making behaviour. The situation changed sharply after epidemiological studies showed an associa-

---

[22] A plot of gambling preference against the potential win showed an inverse relationship (i.e. proportion gambling <u>fell</u> as potential winnings rose) which explained only 19.4 percent of the variance: thus subjects became increasingly risk-averse as the size of the potential win rose.

tion between illnesses – particularly cancer and heart disease – and life-style and personality factors. There is now an impressive body of research linking risk taking to unique personal attributes, including personality.

Hartog et al. (2000) found that risk aversion is more strongly associated with female gender and lower income, employment as an employee especially in the public sector, and a shorter period of education. Donkers et al. (2001) also found that women and those on low income were more risk averse, and that risk aversion fell with higher education. However, in contradiction of other studies, their analysis showed that older people were more risk averse.

A different psychometric view of risk attitudes was given by Balabanis (2001) who links personality to gambling, and hence to risk taking. His survey of the literature found mixed results, but suggested that gamblers are more likely to be male and older; drink alcohol and smoke cigarettes; and participate in several types of gambling. His own study confirmed previous findings that gamblers are characterised as extraverts (sociable, assertive, adventurous and compulsive), antagonistic (not trusting, altruistic or compliant), and of lower intelligence.

An interesting feature of these studies is that they find conflicting impacts of age on risk taking. Although the majority of analyses show that older people are more risk prone, a number support the intuitive conclusion that older people are more conservative and take fewer (although perhaps better-judged) risks.

Zuckerman and Kuhlman (2000) showed strong links between personality and risk taking in sports and vocations, and in personal habits such as smoking, drinking, drug use, reckless driving and gambling. They found that subjects were likely to exhibit multiple risk behaviours. Those who embraced risk had personality traits such as sensation seeking (seeks novel experiences and will take risks to get them) and impulsivity (rapidly responds to cues; not inhibited from risk-taking).

A number of studies have probed the evidence of lower risk-propensity by women following the argument that this behavioural trait might harm their promotion prospects and contribute to the corporate 'glass ceiling'. Schubert et al. (1999: 384-385) used 141 Swiss university students with roughly equal numbers of men and women in an experiment to test investment and insurance decisions:

"Under controlled economic conditions, we find that female students do not generally make less risky financial choices than male subjects ... Gender-specific risk behaviour found in previous survey data may be due to differences in male and female opportunity sets rather than stereotype risk attitudes."

A somewhat different approach was taken by Croson and Buchan (1999) who used a trust game to examine differences in behaviour between

50 female and 136 male students from China, Japan, Korea and the United States. They found no significant differences in risk-taking behaviour between nationalities, nor any gender biases. However, women subjects exhibited significantly more reciprocity in their behaviour than men.

Byrnes, Miller and Schafer (1999) conducted a meta-analysis of 150 studies to compare male and female risk-taking behaviours. Differences were greater than the cut-off for small effects (Cohen's d > 0.2) in about half the situations studied. Men were particularly likely to take greater risks in playing games involving skill; and were more willing to participate in an experiment described to them as risky, and in tasks involving complex mathematical or spatial reasoning skills. Differences between men and women in risk-taking were small or non-significant in relation to sexual activity, drug and alcohol use, actual driving behaviour, and gambling. Overall the study showed that the proportion of women accepting any risk is an average of six percent less than the proportion of men offered the same risky choice. It seems, then, that the effect of gender is relatively small and somewhat inconsistent.

Personality was examined at the macro level by McClelland (1961) in a wide-ranging (if a little bigoted) study of why some societies succeed. He concluded it stemmed from citizens' strong work ethic and the importance of the achievement motive. The latter is measured in psychological terms as need for Achievement, or n-Achievement, which is a measure of people's drive to do something better, faster, more efficiently and more easily. People high in n-Achievement agree with statements such as: 'I set difficult goals for myself which I attempt to reach.' McClelland pointed out (pages 210-225) that successful executives and entrepreneurs are critical to economic development and their success requires accurate decision making under uncertainty which in turn involves calculated risks in which luck and skill play a role. People with high n-Achievement succeed because their good judgement is able to favourably affect the result.

In a pointer to why innovation can sometimes deliver poor outcomes, McClelland concluded that high n-Achievement decision makers have strong expectations, bordering on over-confidence, that their ability will enable success in an uncertain situation. Thus they "tend to perceive their probability of success as greater, particularly when there are no facts to justify an estimate." But when probabilities are relatively well-known from history, the over-confidence disappears. In the former case, probability of success is only quantifiable in terms of the decision maker's expertise and expectations, whilst hard data offer an indication in the latter case.

This explains the *illusion of control*, or belief that decision makers can foster success through their efforts despite the absence of supporting evidence. This was a popular subject of research during the 1960s and 1970s, and a number of exotic experiments were performed to replicate the finding that people have most confidence in events they can control. Howell (1971) tested students who threw darts at a board and were rewarded in proportion to their score multiplied by a number obtained at random from spinning a roulette wheel. This gave multiple paired outcomes determined by the combination of a factor which is within the students' control (dart score) and a factor beyond their control (roulette wheel's result). After a familiarisation period, students played for money and – when able to choose the criteria for a win – consistently preferred outcomes where the greatest uncertainty related to the dart; in other words, they preferred to back their own skill, rather than trust to chance.

Another personality-related perspective is provided by Slovic (2000) who reported that 'worldviews' – or attitudes towards society and its structures – are powerful risk paradigms. People with an egalitarian preference for equal sharing of wealth in society have a higher perception of the risk of a range of hazards; whereas people who prefer a hierarchical society with experts in control have lower perceptions of risk. A subset of respondents – white males, with better education and income, and conservative political views – have a significantly lower perception of risk.

This led Slovic (2000: xxxiv) to restate the (now-forgotten) 1970s tenet that perceived control is important:

"... risk perceptions may reflect deep-seated values about technology and its impact on society. White males may perceive less risk than others because they are more involved in creating, managing, controlling and benefiting from technology and other activities that are hazardous. Women and non white males may perceive greater risk because they tend to have less control over these activities and benefit less from them."

Other important psychological influences on risk taking include: locus of control (by powerful others, internal control and chance) [Levenson (1974)]; and tolerance of ambiguity [Budner (1962)] [23].

A factor related to decision maker control is advice from experts. Whilst considerable work has been done on evaluating expertise, little has examined the influence of expert inputs on decisions. Eeckhoudt and Godfroid (2000) showed mathematically that expert input is of less value to risk averse decision makers than it is to risk neutral decision makers. Although

---

[23] There is a rich literature containing surveys of attitudes towards risk. An example developed by Simons (1999) looks at company level risks. Zaleskiewicz (2001) provided scales that measure stimulating and instrumental risk taking, respectively, using questions such as the following: If I play a game (e.g. cards) I prefer to play for money; to achieve something in life, one has to take risks. A large number of other studies have provided questions on risk, including: Austin et al. (2001), Casssidy and Lynn (1989), Goldberg (1990), Griffin-Pierson (1990), Levenson (1974), Pennings (2002), Robinson and Shaver (1973) and Rohrmann (1997).

both groups will value expert opinion after they have decided to take a decision, the risk-neutral group gives it most weight because their decision is based on facts, rather than risk evaluation.

A further interesting finding of behavioural studies is the way that risk attributes interact with time preference. The economic assumption behind time discounting is that an immediate reward is preferred over a distant, equivalent reward. In most cases the reduction in value is not linear, but decreases as the length of the delay increases.

Lawrance (1991) used panel data collected annually from 1,513 US households since 1968 to conclude that the discount rate matched for age and family composition ranges from 12 percent for educated, high income groups to 19 percent for least educated, low income groups. Although the paper concluded that poor people are 'less patient', the data are also consistent with delay aversion by socio-economically disadvantaged groups whose negative situation encourages them to accept an immediate risk rather than avoid delay to a possibly favourable outcome[24].

An experiment by Sagristano et al. (2002) shows that the more distant is a result, the greater the weight that is given to the outcome (e.g. win or reward), with decreasing weight to the probability or cost of achieving the outcome. As an illustration, they point out that people overweight the enjoyment of a distant event (e.g. a ski trip) and underweight its costs (a long drive and queue for entry and tickets); this gives rise to the familiar lament that 'it seemed like a good idea at the time'. Also subjects have a lower discount rate for uncertain outcomes than for certain outcomes: thus they are more risk embracing (tolerant of variability) with distant choices than with near term choices.

An important consequence of this is that - in the case of near term outcomes - the feasibility or probability of an event is the key consideration, rather than its benefit or desirability. This means that gamblers, for instance, should prefer games of skill for short term payouts, and games of chance when payouts are delayed. In fact exactly this applies: without exception, gambling alternatives with the illusion of control - such as cards and horse races - have an immediate payout[25]; whereas the only gambles with a longer term payout are lotteries ruled by chance. This was not considered by Sagristano et al. (2002) but is confirmed by their results: when testing subjects' relative rankings, they found that the desirability of a con-

---

[24] Kacelnik and Bateson (1996) similarly report that animals are universally risk embracing when variability is in delay: they are more willing to take a risk and accept variability in outcome than they are to accept variability in time and a possible delay to the outcome.

[25] The reverse is not true: a popular game of pure chance with immediate payout is poker machines (fruit or slot machines in some locations).

trollable outcome is subjectively more important than its feasibility; the opposite applies when chance rules the outcome.

A different way to measure chronological effect on decision makers facing risky alternatives is to create time pressures on subjects. An example is given by Finucane et al. (2000) who asked University of Western Australia students to rank a variety of activities and technologies by their risk to Australia. Half the students were put under time pressure with a limit of 5.2 seconds per answer (this was one standard deviation shorter than the average response time established in pilot tests) and the negative correlation was stronger under the time pressure. The researchers concluded that the reduced time available for analysis switches people to more time-efficient judgement styles so that they make greater use of affect, association and prejudgements. This supports the affect heuristic in which risks are associated with outcomes that exhibit negative feelings and costs.

An alternative interpretation is that subjects become more risk averse (as evidenced by greater perception of risk for a given benefit) under time pressure. This was confirmed by Mano (1990) who summarised a range of studies and concluded that time pressure: simplifies decision techniques and speeds up the process; leads to overweighting of negative data; and reduces the quality of decisions made[26]. Risk-aversion under time pressure complements other risk-averse attitudes, particularly the ambiguity effect, which emerges when people have insufficient resources (in this case time) to make a decision. An important implication of this evidence is that bounded decision makers err on the side of risk aversion unless they have adequate justification to take on risk.

Moving on from time, nationality also seems to play a role in risk attitudes. This is logical given the demonstration by Hofstede (1997) that nationalities differ in a number of personality traits that impact decisions. Despite numerous cross-cultural studies involving risk, most involve pure gambles such as lotteries whose expected return is not amenable to application of skill; moreover it has proven difficult to control for demographic variables. Thus, although a number of studies have yielded interesting findings, they are not always consistent and conclusions can only be tentative.

Roth et al. (1991) conducted experiments in Israel, Japan, USA and Yugoslavia using a bargaining situation and simple markets. They followed standard protocols to control for obvious potential biases (such as differences in language and currency) and found that subjects in Japan and Israel have higher risk aversion than subjects in the United States and

---

[26] Conversely, Perlow et al. (2002) concluded that the influence of time pressure on the decisions of individuals and organisations is not clear or consistent.

Yugoslavia. Weber and Hsee (1998) recruited 283 students at four universities in China, Germany, Poland and USA and gave them questionnaires relating to risky investment alternatives, each with three possible outcomes ranging from gain to loss. The study measured the value and perceived risk of each alternative. The Chinese students were most risk prone and perceived risk to be lower; whilst American students were least risk prone.

Yates (1990: 98) reports studies of two groups of Chinese and American university students who were asked 'almanac' questions of the type: does London or Paris have more residents? Subjects were then asked to indicate the probability that their answer was correct. Although the average number of correct responses by the groups was almost identical, the Chinese students were more overconfident and they were much more likely to be 100 percent confident. This matches the finding reported by Camerer (1995) that Asians tend to have poor overall assessments of probabilities which leads them to assign a higher probability to extreme outcomes. And it matches the findings of Hsee and Weber (1999) whose tests involving standard gambles showed that Chinese students were significantly ($p<0.001$) more risk seeking than American students.

In summary, results are not always conclusive and in agreement, but most studies have discovered statistically significant links between risk taking behaviour and personal attributes. Thus risk embrace increases with male gender, income, education, a history of risky past decisions, and – less certainly - with Asian heritage. Conversely it decreases with assets and marriage, and perhaps age. Risk embrace is also linked to a number of personality traits such as sociability, assertiveness, adventurousness and compulsiveness; untrusting, altruistic and compliant; and preference for a hierarchical society.

Summary of Experimental Findings

The previous section described the role of risk in decision making to lay the foundation for a model of risk and decision making. In theory, decision makers should choose the best from available alternatives irrespective of prior outcomes and their preferences should not respond to valuations determined by their endowment. However, it is clear that humans and animals display non-optimising (or paradoxical) behaviour. Typically this is taken as evidence of use of heuristics, or simple rules, that lead to cognitive errors. According to Kahneman et al. (1982: xii) the heuristics reduce task complexity so they are "tractable for the kind of mind that people happen to have … [but] sometimes lead to systematic errors."

What are we to make of behavioural anomalies which fly in the face of normative assumptions such as utility maximisation? Waite (2001) provided the likely explanation that they stem from successful natural selection of an optimum decision making methodology. These automatic responses shortcut decision making, much as making all warning lights red simplifies recognition of alerts. At the very least, the anomalies provide important insights which must be taken into account when analysing the way that people reach decisions. The behaviours may be curious and illogical, but they are real. None can be dismissed as an aberration, nor abandoned in preference to normative, value maximising approaches.

Even so, it is quite unusual to suggest that anomalies could be associated with employment of sophisticated decision processes. This is puzzling because the most reliable anomaly, instinctive risk-aversion, is logical given that survival of forebears of all current beings means that the average animal or human faces a positive expected outcome: there is no need to adopt risky behaviour for its own sake; and automatic risk aversion is a sensible first assumption. The natural tendency to evolve towards intuitive risk aversion (rather than (say) enhancing cognitive skills to better judge and manage risk) is also consistent with experimental findings that beings subjected to environmental stresses adapt to avoid the stresses, rather than evolve to cope with them [e.g. Stanton et al. (2000)].

In her update of animal foraging studies, Bateson (2002) observed that foraging decisions literally have a life-or-death outcome and so natural selection would have acted to optimise their behaviour. The difficulty for researchers has been to develop a unified explanation of how animals choose between different alternatives. Logically the long term goal is fitness to survive environmental pressures, but this needs to be operationalised through short-term guides. Experiments designed to elicit these guides have reached the conclusion that animals do not maximise the immediate value of choices facing them[27]. She pointed to several obvious conclusions from experiments: animals are risk sensitive, and tend to be risk-averse unless facing a negative energy budget when they turn risk-prone. Animals are averse to taking a risk on amounts of food, but will accept a risk in terms of the timing of food availability rather than accept a certain delay.

Such examples of Nature responding so clearly to risk make it hard to argue with Lo (1999) that the fundamentals of risk – its heuristics – have been inspired by evolution so that there is a genetic basis to risk (as there is to so many other psychological and behavioural traits). Krebs and Davies (1984: 18) are unequivocal: "behaviour is influenced by natural selection"

---

[27] This is analogous to findings of behavioural economists' experiments where people do not target maximisation of the choices facing them.

and evolution shaped modern day norms. Thus our key institutions – ranging from language to family - evolved to optimise human survival.

This is bolstered by experimental studies showing a link between neurochemical activity and risk taking which led Schoemaker (1993: 53) to conclude "that global risk attitudes may contain agent-specific biological components in both humans and animals". This also matches the argument by Hamer and Copeland (1998) that personality has genetic roots and that DNA can impact our decision making processes.

The deterministic interpretation of decision making gains weight from experiments conducted by Greene et al. (2001) which monitored subjects' brains using MRIs. These showed that different types of decisions lead to significant variability in levels of activity in parts of the brain associated with emotion and cognition. Where decisions trigger emotional engagement – for instance through positing a moral dilemma – they engage activity in a part of the brain which is not utilised in impersonal decisions such as mathematical calculations. Because different parts of the brain are used to evaluate decisions with different features, the criteria for decision making will differ. This may be a partial explanation of the compatibility principle discussed above where decision makers use different criteria in what appear to be similar decisions.

The intensity of behavioural anomalies is related to the perceived risk of the decision. Despite the general aversion of humans and animals towards risk and loss, most will vary their risk attitudes according to the environment. This means that the relative attractiveness of options is not stable or objectively established: decision makers are risk-sensitive. In humans at least, risk attitudes and risk sensitivity are related to personality characteristics, largely because embracing risk requires traits such as tolerance of ambiguity. Wally and Baum (1994: 939) summarise the evidence: "Tolerance for risk ... appears to be associated with psychological flexibility. Flexible individuals display informality, adaptability, optimism and adventurousness." The key implication is that any decision model which is blind to the players and their context will be of sorely limited value.

Although most biases and paradoxes tend to be dismissed as cognitive illusions, they suggest that decision makers do not target maximisation of value or utility: behaviour is designed to maximise the probability of survival. The difference between the concepts of utility maximisation and risk sensitivity is pictured in figure 3.3. Normative theory holds that decision makers choose the greatest expected utility, irrespective of the prospects that it offers for survival.

Risk-sensitive foraging argues that animals and humans are outlook-sensitive in their risk-taking: they are continually alert to the risks of worst case, survival-threatening outcomes and their primary motivation is to

avoid catastrophic loss. This motivates decision makers to choose alternatives which maximise their chances of survival, irrespective of whether
they offer the highest utility. As Singh (1986: 565) noted: "organizations
seek to maximize their chances of survival when faced with uncertainty."

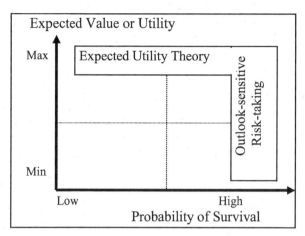

Fig. 3.3. Utility and Risk Sensitivity

Another important feature shown in the next diagram is the expected
outcome: if it exceeds a survival or satisficing level, then the decision
maker is risk averse; and vice versa. The implication – as summarised in
the next figure – is that risk propensity shifts abruptly around a satisficing
level which - at its most basic - is related to survival.

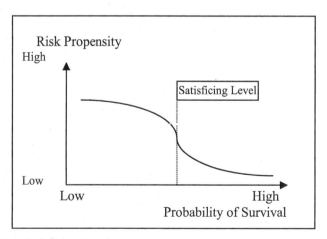

Fig. 3.4. Satisficing Level

Decision makers provide much greater support for unlikely events than is justified by their objective probability of success. Apart from situations of near certain ruinous loss where extreme risk provides the only survival chance, this behaviour is confined to situations involving skill. In accord with the competency effect, decision makers believe that their judgement is influential in the outcome of risky decisions and select a risky alternative with a high payout. The implicit calculation according to Expected Utility Theory might be:

$$\text{Payout} = \sum_{Allchoices} (\text{Probability} + \text{Skill margin}) * \text{Return}$$

A complex environment and constraints on decision makers' resources (both data availability and cognitive capability) mean that they physically cannot implement the ideal decision strategy. The inevitable simplification renders decision makers boundedly rational [Simon (1955)] and thus forced to constrain their options. As a result, decision makers adopt heuristics – or rules producing automatic responses – such as risk aversion in order to streamline complex decision making.

One of the most significant bounds (at least for its challenge to normative assumptions behind decision making) is that decision makers have poor estimates of the distribution of most decision events. This is because obtaining certainty imposes delay while significant sampling takes place; it is intellectually demanding to remember and process additional data; and – because not all distributions remain constant over time - opportunities can quickly evapourate and so decision makers avoid the delay inherent in deeper research.

In amusing fashion, Miller (1956) put a limit of seven on humans' recall capacity, although it can be increased by several tricks[28]. Making a choice using a sample of (say) ten gives 70 percent confidence that the estimate is within ±30 percent of the distribution's true mean[29]. Clearly small samples and simple calculations of probability are appropriate when memory and analytical capability are limited; and pursuit of stable functions does not

---

[28] Animals use similarly small samples: Caraco et al. (1990) found that birds choose after eight tests, whilst Real (1991) shows bees make 15 tests.

[29] Under a binomial distribution, the confidence interval attached to any estimate (or its associated level of accuracy) is given by $\pm z \sqrt{p(1-p)/n}$ where p is the probability of one outcome, n is the number of observations and z corresponds to the level of confidence. Assuming two tails, at the 70% confidence level z = 1.04; at 80%, z =1.28; and at 90% z=1.65.

`make sense when ambient conditions are changing. Inevitably, then, decision makers accept considerable uncertainty about the choices they face, both in terms of limits on the range of alternatives they can consider and on the risks and outcomes.

There is also a bias in data collection pointed out by Zackay (1984): we tend to require less information to support a desirable event than we do before concluding that an undesirable event may occur. Together this becomes what Tversky and Kahneman (1971) termed the *law of small numbers* in which people overgeneralise from limited data, rather than committing resources to collect and analyse a statistically robust sample. The result is an overweighting of recent experience or data (and underweighting of longer term evidence and the population distribution).

The empirical data above make it clear that - although animals and humans are conditioned to recognise risks - they normally have a strong bias towards loss aversion: they consistently prefer strategies with low variance and therefore a high probability of achieving the expected result. When faced with a decision, they are relatively quick to identify a positive expected outcome and appreciate whether their situation is solely dependent upon chance, or offers the opportunity to profit by skill. Where outcomes are ruled by chance, bees, birds and people all prefer certainty!

Moreover, `risk' is not just the probability of an adverse outcome but uncertainty about the outcome. Thus decision makers equate choices which are ambiguous and which have high variance: each is a diversion from the greater level of certainty that can be obtained by risk aversion. This explains why test subjects prefer a lower expected outcome to an ambiguous outcome.

Despite impressive progress in the last few decades, there are clearly significant gaps in our knowledge of risk and decision making. One is the role of personality and how it might impact on risk propensity. For instance the signs associated with age and gender are different in various studies, and ethnicity's role is similarly unclear. Another is confusion in terminology such that two sets of apparently identical behaviours can be variously attributed to different causes. Similarly there appears to be a lack of clarity between loss aversion and risk aversion.

Another fruitful area of research is replication of human decision making biases in animals, as evidence of cross-species decision rules would even more strongly point to the evolutionary importance of risk propensity.

Finally there is a need to operationalise biases: how, for instance, can one account for apparent confidence of Asians, or of decision makers who misguidedly believe they have a relevant skill? And what leads to the cross-over between risk aversion and risk embrace?

CHAPTER 4   Real-World Decision Making Under Risk

This chapter provides a summary of the literature on real-world decisions by individuals who face risk, and complements previous discussions which looked at the theory of risk-taking and reported the findings of experimental behavioural studies.

The chapter begins with a description of the principal studies which are representative of individuals' risky problem solving in the real world; then reports relevant findings from studies of racetrack wagering markets; and closes with a summary and brief conclusions.

Principal Studies

Empirical studies which illuminate real-world decision making under risk or uncertainty fall into two broad categories. The first measures individuals' *ex ante* beliefs, for example by using case studies describing a typical real-world decision [e.g. Sitkin and Weingart (1995)], or in controlled experiments that simulate real-world outcomes [e.g. Fox and Tversky (1998)].

The second type of study involves *ex post* analysis of micro-economic data which reveals the collective outcome of many people's individual decisions in relation to the same question. An example is Lease et al. (1974) who accessed the trading history of customers at a New York broking house and sent them a questionnaire. A warning to readers, though, is that studies of this type are few as most field studies have not attempted to incorporate personality or demographic measures, but deduced risk attitudes from large, anonymous groups.

Personality and Risky Decision Making

Common management strategies (such as personnel selection, training and placement) rely on stability in individuals' personality and assume that managers make similar decisions across varying situations. Thus it is not surprising to find a considerable number of real-world studies link personality to risk-taking.

MacCrimmon and Wehrung (1990) obtained comprehensive data on the characteristics and behaviour of 509 senior executives in North America, and developed 13 measures of personal and business risk. They found that risk taking rose with professional success, and declined with age and education. Williams and Narendran (1999) included a test to evaluate the need for achievement in their study of managerial risk-taking and found it correlated (r=0.33, p<0.01) with managerial risk preference.

Smith and Friedland (1998) obtained survey responses from 102 mid level nurse managers in 14 US hospitals. Risk taking was more likely amongst managers with at least a bachelor's degree, higher autonomy orientation (a world that is supportive of free choice), and lower control orientation (the environment constrains behaviour to norms). Trimpop (1994: 281) prepared a comprehensive study entitled *The Psychology of Risk Taking Behavior* and concluded that: "personality risk factors play a significant role in risk taking behavior, but they play a less important role (5-25 percent of variance explained) than situational factors do."

This may be too low an estimate based on the table below which summarises the amount of variance in risk-taking which published studies found was explained by personality. These contemporary studies in real-world settings suggest that about 30 percent of risk propensity is explained by personality.

The minority influence of personality on risk taking is consistent with evidence that individuals' risk behaviour is not stable across different settings [Isaac and James (2000)], but depends on situational factors such as control over the outcome, and the environment.

Although it should be a particularly fruitful research topic, little work has attempted to evaluate risk propensity by linking actual risk behaviour such as investing (i.e. revealed risk preferences) to personal characteristics and psychometric factors. Many researchers believe that this is impractical, including Kahneman and Tversky (1979: 265): "Field studies can only provide for rather crude tests of qualitative predictions because probabilities and utilities cannot be adequately measured in such contexts" [30].

Table 4.1. Proportion of Variance in Risk-Taking Explained by Personality

Reference	Sample and Testing Material	R^2
Austin et al. (2001)	252 Scottish farmers provided data on their production orientation, personality and cognitive ability	~0.3
Grable (2000)	Sample of 2,065 faculty and staff at large US university provided measure of propensity for financial risk and details of education, income and occupation	0.22
Halek and Eisenhauer (2001)	2,376 Michigan households: explanatory variables include demography, workforce status, and depression as well as personality	0.47
Smith and Friedland (1998)	102 mid level nurse managers in 14 US hospitals	0.19
Williams and Narendran (1999)	285 ethnic Indian managers completed risk preference and personality questionnaires	0.26
Zuckerman and Kuhlman (2000)	260 psychology undergraduates completed measures of risky behaviour and personality	0.29

A comprehensive study examining personality and risk taking by Halek and Eisenhauer (2001) used a survey to obtain details of insurance coverage (a real-world measure of risk propensity) for 2,376 Michigan households. They found that risk embrace increases with age (by about one twentieth per year), male gender (55 percent risk prone, versus 50 percent for women), non-white race, and a record of immigration. Risk embrace decreases with assets (but at a declining rate) and marriage.

Somewhat less successful was Pålsson (1996) who took a random cross-section of 7,000 Swedish households from 1985 and calculated a risk-aversion coefficient based on the proportion of total wealth held in risky asset classes, particularly equities. She then looked at the relationship between risk aversion and a variety of socio-economic, geographic and demographic household indicators (gender, age and marital status of household head; the household's number of children, net wealth, city and

---

[30] They added: "By default the method of hypothetical choices [i.e. laboratory gambles] emerges as the simplest procedure by which a large number of theoretical questions can be investigated." This explains the considerable amount of work described in previous chapters where laboratory experiments have been used to assess personality aspects of risk taking.

dwelling; and the labour force status, occupation, employer and income of occupants). Unfortunately these variables provided minimal ability to explain risk aversion ($R^2 < 0.1$), and none was statistically significant at the 5 percent level.

Arrow (1982) reported the results of a 1940s study[31] which used data from brokerage houses on grain futures trading to examine the record of large hedgers (mainly millers), professional speculators and non-professional speculators. The first group lost, which was expected as they are risk averse and buying insurance; the second group won; and the third group lost.

Another useful example is that of Burns and Wilde (1995) who posed as taxi passengers to observe driver behaviour, and then asked drivers to complete personality tests, self report on driving traits, and release their driving records. The researchers found that a third of driving behaviour could be classified by two factors: abrupt handling of the vehicle, and intentionally fast driving. The second factor is a clear indicator of risky behaviour and correlated significantly ($p<0.01$) with the high-risk personality measure developed by Keinan (1984), and only slightly less significantly ($p<0.05$) with the Experience Seeking measure in the Zuckerman and Kuhlman (2000) sensation-seeking-scale.

Published analyses of the link between individuals' real-world risk attitudes and personality are sorely limited and their results are far from unequivocal. However, they clearly challenge the normative assumption that decision makers are typically risk averse; and suggest that at least a quarter of risk behaviours are due to decision makers' unique traits.

Nationality and Risky Decision Making

Given the link between nationality and personality traits, it is no surprise that nationality plays a powerful role in determining risk attitudes. Hofstede (1997: 4) drew an analogy with computer programming to argue that national culture is "the software of the mind ... which indicates what reactions are likely and understandable given one's past." Thus different cultures react in different, but predictable, ways to the same stimulus.

Hofstede (1997) used data drawn from personality tests on IBM executives to develop a concept called *uncertainty avoidance* (the extent to which unknown situations are resisted as threatening). This is related to loss aversion, and Hofstede's measures cluster Australian managers with

---

[31] Stewart, B (1949), 'Analysis of Speculative Trading in Grain Futures' *USDA Technical Bulletin* Number 1001

those in Britain, Canada, Ireland, New Zealand, and USA in a more risk prone, Anglophone group.

Several other studies have reported risk attitudes by nationality. Rothman (2000) surveyed 324 US managers who self-indicated their ethnicity as African-American, Asian-Pacific Islander, Caucasian, or Hispanic-Latin. He found that Asian-Pacific Islanders were high in socialisation (the extent to which individuals conform to collective social values) and Hispanic-Latino managers were low on the responsibility scale (a measure of dependability and acceptance of rules).

Lee et al. (1994) surveyed 155 executives from Canada, China, and Hong Kong to examine the influence of national environment on responsible business strategy in relation to the corporation, customer and competitor. As shown in the accompanying table (drawn from Lee et al's table 3.2), three factors explained 65 percent of the variance: Hong Kong managers were highest on ensuring survival of the firm, whilst Chinese managers were lowest with Canadians in the middle; co-operation with competitors showed the same polarisation with high scores in Hong Kong, low in China and Canada in the middle; managers in Canada scored lowest on creating win:win relationships with customers, with China highest and Hong Kong managers in the middle.

Table 4.2. Responsible Business Behaviour

Factor	Mean Factor Score		
	China	Hong Kong	Canada
Serving as the guardian of the firm	-0.26	0.29	-0.01
Maintaining a healthy relationship with competitors	-0.03	0.40	-0.28
Creating win:win relationships with customers	0.76	-0.09	-0.60

Such studies reveal an international dimension in risk-taking; and point to strong influence on a firm's internal and external strategy (including business ethics and risk propensity) from national cultural and regulatory environments.

Combining the studies suggests the following ranking of nationalities from risk-averse to risk-embracing: Southern Europe (Greece, Portugal), Japan and Korea, Latin America, Middle East (Israel, Saudi Arabia) and West Asia (Turkey), Western Europe, Scandinavia, Australia, North America, and East Asia.

Environmental, Temporal and Framing Effects on Risky Decision Making

Unfortunately few studies have tested the hypothesis that human behaviour responds to environmental pressures. Pietras and Hackenberg (2001) conducted a human version of animal energy budget experiments by giving test subjects choices between two coloured keys which delivered either a fixed number of points (two) or a variable number (equal probability of either one or three points); the points were exchangeable for money, but only if a minimum value were achieved by the end of each block of choices. The minimum value was varied from positive earnings budget conditions (ten points required from five trials) to negative (12 or 13 points). The results paralleled those of animal studies with risk embrace by human subjects under negative budget conditions.

Although it is hard to change humans' environment, individuals and organisations do modify their behaviour when faced with an unfavourable environment. Good examples are the decisions of farm managers as drought approaches, and the strategies of taxi drivers (i.e. cruise around and `forage' for passengers, or wait on ranks [Camerer et al. (1997)]).

Experimental evidence in the previous chapter showed that time is an important lever on human behaviour and induces preferences for an immediate reward over a distant payout. Although decision makers will embrace risk to avoid a delay, the cause-and-effect can be reversed so that risk aversion promotes delay. Pablo et al. (1996), for instance, provide evidence that risk-averse managers will slow implementation of strategies to gain more data and institutional support, and thus reduce or spread risks.

When individuals face decisions, an important factor is framing, or the tendency to change preferences when a decision is repackaged. A tangible example in the real world came from a New Zealand research project which counted visitors to a regional shopping centre and – after normalising numbers for day of the week and holiday impacts – regressed visitor traffic against weather. It found that an increase in rainfall and maximum temperature decrease patronage by up to a quarter [Parsons (2001)].

Highhouse and Yüce (1996) conducted experiments on 244 psychology undergraduates to test the importance of framing on decisions. They found that decision makers consistently prefer a risky alternative which is framed as an opportunity over one framed as a threat; and take more risks when facing a loss than when facing a gain.

One of the most graphic depictions of the power of framing was provided in a study which set out to validate the intuitively obvious conclusion that the public places a lower value on the lives of future generations than on the lives of people alive today. Studies had typically shown that people value one life today as equal to six lives in 25 years and 45 lives in 100 years (implying respective discount rates of 7.4 and 3.9 percent per year). Frederick (2003) used a sample of 401 voters and undergraduates, and seven different methods (including the exact wording of questions used in the best known previous study) to elicit their intergenerational time preferences between lives saved today and in the future. He replicated the previous findings, but obtained dramatically different results from alternative elicitation procedures: one life today was equivalent to a range of values from <1 to six lives in 25 years, and to a range from <1 to 45 lives in 100 years. For both time periods, at least one measure placed similar values on current and future lives. This showed that respondents could equate present and future lives, but their answer depended on the survey method.

As an aside, one of the reasons for the quite different results is that none of the elicitation methods directly measured the target variable (e.g. 'Do you care less about future generations than this generation?'). This, in fact, is a common shortcoming of many experiments where the motivation of the subjects is either assumed and tested, or inferred from the data. Examples discussed later in this chapter include Odean (1998) who attributes investors' trading activity to loss aversion without asking why they made the choices; and Camerer et al. (1997) who explain taxi drivers' working hours without enquiring about the driver goals (although they surveyed owners about institutional factors). An enhancement to many experimental procedures would be to include even a few questions about subjects' motives and objectives.

Framing can also complement a natural aversion to extremes and preference for 'normal' choices. This leads to the common experience (not infrequently abused in unscrupulous opinion surveys) that people tend to cluster their preferences or decisions around the middle of a range, irrespective of whether it makes objective sense or not. Thus simply adding an outlier value to a survey can shift respondents' apparent preferences.

Framing shapes group perceptions, too. An example of its power is given by Japanese management scholar Ohmae (1990: 180-181) who pointed out that Japanese textbooks teach children that their country is poor with no natural resources, whilst Brazilian children learn that their nation is rich and blessed with every known kind of natural resource. This is his explanation for why Japanese add value to imported raw materials whereas Brazil stagnates.

Pablo et al. (1996) suggest that framing can be used to modify the attitudes of those involved in planning and implementing major strategic decisions, and thus increase or reduce their level of risk. For instance, organisations which measure performance against outcomes and reward success will increase risk-taking; conversely focussing on adherence to process and providing minimal individual incentives will promote risk-aversion.

Kessler (2003: 26-27) described how CIA Director John Deutch

"diminished its effectiveness by creating a risk-averse atmosphere ... Deutch imposed a rule requiring special approval before a CIA officer could recruit a spy who was not an upstanding citizen ... His rule on recruitment of assets had a chilling effect ... [as it] implied that assets who were bad guys were less desirable than those who were squeaky clean ... The extra hassle of obtaining approval meant many CIA officers simply avoided anyone with a history of problems ... Yet exactly that kind of person was what the CIA needed to penetrate organizations like al Qaeda."

Kessler (2003: 206-208) also looked at FBI processes and reported that Louis Freeh, who became FBI Director in 1993, was averse to technology. His refusal to have a personal computer sent a powerful anti-technology message to the organisation. Thus in the months prior to terrorist attacks on 11 September 2001, the FBI's paper-based system and minimal electronic capability were weak in detecting patterns of threat.

In similar vein, the way a proposal is presented will shape its appeal. Risk seeking executives tend to overweight opportunities: they focus on projects with high payout and pay less attention to difficulties that may bring the outcome below the upper bound. Conversely, risk averse executives overweight the worst-case outcome and divert effort towards minimising ambiguity, diversity and threats: they perceive a higher level of risk attached to any venture [Lopes (1987)].

The way an issue is presented (threat or opportunity; possible loss or probable gain) influences the decision: stylising a decision as low-risk will gain more broad based support, especially from risk intolerant executives; whereas focussing on its upper bound is more attractive to risk seeking executives[32].

A different aspect of framing which can promote risk-taking is reduction of bounds by providing an excess of data. For instance Yates (1990) discusses the Oskamp Study where psychologists were asked to read a patient's clinical history, build up a personality profile, and then answer questions about his condition and indicate their confidence in the answer. The test was carried out in four stages as subjects were given progressively more information about the patient. Whilst the accuracy of the answers changed little through the study (roughly 30 percent correct), the psychologists' confidence almost doubled. Thus the doctor who is able to ask many questions of a patient or the stock analyst of a CEO and thereby gain contextual information may only be lifting his or her confidence, not the accuracy of the prediction.

---

[32] Despite many examples of the power of framing, a meta-study by Kühberger (1988) concluded that the effect is relatively small.

Another decision feature related to framing is the importance of reference levels such as milestones which most empirical studies reveal as influencing decision makers.

A good example involving a large volume of financial data comes from interesting studies of the patterns of exercise of stock options which were granted to over 50,000 employees at seven publicly traded US corporations during the decade to the mid 1990s. Heath et al. (1999) found that option holders defer exercise (and hence accept risk) following recent falls in the stock's price and in proportion to the amount by which the share's price is below its maximum for the past year. Exercise rates are sensitive to historical extremes and increase when the stock price rises above peaks recorded during the preceding few years. The studies also show application of judgement through higher levels of exercise in periods when stock prices rebound from a fall.

If option recipients were risk neutral, they would exercise options at a price around their expected value, which is about 1.5 times the strike price (given that the market value of a ten-year option at the time of its grant is around half the strike price). In fact few options are exercised to capture modest, but certain, returns: the mean market price at the time of exercise is 2.2 times the strike price, which shows option holders defer exercise until the return is well above the ex ante expectation. Overall these behaviours are consistent with risk embrace by the option holders, and their incorporation of reference levels in decision making.

One of the few studies to tease out how reference levels are set was by Gaba and Viscusi (1998) who surveyed 335 workers in four US chemical plants to determine their subjective evaluation of risk thresholds. They found that the most significant impact came from education, with college-educated workers reporting that a 'dangerous job' has an objective accident rate which is more than a third lower than the rate reported by those without a college education. Thus better educated workers see any job as more risky than it is perceived by less educated workers.

Laughhunn et al. (1980) found that reference levels are important to managerial decision making. They surveyed the risk preferences of 237 managers from North America and Europe and found that – when returns are below target – 71 percent of the managers were risk-seeking. However, when the losses were ruinous, only 36 percent of the managers were risk seeking.

Style Effects in Risky Decision Making

During the 1970s, the prevalent view in management literature was that decision makers are uniformly risk averse. Gradually, though, it became clear that risk preference is influenced by the style of decision makers, particularly the way they evaluate information, modify its associated risks, and implement the decision. This led to an increasingly vigorous search for factors which influence managerial risk-taking.

March and Shapira (1987) found that executives do not see risk as a probability concept, but as one involving uncertainty and the magnitude of a bad outcome: for them risk is a question of the quantum of exposure to loss, not the probability of variation. These and other studies indicate that individuals do not make precise calculations of probability, but compare alternatives against realistic outcomes. Arguably many of them do not even think in terms of probabilities as the data are inadequate to support such differentiation. March and Shapira, for instance, found a direct link between risk propensity and managers' control over the outcome as the latter impacts on probability of success.

MacCrimmon and Wehrung (1984) used a 16-page (!) questionnaire to evaluate the responses of 464, all male, North American executives to four risky business situations. Their subjects tend to use similar risk modification strategies, but had wide disparities in risk propensity (depending on perceived risk and their level of control). For instance, executives have different attitudes towards risks that involve their own money and their company's money, and between risks with their finances and recreation. Using a similar methodology, Wally and Baum (1994) studied the decision making attributes of CEOs of Pennsylvania manufacturing firms and found those who embrace risk are confident and able to make decisions quickly. Cognitive styles and personality characteristics – particularly the degree to which executives utilise intuition along with their intelligence, risk tolerance and propensity to act – speed up strategic decision making and generate superior financial performance.

An important feature of any decision is the depth of relevant information available to the decision maker. Di Mauro and Maffioletti (2001) examined decisions under ambiguity by conducting a screen-based auction to determine the price people would pay to insure against a loss. They found weak ambiguity aversion which did not impact valuations with statistical significance. Conversely Fox and Tversky (1995) report studies which found substantial evidence of ambiguity aversion in a market setting. Ambiguity aversion is also clear in work by French and Poterba (1991) which documents the near-universal preference amongst investors for assets in their own country. The evidence suggests, then, that decision maker confidence rises as a problem's dimensions become less ambiguous and more familiar: this is the competency effect discussed in the previous chapter. Affect seems to play a role in managerial decision making. For instance, Antonides et al. (1997) surveyed 200 subjects in each of Hungary, Netherlands, Poland and UK to determine their attitudes towards a variety of common activities such as employment. The authors provided cross-correlations between 11 evaluation measures and the question `To what extent is this activity risky?' This showed a significant inverse relationship between risk and four measures (correlation coefficients in brackets):

- Moral (0.74) - To what extent is this activity moral?
- Beneficial (0.67) - To what extent is this activity beneficial to society?
- Known (0.66) - To what extent is this activity known to you?
- Prestigious (0.53) – To what extent is this activity prestigious?

Thus low-risk activities are judged to be moral, beneficial, known and prestigious (although the direction of causality is problematical: is the activity judged as positive and hence low risk, or vice versa?). The important aspect is that decision makers facing risky alternatives choose between them based on mental images of their associated benefits and costs: preferred choices are not expected to lead to bad outcomes, including losses.

To assess decision making style, Amsel et al. (1991) presented a variety of scenarios to psychologists, lawyers, police officers and undergraduate psychology students. Each scenario started with a conclusion involving a cause and effect, and then presented evidence of the relationship; subjects were asked to choose the most probable scenario and rate the causal relationship and the most logical cause and effect. Lawyers were convinced by statements such as `If X had not taken place, the event would not have occurred'; psychologists favoured previous historical links such as `X and Y have been associated in the past'; and more novice decision makers - police and undergraduates - relied on several causes. This is typical of anecdotal reports of differences in professions' cognitive styles: engineers, for instance, are said to think in systems terms, and thus remember processes that can be used to solve problems; whereas doctors think in facts and remember the solutions to past problems.

Forlani and Mullins (2000) set out to identify factors in entrepreneurs' risk preferences. Their subjects were 78 CEOs drawn from a sample based on popular rankings of the fastest growing public companies in the United States in the mid 1990s. The entrepreneurs preferred ventures with low variability in expected returns, and differences in choices responded to personal risk propensity and perceived risk in the venture. When offered choices with different magnitudes of potential loss, the entrepreneurs generally proved to be loss prone.

These results are interesting in light of the finding by Skaperdas and Gan (1995) that risk averse participants are more fearful of loss than risk seekers, and - because this encourages them to expend more effort as a form of insurance - they have greater chance of success. The authors proposed that risk-averse decision makers could actually enjoy an advantage in risky settings: if they self-select to participate in risky activities, particularly in business, this leads to the counter-intuitive finding that entrepreneurs who survive are more likely to be risk-averse. This explains why the risk propensity of successful entrepreneurs is <u>not</u> high.

Busenitz and Barney (1997) used survey techniques to examine decision making by entrepreneurs and a sample of managers in large organisations. The first sample comprised the founders of 573 newly formed, manufacturing firms. The second group comprised general managers (defined as having responsibility for at least two functional areas) from three publicly owned organisations with over 10,000 employees. Results showed that – by comparison with managers in large organisations - entrepreneurs were more overconfident and tended to adopt a more instinctive, heuristic approach to decisions rather than use statistical analysis. The authors found that these two variables predicted more than 70 percent of the variance in decision style between entrepreneurs and managers, and concluded (page 23): "entrepreneurs and managers in large organisations think differently."

The high explanatory power of just two variables explicitly left little room for factors such as personality and demography. This has two interesting implications. The first is that organisational climate has a strong link to decision making style. Secondly, that differences in occupation are accompanied by differences in thinking, and – by extension – in performance measures and goals. This explains how individuals can be successful in one type of organisation, but fail elsewhere; and why intra-organisational conflicts can be so chronic and damaging.

A further important aspect of decision making style is the strategy employed to implement a decision. Wehrung et al. (1989) studied 50 experienced managers using the `in-basket format' where participants are asked to respond to business situations described by hypothetical memos. They found that executives facing a risky choice typically try to modify it through negotiation, exploring other options, or delay. Executives will also use expenditure, bargaining or influence to enhance the probability of a favourable outcome and/or diminish the prospects of an unfavourable outcome. These interventions can occur several times in the chain of steps from first considering a risky decision until its execution.

Decision makers will also influence the context of their decisions – particularly to reduce ambiguity and manage risk - through delay, changing parameters, identifying alternatives and risk sharing [Wehrung et al. (1989)]. For Pablo et al. (1996: 724), it was clear that "risk affects decision behaviour [in acquisitions] by influencing perceptions of the decision situation, evaluation of alternatives, choices made and other decision-related actions taken in response to risk."

During the 1960s and 1970s, a subject of compelling interest in decision research (which seems of little interest today, although Forlani (2002) may have begun a revival) was that people's confidence in their decisions is related to control over the result, so they take greater risks when able to affect the outcome. Clear experimental evidence was offered by Langer (1975) who sold office workers lottery tickets in the form of a card featuring a famous footballer: the prize was $50 and each ticket cost $1; half the subjects chose their own footballer, whilst the other half received a card at random. Then just before the draw, Langer went around the subjects asking if they would sell their choice: the average selling price of no-choice participants was $1.9, but $9.0 for those who had chosen their own cards! (Conversely this could be evidence of the endowment effect discussed in chapter three).

Forlani (2002) conducted an experiment to confirm his hypothesis that – when a decision maker has (or perceives he has) significant control over the outcome – the expected return is more certain and so the magnitude of loss is of less importance than the probability of loss. He used 45 part-time MBA students in an exercise which manipulated their decision domain (relatively favourable or unfavourable position) and their control over the decision outcomes. Decision makers with high perceived levels of control took risks, irrespective of their domain. These results negated the now common presumption that risk taking is always more common below a satisficing threshold and after an experience of losses.

Howell (1971: 240) neatly encapsulated the essence of these studies with the argument that the locus of uncertainty of an outcome is important as "people tend to be overconfident in the outcome of events over which they have some control"; whereas they are underconfident over events which are beyond their control. When this skill is illusory and decision makers have less control than they think, risk of failure is high. Following a review of literature in a different context, Balabanis (2001) concluded that gambling games which are most addictive are ones that engage the players' skill. However, this could just as easily apply to managers whose professional satisfaction is so tied to demonstration of skill that they repeatedly seek out challenging opportunities. This would explain the finding by Kahneman and Lovallo (1993: 17) that managerial "decision makers are excessively prone to treat problems as unique, neglecting both the statistics of the past and the multiple opportunities of the future."

Bayesian Considerations in Risky Decision Making

A significant number of risky decisions occur sequentially, for instance: credit approvals in a bank, commodity trades in a Treasury, cycles in a manufacturing plant, or launches of a space shuttle. One of the important reference levels, or ledgers of mental accounting, is the risk associated with each successive decision: specifically, does risk remain constant irrespective of the outcome of decisions?

Starbuck and Milliken (1988) use the example of NASA's successful launch of 24 space shuttles before the 1986 *Challenger* disaster to discuss the implications of different beliefs about the outcomes of separate, risky events. Each shuttle launch was one of a finite population of events that are qualitatively similar and driven by common human, organisational and technical factors. This makes them different to random, mutually independent events such as successive spins of a balanced roulette wheel.

Decisions on whether to launch a shuttle or not have much in common with many other risky real-world decisions involving sequential events as their estimated risks are subject to re-assessment. Although risk estimates may be based on hard data (e.g. the record of similar technologies, or an aggregate of the performance record of a system's component parts), they inevitably contain elements of subjectivity. These subjective probability estimates are subject to three possible changes following the outcomes of a series of similar decisions.

The first possible response to similar outcomes of comparable events is that the original estimate of the probability of their success has not changed: each outcome is independent of the others, and results do not alter the population-based probability. This is the *representativeness bias* in which the decision maker prefers to rely upon original estimates rather than incorporate new data.

An alternative view is that there is no statistical validity in the assumption that initial probability estimates are correct, nor even that probabilities remain constant over time: thus each outcome adds new information. In other words, decision makers should continually update probability estimates in light of how well they predict each event. At an extreme this becomes the *gambler's fallacy*, where (say) a roulette player may initially believe there is a 50 percent probability that any spin will come up red, but adjust the probability down after a series of reds.

If notionally independent events are actually linked, then history provides a guide. Consider, for instance, that a set of risky decisions is subject to a risk management program which is designed to encourage good decision making and provides careful monitoring to assist favourable outcomes. A series of successes could indicate the program is working well, and so increase the expected probability of future success; similarly a run of failures could promote an expectation of continued poor outcomes. A series of failures, though, may also lead to a search for improvements to the risk management program and enhanced prospects of success; whilst a run of successes may promote complacency, relaxation of standards and poorer performance.

Thus after several outcomes have been observed, a decision maker may leave the subjective probability estimate of success unchanged; lift (reduce) it following success (failure); or reduce (lift) it following success (failure). These changes reflect, respectively, assumptions that the outcomes are described by random walk, trend following, and mean reversion.

In expanding on this process, it is useful to use some simple mathematics. The starting point involves Bayes Theorem [Beach (1997)] which is defined by the following expression[33]:

$$P[H|E] \quad = \quad \frac{P[E|H] * P[H]}{P[E]}$$

In words this says: the probability of an event H given the occurrence of event E is equal to the probability of event E given the occurrence of event H times the probability of event H divided by the probability of event E. This expression is useful because it allows validation of probabilistic data when it is presented in a form that is different to population statistics.

As an example, consider the space shuttle. Assume that - prior to its first launch - NASA engineers believed that the shuttle had a 70 percent probability of safe performance, and that they were 70 percent confident in this assessment. Should they change their estimate after (say) ten successful launches? Using the formula above:

P[Prob of safety = 0.7|Ten successful launches]
= $\frac{P[\text{Ten successes}|\text{Prob of safety} = 0.7] * P[\text{Prob of safety} = 0.7]}{P[\text{Ten successful launches}]}$

---

[33] This is derived from conditional probabilities where: P[H|E] = P[H&E]/ P[H]. In words this says: the probability of an event H given the occurrence of event E is equal to the probability of both E and H divided by the probability of H. Alternatively: P[E] = P[E|H] * P[H] + P[E|≠H] * P[≠H]

The probability that ten successful launches will occur if the probability of a successful launch is 70 percent comes from a binomial distribution (success or failure) with a mean probability of success of 0.7 and a standard deviation of $[\sqrt{0.7*(1-0.7)} =]$ 0.46, which gives a sample standard deviation of 0.14 for ten launches. Using a two-tailed test with a sample mean of 0.7 and standard deviation of 0.14, the probability of ten successful launches is 0.04.

Thus P[Prob of safety = 0.7|Ten successful launches]

$$= \qquad \frac{0.04 * 0.7}{0.7^{10}}$$

$$= \qquad 0.99$$

A similar calculation gives a probability of 0.83 that the probability of safe performance is 0.7, a probability of 0.74 that it is 0.8, and a probability of 0.60 that it is 0.9. These results suggest that - after ten successful launches - NASA should revise its estimate of the 70 percent confidence level of a safe launch upwards to at least 83 percent.

By extension, serious errors in risky decision making (including crises) can emerge from success. One attitude that a successful decision maker can adopt is to assume that decisions have been too conservative, and then reduce safety margins, oversight and other expensive risk management practices. This `fine tuning' can continue until failure occurs. Starbuck and Milliken (1988) concluded that NASA followed exactly this line of reasoning through the 1980s. Each successful launch lowered the perception of the shuttle's risk and encouraged NASA to fine tune its processes to reduce wasteful safety factors. NASA became complacent and overconfident, anticipated the successful trend would continue, and thus treated shuttle decisions as less risky, and in less need of care and resources. Unfortunately for NASA, success bred failure as favourable outcomes from a series of risky decisions sowed the seeds for the organisation's near destruction.

People in an organisation where risk and problems are endemic (in NASA's case because it is at the cutting edge of technology) embrace a culture which treats as normal risks which elsewhere would be considered intolerable: risk taking becomes the norm. Because success in risk-taking comes to be seen as a measure of skill and control, the absence of disaster can encourage ever higher thresholds of acceptable risk. When a disaster eventually occurs, the post-audit takes a reductionist view of the incident's proximate, physical causes and finds an `obvious' chain of errors by individual managers and engineers who were close to the failed system.

Crises can also emerge from failure. Staw et al. (1981) cite numerous examples of corporations collapsing after refusing to alter in the face of dramatic change in their industry environment. They propose that external threats concentrate power and restrict information processing so that behaviour is less flexible. Thus when decision makers – whether acting as individuals or in groups such as firms – face a threat or crisis, they tend to respond by rigid, inflexible behaviours. They are unwilling to change, even in the face of evidence that risk is very high.

The shuttle is not the only example of sequential risky decisions. Baucus and Near (1991) searched court records for criminal convictions of Fortune 500 companies between 1974 and 1983, and found that firms were more likely to break the law if they had a previous conviction. As the probability of law breaking rose with the number of previous convictions, adverse outcomes (conviction) do not deter managerial decision makers: they must expect the probability of success (i.e. avoiding detection of illegal action and/or avoiding subsequent conviction) remains acceptably high, and thus assume mean reversion.

Camerer et al. (1997) analysed the time sheets of New York City cab drivers to determine the influence of their earnings (which comprise a share of the fares collected) on the number of hours worked each day. The daily number of hours was inversely related to earnings per hour; and their wages were virtually uncorrelated ($p > 0.7$) between successive days. Thus drivers stopped work earlier on days when they were busier, even though the statistics showed a strong autocorrelation between earnings from one hour to the next, and between earnings in the first and second halves of a driving shift. Assuming that the drivers irregularly consider during their shift whether to discontinue work, Camerer et al. (1997) concluded that their decision follows daily targeting of a specific income or income band; or reflects decreasing utility of work, with strongly concave utility around average daily income. Alternatively the drivers' decision could be based around an erroneous assumption of mean reversion in hourly earnings.

The analysis by Heath et al. (1999) discussed earlier which looked at factors contributing to the exercise of employee stock options found that the rate of exercise increased following a rise in stock price. Thus if the option-holders irregularly consider whether to exercise, they also seem to assume mean reversion.

In wagering markets, this assumption of mean reversion is termed the gambler's fallacy because decision makers expect an early end to a trend of identical outcomes. This has been demonstrated in the laboratory by Morrison and Ordeshook (1975), and in real-world settings by Clotfeller and Cook (1993) and Terrell (1997).

Another example of mean reversion in financial markets is the disposition effect, which is the tendency for owners of assets such as houses and shares to sell their winners in preference to their losers [Odean (1998)]. This is typically assumed to be loss aversion, because realising a loss on an investment is a clear admission of failure. However, the data also match the assumption of mean reversion that would suggest that losing investments are likely to outperform profitable investments.

Although these studies of Bayesian decision making are not conclusive, most of them support the conclusion of Heath et al. (1999: 604) that decision makers anticipate mean reversion "unless they had a causal belief why a trend might continue" [34].

Other Influences on Risky Decision Making

Apart from the rational approaches discussed above, there are less concrete, largely neglected, determinants of risky decision making. Kahneman (2003: 1470) made the important point that recent research has "restored a central role [in judgement and decision making] to emotion." This had previously not been studied as intensively as other decision features.

Another intangible decision making tool is intuition, which was evaluated by Khatri and Ng (2000) who found that it is most useful in an unstable environment. Other decisions can look like wilful refusal to face facts. At the time of writing, for instance, a scandal is brewing over the use of performance enhancing drugs by US athletes with the apparent approval of the Track and Field Association. These decision makers seem to have long ignored data that challenges a favourable position. This is possibly an extreme amplification of the mildly optimistic instinct of most humans; or perhaps the affect heuristic in which authorities simply block out the consequences and risks of an overwhelmingly desirable course.

A variation on this is the tendency for decision makers to seek a major explanation for a major event, such as the violent death of a popular figure or a shocking accident. Even when there is convincing evidence that it is largely related to chance (either an unfortunate alignment of random events, or a lone rogue), people will still look for a powerful force and this often sustains conspiracy theories. For instance, in discussing the surge of

---

[34] Another example of similarity in decision making processes by different species is the report by Waite (2001) of experiments involving birds in sequential decisions which – although not addressing the issue of mean reversion – showed that their preferences were influenced by prior choices.

conspiracy theories following the assassination of President Kennedy, Brogan (1996: 207) wrote:

"Kennedy's murder had been too shocking; in the best of circumstances many Americans (including zealous journalists and historians) would have found it impossible to accept that so great an event could have such trivial causes as the odious personality of Lee Oswald and the absence of a Secret Serviceman from the rear of a presidential limousine."

Such anecdotal reports have been confirmed by controlled studies, including research conducted at University of London (which was described in *The Economist* of 20 March 2003) where students were given specially prepared newspaper clippings reporting four versions of an assassination attempt on the president of a fictional country. Subjects were more likely to suspect a conspiracy if the president died, rather than if he was shot and survived, or if the shot missed. Thus the more important the event, the greater is the probability that people will look for a complex cause.

Another intangible decision influence is prestige, the phenomenon whereby people identify traits that have led others to success and then emulate them. People with prestige are admired by others, which perhaps explains the proliferation of media depictions of successful people's lifestyles. Henrich and Gil-White (2001) develop a theory of cultural transmission whereby decision makers reproduce successful behaviours rather than expending the effort to learn them. This suggests that many decisions can be mere copying of the behaviour of someone who has excelled in a valued sphere of activity.

Decision Making Evidence from Racetrack Gambling

Racetrack wagering markets provide illuminating insights into individuals' decision making as they provide a real-life financial environment, with the advantages that the stock of information is fixed, participants know payouts in advance, and each bet has a clearly defined value and end point [Brailsford et al. (1995)].

If there is no bias in betting markets, then the efficient markets hypothesis would argue that the starting price of each horse provides the best forecast of its probability of winning. And if the betting market is efficient, then the expected return at all odds will be the same, and equal to the negative take of the market's operator [Asch et al. (1984)]. Moreover prices should continuously reflect all available information: hence no wagering strategy using publicly available data can have a positive expected return (in practice no better than the negative take which the operator deducts from the pool of wagers) [Asch and Quandt (1987)].

This normative theory is overturned by a striking behavioural anomaly in wagering markets: the *longshot bias*. It arises because more money is wagered on longshots than is justified by their objective chances of winning; and it acts counter-intuitively to ensure that the expected return of any bet increases with the probability that the horse will win [Potters and Wit (1995)]. The bias was first documented by Griffith (1949), and has been confirmed in more than 25 studies using statistically large numbers of horses and greyhounds on racetracks in Australia, North America and the United Kingdom. It can justifiably be described as "one of the most robust anomalous empirical regularities in economics" [Walls and Busche (2002: 2)].

The existence of a bias in wagering markets, longshot or otherwise, is identified by evaluating the return from wagering as a function of the dividend payable for a win. Published studies of the longshot bias have typically found that over 80 percent of the variation in returns can be explained by an expression of the following form:

$$\text{Expected Return (\%)} = \beta_1 - \beta_2 * \text{Ln (Dividend)}.$$

where β_1 and β_2 are positive constants equal to an average of 10.9 and 11.9, respectively [Coleman (2004)].

The data reveal a number of other interesting behavioural patters.

First, although the longshot bias is common in betting markets, it is not apparent in all of them. Significantly, though, betting markets without a longshot bias (where returns – as predicted by CAPM – rise with risk) are confined to Japan and Hong Kong: in a sample of 20+ studies, the absence of a longshot bias only on Asian racetracks is highly significant as – even assuming an equal probability that the bias exists or is absent – this would be expected to occur by chance on less than one percent of occasions.

The absence of a longshot bias is indicative of lower risk propensity. Thus the Japanese result is consistent with other evidence discussed in this chapter and suggests a behavioural explanation. However, studies pointing to higher risk propensity in Hong Kong suggest that the absence of a longshot bias there may be due to market factors such as larger pools.

A second finding of relevance to risky decision making is that the longshot bias becomes more pronounced when bettors have less capital. This was documented in the study by Ali (1977) of on-course betting patterns at three New York tracks which found that risk-embrace is higher when the average bet drops; and by the conclusion of Busche and Walls (2000) that the longshot bias is stronger when pools are small. Further confirmation comes from studies which show that the longshot bias at race meetings strengthens through the day [e.g. McGlothin (1956) and Metzger (1985)] as bettors' stakes are eroded. This greater risk taking by capital-poor bettors conforms to the prediction of risk-sensitive foraging that risk embrace rises as wealth falls.

The longshot bias arises because bettors' decisions distort the market, and behavioural explanations fall into two sub-categories: conscious embrace of risk, and subconscious misjudgement of true win probabilities.

Thus risk seeking gamblers bet more on long odds horses than justified by their objective chances of winning (thus depressing their odds and raising odds on shorter priced horses). Thaler and Ziemba (1988: 171) argued that, in the absence of short selling in wagering markets, less informed bettors support longshots, "with the 'smart money' simply taking the better bets on the favourites." Quandt (1986) postulates that bettors are risk loving. Bird et al. (1987) attribute bettors' decisions to a preference for positive skewness in returns which provides an occasional longshot win to compensate for the negative expected return[35]. Another possibility is that longshot decision makers may be adopting the Laplace Rule of Insufficient Reason which says that all outcomes are equally likely (at least on a risk-adjusted basis) and therefore you may as well go for a decent return.

Further evidence that gamblers misunderstand the statistically obvious comes from the gambler's fallacy, or belief that the recent occurrence of an outcome (e.g. win by red, or horse number one) lowers the probability of re-occurrence in an identical, statistically independent event. This is consistent with the conclusion of Heath et al. (1999) that – in the absence of contrary evidence - most decision makers anticipate mean reversion.

Metzger (1985) undertook a comprehensive study of gambling behaviour and her key results are summarised in table 4.3 which shows the ratio of subjective win probability to objective win probability for the favourite in percent: thus a number below 100 indicates underbetting on the favourite as the proportion of bets is less than the objective probability that a horse starting at those odds will win.

The data are somewhat mixed. The three left columns evidence the gambler's fallacy because support for favourites decreases with the length of their run of success. But the three right columns show the opposite by reference to longshots (which she defined as any horse other than first or second favourite): as their winning streak extends, support grows. This, too, is a well-known fallacy termed *hot hands* when applied to basketball players who are assumed to be more likely to score after making a basket

---

[35] This argument gains support from the fact that the longshot bias is also apparent in games involving pure chance and no skill. Anecdotal evidence [for instance Oldman (1974)] suggests that roulette gamblers prefer to bet on single numbers with a one-in-37 chance of a payout rather than even chances.

than after missing a shot. The gambler's fallacy assumes that outcomes mean revert, whereas hot hands is trend following. Significantly both approaches incorporate Bayesian probabilities, rather than assuming there is no statistical link between independent events.

Table 4.3. Ratio of Subjective to Objective Probability of Favourite Winning (Percent)

Mean subjective probability of win	Last three races won by 1st or 2nd favourite	Last two races won by favourite	Last race won by favourite	Last race won by longshot	Last two races won by longshot	Last three races won by longshot
0.51 ($2.0)		85	92	94	104	
0.35 ($2.9)		97	99	103	103	
0.27 ($3.7)		96	96	111	96	
0.24 ($4.2)		89	94	107	98	
TOTAL	86	91	96	104	100	94

It would appear that two populations of gamblers are involved in Metzger's sample: those backing favourites who believe they can only win a fixed proportion of races; and those who back longshots and believe they can have runs of success.

With Occam, let us use the data above to deduce the blindingly obvious: there are basically two groups of bettors. The first is informed or skilled, predominantly backs relatively short priced horses, and has a positive expected return: this group is risk averse. The second, and larger, group is unskilled and uninformed, and places bets largely in accordance with chance: these are gamblers and risk lovers.

The clearest evidence for this split between bettors is in the shape of the relationship

$$\text{Expected Return} = \beta_1 - \beta_2 * \ln (\text{Dividend})$$

This shows a transition from risk aversion (positive Expected Return) to risk embrace (negative Expected Return) at a dividend equal to e^{β_1/β_2}. In wagering markets with a longshot bias, the crossover from risk aversion to risk embrace occurs as the dividend moves above a value in the range 4 ± 3, which is equivalent to a move in the objective probability of a positive outcome to below a value in the range 0.2 ± 0.2.

This transition to risk embrace (or overweighting of longshots) has been of interest to researchers since Preston and Baratta (1948) estimated that probabilities of less than 0.25 are subject to systematic overestimation.

Camerer (1995: 625) proposed that the crossover from risk-aversion to risk-embrace occurs as the objective probability of success moves below a point somewhere in the range of 0.1-0.3. Tversky and Fox (1994) put the crossover at around 0.3. Such studies are consistent with the existence of two groups on the racetrack (knowledgeable bettors and true gamblers who trust to chance) and a transition from one to the other at an objective probability of success of around 0.2. This is comparable to the probability where oil explorers transition from risk aversion to risk embrace [Coleman (2005)].

Thus the explanation which best fits data on the longshot bias is behavioural: bettors know the returns on offer at the racetrack and consciously decide either to be risk averse or risk embracing. The split, respectively, leads them to back horses which offer a win dividend of less than or greater than about $4 (probability of success = 0.2).

This conclusion challenges existing theories of decision making under risk or uncertainty because it violates what Tversky and Kahneman (1992: 299) describe as a key decision element whereby "transparently dominated prospects are eliminated." Although the concept that decisions are based on intrinsic risk attitudes has been discredited [e.g. Schoemaker (1993)], on the racetrack affect and hedonics clearly rule bettors' risk taking.

Discussion

Tversky and Wakker (1995: 1255) point out that "classical theory of decision under risk and uncertainty combines the principle of mathematical expectation with the assumption of decreasing marginal utility, which jointly imply risk aversion." The discussion above and elsewhere [e.g. Camerer (1995)] shows conclusively that people frequently diverge from normative expectations. This has confounded most economists' models (including those from finance and management) which rely upon the assumption that decision makers use monetary values and continuous distributions of probability when evaluating decision outcomes. It is easy, then, to agree with Halek and Eisenhauer (2001) that the existing literature provides little consensus even on indicative drivers of risk aversion.

Whilst many of these 'violations' are systematic, few prove predictable, and so this section syntheses the influences, behavioural biases and paradoxes on individuals' real-world decision making. These can be boiled down into seven key groups of decision making characteristics[36]:

---

[36] McFadden (1999) also provides a neat tabulation of cognitive anomalies

Decision makers are instinctively loss averse with a preference for low risk strategies that minimise variability, and the possibility of an adverse outcome. However, risk sensitivity has evolutionary advantages and so decision makers have a flexible approach which is determined by their own personality and culture, and alters in light of situational and contextual cues.

Reference levels are important in determining attitudes to risk, as decision makers tend to embrace risk when the outcome appears unfavourable. Thus risk aversion grows with rising value or utility of the worst outcome (the Common Consequence Effect) so that people adopt satisficing, rather than optimising, goals. If a favourable outcome is almost certain, risk aversion is high. Risk aversion also grows with increasing bounds on decision making (e.g. uncertainty, lack of data, and reduced time for analysis).

Decision makers are willing to trust their judgement and are more likely to embrace risk in areas where they have a perceived skill that offers advantage (the Competency Effect). Overconfidence is common, even with uncontrollable events (the Illusion of Control).

Different presentations of identical data elicit different responses from the same individual (the Framing Effect) and from different individuals (a function of personality traits). Through the affect heuristic, people mentally tag objects and events with positive or negative feelings or emotion, and thus create an inverse relationship between risk and benefit which sees selection of preferred or liked outcomes. Decision makers' mental images of events can over-ride facts and thus overstate the subjective probability of a favourable or dreaded event and understate the probability of an unwanted event (thus prediction is linked to outcome preference). These biases can be particularly strong in the face of new problems

Decision makers place minimal reliance upon probability calculations in making judgements as evidenced by overweighting of low probability events and seeing independent events as related. They tend to rely on small, recent samples; and - in decisions involving an object (or event) - place greatest weight on its characteristic(s) which is most closely related to the terms of the response (Principle of Compatibility).

Personality and experience determine people's attitudes towards risk, their perception of risky decisions, and their decision making style. This confines most people to a small number of decision making strategies which they use invariably even though situations alter in terms of event, environment and consequences. Even so, framing and other cognitive pressures induce different rules for different situations: people do not have stable decision making techniques.

When facing choices involving future events, decision makers place greater weight on the outcome and benefits, with relatively less weight on the costs and probability of occurrence. This is consistent with optimism, goal orientation and inherent unpredictability of details such as impediments and probabilities. It also incorporates recognition of optionality: why sweat the small stuff when the decision may change?

`The proposal that behavioural biases and paradoxes form seven key groups of decision making characteristics is supported by real-world evidence. An interesting enunciation is the maxims of common folklore which can be dismissed as trivial but actually encapsulate the decision making biases as shown in table 4.4 using a sampling of folk advice on risk and decision making drawn from Pickering (1999) and Simpson (2000). Although these largely advocate risk aversion (`better to be late alive than dead on time'), the maxims also offer advice for those wishing to embrace risk (`no rose without a thorn') and reflect a number of biases including regret aversion (`better to be safe than sorry') and a high discount rate (`time is money'). Even the framing effect is recognised in `look before you leap'.

Table 4.4. Maxims for Risk and Decision Making

Decision Making Bias	Maxim
Instinctive Risk Aversion: natural tendency to avoid variability and uncertainty	Better to be safe than sorry
	A stitch in time saves nine
Common Consequence Effect: risk aversion grows with rising value or utility of the worst outcome	A rising tide lifts all boats
	Slow and steady wins the race
	A bird in the hand is worth two in the bush
Risk embrace increases when outcome appears unfavourable	No rose without a thorn
Competency Effect: willingness to trust judgement and to embrace risk grows with perceived skill	There is always room at the top
	The tree is known by its fruit
	When you are on a good thing stick to it
Framing Effect: different presentation of identical data elicits different responses	Look before you leap
Minimal reliance upon probability as evidenced by overweighting of low probability events and seeing independent events as related	Time is money
	It takes two to make a bargain
	Caveat emptor
Principle of Compatibility: for a decision involving an object (or event) people place most weight on its characteristic(s) which are most closely related to the terms of the response	When in Rome do as the Romans do
	There is safety in numbers

Whilst heuristics are clearly useful, a detailed discussion of moral heuristics (e.g. punish betrayals) by Sunstein (2003) made it clear that they can lead to serious mistakes in political and legal decisions. Take the 6th Commandment ('Thou shalt not kill') which appears an admirable rule. But what about self-defence, war, capital punishment, the greater good and so on? What about products which are generally beneficial, but occasionally kill (everything from guns and cars to pharmaceuticals)? Sunstein (2003: 3) points out that "good heuristics misfire in the factual domain". A corollary is that decision making heuristics and simple decision rules can also prove ill-suited to the real world.

Another important influence on many decisions appears to be the assumption of mean reversion. Even when decision makers understand that sequential outcomes are unrelated, they seem to agree with Dostoevsky (1914: 19) that "though there is no system, there really is a sort of order in the sequence of casual chances." People do not believe that sequences will continue, and this is an important element in their decisions.

Personality is another significant influence on risk-taking, although little work has asked why. An exception is Lopes (1987: 275-276):

"Risk-averse people appear to be motivated by a desire for security, whereas risk-seeking people appear to be motivated by a desire for potential. The former motive values safety and the latter, opportunity... Risk-averse people look more at the downside and risk seekers more at the upside."

Thus personality mediates motivation to drive subjective weighting of decision cues.

This concept of different motivations of risk-averse and risk-embracing decision makers matches results from a number of studies in this chapter. Its strongest implication is that risk attitudes cannot be described by a continuous distribution: human decision makers seem to focus on either gains or losses, rather than aggregating all possible outcomes into a probability-weighted sum.

Two sets of studies provide physiological support for the contention that decision makers separately consider good and bad outcomes. The first studies were discussed in chapter three and involved MRI monitoring of brain activity; subjects use different parts of their brain for different types of decisions such as ethical choices and mathematical calculations [Greene et al. (2001)]. The second type of study has examined the ways that humans use their left and right brain hemispheres. The brain halves, respectively, have quite independent perspectives on any issue: optimistic and big picture; and detail focussed and cautious. There is a switch between the brain halves which leads decision makers to have alternating views of the world [Miller et al. (2000)].

Given that human brains use discrete components to evaluate different problem types, it is not surprising that decision makers place different emphases on various decision aspects. This can be operationalised by a model proposed by Weber et al. (2002) which decomposed benefit and risk:

Preference (X) = a*(Expected Benefit (X)) + b*(Perceived Risk (X)) + ε
This allows for domain-specific attitudes: for example, risk preference as expressed by the strength of b could be high in personal recreation (e.g. skydiving) but low in vocational or financial matters (e.g. conservative employer and investments).

Summary

In the chapters above, we have steadily unpeeled the layers around risk and decision making: apart from the facts of the decision, there are psychological aspects such as preference reversal, situational parameters such as framing, and contextual influences which impact on decision making strategy. Taken together they mean that the relative attractiveness of decision alternatives is not stable or objectively established: decision makers are risk-sensitive.

This leads to an obvious gap in decision theory: any decision model which is blind to the players and their context will be of sorely limited value. Such models can probably give reasonable results for point-in-time decisions by large groups. However, they will not be able to model individuals' decisions, nor even group decisions as their situation alters (e.g. changes in decision making by equity market participants as the market's valuation shifts). It is essential, then, to develop models of decision making which take account of the personality and situation of the decision maker, and which respond to changes in these circumstances.

A second, related gap in the literature is the dearth of real-world studies of decision making behaviour. There is no doubt that these are hard to conduct because it is difficult to obtain representative subjects, and virtually impossible to eliminate confounding effects. However, there is enough evidence to show that laboratory type experiments using students cannot be generalised to the actions of more experienced decision makers in the real world. Creative investigators have studied taxi drivers, bankers and others in their natural settings: more work needs to be done in this arena. In particular, research needs to address the actual objectives of decision makers, their criteria for making choices, the balance between stable and situational determinants of risk propensity, and the parameters that determine decision choices.

CHAPTER 5   Risk-Taking and Organisation Performance

This chapter examines literature relating to the book's second research question: what determines whether choice of a risky alternative proves successful? Success here is measured by the financial performance of the decision maker's organisation.

The chapter first uses risk with its meaning of variance to explain differences in firm-specific performance; it then takes risk with its managerial meaning of adverse outcome and summarises studies of its influence on organisational performance. The last section discusses the implications of this material and contains brief suggestions for future work.

Financial Risk and Performance in Organisations

Although risk with its financial meaning of variance is not the principal focus of this book, a number of studies have shown that it is statistically associated with other measures of risk, including the managerial definition that it is the possibility of adverse outcome. For instance Miller and Bromiley (1990) grouped nine different measures of a firm's risk into income stream risk, stock returns risk and strategic risk, and found statistically significant ($p < 0.05$) correlations between the principal component variables of these risk factors. Miller and Reuer (1996) derived 13 measures of downside risk and found that half the correlations were highly significant ($p<0.001$). Aaker and Jacobson (1987) found a link between unsystemic risk and investor return.

Such studies suggest that – despite significant differences in definition - the various risk parameters are measuring similar latent variables. If this is true, then different concepts of risk should have qualitatively similar impacts on organisation performance. As demonstration of such a link would be powerful reinforcement of the important role of risk in organisation results, this section looks at the influence on firm returns of risk with its meaning of variance in earnings.

Economists have traditionally had limited interest in any cause-and-effect links between risk and the outcome of organisations' decisions. Finance, for instance, advocates portfolio diversification as a strategy for investors (who are assumed to be risk averse) to eliminate risk or uncertainty associated with performance of any firm (that is firm-specific or non systematic risk) [Peirson et al. (2002)]. Thus modern capital markets theory largely ignores risks that are specific to an individual firm. In similar vein, paradigms in management theory rarely allow any significance to risk. For instance, the Porter (1980) model explains a firm's performance through its relative competitive position which is an outcome of strategic decisions relating to markets, competitors, suppliers and customers. Risk has no contributory role, and is dismissed by Porter (1985: 470) as "a function of how poorly a strategy will perform if the 'wrong' scenario occurs." A third perspective – that of behavioural economics – has been applied to firm performance [e.g. Lovallo and Kahneman (2003)], but generally only attends to the shortcomings of managers' cognitive processes.

Textbooks treat it as axiomatic that management decision making follows a disciplined process which defines objectives, validates data, explores options, ranks priorities and monitors outcomes. When risks emerge at the firm level, it is generally accepted that they are neutered using conventional risk management techniques of assessing the probability and consequences of failure, and then exploring alternatives to dangerous paths [Kouradi (1999)]. Systematic biases and inadequate data are rarely mentioned; and the possible significance of chance is dismissed in the quip quoted by McClelland (1961: 211): "The gambling known as business looks with austere disfavour on the business known as gambling".

Although risk does not have a theoretical place in corporate strategy, discussion in earlier chapters strongly supports the intuitively obvious proposition that risk has such a strong influence on decision making that it should be an important factor in firm performance. If this is true, then normative analyses of organisation performance which are blind to risk should have little ability to explain real-world organisation performance. Exactly this was reported by Campbell-Hunt (2000: 147) whose meta-analysis of the Porter competitive model found it has "very limited explanatory power."

This explains why studies show that strategy – including risk propensity – is important at the firm level. For instance, Rumelt (1991) analysed variance in US company profits and found that around 49 percent was explained by firm-specific factors with only 16 percent due to industry-specific factors. Similarly Palmer and Wiseman (1999) found that at least 20 percent of organisational risk propensity is explained by managers' risk attitudes, and relatively little (p>0.1) arises in external factors such as industry structure.

There have been only a limited number of studies linking risk and organisation performance, and these generally employed variance in accounting profits or return (usually ROCE or ROE) as their dependent variable. The first systematic study of firm-level risk and performance was conducted by Bowman (1980), with such striking results that they became known as the *Bowman Paradox* [Nickel and Rodriguez (2002)]. The analysis looked at companies by industry classification between 1972 and 1976 and found that more profitable companies had lower risk, as measured by variability in profits.

As an aside, the Bowman Paradox was quickly linked to the Prospect Theory of Kahneman and Tversky (1979), perhaps because the concepts emerged almost simultaneously (Bowman (1982) was probably the first to make the connection). Prospect Theory – along with strategic and organisational influences and methodological shortcomings – remains the leading explanation for the Bowman Paradox [Henkel (2003)].

Bromiley (1991) defined risk as the *ex ante* uncertainty of a firm's earnings stream, and measured it for any given year as the variance in security analysts' forecasts of that income. He used a decade of data for 288 US companies and found a number of significant relationships: risk was directly related to previous risk and to aspirations (defined as 1.05 times historical ROA for firms with performance above the industry mean, and industry mean for underperformers); whilst risk was inversely related to prior year's performance, and to current ratio (current assets divided by current liabilities), SG&A-to-sales ratio (selling, general and administrative expenses divided by sales) and interest coverage (income before interest and taxes divided by interest).

He used these results to develop several models, including one that projected firm performance measured as Return on Total Assets:

$$Performance_{t+2} = -0.01 + 0.66*Industry\ Performance_{t+2} - 0.02*Risk_{t+1}$$
$$+0.37*Aspirations_{t+1} + 0.004*Current\ Ratio_{t+1} + 0.04*InterestCoverage_{t+1}$$
$$- 0.01*Debt\text{-}to\text{-}equity\ ratio_{t+1}\quad [R^2 \approx 0.40]$$

Bromiley (1991: 54) found that historically poor performance promotes risk taking (p<0.01), but increased risk does not lead to better returns:

"Risk taking has a negative influence on future performance. Thus not only does low performance result in a company's income stream becoming more risky, such riskiness lowers future performance even when factors such as past and industry performance are controlled … Firms performing poorly do indeed make risky and low-payoff strategic choices."

Fiegenbaum and Thomas (1988) made a detailed study of the financial results of companies in 47 US industries during 1960-79. They chose the industry median return on equity as a reference level, and found that the risk: return relationship was negative below the reference level and positive above it. The diagram below interprets their results[37]: the solid lines show the performance prospects of good and bad performing firms. Better performing firms have lower risk and a positive relationship between risk and return; whilst poorer performing firms embrace higher risk and have a negative risk:return relationship. The inverted U-shape of the return envelope is consistent with two decision making populations sharing different risk attitudes.

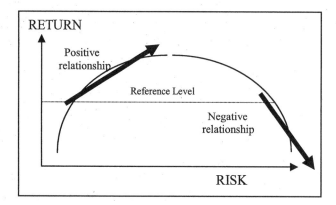

Fig. 5.1. Concave Return:Risk Links

Exactly the same pattern is seen at a macro level in returns from asset classes, and the charts below show two of the many examples[38]. Data in the left chart are returns from financial markets in Australia as reported by Intech (2002). Data in the right chart are from Harvey (1995) for more than 800 listed stocks in 20 countries between 1976 and 1992 (the outlier result for Argentina has been removed). The two equations are:

Australia Return $= -0.26*Risk^2 + 3.8*Risk + 2.0$ $[R^2 = 0.81]$
Global Equities Return $= -0.033*Risk^2 + 3.4*Risk - 45$ $[R^2 = 0.16]$

---

[37] Fiegenbaum and Thomas (1988), however, postulated a discontinuous distribution which comprises nested curves which are concave to the right in the style of ((. Unfortunately their paper does not provide sufficient detail to verify which relationship provides the better explanation.

[38] It is becoming fashionable to reject keystone normative assumptions about individuals' attitudes towards risk. A good example is Barberis and Thaler (2002) `Survey of Behavioural Finance'

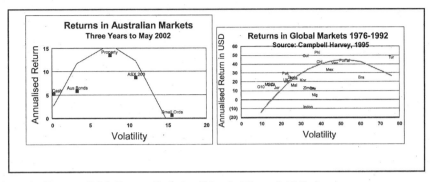

Fig. 5.2. Concave Risk:Return Relationships in Financial Markets

Walls and Dyer (1996) also found a concave, inverted U-shaped relationship between oil exploration companies' returns and their size-adjusted risks. As discussed in the previous chapter, racecourse betting markets display a similar concave pattern between returns and risk as measured by the probability of a horse winning (the relationship derived was: Expected Return = 11 - 12*Ln[Dividend] which is concave in shape).

Miller and Bromiley (1990: 757) examined the numerous exceptions to CAPM's assumed direct relationship between risk and reward and concluded: "the risk-return relation has not had a consistent sign in previous studies".

The link between corporate returns and risk arises in the cost and uncertainties that are associated with strategic risks. Failures, crises and incidents have direct costs and divert management attention, and so reduce profits and thus returns. In addition, risk raises uncertainty over future profitability and creditors require a premium to support risky companies. Higher borrowing costs further reduce earnings. This explains why Amit and Wernerfelt (1990) found that lower business risk (which they defined as variance in stock prices after adjusting for market moves) increases cash flows.

Risk also affects returns to investors because an uncertain income stream will attract a higher discount rate. All things being equal, the share price of risky companies (which equals the discounted value of their future earnings) will be lower than that of less risky companies. Thus risk taking undercuts investor returns. In summary, the mechanism leading to common findings of a negative or concave relationship between risk and return is simple. Good risk management brings fewer shocks and reduced expenses: lower risk translates into higher returns.

As an aside, it is possible that the inverse relationship between return and accounting risk may be at least partly spurious. Henkel (2003), for instance, shows that it could arise if returns are skewed to the left[39] as this simultaneously increases variance and reduces return. He reworked the 1970s data used by Bowman (1980) and Fiegenbaum and Thomas (1988) and suggests that up to 88 percent of the negative risk-return link can be explained by skewed data. Whilst this does not eliminate the negative relationship, it is significantly weakened.

Although Bowman (1980) and his imitators used risk in its variance sense, their results were important for the challenge to the assumed positive relationship between return and risk. They opened up a new field of research, and led to a number of increasingly innovative attempts to explain the links between risk and return. Eventually they were fully vindicated when Fama and French (1992) found a negative relationship between risk and return at the equity market level.

Studies of the Impact of Risk on Firm-Specific Returns

The rational-actor model [Allison (1971)] postulates that organisations act like individuals; by implication, then, the rules driving organisational decision making should be comparable to those driving individuals' decisions. This makes it convenient to evaluate the influences of risk on firm performance under a number of broad headings: industry, institutional framework, governance and financial history.

The following sections discuss the link between firm return and risk.

Company Influences

One of the first attempts to probe how risk might affect corporate performance came in an interesting paper by Singh (1986). He proposed that organisations have a satisficing level of performance, and increase risk when their results are below that level. His study used responses to a questionnaire and publicly available data for 64 medium to large North American firms. Risk taking was measured with questions about biases towards innovation, debt, R&D and high risk-high return investments; competitive pressure was evaluated by questions about costs, marketing and prices. Re-

---

[39] This conflicts with the common assumption in most analyses "that an investment's distribution of returns follows a normal distribution" [Peirson et al. (2002: 201)].

sults showed that risk taking had a statistically significant negative relationship with return on net worth, and a positive relationship with competitive pressure. This justified Singh's simple, but compelling, argument (page 582): "poor performance triggers risk taking." More speculatively: "most firms, when faced with poor performance, would undertake decisions that would only further their decline."

A number of studies have attempted to explain returns using risk with meanings other than variance in total returns. Aaker and Jacobson (1987) obtained financial results for 1,376 business units and calculated unsystematic risk as the error term in the CAPM model, or the diversifiable component of a firm's risk[40]. They found a highly significant ($p<0.01$) positive link between Return on Investment and unsystematic risk, but no correlation with systematic risk, beta. The link between unsystematic risk and return contradicts CAPM, and suggests that return is directly related to the risk consequences of strategy and managerial decisions.

Amit and Wernerfelt (1990) compiled data on 151 US firms to examine business risk (which they defined as the diversifiable component of a firm's total risk, and calculated as the variance of actual return minus the return predicted from market and the firm β). For the dependent variable, they used the ratio of firms' market value to replacement value of their assets, and found a strong inverse relationship ($p<0.001$) with business risk. The authors concluded the negative return:risk linkage arose because lower risk improved operational efficiency and increased cash flows. A similar conclusion emerged in work by Miller and Bromiley (1990) who identified a factor called strategic risk which was related to higher ratios of debt to equity and capital to sales, and a lower ratio of R&D spending to sales. Using data for 493 US firms during 1978 to 1987, they found that strategic risk had a strong inverse relationship ($p<0.001$) with return on equity and return on assets.

Most of these results suggest that managers are more likely to take risks when facing a loss than when facing a gain. Gambles seem particularly common in desperation. This is certainly confirmed by anecdotal evidence with a good example in insurance company HIH that collapsed in March 2001 with debts exceeding \$5 billion. According to an editorial in *The Australian* newspaper [17 April 2003]:

---

[40] CAPM proposes that the expected return on any asset is equal to a risk-free rate of return plus the asset's systematic risk, beta, times the expected difference in return between the market and the risk free asset. Aaker and Jacobson (1987) used the following model: $(ROI_{jt} - R_{Ft}) = \alpha_j + \beta_j \times (R_{mt} - R_{Ft}) + \varepsilon_{jt}$; where ROI_{jt} is the return on investment of business j in year t; R_{Ft} is the interest rate on long term government bonds in year t, R_{mt} is the average return of all business units in year t; α_j and β_j are co-efficients to be measured, and ε_{jt} is the unsystematic risk of a business j in year t.

"The company was destroyed not by hard times or bad luck but by [its executives'] reckless disregard … for the well-being of anybody but themselves … The way [they] contributed to the company's demise was …[that] they kept on trying to shore it up with desperate deals, all designed to provide HIH with the cash flow and capital that it needed to survive. The fact that they were gambling, literally, with the future of ordinary Australians does not appear to have bothered or even occurred to them."

In like vein is the behaviour of one time General Motors vice-president John DeLorean who founded an innovative business that manufactured a revolutionary stainless steel sports cars with gull-wing doors. As car demand crumbled after the oil shocks of the 1970s, his business moved to the brink of collapse. In 1982 he was captured on videotape allegedly conspiring with undercover FBI agents to smuggle $US24 million worth of cocaine into the United States and use the proceeds to bail out his company [Pilcher (1984)]. Although acquitted after arguing entrapment, DeLorean is another example of a decision maker whose desperate straits led to desperate measures.

This pattern of behaviour also seems true of risk-averse politicians who initiate new policies as a reaction to some adverse event that threatens their electoral support. For instance, in his analysis of 1960s US politics Monk (2003: 8) reported Ellsberg's conclusion[41]

"[In every one of the major Vietnam war decisions by US Presidents Eisenhower, Kennedy and Johnson] the President's choice was not founded upon optimistic reporting or on assurances of the success of his chosen course. [On the contrary] escalation was always immediately preceded and accompanied by a breakthrough of gloomy realism, including an internal consensus that the new commitment the president was choosing would probably be inadequate for success."

Reams of academic research were summed up by the comment of legendary Australian Rules Football coach Kevin Sheedy in the *The Australian* newspaper on 21 May 2003: "I have a theory that when things are toughest, you take your biggest risk."

In addition to the influence of firms' recent experience, structural features give them attributes that are analogous to individuals' personality. For instance, Reuer and Leiblein (2000) tested the influence of firm characteristics on risk and performance using data on 332 US manufacturing companies during the early 1990s. They found that downside risk (or the probability of below target performance) is lower for larger firms ($p <$ 0.001) and those with lower levels of slack resources and fewer international joint ventures. This matched the findings of Walls and Dyer (1996) who modelled the risk attitudes of oil explorers in the 1980s and found that

---

[41] Daniel Ellsberg wrote an influential book on decision theory which led to policy appointments at RAND and in various US Presidential Administrations. The latter roles gave him access to classified material which became the *Pentagon Papers* after publication in *The New York Times*.

risk aversion was directly related to size: large companies tended to be more risk averse.

Another pointer to firm personality is the finding of Claessens et al. (2000) that attitudes towards risk by corporates differ between countries. They ascribed this to institutional factors such as legal protections for shareholders, directors and creditors; civil or common law systems; and nature of the financial system. A particularly interesting finding was yet more evidence that lower profitability is associated with higher risk.

Dess and Beard (1984: 52) took a biological perspective on risk and argued that "the resources required for organisational survival are the most relevant focus in defining organisational environments ... [Thus] organisations seek out environments that permit organisational growth and stability." They analysed 52 US manufacturing industries along 23 environmental dimensions and found that three factors explained 62 percent of the variance between firms: munificence or industry capacity to support growth (where significant ($p>0.05$) variables were: increase in sales, margin, employment, value added and establishments); complexity of operations (concentration of sales, value added, employment and establishments); and unpredictability or dynamism (variance in sales, margin, employment and value added). Although the authors did not extend their analysis (for instance by using the factors as independent variables to explain performance), the third factor is related to risk and shows that the level of strategic risk is a significant distinction between firms.

Only a few studies have analysed decisions by managers (as opposed to firm-level results) in their day-to-day environment. McNamara and Bromiley (1997) examined commercial lending practices inside a US commercial bank using annual loan review data for 223 large corporate borrowers. The authors developed a model to explain the risk ratings that loan officers placed on each borrower: 53 percent of the ratings were predicted by a combination of net worth to total assets, net working capital to total assets, and EBIT to total assets. They then examined cases where the bank's rating differed from the model, and sought to explain the variation in terms of independent variables related to industry, branch and customer. This showed that loan risk was under-rated when the customer had a long relationship with the bank, the loan size was large, and the industry was 'exciting' as reported by three banking industry experts. Branch performance had no relationship ($p>0.7$) to loan ratings.

There are several features of these results. The first is that a relatively simple model performs approximately as well in managing risk as an experienced loan officer. The second is that organisational factors proved significant in managerial risk-taking, and demonstrated much more explanatory power than cognitive biases and reference levels. This cautions that many decision anomalies may arise in the experimental design. A third result from the study is that current performance of the branch did not influence the risk propensity of its loan officers. This matches the findings of a number of papers [e.g. Mullins et al. (1999)] that have found that organisations with recent poor performance do not necessarily adopt risky behaviour.

Although the number of studies examining the linkages between business or strategic risk and organisational return is small, they rebut the normative assumption of a positive relationship.

Institutional Framework

Just as company structure is an important influence on risk and decision making, so, too, is the institutional framework because of the way that it shapes facts and frames organisational analysis and conclusions. This can be thought of as organisational heuristics.

According to Wally and Baum (1994), firms with superior financial performance make quicker strategic decisions. Their research showed that the pace of decision making varied between executives, and was accelerated by higher intelligence, greater tolerance for risk, and a strong propensity to act; loss-averse managers act to slow decision making and complicate its process to minimise possibility of failure. The pace of decision making varies between organisational types and is faster in more centralised firms [Pablo et al. (1996)].

Levinthal and March (1993) took a different view and argued that risky decisions by organisations and individuals are subject to a strategy of inertia through: the *hindsight effect* which discounts past errors; and the success trap which leads to inappropriate persistence with previously successful strategies. Those strategies which have proven correct (even for the wrong reasons) and those which are no longer suitable will be pursued because they provide a low risk option, and do not demand the effort involved in analysis and selection of a new strategy. This is defensible given that – once an organisation achieves a minimum acceptable threshold of profit, cash flow, efficiency, and so on - a workable, low risk strategy is preferable to a continuous, never-ending search for the best strategy. Strategy inertia provides certainty and can give good results in a variety of common situations; whereas the optimum solution can only be found after possibly wasteful expenditure of additional resources (with associated risk and delay). Perversely, though, inertia can mean that organisations with greatest need for strategy update are least likely to consider change.

Brouthers et al. (2002) used a survey of the 500 largest firms in the European Union to understand differences in the way that services and manufacturing firms respond to perceived environmental uncertainty, particularly through their preferred mode of international market entry. The uncertainties comprised risks from the actions of government and customers; market demand, and raw materials availability and cost; and the macroeconomy and competitors. Confirming that organisations have individual risk propensities, services firms tended to rely more on wholly-owned subsidiaries for market entries, and were more affected by uncertainties. Manufacturing firms, by contrast, used less integrated approaches.

Bozeman and Kingsley (1998) obtained survey responses from 365 middle and top level managers in various public and private organisations in metropolitan areas of New York State to examine their risk culture. They found that a significant portion of risk propensity (adjusted $R^2 = 0.48$) is explained by organisational traits. In particular, risk taking is promoted when managers trust their subordinates, and when goals are clear; conversely risk is reduced by red tape and insistence on following rules and procedures.

In another setting, Goodrick and Salancik (1996) examined the frequency of Caesarean surgery during 1978-1986 in 319 Californian hospitals with different ownership and operational structures. The authors' aim was to assess whether organisation interests over-ride individuals' preferences. They compared each hospital's Caesarean rate to hospital-specific indicators of direct risk to the baby (size, labour complications) and to inferred risks to the baby (for instance from the mother's age).

The most relevant feature of their findings is that - across a wide range of elevated risks to the baby - doctors at all hospitals were risk averse and opted for delivery by Caesarean section. At lower levels of risk where empirical evidence is equivocal, discretion is used to the institution's advantage, most obviously in a higher Caesarean rate in for-profit hospitals. Not surprisingly the interests of an organisation influence its members' decisions. Goodrick and Salancik (1996: 2) concluded that "the environment consists of taken-for-granted beliefs and rules that penetrate organisations, creating the lenses through which actors view and construct the world... [Thus] institutional frameworks define the ends and shape the means by which interests are determined and pursued."

The institutional influence on risk propensity flows over to group thinking. Since the 1960s it has been apparent that the mere interaction from group discussion will lead people to adopt more risky decisions than they will advocate as individuals [Stoner (1968)]. This is further evidence that organisations develop a personality in the same way that demographic and psychometric attributes give personality to executives.

Gummer (1998) evaluated the role of conflict within top management teams and found that it is promoted by age differences (a decade or more), a history of interaction between members that promotes mutual understanding, and distinct roles. Conflict proved valuable in decisions because it promotes better strategy by encouraging consideration of more choices and evaluating them in greater depth. Thus the way a team is structured and tasked (i.e. framed) shapes its effectiveness and the quality of its decisions. A group which is confident of success will choose an alternative with potentially high payout; one in a pessimistic frame of mind will contemplate disaster.

A little speculatively, groupthink resulting from lack of conflict and diversity is probably the root cause of the pattern noted by Band (1989: 39) that "cover stories in [*Time, Newsweek, Business Week* and *Fortune*] often signal that a trend of ... importance has gone to an unsustainable extreme." He reports a study of *Time* covers between 1924 and 1983 relating to financial issues which found that 80 percent of the outcomes after a year were the opposite of the magazine's predictions. This became enshrined as the `Time Indicator' which is used by contrarian economists. Even the world's most prestigious weekly, *The Economist*, is infamous for the frequency of major blunders on its front covers: a detailed list is provided by Sullivan (1999). The best-known recent example is the 1999 cover story entitled 'Drowning in Oil' which predicted that oil prices would head down just before they began to treble[42]. Another glaring example of the magazine's uncanny ability to misread reality came with a piece in late 2000 under the heading: 'The invisible enemy - Has the threat of bioterrorism been overstated?'[43]. Other well-regarded magazines are as bad. For instance, a cover story entitled 'The Crazy Things People say to justify stock prices' appeared in *Forbes* in 1992 when the US S&P 500 was only a quarter of its March 2000 peak [Baldwin (1992)].

In summary, the framework and setting of an institution shape the decision style and conclusions of its managers. These can be structural factors such as Board composition and financial objectives. They can also be fluid and arise in the framing of goals, response to uncertainty and willingness to accept change.

---

[42] Not to be cowed by its predictive shortcomings, *The Economist* had a cover story on 25 October 2003 entitled "The end of the Oil Age" which said (page 11): "Advances in technology are beginning to offer a way ... to diversify supplies of energy and reduce demand for petroleum, thus loosening the grip of oil ..."

[43] *The Economist*, respectively, 6 March 1999 and 18 November 2000

Longshot Bias in Organisations

A striking feature of many organisational strategies is their consistently poor outcome: routine strategic decisions have a statistically low probability of success – they are high risk. This matches evidence that individuals are overconfident and overweight low probabilities, and is also consistent with the inverted-U relationship between risk and reward which was discussed above.

There are numerous examples of real-world management initiatives - particularly those with strategic implications – which routinely produce a negative outcome. An indicator at the macro level is that the average life of an S&P 500 firm is between 10 and 15 years which is well down on the 50 year lifetimes of the 1930s [Foster and Kaplan (2001)]. According to Fama and French (2003), the ten year survival rate for new firms which have listed in the United States since 1980 is no more than 38 percent. In a related area, Park and Ungson (1997) studied 186 joint ventures which started operating in the electronics industry between 1979 and 1988 and had at least one US partner. At the end of 1995, only 27 JVs survived (85.5 percent failure rate); and the average JV lifetime was five years.

An even worse outcome awaits micro decisions as shown in a study by KPMG (1999: 2) of large cross border mergers and acquisitions between 1996 and 1998. The study

"... found that 82 percent of respondents believed the major deal they had been involved in had been a success. However, this was a subjective estimation [as] ... less than half had carried out a formal review process. When we measured each one against our independent benchmark, based on comparative share performance one year after deal completion, the result was almost a mirror opposite. We found that only 17 percent of deals had added value to the combined company, 30 percent produced no discernible difference, and as many as 53 percent actually destroyed value."

Although managers felt their strategy had succeeded, objectively the vast majority fail[44].

Rau and Vermaelen (1998: 246) examined the performance of bidders in over 3,400 mergers and acquisitions in the United States between 1980 and 1991. They adjusted returns in the three years following the transaction for differences in firm size and book-to-market ratio, and concluded that the acquiring companies suffered a statistically significant four percent underperformance. The authors argue that the result is due – even after adjustment – to the decisions of `glamour bidders' with low book-to-market ra-

---

[44] I contacted the lead author to see if there was any correlation between the size of a takeover (arguably a function of its probability of success) and outcome. The study did not find a link and concluded that "small deals can be every bit as tricky as big ones" (Personal communication, John Kelly, 17 September 2002)

tios which "tend to over-estimate their ability to create synergies in the target and should therefore be willing to pay more than managers of value firms": as a result the glamour firms earn a significant negative return of 17 percent. The average M&A is unsuccessful because managers consistently overestimate the probability that complex strategy will succeed [Roll (1986)], particularly the myriad decisions involved in post acquisition integration [Pablo (1994)]. Managers involved in mergers have a longshot bias and preference for risky strategies[45].

The weak record of mergers and acquisitions is a good example of the *winner's curse* or tendency for winning bids to provide poor financial results. The issue was given real immediacy by ARCO geologists, Capen et al. (1971: 641), who had been puzzled as to why oil fields acquired through successful tender bids did not make a profit: "while there seems to be a lot of oil and gas in the [Gulf of Mexico] region … [since 1950, oil production in] the Gulf has paid off at something less than the local credit union." They concluded that competitive bidding for leases had drained all economic rent and – on average - left no available margin.

Other good examples of risk sensitive decisions with negative expected return can be seen in mineral exploration, development of pioneering technologies such as pharmaceutical research, and innovative business models.

For instance, my analysis [Coleman (1984: 63)] of the expected returns from uranium exploration in Australia found that:

"After committing a minimum exploration budget of $10 million, ... an explorer has one chance in between 7 and 12 of discovering a deposit that will repay the exploration investment."

This suggests that geologists are prepared to adopt a risky decision (explore for uranium) when the population-based probability of success is in the range of 8-15 percent.

A later analysis by Mackenzie and Doggett (1992) found that mineral exploration in Australia had consistently generated a rate of return below ten percent: on average the cost to discover an economic mineral deposit was $41 million, but the present value of the contained minerals using a discount rate of 10 percent was $30 million (i.e. a net present value of negative $11 million!). The study's tables 30 and 31 are reproduced below and clearly show low returns at all deposit sizes. There is also an inverse relationship between return and deposit size because of rising discovery costs and declining present value of contained minerals (largely reflecting long delays in environmental and development approvals for major mining projects). Their analysis concluded that a typical exploration budget of

---

[45] Shareholders may take a different view given that the price of an acquiring firm typically falls after an acquisition is announced.

$A(1990)10 million has a 28 percent probability of finding an economic deposit. As the result from comparable expenditure in Canada during a different period is little different at around 35 percent [Mackenzie (1981)][46], the low probability of success from a risky strategy is not an anomaly of the Australian experience. Exploration companies have a longshot bias.

Table 5.1. Australian Mineral Exploration 1955-1986[1]

Minimum in situ value : $ mill	Discoveries #	Discovery Cost Av $ mill	Return Av $ mill	Expected Value : $ mill	Rate of Return : %
20	102	34	35	1	10
100	75	40	34	-6	9
250	43	51	23	-28	7
500	27	47	10	-47	5
MEAN		41	30	-11	9

[1] All prices are in 1990 Australian dollars and discounted to the start of exploration

The same bias in managers' decisions towards low probability outcomes is evident in the oil industry. Pesaran (1990), for instance, calculated that the price of oil required to justify exploration in the United Kingdom in the 1980s was several times higher than the value of oil in the ground. This is confirmed by Morris (2001) who analysed costs faced by the 11 major international oil companies in replacing their reserves: in the five years to 1999, companies spent about $US4.4 per barrel to discover oil through exploration; whereas the cost of purchasing oil was 42 percent lower. These data show that the companies seeking to replace depleted oil reserves do not move away from a risky strategy (exploration) to a risk-averse strategy (purchase of proven reserves) until the probability of success from the risky strategy drops below about 15 percent [Coleman (2005)].

Taken together, this material on oil and mineral exploration points to the harsh reality that discovery is problematical, particularly of large deposits. Even so, every geologist yearns to find an 'elephant'. This is a classic example of the longshot bias in operation: geologists know (or should know) that the high cost and low probability of finding a massive deposit make it

---

[46] Mackenzie (1981) analysed Canadian post War (1945-1979) base metal exploration economics using the following model: $A = C \, Log(1-Pr)/Log(1-p)$; where all costs are in 1979 Canadian dollars, and A = exploration budget, C = average cost of finding any mineral deposit, Pr = probability that the budget will discover any economic deposit, and p = probability that a deposit is economic. Mackenzie calculated: p=0.02-0.04 and C=$0.45 million. Based on inflation such that $[C1979]1=$[C1990]1.7 and a 1990 exchange rate of $A1=$C1.07, for p=0.03 and A=$(A1990)10 million, Pr=0.35.

economically unwise to search for them. Investors should know to steer away from explorers with ambitious objectives. But it is rare to find an investor or geologist who prefers to seek out 'favourites' in the form of small, more easily found deposits.

In like vein, decisions to fund research and development involve high risk expenditures with long payout periods and low probability of success. Biggadike (1979) sampled 200 Fortune 500 companies to evaluate financial returns from their launch of a new product or service in the late 1960s and early 1970s. He found that these strategic initiatives by large corporations suffer severe losses with an average ROI in the first two years of –40 percent, and –14 percent in the next two years[47]. Only 12 out of the 60 ventures were profitable in the first two years. This was not due to cash requirements as most had negative income before tax and interest expense. He concluded (page 106) that "new ventures need, on the average, eight years before they reach profitability." A different study by Davis (1985) found that the average ROI for start-up ventures is near zero for the first five years. Camerer and Lovallo (1999) report other statistics showing poor survival rates for new ventures.

According to Palmer and Wiseman (1999: 1043): "only 27 percent of R&D projects achieve financial success." A similar experience is reported for information technology projects which are commonly reported to have a small chance of coming in on-time, under budget and with the promised functionality: The Standish Group (1995) put the figure at one in six, whilst Whiting (1998) put it at one in four.

Another indication of the longshot bias in management decision making came from the large scale study of 258 major transportation projects by Flyvbjerg et al. (2002).The authors found that costs are systematically biased, and are under-estimated in almost 90 percent of projects by an average of 28 percent. They concluded (page 279): "cost estimates ... are highly and systematically misleading. Underestimation cannot be explained by error and is best explained by strategic misrepresentation, that is lying." According to the authors (page 288): "the most common psychological explanation is probably 'appraisal optimism'... Promoters and forecasters are held to be overly optimistic about project outcomes ...". These results were confirmed by Davis (1985: 95) who reported a study's conclusion that "first estimates of the construction cost of pioneer plants are typi-

---

[47] Perversely the biggest loss-making initiatives were those whose sponsors had deliberately chosen a small scale relative to market share and breadth of supply (number of customers and product lines), apparently in the mistaken belief that a risk-averse strategy provides the lowest probability of loss. This is another result which is consistent with a concave return-risk relationship.

cally less than half the eventual cost"; and more than 80 percent of projects do not meet their expected market share.

Cooper and Kleinschmidt (2000) surveyed 55 Australian industrial firms on the outcomes of their successful and not so successful product launches; and then sought explanations for the different outcomes. The authors included a factor called 'perceived risk at start [of project]', and found that the worst performers had the highest perceived risk (6.1 versus a sample mean of 4.8), whilst the best projects had only slightly lower risk (mean perceived risk of 5.8). Indicating that good risk management is key to project success, factors contributing to project failure included poor co-ordination, few customer benefits and low senior management support.

In summary, it is clear that there is a complex, non linear relationship between risk and reward. Decision makers are outlook-sensitive in their risk-taking and look at probable results in light of their abilities. This renders most decision makers risk-averse in the case of pure gambles. When decision makers' skill is relevant, they prefer an alternative with a high payout, even though it may have a low objective probability of success.

Summary and Conclusions

The first conclusion from the material above is that - contrary to common financial wisdom – reward is not directly related to risk, but has a concave relationship that is consistent with two populations of decision makers. One is more risk averse, successful and expects that higher risk will bring greater reward. The other group is less successful with a lower level of endowment, and seeks risk for the small possibility it offers to make a large return. Their motivation is clear from suggestions that the distribution of returns is typically skewed, with a small number of very positive outcomes.

Importantly the concave relationship applies to risk with both of its meanings as variance in some accounting measure and possible loss. This contradicts a key assumption of financial analysis – explicit in capital markets models – that investment decisions have a risk-neutral outcome: and higher risk brings a proportionately higher reward, decision makers can expect the same risk-weighted outcome, irrespective of risks accepted.

The concave relationship is not new and - according to an early edition of *Dictionary of Political Economy* [Higgs (1926: Volume III page 224)]:

"... the classes of investments which on the average return most to the investor are neither the very safest of all nor the very riskiest, but the intermediate classes which do not appeal either to timidity or to the gambling instinct."

This concave return-risk relationship has been recognised several times in earlier discussion. It is apparent in company profitability, investment returns, oil exploration, and racetrack wagering.

Assuming that the relationship between return and risk is concave with a positive relationship below a prudent level of risk and a negative relationship above, the curve will be of the type:

Return = $-\alpha_1*\text{Risk}^2 + \alpha_2*\text{Risk} + \alpha_3$; or perhaps
Return = $-\alpha_1 + \alpha_2*\text{Ln(Risk)}$

where α_1, α_2 and α_3 are positive constants.

An example meeting these criteria is shown in the next chart with a relationship of the following form[48]:

Return = $-90*\text{Risk}^3 + 60*\text{Risk}^2 + 25*\text{Risk} + 2$

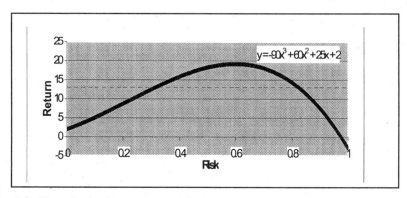

Fig. 5.3. Hypothesised Return vs. Risk

This model incorporates a risk-free rate of return, has CAPM as a particular case in the low risk domain; and – to match the longshot bias - offers a 20 percent probability of achieving a return above 13 percent.

Risk's important influence on return confirms the intuitive belief that managing firm-specific risk is of benefit to employees through job protection; to creditors through lower possibility of default; and to shareholders through enhanced financial performance. As Chatterjee et al. (2003: 62) point out: "failure to control risk increases a company's cost of doing business... and market perceptions of risk play an important role in determining stock price." Good risk management results in fewer shocks: this

---

[48] A third order polynomial term, Risk³, is incorporated to allow the curve to be asymmetrical about the vertical axis

lowers the cost of debt and – by improving cash flow and reducing uncertainty – leads to a higher share price. The higher share price lifts the average cost of capital and so increases the hurdle rate of return for new investments; assuming unlimited availability of new investments with a continuous distribution of risk:reward trade-offs, this promotes a virtuous cycle which produces higher return for lower risk.

A second set of implications from the material above arises in what is arguably the most striking feature of organisational decision making: prevalence of the longshot bias. The evidence is that mergers and acquisitions, research and development, mineral exploration, new projects, product launches and company start-ups have low probability of success. Even so, they are a preferred managerial strategy.

Table 5.2 summarises a sample of decisions to show that a low success rate is chronic: a Chi-squared test, for instance, shows that success rates do not significantly ($p<0.1$) differ from their mean of 21 percent. It is apparent that managers adopt a variety of high risk strategies even though the population-based probability of success lies in the range 10-30 percent. That is, there is consistent evidence across a range of ventures that the average manager or firm has just one chance in five of achieving financial success from a risky new strategic initiative. Only top quartile performers can expect a positive return from their strategic initiatives[49].

Despite the probability of failure, high risk strategies are common in business: in 2002, Australian companies were involved in 433 M&A deals valued at $US22.4 billion [The Thomson Corporation (2003)]. The bias towards over-weighting of low probability outcomes is also evident in asset markets which evidence a longshot bias almost as strong as that in betting markets[50]. For instance, longshot growth stocks consistently perform worse than predicted, whereas the favourites (with low prices relative to book, earnings and other divisors) perform better [Cochrane (1999)].

Why should this longshot bias be so prevalent amongst managers, and how can it persist after repeatedly delivering poor results?
One possibility is that longshot investment decisions are a sophisticated version of gambling: managers know that the distribution of returns from these high risks is positively skewed and so – even though the expected return is low or negative - they can occasionally have spectacular payouts. The limited amount of work in this area is well captured in a paper by

---

[49] Assume the decision results in either success or failure with a 0.21 probability of success. Each event will be similar to a binomial distribution with a mean of 0.21 and standard deviation of ($\sqrt{(0.21*0.79)}$=) 0.41. Using a two-tailed test, any decision makers who expect to have a greater than 50 percent probability of success need to be in the top 24 percent of the distribution of their peers.

[50] A cynical friend calls stockbrokers 'bookmakers-to-the-rich'

Golec and Tamarkin (1998) entitled `Bettors love skewness, not risk, at the horse track'. Even low probabilities of large payouts are attractive to managers who have a financial interest in the outcome (either as part owner or through improved professional prospects from success) or managers who have a sensation-seeking personality as they can anticipate, respectively, additional pecuniary and psychic benefit from the risky strategy. Another group which embraces risky initiatives is ambitious managers who see them as sources of prestige [Roll (1986)].

Table 5.2.   Population-based Outcomes of Managerial Decisions

Decision Setting	Success Rate
R&D projects that meet their expected market share	20 percent
R&D projects that achieve financial success	27 percent
Information technology (IT) projects which come in on-time, under budget and with the promised functionality	16- 25percent
Proportion of major transportation projects where cost estimate is met	14 percent
Probability of making an economic mineral discovery from a typical exploration budget:	
• Australia (1955-1985)	28 percent
• Canada (1945-1979)	35 percent
Probability of successful uranium exploration in Australia	8-16 percent
Proportion of mergers and acquisitions which yield a positive financial outcome	17 percent
Ten year survival rate for new firms in the United States	
• listed since 1980	< 38 percent
• manufacturers between 1963 and 1982	20 percent

It is easy to focus on self-interest and cognitive biases as contributing to risky decisions, and blame them on the human trait that was obvious to Adam Smith (1776, reprinted 1937: 107) when he wrote of: "the overweening conceit which the greater part of men have of their own abilities [because of] their absurd presumption in their own good fortune." However, it is also likely that a significant number of managers do not see such decisions as gambles, but as business challenges where their skill and judgement can improve the objective probability of success [March and Shapira (1987)].

This latter position is supported by the consistency of the 20±10 percent success rate across varied decision domains, and by evidence that there might be a logical underlying mechanism. A clue to the latter comes in a well-cited study involving self-perception of skill where Svenson (1981)

asked 81 American and 80 Swedish students to compare their driving skill with that of other people in the experimental group. 83 percent of the Americans and 51 percent of the Swedes (average 67 percent) put themselves in the top 30 percent on safety; and 59 and 40 percent, respectively, (average 50 percent) put themselves in the top 30 percent on skill. In experimental studies decision makers self-report their skill as being significantly higher than is objectively possible. This has been confirmed in various studies, including one by Camerer and Lovallo (1999) which employed business students in an industry-like experiment.

These findings are part of a pattern which psychologists term self-enhancing biases. According to Rabin (1996: 50):

"We are over-optimistic regarding our health and other aspects of our life; we feel we are less vulnerable to risk than others; and we are more responsible for our successes than we are for our failures. We think that we are superior to others in all sorts of ways: we are better at controlling risk, better drivers, and more ethical."

Although this may appear to be merely wishful thinking, anxiety reduction, or a reflection of the salience of personal actions, the biases also arise in cognitive errors, especially filtering out information that might disprove a comfortable self-delusion.

Combining this evidence shows that managers behave as if their skill is in the top 25 percent of their peers. If skill is even minimally distributed, not everyone can fall in the top quartile, yet that is how managers behave. This over-confidence seems to be an important economic factor. In particular it directly leads to a 70-80 percent failure rate for risky decisions.

All of this sets up a neat tension between strategic options. Consider a company that wishes to grow. It can decide on an acquisition with a 20 percent probability of adding shareholder value. Or it can decide to grow organically with R&D projects that are rarely profitable, major capital projects that massively over-run their budgets, and very long lead times from new products. Is it more risky to grow organically or abruptly?

If it is unclear why longshot strategies exist, it is even less clear on how they can persist after repeated failures. The most likely explanation is that they are driven by aspirations and goals established by third parties such as shareholders, analysts or peer activities so that risk taking becomes an expectation. This matches the appearance of waves of similar strategies – M&As, diversification, aggressive downsizing – that seem to sweep whole industries. Also, because major strategic risks are relatively infrequent experiences for any individual, few risk-embracing decision makers receive sufficient feedback to modify their behaviour.

Normative economic theory a'rgues against these high risk strategies because they have negative expected returns. Yet they are essential to produce new technologies, minerals and consumer products at low cost[51]. Moreover, as expressed neatly by Berg (2003: 414), they show net economic benefits: "[There are] decision environments in which anomalous behavior leads to surprising social benefits. That is, systematic 'mistakes' can have pro-social consequences". His examples include overconfidence by participants in financial markets which improves liquidity; the beneficial 'informational externality' when individuals leave the herd to strike out on their own and demonstrate the merits of unsuspected initiatives; and success in bargaining situations by those with inflated beliefs about the value of their goods. Thus non-optimising decision making can result in significant benefits to the economy and consumers.

The third set of implications is that achieving the right level of business or strategic risk is critical to firms' financial performance. Not all business decisions are strategic, nor involve the longshot bias discussed above. But at the very least, there is an imbalance between firms' risk propensity (which is the tendency to take or avoid risks and so fixes what risks are acceptable) and risk perception (which is judgement of the quantum of risk inherent in an action) [Pablo et al. (1996)].

Despite a growing richness of literature on firm risk and performance, there remain several significant gaps. The first, already covered at length, is the lack of an agreed definition of risk, and uncertainty over the validity of measures which are commonly used (especially the assumed normal distribution of firm returns). The second gap is in measures of the risk propensity of firms. A third gap is the limited analysis of performance as a function of organisation parameters and internal structures.

A fourth gap in our knowledge relates to the parallel influences on firm performance of risk with its meanings of possible adverse outcome and variance in accounting returns. Intuitively one might expect that different factors contribute to firm risk in its financial and managerial definitions. However, as discussed in chapter 2, the various measures of risk are not independent. Even more surprising are the findings in this chapter that both measures of risk share common drivers as each increases in line with poor historical performance and smaller organisation size; and increases in both measures of risk lead to reduced firm performance. This significantly

---

[51] If investment in low probability outcomes provided a return commensurate with their risk, then the economic rent would be much higher, and increase the price of end products. In other words, "if there is a 'sure thing' and an efficient market or the possibility of arbitrage, all rents will be bid away" [I am indebted to an anonymous examiner for this observation].

strengthens conclusions about the role of risk in firm performance. Whilst this link is not pursued here, it offers scope for considerable research.

An intriguing research gap arises in strong real-world evidence of the nexus between managers' over-estimates of the probable success of high risk initiatives and their preference for such strategies. Finally there has been little work exploring the behavioural dichotomy between firms which decide to grow through risk embrace (such as acquisition or exploration) and those which adopt more conservative strategies.

CHAPTER 6 Published Models of Decision Making Under Risk

This chapter extends the discussion in chapter two and discusses models which have been developed to explain risky decision making. The evaluation starts with a description of a representative selection of models; then provides a detailed evaluation of Prospect Theory which has become a leading explanation for risk-taking behaviour and forms much of the orthodoxy in decision theory; and closes with a discussion of the gaps in current models.

Models of Decision Making Under Risk

In brief, contemporary models of managerial decision making can be classified as either mathematically based or descriptive; and are developed by back-fitting to measured data or as explanations of observed behaviours.

Mathematical Models

A good starting point for mathematical models of decision making is the analysis by Bromiley (1991) which was discussed in the previous chapter. He compiled data on the structure, performance and earnings forecasts for 288 US manufacturing companies between 1976 and 1987, and then explained nearly half the variation in their risk through seven significant ($p<0.05$) variables:

$$\text{Risk}_{t+1} \tag{6.1}$$
$$= 0.36 + 0.21*\text{Risk}_t - 3.1*\text{Performance}_t - 1.3*\text{Industry Performance}_t + 2.6*\text{Aspirations}_t - 0.02*\text{Current Ratio}_t - 0.45*\text{SG\&A-to-sales Ratio}_t - 0.06*\text{Interest Coverage}_t \qquad [R^2 \approx 0.40]$$

where: Risk in any given year is the variance in security analysts' forecasts of income; Performance was reported as Return on total assets

(ROA); Aspirations equalled 1.05 times historical ROA for firms with performance above the industry mean, and industry mean for underperformers; Current Ratio equals current assets divided by current liabilities; SG&A-to-sales Ratio equals selling, general and administrative expenses divided by sales, and is a measure of 'slack'; and Interest Coverage equals income before interest and taxes divided by interest.

This shows that risk at any time is directly related to previous risk; and is inversely related to prior year's performance, and to the prior year's current ratio, SG&A-to-sales ratio, and interest coverage. The most obvious implications are that risk propensity is sticky and that firm risk is reduced following good performance.

An interesting result is the influence of slack, which is a measure of the extent to which a firm can free up resources or readily obtain additional resources. Available slack is measured by the current ratio and points to how much working capital can be immediately released; recoverable slack is measured by overhead expenses relative to sales which indicates the proportion of non volume-related expenses that could be cut; and potential slack is indicated by interest coverage and a low debt to equity ratio which points to untapped borrowing capacity. In general, higher slack reduced risk taking. This is consistent with other findings that better endowed individuals and organisations are less likely to take risks.

A second type of mathematical model is an extension of normative assumptions about decision making, usually incorporating experimental observations. After Prospect Theory first emerged in 1979, Quiggin (1982) developed a concept called rank dependent expected utility (RDEU) which appears similar to expected utility but has weightings which are relative to other possible decision outcomes rather than to some absolute measure; its payoff is utility. Tversky and Kahneman (1992) then developed Cumulative Prospect Theory which is similar to RDEU but has payoffs which are measured relative to a reference point (it is only briefly discussed here as it forms much of the material in the following section). Because of the intertwining of the concepts, there is some tension between their proponents: RDEU is popular in Europe, while CPT is the dominant North American paradigm.

An improvement suggested by Fox and Tversky (1998) is to model risky decisions through two elements: the first involves the decision maker in estimating the probability of the decision outcome(s); and the second element is to weight the outcomes and so put an overall value on the decision. Consider an event, A, with a particular, but uncertain, outcome, x; the decision maker assigns a value to x of v(x) and develops a probability distribution of A, P(A). If w is the function that weights the choices, then the overall value of the event, V, is given by:

$$V(x,A) = v(x).\ w[P(A)] \tag{6.2}$$

Another good example of a model which specifically incorporates risk is given by Sarin and Weber (1993). They recognised that many studies had separately considered risk measurement and decision strategies, to such an extent that some models – including Prospect Theory – treat risk as independent of the decision maker's preferences (others, including expected utility, ignore risk). They synthesised the two analytical approaches and developed a risk-value model which allows comparisons between attractiveness of alternatives in the following form:

$$f[V(X), R(X)] \geq f[V(Y), R(Y)] \tag{6.3}$$

where V and R are the value and riskiness of alternatives X and Y.

Descriptive Decision Making Models

The principal alternative to mathematical models of decision making are descriptive models which describe the behaviour of decision makers and/or the processes they follow in making a decision. These models are the why and the how of decision making.

A particular subset of process descriptions is *behavioural decision theory* which Camerer (1990) described as "a catalogue of ways in which judgements and choices deviate from normative decision theory and of psychological explanation of these deviations." According to McFadden (1999: 74):

"Choice behaviour can be characterised by a decision process, which is informed by perceptions and beliefs based on available information, and influenced by affect, attitudes, motives and preferences."

These models are useful, but not universal. For instance, there is still a gap between the outlook of economists and psychologists. Thus, according to McFadden (1999), where economists focus on the direct links between information and choice, behavioural decision theorists see multiple linkages and mediating variables.

A comprehensive depiction of how individuals conceptualise risk is given by Rohrmann (1999). This model recognises that decisions involve complex, compounding pressures from personality, situation, probabilities, outcomes and perspective. Although integrated, wide ranging models such as these are intuitively appealing, they are not common in the literature on risk and decision making. However, the analysis and conclusions of this book conform to the Rohrmann model.

The fourth approach to explaining risky decisions uses process models, and management science is currently leading in this field. Although a number of branches of economics have given an important role to decision making (e.g. in consumer behaviour, micro-economic theory of the firm and the revealed preferences of markets and populations), they have not tended to look at the decisions of *individuals* and what leads them to make specific choices. Management, however, emphasises the importance of the role played by individuals. The second reason is management's embrace of the psychologist's interest in the *why* of processes: psychologists seek to understand individual elements of decision making, and management scientists link them into a holistic explanation which is suited to the complex process of risky decision making. This recognises the perspective of Brehmer (1992) who pointed out that most decisions are dynamic: far from being an end, they form part of a broad objective, depend on preceding decisions, and must be made when demanded by the circumstances.

A comprehensive example from the management literature is provided by Sitkin and Weingart (1995) whose work is most closely related to the model and validation process in this book. They started with the framework of Sitkin and Pablo (1992) whereby judgements about the type of risk being faced (either gain or loss) are mediated by the decision maker's risk propensity because risk prone decision makers perceive a lower risk from any given situation: their decision is driven by risk propensity rather directly by than the 'facts' of the situation as assumed by normative models. They concluded (page 9) that: "risk propensity dominates both the actual and perceived characteristics of the situation as a determinant of risk behaviour." Aggregating the factors in this way was an important breakthrough.

Sitkin and Weingart (1995) confirmed the model's applicability in an experiment using MBA students in a class exercise where students answered questions in relation to a case study which was similar to the circumstances leading up to the *Challenger* space shuttle explosion in 1986[52]. They found that risk perception and risk propensity – whilst determined by numerous individual variables – are the prime determinants of risk taking behaviour and explained 38 percent of the variance in results. The researchers took a reductionist perspective by looking at organisation attributes, and determined that factors which had previously been thought to

---

[52] This is the Carter Team case study which is used to compile data for the book. The methodology and results are described in chapter seven.

impact directly on risky behaviour actually acted on the decision maker's risk perception and risk propensity.

Palmer and Wiseman (1999) examined organisations as a whole and assumed that their risk propensity is determined by corporate governance, and by the environment and firm structure. They hypothesised that risk is related to environmental characteristics of the industry (complexity, growth and dynamism) and to those of decision makers (managers' traits, firm ownership); and to the firm's target and actual performance (respectively, managers' aspirations and expectations) and its resources. Palmer and Wiseman (1999: 1038) defined managerial risk as "management's proactive strategic choices involving the allocation of resources" and measured it by R&D investment relative to firm sales and by the extent of diversification (the average number and importance of four digit SIC industries that each firm competed in). They chose organisational risk as income stream uncertainty (variance in ROA), and used data for 235 US firms in 64 industries between 1984 and 1991 to develop a structural model.

Manager risk taking proved to be strongly ($p<0.001$) promoted by equity participation and previous managerial risk taking; it is less significantly ($p<0.05$) promoted by shortfalls in firm returns (industry benchmark ROA and ROE less firm actual) and low slack (combination of excess liquidity, high expenses relative to sales, and low debt:equity). Organisational risk is driven by managerial risk taking and shortfalls in returns, and thus has behavioural causes which are independent of the firm's environment. The study was silent on the relationship between risk and returns.

In summary the processes underpinning individual risk taking remain ill-defined, but there is evidence that they respond to a combination of environmental, situational and definitional aspects of the decision.

Prospect Theory: Does It Describe Reality?

There can be little doubt that Prospect Theory is one of the most successful concepts in the social sciences. It was developed by Nobel laureate Daniel Kahneman and his brilliant collaborator Amos Tversky [Kahneman and Tversky (1979)] and then updated to Cumulative Prospect Theory [Tversky and Kahneman (1992)].

Prospect Theory and Cumulative Prospect Theory (hereafter referred to generically as 'prospect theory', or PT) form a descriptive model of decision making under risk which argues that people derive value or utility from changes in wealth relative to a reference level, rather than from absolute wealth levels [Barberis and Huang (2001)]. Decision makers weight alternative outcomes by dynamic factors which are related to cumulative experiences, and are independent of absolute monetary values.

These two seminal papers are amongst the most cited in economic science[53]. It is interesting that – even though CPT is later and more general than PT – the latter's citation rate is currently four times higher. The implication is that scholars see the concepts in Kahneman and Tversky (1979) as far more relevant than those in Tversky and Kahneman (1992). Whatever the assumptions, Prospect Theory's tenets are all but unquestioningly accepted as guidance for decision making studies in fields as far apart as corporate strategy [Miller and Bromiley (1990)], racetrack gambling [Jullien and Salanié (2000)], and investment [Barberis et al. (2001)]. Prospect Theory is credited with explaining behaviour in subjects as diverse as starlings [Marsh and Kacelnik (2002)] and market traders [Willman et al. (2002)]; and in settings from hospitals [Treadwell and Lenert (1999)] to war rooms [Haas (2001)].

Edwards (1996) undertook a literature review of PT and included a description of its principles and development. Most of her examples (34 out of 38 papers) support PT. Camerer (1998: 1) used PT to explain ten anomalies in real-world data in order "to inspire economists and psychologists to spend more time in the wild." He reached the favourable conclusion (page 10) that "there is no good scientific reason why it [PT] should not replace expected utility in current research, and be given prominent space in economics textbooks."

The theory's wide embrace and universal recognition as a description of decision making behaviour meets what Kuhn (1970, 2nd edition) proposed as the test of a paradigm.

Although PT dominates behavioural economics, in conformance with the techniques of that discipline, many of its applications have been in a laboratory setting. This is not surprising as behavioural economics grew out of psychologists' experimental methodology which is directed at understanding single hypotheses [Kahneman (1991)]. In a typical study, Blondel (2002) set out to test six competing theories of choice under risk and used a laboratory experiment. Reliance on artificial results is also consistent with the observation by McDermott (2002: 31) of practice in

"the hard sciences, including biology, chemistry, physics, and medicine [which] all rely primarily on experimentation to examine and illuminate basic processes… implic-

---

[53] Laibson and Zeckhauser (1998) report the economic folk wisdom that Kahneman and Tversky (1979) is the most cited paper published in *Econometrica*. In early 2004, the ISI Web of Knowledge had 3,146 citations for Kahneman and Tversky (1979); some 500 had appeared in 2002 or later. In addition, there were 437 citations for Tversky and Kahneman (1992), about 130 of them since 2002.

itly trusting in the power and validity of experiments as applied to real-world contexts."

In such settings, the term 'empirical' means data which have been derived from experiments, rather than proven by observation or guided by practical experience.

It is not hard to be critical of evidence obtained in an artificial environment such as a laboratory, using non-representative subjects such as undergraduates, and posing hypothetical questions (how much money would induce you to quit your job?). When this experimentation displays little meaningful variation and is performed to test a single hypothesis, it leaves the results blind to the complexities of decisions, especially when homogenous subjects cannot reveal the significance of individual factors such as personality, perceptions of the decision's risks, competencies and experience. As a result, most findings from experiments in controlled environments have low explanatory power (few papers indicate any measure of confidence, but typical values of R^2 fall well below 0.2).

Further contributing to the difficulty in applying PT to real-world topics is that its authors have not detailed some of the theory's key aspects, especially specification of the reference level and components of gains and losses. Another gap is the absence of any rules for the editing phase: for example, in the case of prior gains and losses, it is variously suggested that a decision maker considers "only the direct consequences of the act" [Tversky and Kahneman (1981: 456)] and ignores prior gains and losses; or that one "who has not made peace with his losses is likely to accept gambles that would be unacceptable to him otherwise" [Kahneman and Tversky (1979: 287)] and take into account prior gains and losses.

A significant deterrent to comprehensive tests of PT in the real world has been the opinion of Tversky and Kahneman (1992) that it is impractical, and they offer few applied examples. Despite the analytical inconvenience, researchers have recently begun to subject this paradigm to increasingly creative tests using real-world applications, even if some of the evaluations are only approximate. In many cases PT fails the test.

For instance, Treadwell and Lenert (1999) used medical literature to evaluate Prospect Theory on the assumption that it could explain different perceptions of medical states and treatments between sick and healthy people. Although PT proved useful, results were mixed and there were a number of confounding behaviours.

This unsatisfactory outcome has been shared by other papers which could only employ PT in a conceptual sense because it would not fit the observed evidence. An example is Barberis and Huang (2001) who attempted to use PT to explain moves in equity markets, but found it had trivially low explanatory power with values of R^2 smaller than five percent. de Blaeij and van Vuuren (2003) attempted to use PT as a basis for analysing traffic risk perceptions, but half of their 33 subjects could not answer the questions posed to them. Bradley (2003) examined consolidated data on bettor behaviour, but could not decide if it matched or contradicted PT. Neilson and Stowe (2002) had a similarly unrewarding experience when they attempted to explain common behaviours using PT.

Several studies [e.g. Thaler and Johnson (1990)] have shown that prior success led to a greater willingness to take risks in gambling and investment: thus – in contradiction of PT - people were risk taking in the domain of gains. This was confirmed by March and Shapira (1987: 1413) in their study of managers' attitudes to risk: "if performance is well above the survival point, the focus of attention results in a predilection for relatively high variance alternatives, thus risk prone behaviour." Starbuck and Milliken (1988: 319) analysed the 1986 *Challenger* tragedy and concluded: "organisations often interpret past successes as evidencing their competence" and will accept increasing risk[54].

Birnbaum (2004) reported a number of largely experimental studies which showed evidence of seven behaviours that disprove PT's description of decision making under risk. Sitkin and Pablo (1992: 10) list real-world studies that contradict Prospect Theory[55] and lament that "they have not even been recognised in the literature." Other empirical studies which fail to replicate PT include: Hollenbeck et al. (1994), McNamara and Bromiley (1997), Mullins et al. (1999), and Slattery and Ganster (2002). In addition several studies – such as Forlani (2002), Miller and Bromiley (1990) and Schneider and Lopes (1986) – found that the predictions of PT apply only under specific assumptions. With disappointing results, PT remains a theory that is not widely applied and has been slow to move into the management literature.

Prospect Theory was developed in a laboratory, where tests usually provide clearly defined probabilities and outcomes. This is in marked contrast to most economic settings where the facts are unclear, and decision makers suffer bounds from lack of computational power, skill and data. The real world is also dynamic and uncontrolled. Moreover, decision makers self-select, opting to participate in events with particular economic features, including uncertainty and returns to skill.

---

[54] As an aside, the opposite does not apply: consider, for instance, bettors who face a negative sum outcome and persist in risk-taking despite consistently unprofitable performance.

[55] They cite: Osborn and Jackson (1988), Thaler and Johnson (1990) and Staw et al. (1981). But note that West and Berthon (1997: 29) consider Thaler and Johnson (1990) is one of the "many studies that have supported prospect theory in the business environment."

Whilst the controlled environment of laboratory experiments can provide useful foundations for developing new theories, it remains essential to provide empirical validation of paradigms. And although the usual subjects of experimental studies – undergraduates – are in common supply, Frederick (2003) and Potters and van Winden (2000) have shown that there are statistically significant differences in the responses of students and less naïf subjects. Thus generalising laboratory studies using students is problematical.

Patchy real-world validation of PT remains a void that this survey fills by examining a representative selection of appropriate studies. The scrutiny is broad in time and ranges across disciplines in search of empirical data.

The conclusion is that Prospect Theory has not successfully transitioned to Kuhn's 'normal science' because it does not yet provide a comprehensive foundation for explaining actual behaviours. Although some of its elements prove true in the real world, other important assumptions are either inconsistent or are contradicted by the evidence. PT remains a powerful theory, but is a theory nonetheless, with all the limitations this implies.

Description and Implications of Prospect Theory

Like all good paradigms, Prospect Theory draws widely on earlier research, and embraces much in the concepts of risk-sensitive foraging [Stephens (1981)], rank dependent utility [Quiggin (1982)], importance of changes in wealth and reference levels [Markowitz (1952)], and non-linear weighted utility [Edwards (1954)].

When Prospect Theory first emerged, it was heavily descriptive and Kahneman and Tversky (1979) used figure 6.1 which has become one of the most reproduced relationships in finance. The vertical axis is termed 'value' (not 'utility'), and the horizontal axis measures deviation from a neutral reference outcome.

The diagram shows the classic features of: a convex curve for losses evidencing risk embrace; greater sensitivity to losses than equivalent gains as the curve is steeper in its left portion with a more rapid drop in value per unit loss; and a concave curve for gains where individuals are risk averse. This non-linearity in probabilities means that lower probabilities are overweighted (and unlikely events are typically ignored) whilst people underweight moderate and high probabilities; this leaves decision makers relatively insensitive to differences in probability between events which are commonly encountered.

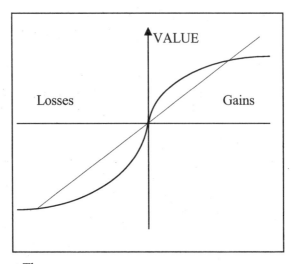

Fig. 6.1. Prospect Theory

The S-shaped curve is an amalgam of ideas. Economists generally assume that marginal utility falls and hence utility functions are concave: but this implies universal risk-aversion, not only in the domain of gains. By contrast, psychologists think in terms of diminishing sensitivity to changes in wealth that leads to risk seeking over losses (convex utility function) and risk aversion over gains.

Under PT, decisions come in two stages. The first, editing phase simplifies the range of possible choices, often as decision makers eliminate obviously inferior possibilities to shape a realistic set of alternative choices: this becomes the source of a number of behavioural anomalies. The second, evaluative phase chooses the optimum alternative. An important feature is that value is measured by changes in wealth, rather than absolute levels, that harks back to older concepts such as 'happiness is relative'.

The process requires the decision maker to select between prospects that are defined by a finite probability distribution and yield outcome x with probability p. It is described by:

$$E(U) = \sum_{i=1}^{n} w(p_i).u(x_i)$$
(6.4)

where: $w(p_i)$ is a function that turns probabilities, p, into decision weights. It is typically assumed to have an inverse S-shape which is concave for low probabilities and convex for higher probabilities; and $u(x_i)$ is the utility of outcome x_i and is measured by gains and losses rather than absolute values.

Different weights can be assigned according to both the event and to its outcome, particularly when ambiguity is involved.

This is an extension of work by Friedman and Savage (1948) who used a similarly shaped curve and axes marked utility and income to explain why the same consumer will buy insurance (a risk averse behaviour in the domain of losses) and gamble (a risk embracing behaviour in the domain of gains).

A decade after launching PT, Tversky and Kahneman (1992) pointed to the importance of framing, non-linear risk preferences, overweighting of low probability events, perceived competence, and risk seeking when facing losses. Their resolution of these various features of decision making involved *Cumulative Prospect Theory* (CPT). CPT is more general than its predecessor as it allows for multiple outcomes rather than just two; and it enables different treatments of gains and losses by assigning a separate weighting function to each.

CPT starts by ranking all outcomes, x_i, from least to most preferred, after which:

$$V(f) = \sum_{i=-m}^{n} \pi_i.v(x_i) \tag{6.5}$$

where: $V(f)$ is the value of an uncertain prospect f, and f is preferred to g iff $V(f) > V(g)$; π_i is a decision weight equal to the marginal contribution of x_i (the values of π_i can be different for gains and losses, and do not necessarily sum to 1). People transform actual probability to subjective probability through a non-linear expression of the following form:

$$\pi = w(p) = \frac{p^\gamma}{[p^y + (1-p)^\gamma]^{\frac{1}{\gamma}}} \tag{6.6}$$

The authors conducted experiments and found that subjects shift between risk embrace and risk aversion at a probability of success of around 0.35-0.4.

Testable Hypotheses of Prospect Theory

This section lists those hypotheses of Prospect Theory that can be tested using real-world data.

The primary source of PT's hypotheses is Kahneman and Tversky (1979: 274-278):

"Prospect Theory distinguishes two phases in the choice process: an early phase of editing and a subsequent phase of evaluation … People normally perceive outcomes as gains or losses, rather than as final states of wealth or welfare. Gains and losses, of course, are defined relative to some neutral reference point [which] usually corresponds to the current asset position … [but] can be affected by the formulation of the offered prospects, and by the expectations of the decision maker … The preference order between prospects need not be invariant across contexts, because the same offered prospect could be edited in different ways depending on the context in which it appears … the value function for changes of wealth is normally concave above the reference point and often convex below it."

Further amplification was provided in Tversky and Kahneman (1992: 297-316):

"The key elements of this [i.e. prospect] theory are (1) a value function that is concave for gains, convex for losses and steeper for losses than for gains; and (2) a nonlinear transformation of the probability scale, which overweights small probabilities and underweights moderate and high probabilities …The carriers of value are gains and losses, not final assets … The reference point serves as a boundary that distinguishes gains from losses … people are relatively insensitive to probability difference in the middle of the range … The weighting functions are inverse S-shaped."

These papers generate the following hypotheses of Prospect Theory:

H1   Individuals make decisions based on changes in wealth or endowment

H2   In evaluating choices, decision makers use reference points or target levels equal to current or anticipated wealth

H3   When outcomes drop below the reference level, decision makers are risk seeking

H4   When outcomes are above target, decision makers are risk averse

H5   Decision makers are more sensitive to losses than equivalent gains (i.e. loss averse)

H6   Preferences can be described by a non-linear, inverse-S shaped function

H7   Low probabilities are overweighted

H8   Moderate to high probabilities are underweighted

H9   The crossover from overweighting to underweighting occurs at a probability of around 0.4

Consideration of how the hypotheses should apply in real-world settings leads to a number of extensions and corollaries. These are listed below and draw on suggestions from a variety of sources, especially Bauer and Rotte (1997), Fiegenbaum and Thomas (1988), Mullins et al. (1999), and Slattery and Ganster (2002). Each is linked with one of the principal hypotheses derived above (i.e. Hx, where x = 1, 2, …9) and thus numbered Hxα (where α = a, b …).

In the decision making process, individuals are not immutably risk-averse or risk-embracing, but evaluate alternatives in the light of their personal reference levels and assessment of the facts of the decision. Hence:

H1a Different decision makers facing identical decisions reach different conclusions

H1b Individuals are risk sentient and can be both risk averse and risk seeking when facing different decisions

H1c Risk propensity in decision making is not impacted by whether the outcome is near-term or distant

Decision makers embrace risky alternatives because they have experienced or anticipate a deterioration in wealth. Incorporating reference levels in decision making leads to a distinct behavioural change around specific quanta of wealth where decision makers shift between risk-embrace and risk-aversion. Thus:

H2a Reference points such as milestones and symbolic numbers are associated with a disproportionate frequency of decisions

H3a Workers target a satisficing income level and are income (risk) averse above that level, and income (risk) seeking below.

Another aspect of PT is the *framing effect*. The frame follows subjective evaluation of a decision's components and consequences, and thus is a function of the way a choice is presented and apprehended, particularly in relation to the decision maker's reference level at the time. A framing effect is a change in preference after the same decision is presented in a different formulation, or frame.

H2b Identical datasets presented differently elicit different responses from the same decision makers

H3b When outcomes are negatively framed (i.e. only losses are posited), decision makers choose more risky outcomes

H4a When outcomes are positively framed (i.e. only gains are posited), decision makers choose less risky outcomes

The S-shape which is subjectively assigned to value weightings has a number of implications. One is that risk propensity as measured by the relationship of value to wealth changes will differ between the regions of losses and gains. Another implication from the perception that unlikely events have a greater probability of occurrence is a tendency towards what is called the *longshot bias* on the racecourse where bettors provide greater support for long odds horses than is justified by their objective chances of winning. Thus:

H6a Risk propensity in the different domains of gains and losses is not positively correlated

H7a Decision makers adopt a longshot bias

Prospect Theory's hypotheses should apply to a variety of personal and financial decisions. Because decision makers are more sensitive to losses than equivalent gains, a fall in the value of any investment will induce proportionately greater risk-embrace than the risk-aversion which is induced by an equivalent rise in value. Thus in choosing strategies to partially liquidate a portfolio, investors will sell winners in preference to losers (this is termed the *disposition effect*).

A second situation arises around reference levels where decision makers are more sensitive to losses than gains. Those with a low level of endowment (ranging from being poor to being in ill-health) will perceive any given level more favourably than better endowed decision makers; and if the wealthier people are brought down to the given level, they will experience a greater loss than the gain felt by those brought up to the higher level. In the case of sick people, this effect can be evaluated using time trade-off which is the proportional shortening of life in their current ill state that decision makers would hypothetically accept in exchange for enjoying excellent health (e.g. for a kidney patient, ten months of life without dialysis might equate to a year on dialysis). If PT holds, then the time trade-off should be greater for healthy subjects as they see any hypothetical ill state as more of a loss than would sick people [Treadwell and Lenert (1999)]. A parallel arena is litigation where plaintiffs anticipate gains and defendants anticipate nothing or a loss. When a settlement is proposed, this represents a lower risk alternative than proceeding to trial: it should be more acceptable to risk-averse plaintiffs than to loss-averse defendants [Guthrie et al. (2001)]. Thus:

H5a   Investors realise gains more readily than losses

H5b   Poor or sick people view any wealth or health state more favourably than rich or healthy people.

H5c   The time trade-off (or proportional shortening of life that a person would accept when offered a hypothetical move from an ill state to perfect health) is less for an ill person than for a healthy person.

H5d   The wage premium for employment in a dangerous industry or workplace is proportionately greater for higher paid employees.

H5e   In litigation, plaintiffs are more likely than defendants to prefer settlement

As decision makers use reference levels in distinguishing gains from losses, a run of sequential gains (or losses) moves them further towards (or into) the domain of gains (losses) and should be followed by growing risk-aversion (risk-embrace). This suggests, for instance, that when gamblers have been winning they are more firmly in the domain of gains and should be risk-averse. Conversely when gamblers are behind, their risk-embrace should rise. This will be evidenced by mean-reverting expectations in successive, similar decisions: after wins the decision makers change to adopt less risky choices; after losses, they continue risk taking in the expectation of a reversal of the trend. Because most gambling has a negative expected outcome (which can be as high as minus 25 percent in pari-mutuel gambling where the operator takes a fixed proportion out of each pool), when prolonged gambling occurs such as at race meetings average wealth is continuously declining. Thus:

H4b   Risk taking declines as gains mount: the *house money effect* (the low-risk feeling that gamblers express when they are ahead and playing with the house's money) is negative

H4c   Wealthier people are more risk averse

H2c   Decision makers display mean-reverting behaviour in successive choices

H3c   As gamblers take more risks when losses increase, the longshot bias on racetracks strengthens through the meeting

H3d   Support for risky bets strengthens over the meeting

It is commonly proposed [e.g. Fiegenbaum and Thomas (1988)] that rational-actor models should see Prospect Theory apply to organisations in the same way as it does with individuals. Thus the longshot bias should be evident in firms through support for improbable strategies, and organisational propensity towards risk-taking should increase following poor returns (and *vice versa*). As poorer performing firms increase their risk taking, risk and return will be negatively correlated in the domain of losses, but positively correlated in the domain of gains (this is the *Bowman Paradox*). Thus:

H7b   Firms have a bias towards high-risk strategies

H3e   As risk-taking leads to corner-cutting, poorer performing firms have more safety and legislative breaches and more operating incidents and crises

H3f   Poorer performing firms will further reduce returns to increase their risky expenditures (e.g. on advertising, acquisitions, market entries, product launches)

H6b   Risk and return are not positively correlated

The principles of PT should similarly be apparent in relations between nations, most obviously through warfare which is the pre-eminent arena for decision making under risk. Countries which expect a deterioration in their position will be more willing to take aggressive, risky positions [Watman et al. (1995)]. Successful nations will be risk-averse and prefer the *status quo* where no risk is involved. As losses are more highly valued than equivalent gains under PT, conflict is more likely to occur over allocation of scarce resources (e.g. water, land) and costs (e.g. environmental clean-up). In wars, leaders who have experienced losses (typically measured as casualties) should embrace risk and so prolong a losing conflict for longer than prudence dictates [Bauer and Rotte (1997)]. Thus:

H3g   After experiencing losses, attackers become more aggressive

H5f   Warring nations value their own casualties (i.e. losses) higher than their opponent's casualties (i.e. gains)

This gives 35 testable hypotheses in the first two columns of table 6.1. Although not pursued here, it is also possible to examine hypotheses resulting from the various observations that led to development of PT such as the isolation, certainty and reflection effects; and the operations presumed to occur in the editing and evaluation phases of decision making.

Real-world Applications of Prospect Theory

Literature with real-world applications of PT falls into two groups. The first offers a specific test of PT and concludes whether the data confirm one or more of its tenets. The second type of study is silent on the salience of PT, but examines hypotheses set out in table 6.1. Typically these latter incidental tests were published prior to emergence of PT in the mid 1980s, or come from fields unrelated to behavioural decision making.

I have been able to locate over 50 papers which provide specific tests of the real-world operation of PT. The 37 most significant examples are summarised in table 6.2. This is not an exhaustive list; other additions, though, would make little qualitative contribution to the debate as they essentially duplicate the findings of those noted.

The two right columns of table 6.1 distribute the papers listed in table 6.2 according to the hypothesis(es) which they test, and provide an assessment of whether the papers' conclusions support or contradict Prospect Theory.

Out of the 35 hypotheses, some 26 are supported by real-world evidence, whilst six receive a mixture of support and contradiction, and three are contradicted. The nine hypotheses of Prospect Theory which are not conclusively supported by real-world data comprise:

H1c Risk propensity in decision making is not impacted by whether the outcome is near-term or distant

H2c Decision makers display mean-reverting behaviour

H3 When outcomes drop below the reference level, decision makers are risk seeking

H3b When outcomes are negatively framed (i.e. only losses are posited), decision makers choose more risky outcomes

H3e   Risk-taking leads to corner-cutting, and so poorer performing firms have more safety and legislative breaches and more operating incidents and crises

H4a   When outcomes are positively framed (i.e. only gains are posited), decision makers choose less risky outcomes

H4b   Risk taking declines as gains mount: the *house money effect* (the low-risk feeling that gamblers express when they are ahead and playing with the house's money) is negative

H6   Preferences can be described by an inverse-S shaped function

H9   The cross-over from overweighting to underweighting occurs at a probability of around 0.4

These exceptions fall into three clear groups:

1. Individuals are not homogeneous in evaluation of risk. It seems that uniquely personal attributes – education and experience, personality and risk propensity – play a significant role in decision making. Moreover the time until a decision's outcome shapes preferences, and the effects of framing are inconsistent.
2. Risk-taking below the reference level and risk-aversion above is moderated by the opportunity cost of risk-sentience. Below the reference level, loss aversion can be more powerful than risk embrace.
3. Preferences are not described by a continuous distribution, particularly not an S-curve; and decision makers exhibit a longshot bias so that the cross-over from overweighting (i.e. risk embrace) to underweighting of probabilities occurs in the range 0.2 ± 0.2.

An overall evaluation of PT is not obvious. Based purely on the weight of numbers – three quarters of the hypotheses are supported – PT seems relatively robust. However, the exceptions show substantial lack of support for key PT tenets, including reference levels, framing and structure of the preference weightings. The exceptions undermine the generality of PT, so that it only selectively explains decision making under risk: Prospect Theory is not universally applicable, which is why it has been shown to lack predictive capability.

Table 6.1. Prospect Theory Hypotheses and Real-World Tests

Hypothesis		Reference	Implication for Prospect Theory
H1	Individuals make decisions based on changes in wealth or endowment	Camerer et al (1997)	Supported
		Hollenbeck et al (1994)	Supported
H1a	Different decision makers facing identical decisions reach different conclusions	Guthrie et al (2001)	Supported
		Harries et al (2000)	Supported
		McGlothin (1956)	Supported
		Tsevat et al (1995)	Supported
H1b	Individuals are risk sentient and can be both risk averse and risk seeking when facing different decisions	Loughhunn, Payne and Crum (1980)	Supported
		Qualls and Puto (1989)	Supported
H1c	Risk propensity in decision making is not impacted by whether the outcome is near-term or distant	Sagristano, Trope and Liberman (2002)	Contradicted
H2	In evaluating choices, decision makers use reference points or target levels equal to current or anticipated wealth	Camerer et al (1997)	Supported
		Heath, Huddart and Lang (1999)	Supported
H2a	Reference points such as milestones and symbolic numbers should be associated with a disproportionate frequency of decisions	Heath, Huddart and Lang (1999)	Supported
H2b	Identical datasets presented differently elicit different responses from the same decision makers	Guthrie et al (2001)	Supported
		Kuhnberger (1988)	Moderate support
		Qualls and Puto (1989)	Supported
H2c	Decision makers display mean-reverting behaviour in successive choices	Camerer et al. (1997)	Supported
		Heath et al. (1999)	Supported
		Thaler and Johnson (1990)	Contradicted

Table 6.1. (cont.)

		Reference	Result
H3	When outcomes drop below the reference level, decision makers are risk seeking	Fiegenbaum and Thomas (1988)	Supported
		McGlothin (1956)	Supported
		Qualls and Puto (1989)	Supported
		Slattery and Ganster (2002)	Contradicted
		Willman et al (2002)	Contradicted
		Camerer et al (1997)	Supported
H3a	Workers target a satisficing income level and are income (risk) averse above that level, and income (risk) seeking below.	Loughhunn, Payne and Crum (1980)	Mixed results
		Staw, Sandelands and Dutton (1981)	Contradicted
H3b	When outcomes are negatively framed (i.e. only losses are posited), decision makers will choose more risky outcomes	Ali (1977)	Supported
		McGlothin (1956)	Supported
H3c	The longshot bias strengthens through the day,	Metzger (1985)	Supported
H3d	Support for risky bets (i.e. win vs. place) strengthens through the day	McGlothin (1956)	Supported
H3e	Risk-taking leads to corner-cutting, and so poorer performing firms have more safety and legislative breaches and more operating incidents and crises	Baucus and Near (1991)	Contradicted
		D'Aveni (1989)	Supported
		McNamara and Bromiley (1997)	Contradicted
		Osborn and Jackson (1988)	Supported
H3f	Poorer performing firms will further reduce returns to increase their risky expenditures (e.g. on advertising, acquisitions, market entries, product launches)	West and Berthon (1997)	Supported
H3g	After experiencing battle losses, attackers become more aggressive	Bauer and Rotte (1997)	Supported
H4	When outcomes are above target, decision makers are risk averse	Fiegenbaum and Thomas (1988)	Supported

Table 6.1. (cont.)

H4a	When outcomes are positively framed (i.e. only gains are posited), decision makers will choose less risky outcomes	Qualls and Puto (1989)	Supported
		Slattery and Ganster (2002)	Contradicted
H4b	Risk taking declines as gains mount: the house money effect (the low-risk feeling that gamblers express when they are ahead and playing with the house's money) is negative	Barberis, Huang and Santos (2001)	Contradicted
		Hollenbeck et al (1994)	Contradicted
		Thaler and Johnson (1990)	Contradicted
H4c	Wealthier people are more risk averse	Schoemaker and Kunreuther (1979)	Supported
H5	Decision makers are more sensitive to losses than equivalent gains (i.e. loss averse)	Slattery and Ganster (2002)	Supported
		Willman et al (2002)	Supported
H5a	Investors realise gains more readily than losses	Odean (1988)	Supported
		Shapira and Venezia (2001)	Supported
H5b	Poor or sick people view any wealth or health state more favourably than rich or healthy people.	Brickman, Coates and Janoff-Bulman (1978)	Supported
		Sackett and Torrance (1978)	Supported
H5c	The time trade-off (or proportional shortening of life that a person would accept when offered a hypothetical move from an ill state to perfect health) is less for an ill person than for a healthy person.	Tsevat (1995)	Qualified Support
H5d	The wage premium for employment in a dangerous industry or workplace is proportionately greater for higher paid employees.	Gaba and Viscusi (1998)	Supported
H5e	In litigation, plaintiffs are more likely than defendants to prefer settlement	Guthrie, Rachlinski and Wistrich (2001)	Supported
H5f	Warring nations value their own casualties (i.e. losses) higher than their opponent's casualties (i.e gains)	Bauer and Rotte (1997)	Supported

Table 6.1. (cont.)

H6	Preferences can be described by a non linear, inverse-S shaped function	Jullien and Salanié (2000)	Weakly supported
		Levy and Levy (2002)	Contradicted
		Neilson and Stowe (2002)	Contradicted
H6a	Risk propensity in the different domains of gains and losses is not positively correlated	Bowman (1980)	Supported
		Fiegenbaum and Thomas (1988)	Supported
H6b	Risk and return are not positively correlated	Bowman (1980)	Supported
		Fiegenbaum and Thomas (1988)	Supported
H7	Low probabilities are overweighted	Bernasconi (1998)	Supported
		Preston and Baratta (1948)	Supported
H7a	Decision makers adopt a longshot bias	Ali (1977)	Supported
H7b	Firms have a bias towards high-risk strategies	Palmer and Wiseman (1999)	Supported
		Whiting (1998)	
H8	Moderate to high probabilities are underweighted	Ali (1977)	Supported
H9	The cross-over from overweighting to underweighting occurs at a probability of around 0.4	Preston and Baratta (1948)	Contradicted

Table 6.2. Papers Providing Real-World Tests of Prospect Theory

Reference	Setting	Sample	Results
Ali (1977)	Examines behaviour of bettors on harness racing in New York	20,247 races in 1970-4	Bettors' risk-taking increases as capital dwindles. Favourite-longshot bias exists
Barberis et al. (2001)	Develops a model for testing against actual returns from 1926 to 1995 in US Treasury Bills and NYSE stocks		Investors display loss aversion which increases after poor investment performance, and decreases after a run of profits
Baucus and Near (1991)	Searched court records for criminal convictions by companies, and examined criminal disposition (risk taking) in light of size and financial performance	Fortune 500 companies between 1974 and 1983	Larger firms were more likely to be convicted of criminal offences; good performing firms were (not statistically significantly) more likely to offend
Bauer and Rotte (1997)	Analyses the duration of large, modern battles	US Army database of 301 battles in 20th century where attackers involved more than 10,000 soldiers	Increasing losses prolong battles; attackers value own losses about three times higher than gains
Bernasconi (1998)	Explanation for the high rate of observed tax compliance in the United States		Overweighting of small probabilities explains compliance
Brickman et al. (1978)	Test of current and anticipated happiness to see if poorly endowed people view any state as better than more richly endowed people	Studied three groups: people who had recently won a major lottery (minimum $50K, average about $600K); people who had been rendered paraplegic following an accident; and controls.	Lottery winners were not much happier than the controls and looking ahead did not expect to be as happy as the accident victims.

Table 6.2. (cont.)

Camerer et al. (1997)	Examination of income elasticities of self-employed New York City cabdrivers	1,826 daily trips sheets in 1988, 1990 and 1994	Negative wage elasticities: drivers stop work when a daily income threshold is reached. Shows expectation of mean reversion
D'Aveni (1989)	Tests a model of organisational bankruptcy based in part on Prospect Theory	57 large bankrupt US firms and 57 matched firms	Creditors are loss averse and will become risk-seekers with ailing firms
Fiegenbaum and Thomas (1988)	Explanation for Bowman's (1980) Paradox	COMPUSDAT database of financial returns for firms and industries from 1960 to 1979	Negative relationship between the average and variance of firm ROE for firms with below target level ROEs; and positive relationship above target level
Gaba and Viscusi (1998)	Examined differences in scales which people use to measure risk	335 workers exposed to hazardous chemicals	College-educated workers see jobs as more risky than those without college education who have lower current income and lower lifetime wealth levels
Guthrie et al. (2001)	Empirical study designed to identify whether decision making is influenced by cognitive illusions	167 US federal magistrate judges	Shows significant variation in decisions
Harries et al. (2000)	Tests repeatability of doctors' judgements in prescribing treatments	32 British General Practitioners	Correlations between decisions in similar cases ranged from 0.3 to 0.7
Heath et al. (1999)	Examines factors which lead employees to exercise stock options granted by their employer	50,000 employees at seven corporations in 1985-94	Exercise is positively related to recent price moves and negatively related to longer term price moves. It accelerates around reference points, including historical price maxima. Shows expectation of mean reversion

Table 6.2. (cont.)

Hollenbeck et al. (1994)	Computer based decision task involving acting as an airspace controller around a naval squadron monitoring for incoming, possibly hostile, aircraft	135 undergraduate management students	Poor performance was followed by risky decisions. Under instructions to 'do their best', winners took more risk than losers. Confirms 'house effect'.
Jullien and Salanié (2000)	Uses data from racetrack betting markets to make econometric estimates of CPT	Bets with UK bookmakers on 34,443 thoroughbred races between 1986 and 1995	Significant concave result for losses; not statistically significant convex result for gains
Kuhberger (1988)	Meta-study of framing effects		Effect is only small to moderate
Levy and Levy (2002)	Uses investment case studies to examine the nature of risk preferences	51 fund managers and 129 finance students	At least 60 percent of choices do not conform to S-shaped function
Laughhunn et al. (1980)	Evaluated risk-propensity of managers in loss-making situation	224 managers in Europe and North America	71% were risk-seeking in the face of non-ruinous losses, and 36% were risk-seeking in the face of ruinous losses
McGlothin (1956)	Studies bettor behaviour on California thoroughbred race tracks	9,605 races in 1947-53	Bettors increase their stake more after losing than winning. Risk-taking (as evidenced by the proportion of bets for a win) rises through the day as losses mount
McNamara and Bromiley (1997)	Explanation of commercial lending practices by a large US commercial bank	223 firms which had borrowed over $100,000 at five branches	Lending in loss-making branches was not more risky
Metzger (1985)	Examines bettor behaviour to see if race outcomes are progressively framed as losses, thus increasing the longshot bias	11,313 US thoroughbred races in 1978	Support for longshots rises through the day

Table 6.2. (cont.)

Mullins et al. (1999)	Case study involving new product developments to identify factors that account for variability in managers' risk-taking	164 evening MBA students, most of whom were (or had recently been) employed as managers.	No impact of recent performance on risk-taking; and risky choices were made by those in gains
Neilson and Stowe (2002)	Calculate weighting functions that explain two specific behaviours – gambling and the Allais paradox		No parameter combinations allow for observed behaviours
Odean (1998)	Accesses trading history of clients at a US discount brokerage house to test whether investors hold losers longer than winners	Records of all trades in 10,000 accounts in 1987-93	Clear evidence of the disposition effect
Osborn and Jackson (1988)	Study of operating safety of US nuclear power stations in light of earnings	Examined reliability and safety violations at 41 plants between 1975 and 1981	Higher reliability was associated with higher prior earnings
Qualls and Puto (1989)	Uses 12 hypothetical purchase decisions typical of those facing buyers to test for framing of choice by organisational climate and decision maker's predisposition to risk	101 members of National Association of Fleet Administrators	Clear evidence of framing effect: subjects viewed outcomes above reference level as gains and below as losses, and chose low and high risk outcomes, respectively.
Sackett and Torrance (1978)	Developed scenarios for 10 well-understood health states and examined time trade-off	240 random subjects and 34 home dialysis patients	Dialysis patients place higher utility on treatment states for renal failure than general public

Table 6.2. (cont.)

Sagristano et al. (2002)	Explored changes in evaluation of events by comparing subjects' time-dependent gambling decisions	Undergraduate students at New York and Tel Aviv Universities	Time shifts the balance between payoff and probability in decisions
Schoemaker and Kunreuther (1979)	Choice of insurance including deductibles, breadth of cover and premia.	240 Wharton students and 101 clients of a Philadelphia insurance agency	Clear evidence of framing, and lower risk propensity as income and wealth rise
Shapira and Venezia (2001)	Tests whether investors hold losers longer than winners	Records of all transactions for 4,330 clients at an Israeli brokerage house in 1994	Clear evidence of the disposition effect with both professional traders and independent investors
Slattery and Ganster (2002)	Studies decision making in a dynamic environment resembling managers' workplace	292 business studies students	No significant framing effect; past failure promoted risk aversion
Staw et al. (1981)	Meta-survey of literature on how adversity affects organisations		Risk aversion grows under external threats which lead to rigidity through restriction, control and well-learned responses
Thaler and Johnson (1990)	Studies how risk behaviour is influenced by prior gains and losses	Cornell MBA and undergraduate students	Prior gains can increase gamblers' risk-taking (the house money effect), and prior losses can decrease willingness to take risks. Generalising risk preferences is difficult

Table 6.2. (cont.)

Tsevat et al. (1995)	Assessment of health values and reliability of opinion of patients' proxy decision makers	1,438 seriously ill patients with at least one of nine diseases which had a projected overall 6-month mortality rate of 50%; also interviewed their surrogates and physicians	Patients equated living one year in their current state of health with living 6.9 months in excellent health; the equivalent measures were 6.0 months for surrogates, and 5.1 months for physicians. Although supports PT, results were mixed; and there were a number of exceptions
West and Berthon (1997)	Examines willingness to take advertising risks	Survey of 75 senior marketing directors and CEOs in North America in 1995	Propensity to take advertising risk is related to performance, with above-target firms being more risk averse
Whiting (1998)	Reports a survey by Standish Group of the proportion of computer development projects that are expected to succeed		Evidences overweighting of low probability outcomes as success rate of IT projects was 26 percent in 1996 and 25 percent in 1997
Willman et al. (2002)	Examined management of behavioural risk in financial markets	118 equity and bond traders at four London investment banks in 1998	Found loss aversion after losses

Discussion and Conclusions

The most obvious conclusion from real-world examination of Prospect Theory is that risk propensity is subjective and situational. A quarter or more of the variance in individuals' risk propensity is explained by personality factors. Risk propensity is also shaped by the environment, and thus is not an objective measure nor predictable. As Thaler and Johnson (1990: 660) observe somewhat dryly: "Making generalisations about risk-taking preferences is difficult." It seems that many of the real-world exceptions to PT arise because the Theory does not encompass the characteristics of the players and their environment.

A second conclusion is that decision makers are reluctant to accept the neat compartmentalisations of Prospect Theory. Although driven by changes in wealth, they switch between recent and prospective shifts using mental accounting to handle sunk gains and losses in light of expected outcomes. This continuous recalculation of the net position is best seen with sequential decisions, which are common in the real world: financial decisions, for instance, are serially correlated and linked to allied decisions. In such cases, risk-embrace is inversely proportional to cumulative potential losses (i.e. decline in wealth to date plus potential loss from the next decision). Risk will be embraced whilst gains are expected or net losses are low, but will not be preferred in the face of ruinous losses [Laughhunn et al. (1980)].

An allied point is that the propensity towards reward (i.e. personal preference for loss or gain) can be at least as powerful as the propensity towards risk; so decision makers display loss-aversion after losses and gain-embrace after gains. This seems true of animals, too, after Marsh and Kacelnik (2002) found that 86 percent of starlings were risk prone after losses, but did not display significant risk aversion after gains.

The third conclusion is that - although it is analytically desirable to have continuous distributions for weightings of utility and probability - there are so many imprecise factors involved that this seems impracticable. For instance, time is important because the negative aspects of a future decision are discounted more than the positive aspects, and so the weighting or importance given to costs and probabilities is relatively less [Sagristano et al. (2002)]. Moreover, affect (in the psychological sense of associated feeling `or emotion) is a powerful influence during the editing stage of decision making.

The analysis above has a number of profound implications. The first is that the situation or frame of a decision only partially determines the willingness of decision makers to select a risky alternative. Thus the process cannot be treated as a black box where results are driven solely by the quantifiable facts of a decision. A second implication is that conventional decision analysis does not match the way that managers, for instance, actually choose between alternatives with different risks and returns [March and Shapira (1987)]. Thus improving real-world decision making should address deficiencies inherent in the behavioural aspects of the process, rather than suggesting ways to enhance data collection and analysis [Lovallo and Kahneman (2003)].

A third implication of real-world evidence is the recurrence of a pronounced longshot bias. Although this is recognised in PT as overweighting of low probabilities, behaviour exhibiting the longshot bias has usually been dismissed as arising from hubris [Roll (1986)], overconfidence in personal ability [Hvide (2002)], sensation-seeking [Zuckerman and Kuhlman (2000)], or simple misjudgement of reality [Kahneman and Lovallo (1993)]. The prevalence and significance of the longshot bias remain underestimated.

In conclusion, PT provides only a partial explanation of risky decision making. Thus it is a supplement to other theories such as Expected Utility, rather than a replacement. The complexity of the processes involved in decision making under risk do not lend themselves to simple descriptions. Successful decision making models need to better comprehend decision makers' personal traits and the influence of time and opportunity costs; they also need to better specify the distribution of preferences, and account for a pervasive longshot bias amongst decision makers.

Looking more broadly, the approach taken by this survey should have extensions to other paradigms which are struggling to achieve Kuhn's normal science. Examples include the competitive model of firm performance set out in Porter (1980); the capital asset pricing model with its positive relationship between risk and return; principal-agent models of firm behaviour; and a variety of assumptions about the behaviour of organisations and management. In addition, the real-world descriptions of decision making in table 6.2 provide a good set of applied tests for any decision model.

My analysis shows that evaluation of an important paradigm can follow a simple methodology: tease out core hypotheses and list corollaries that should apply in real-world settings; then examine the various hypotheses in light of published evidence. When there is sufficient material, more analytical rigour can be obtained with statistical techniques such as cluster analysis. The example here shows that – despite the doubts of key scholars, including Prospect Theory's authors – there is a relative abundance of data offering applied tests of economics' powerful ideas.

Inadequacies of Current Decision Making Models

Before going further, it is necessary to summarise why current models of decision making are inadequate.

Although a rich literature on risk and decision making has emerged, it suffers a number of inherent shortcomings. The first is that much of the evidence – experimental results – is obtained in an artificial environment, using non-representative subjects, and posing hypothetical questions. Intuitively there is reason to doubt that such analyses can be generalised to explain actual behaviour. Exactly this was identified in a meta analysis by Byrnes et al. (1999) who found that differences in risk taking were considerably larger in actual behaviours than in hypothetical choice situations. Rigorous evaluation requires evidence from revealed preferences and natural environments as opposed to synthetic formulations.

The second shortcoming is that much of this experimentation is performed to test a single hypothesis, which leaves the results blind to the complexities of decisions. Moreover most subjects are homogenous, and they are typically assigned at random to different aspects of the controlled experimental task: thus results are unable to identify the significance of individual factors such as personality, competencies and experience. As most decision making theories are based on experiments with little meaningful variation, there must be considerable doubt about their broader applicability.

Even though choice and decision making confound reductionist explanations, economists look – with Occam – for a simple, mathematically robust explanation. This has encouraged a sameness to experiments (and there have been many) which reflects a concern to test existing concepts rather than seek decision models. A different perspective is taken by management scientists and personality psychologists who accept that choice and decision making can be distinct processes which depend on circumstances. This was nowhere more clear than in the demonstration by Tversky et al. (1990) that people use different criteria in making seemingly comparable decisions: when choosing between bets, subjects emphasise probability; but when selling their preferred bet they emphasise the payoff, or potential price.

The third shortcoming is in how to identify and quantify the 'risk' associated with any decision. Many studies find that decision makers rely on scanty data, with perhaps only a very general idea of the *nature* of the risks involved, and even less precision in estimates of the risks' probability distributions. Moreover any real-world decision is attended by multiple risks, often of quite different character. Thus the econometrician who works *ex post* with a large computerised database has a better understanding of the nature of risks than the decision maker relying *ex ante* on small samples and limited analytical resources.

The fourth shortcoming of current decision making models is a failure to incorporate the complex nexus between risk and decision making. Decades of research by economists and psychologists have relied on the intuition that there must be a strong link between the two. Their results built on the engineering and accounting discipline of risk management and combined with the concepts of social risk to make risk and decision making one of the hottest topics in the social sciences [e.g. Beck (1992)]. Even so, individuals and organisations rely on many factors to make decisions. Some are endogenous: risk attitudes, personal priorities, current resources and circumstances, prejudices, future expectations; whilst others are exogenous: social factors, future trends and peer actions. Most decision makers – whether acting as individuals, investors or managers – are forced to choose from a vast field of alternatives and simultaneously meet conflicting objectives. Thus risk is but one contributor to any decision.

Perhaps the greatest shortcoming of the considerable body of work is that it has not developed a unifying theory of decision making that fits all (or even most) of the evidence. This is not a new point: Arrow (1982: 1) wrote that "hypotheses of rationality have been under attack for empirical falsity almost as long as they have been employed in economics"; Lopes (1987: 255) quipped: "What is most disconcerting [about the efforts of psychologists and economists to explain risky behaviour] is that there has been so much theory for so little substance." Even worse, many decision models simply ignore risk.

Although such criticisms are common, normative assumptions continue to dominate decision making models. It seems that useful old theories are hard to abandon. At one extreme are models which ignore data and rely solely on untested theory: Hartog et al. (2000: 1) report that one economics text[56] included "an entire chapter on 'Measuring risk aversion and risk' without a single reference to empirical work." At another extreme are models with arcane formulae and complex math which render them all but inaccessible except to an initiated few.

---

[56] The book is: Laffont JJ (1993) The Economics of Uncertainty and Information. The MIT Press, Cambridge MA

Drilling down into decision processes, one example of theories' short-comings is that they do not take into account the *gambling effect,* or seemingly different approaches that people use to make decisions that are riskless (either due to simplicity, low potential cost, or relative certainty) and risky. The former is well served by utility theory in which decision makers typically choose the best of a generally good bunch. Although the transition to risky decisions is widely acknowledged, there is not yet a satisfactory depiction of the steps involved.

Another process shortcoming is that models assume decision makers have realistic, quantified approximations of the decision's elements. Despite the proliferation of data and analytical tools, decisions in real-life are rarely amenable to optimisation, and most assume an unquantifiable, indeterminate future without a reliable probability distribution.

In similar vein, decisions are not easily depicted by continuous distributions. Most are Yes/No, Go/Stop type choices rather than a range of alternatives. Thus the gradation of outcomes inherent in a probability distribution is quite irrelevant to most decisions. Although large-scale decision making is amenable to mathematical modelling, that is not true at the individual level except with games of chance. Because the result of a decision is simultaneous optimisation of a number of variables, only some can be independently identified, and few are amenable to quantification. And even when quantification is possible, many decision makers do not bother; and those who do make the effort invariably derive a biased result.

Moreover many models see decisions as a single, clearly defined event whereas they are at once uncertain and dynamic. Decisions are not one action, but a series carried out in changing and uncertain circumstances which are shaped by factors inside and outside the decision maker's control. Many are influenced by the process of making a choice. In particular, decision makers will shape risky decisions by adding expertise, information or resources. Thus a defect in much research is to address the outcome or choice of decisions and ignore the process. It is almost as if researchers agree with the normative attitude of the Queen of Hearts: "Sentence first! Verdict later."

Yet another limitation in conventional models is that they ignore framing and confidence effects, even though these imply that beliefs and perception are key inputs to decisions. Similarly emotion, personality and demographic traits impact decisions: why else would individuals react differently to the same problem set? Unfortunately measuring each of these factors is problematic at best. In the case of framing, for instance, it is frequently unclear in the real world whether this is internal to the decision maker or external (e.g. from advertising). So, too, with intuition and individualised outcome objectives.

Too many models see decisions as having normative objectives: thus, for example, anything involving finance has a purely monetary objective. Reality, of course, is quite different and – even in pure financial risk-taking such as bond trading – there are large roles for ego, competitive instincts, herding and cussedness.

Finally there are a number of behavioural traits – biases or heuristics – which prove robust across different settings, but do not seem to conform to normative concepts of relying upon probability and payoff. Beach (1997) put this well in suggesting that decision makers act more like causal modellers rather than statisticians. People put heavy overlays on statistical artifices in reaching decisions; and they are flexible in decision making behaviour, for instance by making greater use of these overlays when the situation is unfamiliar, demanding or otherwise complicated.

In summary, numerous models of decision making have appeared in recent decades, but none provides a satisfactory explanation of all the evidence. Thus this book seeks an improved model to explain decision making by managers facing risk.

CHAPTER 7   Why Managers Take Risks

Previous chapters traced the patterns of decision making starting with laboratory experiments on animals and humans, and moving through observations of revealed preference in the real world, to an examination of published models of decision making. This produced a consistent catalogue of robust, cross-species decision making behaviours which prove independent of their situation. It is hard to overstate the importance of this convergence of widely shared traits as it provides strong theoretical foundations for any decision making model.

This process is consistent with the research outline set out in figure 1.2 in chapter one. The aim was to draw on a wide variety of materials to analyse risk and decision making and integrate the concepts into an hypothetical model which can be verified by empirical data.

In this chapter and the next, I first set the scene by using the literature survey to summarise hypotheses in relation to decision making and develop an explanatory model. This leads towards the *Risk Budget Theory* of decision making which is proposed as an improved explanation of risk-taking by managers and organisations. A third section describes the basis of the proposed research methodology. The final section sets out the results of the first study which examines why managers take risks.

Summary of Decision Making Behaviours

Although the forces acting on decision makers' attitudes towards risky alternatives are complex, they can be boiled down into seven groups

1. Decision makers are instinctively loss averse with a preference for low risk strategies that minimise variability and uncertainty and the possibility of an adverse outcome. However, risk sensitivity has evolutionary advantages and so decision makers have a flexible approach determined by their own personality and culture, and in light of situational and contextual cues

2. Reference levels are important in determining attitudes to risk, as decision makers tend to embrace risk when the outcome appears unfa-

vourable. Thus risk aversion grows with rising value or utility of the worst outcome (the Common Consequence Effect) so that people a-dopt satisficing, rather than optimising, goals; this can be seen as instinctive or myopic loss aversion. If a favourable outcome is almost certain, risk aversion is high. Risk aversion also grows with increasing bounds on decision making (e.g. lack of data, uncertainty and reduced time for analysis).

3. Decision makers are willing to trust their judgement in areas where they have expertise and are more likely to embrace risk when they have a perceived skill which offers an effective advantage (the Competency Effect). Overconfidence is common, especially in relation to uncontrollable events (the Illusion of Control).

4. Different presentations of identical data elicit different responses from the same individual (the Framing Effect) and from different individuals (a function of personality traits). Describing a proposed action as low-risk will gain more broad based support, especially from risk intolerant decision makers; whereas focussing on its upper bound is more attractive to risk seekers. These effects can be particularly strong in the face of new problems. When tasks are familiar, decision makers will often rely on mental images of events which can override facts and thus overstate the personal probability of a favourable or dreaded event and understate the probability of an unwanted event (prediction is linked to outcome); they also 'fill in the blanks' and use associations with more complete datasets to reach a judgement with scanty data

5. Decision makers place minimal reliance upon probability calculations in making judgements as evidenced by overweighting of low probability events and seeing independent events as related. They tend to rely on small, recent samples; and - in decisions involving an object (or event) - place greatest weight on its characteristic(s) which are most closely related to the terms of the response (Principle of Compatibility). Decision makers tend to be excessively optimistic and those operating in permanently risky environments can become inured to their risk-embrace. Through the affect heuristic, people mentally tag objects and events with positive or negative feelings or emotion, and thus create an inverse relationship between risk and benefit which sees selection of preferred or liked outcomes

6. Personality and experience determine decision makers' attitudes towards risk (including risk preferences), their perception of risky decisions, and their decision making style. This confines most people to a small number of decision making strategies which they use invariably

even though situations alter through event, environment and consequences.

7. When facing choices involving future events, decision makers place
greater weight on the outcome and benefits, with relatively less
weight on the costs and probability of occurrence. This is consistent
with optimism, goal orientation and inherent unpredictability of details such as impediments and probabilities. It also incorporates recognition of optionality: why sweat the small stuff when the decision
may change?

These driving forces form 13 critical components in individuals' decision making processes which are linked as depicted in figure 7.2.

Although the table and diagram suggest that decision makers adopt a
logical, linear process, successful explanatory models recognise that cognitive processes are much more integrated, intuitive and imprecise. It seems
that decision makers personalise their expectation and utility, and evaluate
the best alternative in any decision through a four-step process.

The first step involves selection of the level of risk to be accepted,
broadly whether to adopt a risk-averse or risk-embracing position. This results from the interplay of psychological influences, particularly: the decision maker's (generally) stable personality traits and the more fluid assessment of the current situation, including endowment and aspirations;
the time to outcome (weighting of the current situation diminishes in influence over time), framing (risk-aversion in the domain of gains, loss-
aversion in the domain of losses), affect (reference to a mental database of
images conveying feelings), motivation (goal or sensation seeking), and
competence (control, skill, knowledge). Also important is the decision
maker's personal risk propensity in the decision situation, particularly its
institutional setting. These factors combine to set a level of risk propensity
which is not strongly related to probabilities or utility.

The second step involves compiling an expectation of possible outcomes of each alternative using a distribution reflecting the uncertainty
and instability of the underlying process. Decisions are typically simplified
to make them Yes/No type choices: although some decisions offer a broad
range of alternatives (such as runners in a race, investment alternatives,
and commodity purchases from meat to cars) most decisions are Go/No
Go, Buy/Sell, Yes/No with few alternatives. Thus individual decision
makers do not rely on continuous distributions (although they may be useful in explaining large scale behaviours).

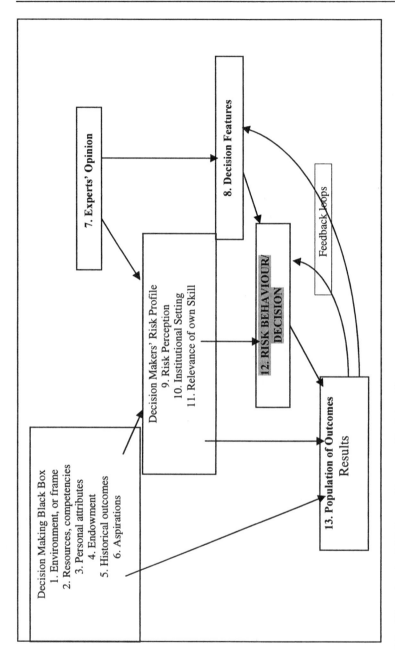

Fig. 7.1. Hypothesised Linkages Between Decision Components

This is part of an approach which operationalises complex, natural distributions using simple heuristics such as pattern recognition built around milestones, realistic extremes and recent changes. Typically this step might start with an assumption that the standard deviation is equal to the mean, which is a property of the exponential distribution that characterises many natural phenomena. The mean is then calculated from a sample of about ten recent values, and may be personalised through a heavy emphasis on recent observations and current rates of change. Alternatively the distribution may be derived by estimating a range that covers 99.9 percent of possible outcomes (i.e. six standard deviations) by selecting realistic extremes as maximum and minimum, or by assuming that realistic values lie between 0.3 and 3.0 times the present level. In other cases a decision maker facing two alternatives will assign them equal probability, or give a high probability to the more desired outcome.

This reflects the reality that decision makers have only a vague understanding of the objective distributions of many events. The most obvious cause is the difficulty in obtaining data. But even when good data are available, distributions change unexpectedly: it requires experience to appreciate the difficulty in isolating likely influences, and projecting future events. Thus people rarely attend to probabilities. Because most decision makers also have limited ability and resources to rigorously evaluate alternative actions, they are quite restricted in their capacity for rational analysis [Simon (1955)].

The next step in personalised decision making is to establish the key features of the decision, particularly the extent to which the outcome is controllable, the relevance of the decision maker's skill, and the advice and opinion of experts in the subject. Each of these factors provides guidance on the impact of factors within decision makers' control and thus can modify initial assessments of the result.

These steps reflect the fact that differences in personality, evaluation and expectation mean that individuals do not share a continuous distribution of outcomes and probabilities. Thus even decision makers who appear to be in the same state and who possess identical data will reach opposite conclusions: some act boldly, whilst others do nothing; and some buy, whilst others sell[57].

In the final step, decision makers determine the most extreme practicable outcome, and weight any alternative in proportion to the change it will bring from their current state. Risk averters consider the consequences of the worst outcome; whilst risk embracers think of the benefits of the best

---

[57] As Mark Twain (1894, reprinted 1996: 120) wrote: "It were not best that we would all think alike; it is the difference of opinion that makes horse races."

outcome. Decision makers compound the weighting using an assessment of their skill set relative to the task: this assumes that the outcome is amenable to influence, if not necessarily control. As skill is generally self-assessed to be high, most decision makers place subjective probabilities on favourable outcomes which exceed their objective probabilities of occurrence (such as might be predicted from historical data). The weights also encompass features such as ambiguity, time to the event, risk management, expert inputs and so on. The decision maker then compares the likely result with other risks which have been assumed or are in prospect, and chooses whether or not to take the risk.

In this way the decision maker evaluates the alternatives, factors in the impact of circumstances and skill, and decides in light of current endowment.

Although these qualitative aspects of individual decision making are useful in understanding the process, their practical application requires an operationalised model which is at least partially mathematical and can explain observed evidence, preferably as verifiable forecasts. Using the process description above, the Model should divide decision makers into risk averters and risk embracers, and assume they evaluate decisions in light of their endowment, application of skill and possible outcomes.

Risk averters look to the relative change which would be caused by the worst outcome, and assess its probability in terms of skill that can be applied, particularly risk management. This weighting can be negative which results in opposition proportional to the adverse impact; or it can be zero when skill is lacking, and thus result in no action. Risk embracers look to the relative change that would be achieved through the best outcome; they then weight the value in terms of the skills they have to achieve the best outcome. When skill is assessed as high, this can result in longshots; when skill is low, the target outcome is reduced.

Research Methodology

The principal research objectives of this book are to explain why managers who are faced with a decision select a risky alternative; and what determines whether the risky choice proves successful.

Although the research questions can be simply stated, their solution is not immediately apparent. Thus this book has been required to pursue a multi-stage process to achieve its objective. The first step – which consumed most of chapters one and two – is to define risk, and – because it is intangible and not directly measurable – develop a means to quantify its derivatives such as risk propensity. The second step is the literature survey set out in chapters three to six which summarises current academic understanding of decision making, particularly in the real world.

This led to the third step in the book which is to derive relevant empirical data which can be combined with published studies to enhance our understanding of risk-taking behaviour by managers. The research is specifically targeted at understanding the risky business decisions of managers, and is required to test the hypothesised linkages shown in figure 7.2. As a minimum, research needs to specifically incorporate decisions which are representative of risky problems faced by managers in their professional lives; examine decision makers' attributes and personality; detail the environment in the decision makers' industry and organisation; and measure the outcomes of the decision makers' actions in terms of risk level and financial performance.

Ideally the research would provide a 'universal constant' of the type found in physical sciences (e.g. the `c' in $e = mc^2$), and thus develop an equation or relationship which has predictive capability. A less ambitious goal pursued here is to develop a process which is able to distinguish the key features of decision problems, and rank the choice of outcomes. This latter, for instance, might specify the objective characteristics of risk-prone organisations so they can be categorised *ex ante* as high, medium or low risk and their performance projected.

There is a multiplicity of techniques available to derive the required data, but they can be simply classified as approaches which are, either, extensive or relatively unobtrusive, and those approaches which are more intensive. Typical unobtrusive methods rely on revealed preferences or secondary data compiled without the subjects' involvement. Intensive approaches include surveys, behaviour monitoring, interviews, focus groups and other field studies.

Chapters four and five used unobtrusive techniques, principally published data on aggregated decisions by option holders and bettors, and obtained useful conclusions. Each suffers the shortcoming that it is blind to decision makers' attributes, personality and environment, and so cannot incorporate them into any decision model.

A number of studies discussed above [e.g. Camerer et al. (1997), Halek and Eisenhauer (2001), and McNamara and Bromiley (1997)] have shown that it is practicable to link decisions to decision maker traits, largely by anonymously observing decisions and then seeking personal data from the subjects. Thus I investigated approaches which would similarly link decision maker traits to decisions, for instance through the co-operation of institutions which arrange financial transactions (e.g. investment houses and wagering firms) and their clients. As initial approaches to a bank and parimutuel betting operator were greeted coolly (largely due to issues involving client privacy and the existence of extensive in-house survey materials), this type of study was not pursued.

The research approach adopted in this book is intensive in the form of surveys involving senior executives as this meets the requirements listed above and gives sufficient granularity in responses to critically examine the influences and outcomes of risky decision making. To counter possible biases in the preferred data collection strategy, two surveys are used so that hypotheses can be confirmed by independent datasets. This strategy also protects against the concern discussed above that some economic theories merely explain the data which have been used in constructing the model: the conclusions are tautological in developing *ex post* rationalisations of observed experimental behaviour.

The first Survey takes the form of a case study involving a decision with two alternative choices, one of them risky and the other safe. Participants are asked to indicate which alternative they would recommend and provide personal details by answering a variety of questions on their demography and personality. The objective of this survey is to identify how the decision to take a risky alternative is shaped by the problem setting and by the decision maker's attributes.

The second Survey obtains the name of the respondent's employer and collects data on the decision maker (which is identical to that in the first survey) and on their organisation's risk environment and strategy. The responses are then matched to information from the organisation's statutory accounts and media reports of crises. The objective of this second survey is to identify links between decision maker's attributes, the risk environment inside the organisation and its risk outcomes (principally financial results and the frequency of crisis-type incidents).

Critical assumptions underpinning the validity of the surveys are that: subjects' responses to a representative (albeit hypothetical) business decision can be generalised to their actual business decision making; their responses are representative of the decision making processes of Australian executives in general, and – where appropriate – are representative of their colleagues in general; the subjects are representative of the employees whose attributes and behaviour shape organisational risk propensity and strategy; and their evaluation of the risk climate inside their organisation is accurate.

The following sections discuss the key elements of the research by describing its approach and the materials incorporated in the surveys; and then address the analytical techniques used and note some deficiencies in the proposed research methodology.

Choice of Survey Technology and Structure

As target respondents were practicing managers, e-mail was used to solicit responses as this is now a common medium of business-to-business contact, and a common mode for decision making. It was not expected to introduce a bias in the sample. Response was facilitated by providing a hot link to the site holding a web-based survey.

This approach has a number of important advantages. It is cheap, typically generates quick responses, and is perceived as environmentally friendly. As responses come electronically, they can be simply compiled and are also obtained anonymously which promotes completion of sensitive questions. The approach chosen has the advantage over personal interviews that no bias is induced by interviewer guidance (e.g. in cognitive processes) or propensity to agree with questions [Dillman et al. (2001)].

A major disadvantage of e-mail surveys is that they have a wide variability in response rate for reasons that are not always apparent, and this can yield response rates of well under ten percent [Smee and Brennan (2000)].

Survey Participants

Subjects were recruited primarily from two sources: the Finance and Treasury Association, which is a professional body whose members have an active interest in corporate finance and are typically employees of major public companies; and the Victorian Division of the Australian Institute of Company Directors. The two surveys were available on University of Melbourne websites, and they took an average of 15 and 25 minutes, respectively, to complete.

Although the Perseus software which was used to develop the surveys also provides the ability to surreptitiously record details of respondents' servers, this was not done. Thus all responses were anonymous.

The first survey is of the in-basket style [Gill (1979)]. Its subject is a Grand Prix racing team, Carter Racing, and the case is loosely modelled on events leading up to the 1986 *Challenger* space shuttle disaster. The case is commonly used to illustrate managerial decision making, with results published by Sitkin and Weingart (1995).

Original material was provided by Professor Sim Sitkin of Duke University [personal communication, 13 February 2003] who is one of the copyright holders. For this study, the case was shortened to one page; and formatted as a memo seeking a typical business decision by providing details of Carter's recent performance and some technical concerns. In keeping with the business style, no irrelevant information was included.

Using an approach which has proved successful on several occasions [e.g. Forlani (2002), Mullins et al. (1999), and Sitkin and Weingart (1995)], the case was internally manipulated to provide varying levels of risk along four dimensions. The case in this Survey incorporates opposing yes-no values to four elements which intuitively seem essential to the decision: finishing position in the last ten races; number of blown engines in the last ten races; expert opinion on the cause of engine failure; and the anticipated consequences of a wrong decision.

The Survey is in three parts. The first obtains the dependent variables through the critical question: 'Should Carter compete in the race tomorrow?'; a second question identifies the probability that the team should race. The second section examines reasons for the decision; and the third section obtains personal data about each respondent.

The second Survey compiles data on the attributes of senior managers and on their opinions of the risk environment inside their company. This is linked to companies' statutory accounts and a listing of corporate crises during the 1990s to evaluate the revealed impact of managers' attributes and institutional settings on companies' actual risk and financial performance.

The survey is in four parts. The first part collects similar personal data on respondents as in the decision making survey (48 questions). The second part of the survey asks for the name and street address of the respondents' employer; and then asks about the environment inside the employer and across its industry (45 questions). These questions were largely derived from Simons (1999) and suggestions provided by the Australian Institute of Company Directors [personal communications from Tony Harford, 16 September and 16 October 2003].

The third section seeks information about crises and potential crises experienced by the employer in the previous three years (four questions).

The fourth part of the Survey adopts several common techniques to elucidate decision makers' utility function, or the way they equate outcomes of different value and probability. Decision makers are assumed as having an exponential function of the type $u(x)=e^{-x/\rho}$, which has a single variable and so can be specified by one data point. The approach is to set up a hypothetical decision with a pair of alternative choices and specify three out of the four 2x2 (i.e. value x probability) outcomes; the decision maker provides the missing data point and hence the shape of the utility function.

The first example is based on an approach developed by Samson (1987); the second and third examples follow Howard (1988); whilst the fourth example has been developed to capture the assumed riskiness of acquisitions:

Consider your company is suing one of its contractors for damages after the contractor's alleged negligence caused a major accident during construction of a new facility. The best legal advice available to you is that the maximum damages the court would award is $20 million. The contractor has now offered to settle for $10 million. Your legal team is considering its advice and wants to know the company's attitude towards the risks of going to trial. What is the minimum probability of a favourable judgement from a trial which your company would expect for it to reject the settlement and allow the case to go to trial?

Consider your company is offered the opportunity to participate in a new investment. The project has a 50 percent probability of success which would pay your company $20 million; and the project has a 50 percent probability of failure in which case half the investment would be lost. How much would your company invest to participate in the project?

If the payout from the project were $5 million, how much would your company invest to participate in the project?

Consider your company can invest in a new venture which has equal probability of doubling the investment or losing half the investment (e.g. there is a 50:50 chance that $100 would become $200 or $50). How much would you invest?

Consider your firm had a windfall capital inflow equal to about five percent of its asset base, and is considering how to allocate the money between organic growth (building new facilities, developing products in-house) and buying assets (acquisition of existing businesses and plants). What proportion of the windfall would you recommend allocating to acquisition of existing business or plants?

Measures of Survey Respondents' Personal Traits

Both surveys were designed to collect risk-related data about respondents. Published studies have shown that risk propensity is influenced by personal competencies including education, income and decision experience (years in workforce, industry, type of job); and demographic features including age, gender, marital status, and nationality. It is also related to personality factors: locus of control (by powerful others, internal control and chance) [Levenson (1974)]; tolerance of ambiguity [Budner (1962)]; sensation seeking (defined as seeking novel experiences and willing to take risks to have them), impulsivity (rapidly responds to cues; not inhibited from risk-taking), aggression and sociability [Zuckerman and Kuhlman (2000)]; egalitarian preferences; extraversion, emotional stability, and conformity to social norms; autonomy orientation, flexibility and competence; anxiety and susceptibility to boredom; need for tension, risk and adventure; lack of inhibition, feelings of self-efficacy, and self-discipline; worldviews (hierarchic, egalitarian, individualist, and fatalist), and achievement motivation. Other studies have found links between different kinds of risk (sports, vocation, criminal activity and reckless driving), and that risk taking is correlated with smoking, drinking, drug use and gambling.

These attributes were evaluated by asking subjects about their demographic features (15 questions), psychographic characteristics (14), and attitudes toward risk (5 questions). The majority of questions are taken from published sources, particularly papers from the psychology literature providing metrics of risk propensity; and (largely management) studies which used the Carter case study. Table 7.1 shows the objective and source of questions. Whilst altering the setting of questions (i.e. their frame) can elicit different responses, using previously published materials should allow validation of results.

Table 7.1. Sources and Objectives of Personal Questions

Attribute	Question	Source
Tolerance of ambiguity	Many important decisions are based on insufficient information.	Budner (1962)
Need for achievement	I set difficult goals for myself which I attempt to reach	McClelland (1961)
Need for risk	I would like to undertake an interesting experience even if it is dangerous	Keinan (1984)
Instrumental risk taking	To achieve something in life one has to take risks	Zaleskiewicz (2001)
Level of decision maker's control	Risk is higher when facing situations we do not understand	
Impulsivity	I've not much sympathy for adventurous decisions	Rohrmann (1997)
Susceptibility to boredom	I become bored easily	
Interpersonal competitiveness	I have always wanted to be better than others.	Griffin-Pierson (1990)
Sociability	I am calm and relaxed when participating in group discussions	Robinson et al. (1991)
	Successful people take risks	Austin et al. (2001)
Achievement motivation	I prefer to work in situations that require a high level of skill	Casssidy and Lynn (1989)

Table 7.1. (cont)

Locus of control (external - importance of chance)	When I get what I want it's usually because I'm lucky	Levenson (1974)
Type A personality	I regularly set deadlines for myself.	Williams and Narendran (1999)
	Risky situations can be made safer by planning ahead	
	Compared to the average manager, I give much more effort	
	If I play a game (e.g. cards) I prefer to play for money	Zaleskiewicz (2001)
Life satisfaction	I have gotten more of the breaks in life than most of the people I know	Robinson et al. (1991)
	I like to play it safe	Pennings (2002)
Competence	In general I am very confident of my ability	Robinson et al. (1991)
Locus of control (external – powerful others)	My life is chiefly controlled by powerful others	Levenson (1974)
	In general, I am less willing to take risks than my colleagues	
Egalitarian preference	Everyone should have an equal chance and an equal say	Robinson et al. (1991)

Table 7.1. (cont)

Think about each of the following adjectives. Please indicate how well you think they fit your behaviour or beliefs.

Flexibility	Adaptable	
Emotional Stability	Temperamental	
Type A	Hard driving	Williams and Narendran (1999)
Modesty	Modest	Goldberg (1990)
Spontaneity	Impulsive	Goldberg (1990)
Sociability	Companionable	Goldberg (1990)
Self discipline	Controlled	Goldberg (1990)
	Unconventional	
Self reliance	Independent	Goldberg (1990)
Insecurity	Insecure	Goldberg (1990)
	Inhibited	
Aggressiveness	Aggressive	Goldberg (1990)
Type A	Competitive	Williams and Narendran (1999)

Research Deficiencies

It is recognised that the proposed research has a number of deficiencies.

The most obvious is that use of intensive techniques risks contamination of the results through what has been called the *Hawthorne Effect* since experiments conducted by Mayo (1933) at Western Electric's Hawthorne Plant in Illinois suggested that simply observing behaviour can change it[58]. Intensive studies must also recognise what Soros (1994: 2) called his *Theory of Reflexivity* in which "participants' bias can change the fundamentals which are supposed to determine market prices... [Reflexivity] is a two-way feedback mechanism in which reality helps shape the participants' thinking and the participants' thinking helps shape reality ..." When systems (Soros was talking about financial markets) have thinking participants, they are not passive, but are shaped by endogenous events through decision makers' future actions which change the systems' trajectory. In a massive understatement, he argued that reflexivity "introduces an element of indeterminacy into social events", so that it is quite inappropriate to use approaches from the physical sciences which rely upon separation between events and observations of them.

Such concerns are further complicated by the ethical research requirement for informed consent: simply describing the research proposal effectively frames responses. Moreover surveys can do no more than recognise patterns in subjects' reports, and so their validity relies upon the goodwill and accuracy of participants. In a sensitive area such as risk and decisions, there is no guarantee that subjects' responses will reflect their true preferences. Using the framework of reflexivity, subjects may shape the meaning, acceptability and criteria of risky decisions to suit their own behaviour. This means that no survey could isolate the behaviour it is trying to measure from the respondents' society and culture, and from the latter's impacts on respondents' beliefs and motivations.

There are several other deficiencies. The subjects of the study - 'risk' and 'decision making' – are ill-defined concepts, impossible to measure directly, and impacted by a multiplicity of forces. Moreover they may not be stable.

The research relies on survey data to determine decision makers' situation and views. This makes the simplifying assumption that all parameters

---

[58] Note, though, that this study involved only five workers and has been dismissed as a "glorified anecdote" by University of Michigan psychology professor Richard Nisbett [Kolata G (1998) Scientific Myths That Are Too Good to Die. The New York Times. 6 December 1998]

can be quantified without error; and that the absence of real risks does not diminish the real-world validity of the results.

There are no longitudinal and cross-country comparisons. Another limitation is the size of the sample and a practical limit to the number of questions which inevitably restrict the extent to which research questions can be explored.

The research assumes that managers unconditionally seek to maximise firm profitability and are motivated to reduce risk; and that conclusions from the micro-economic analyses can be generalized.

Because the surveys attempt to match real-world conditions, they will be coloured by uncontrolled and unmeasured, possibly confounding, influences which typify field studies. By extension, it was impractical to fully formulate all aspects of decision making processes and so conclusions may be inappropriate.

Despite these limitations, the research strategy has important strengths, especially: strong grounding in the literature, including results of empirical studies; linkage between the various research tools to ensure internal consistency of findings; explicit tie-ins to independent, published statistics; strong emphasis on real-world decisions so that decision makers are operating in a familiar environment without artificial distortions; and use of heterogeneous samples of experienced decision makers. This should develop and test hypotheses in a much more realistic environment than used in most studies.

Managerial Risk Taking: Carter Racing Team Scenario

This first case study is modelled on events leading up to the 1986 *Challenger* space shuttle disaster, and evaluates the reasons why experienced decision makers select a risky alternative. The case was presented as a one-page memorandum with a typical business decision. Its subject was a Grand Prix team, Carter Racing , and the memo gave details of Carter's recent performance and identified some technical concerns. The memo was internally manipulated to provide varying levels of risk along four dimensions so that it came in 16 versions; subjects were randomly assigned to one of the versions.

The memo asked: "Should Carter compete in the race tomorrow?" Recognising that decision risk involves a measure of uncertainty about outcomes [Sitkin and Weingart (1995)] and that the initial forced choice does not allow for any variance that might reflect differences in respondents' confidence, a second question was added to assess the probability that the team should race. The question read: "If you were the owner of Carter Racing, what is the probability that you would decide to race?" and responses were measured using a seven point Likert scale where 1=zero probability and 7=100 percent probability. Thus two dependent variables were obtained: Decision to Race, and Percentage Probability of Racing.

The survey also measured 69 independent variables by asking subjects about the reasons for their decision (18 questions); decision making style (19); their demographic features (15) and psychographic characteristics (14); and attitudes toward risk (5 questions). Most questions were sourced from published studies.

Data and Respondents' Characteristics

Subjects were recruited by e-mails inviting members of professional groups to participate in the survey. Respondents logged anonymously onto a University of Melbourne website and completed a survey which took about 15 minutes. There were a total of 67 useable responses[59], and 56.7 percent chose the risky alternative of racing[60]. As the cases were designed to be 'risk-neutral', the overall result is not significantly different (p>0.27) to that expected from a randomly chosen, risk-neutral sample[61].

The respondents' demographic traits are shown in table 7.2. Respondents are not a random sample of the population as they are: predominantly male (84 percent), tertiary qualified (100 percent), in professional or executive roles (96 percent), with considerable work experience (almost 70 percent have 16 or more years in employment) and relatively high incomes (59 percent earn over $100,000 per year). Conversely the group provides a good spread of ages, and – although almost half the respondents work in finance organisations (banks, insurance companies) – there are significant numbers from services, government, manufacturing, and wholesale and retail trade.

---

[59] Although a larger sample may be desirable, a wide variety of well-accepted studies have used smaller, homogeneous samples of students, including: Abdellaoui (2000) – 64 economics students; Bleichrodt (2001) – 66 health economics students; Fox and Tversky (1998) – 50 students interested in basketball; and Kilka and Weber (2001) – 55 graduate finance students.

[60] This is qualitatively similar to most results using the Carter Team scenario [Professor Carol Kulik, personal communication, 22 September 2003].

[61] Assuming a binomial distribution of race-don't race responses, with a mean of 0.50, standard deviation of ($\sqrt{(0.5*0.5)/67}$ =) 0.061, and two tails, the observed pattern would occur by chance in 27.2 percent of equivalent samples.

Table 7.2. Distribution of Respondents (Percent)

Gender	Male	Female				
	84	16				
Age (years)	≤25	26-35	36-45	46-55	55-65	≥65
	6	24	33	32	5	0
Marital Status	Never married	Married	Separated	Divorced	Widowed	
	18	76	3	3	0	
Education Level	Year 11 or 12	Apprenticeship	Diploma	Bachelor Degree	Postgraduate Degree	
	0	0	7	35	58	
Work Experience (years)	<5	5-10	11-15	16-20	>20	
	3	15	15	19	48	
Industry	Manufacturing	Wholesale or Retail Trade	Agriculture or Resources	Finance	Services	Government
	8	7	3	48	26	8
Occupation	Clerical	Craftsman	Professional	Executive	Student	
	2	0	57	39	2	
Income ($K PA)	<25	25-50	50-75	75-100	100-150	>150
	4	2	11	24	22	37
Investments ($K)	<25	25-100	100-250	250-500	500-999	>$1 mill
	17	15	15	29	20	4

The sample, though, is a reasonably close match to the composition of decision making managers, and so should provide a guide to the methodology of experienced decision makers in the real world. Although the survey measured opinions using a five point scale where 0 = 'strongly agree', the signs have been reversed in the following analysis. This makes the results intuitively obvious in that a positive value of R indicates agreement with the statement.To check for any 'natural groupings' of respondents, they were divided into those who chose to race and those who chose not to race. Factor analysis was then used to examine the two groups of risk embracers and risk averters.

Factor analysis of the first group (i.e. respondents who chose to race) gave a four factor solution which explained 53.1 percent of the variability. The first factor grouped subjects who believed that the race was risky and that the Carter Team had an alternative; they described themselves as modest and not easily bored, and had less employment experience. A second group believed the outlook for Carter was positive; they had a lower education level and were more tolerant of ambiguity. The third group reported themselves as insecure, with low measures of personal risk propensity; they also believed that their life is controlled by powerful others. The fourth group believed that the situation was a threat to Carter, but that the team had a large potential for gain from the race; these respondents reported that they could not be described as calm or controlled.

Factor analysis was repeated on the second group of respondents who preferred the low risk alternative and chose not to race. Again a four factor solution made intuitive sense and explained 45.4 percent of the variability. The most powerful factor – which explained 15.8 percent of the variance – grouped subjects who felt risk was not necessary for success, and did not want to be better than others; these respondents believed that they were less willing to take risks than their colleagues and that they could not be described as confident or hard driving. A second group was not competitive, and did not set deadlines for themselves (thus they lack an attribute of Type A personality types); they did not agree that decisions are often based on insufficient information. A third group was not easily bored and did not have much sympathy for adventurous decisions. The fourth group believed that Carter did not have the necessary skills to decide, and had an alternative to racing; they seem reluctant to make a decision.

To examine the applicability of the factors, eight new variables were constructed by grouping the three independent variables which loaded most heavily each factor. When regressed on the dependent variables they explained a disappointing 33.3 percent of the variance. Ultimately two of the constructed variables stood out and explained 29.9 percent of the variance:

1. Factor 2 in the Race group: expectation of a positive outlook for Carter, lower education level and disagreement that lack of information can increase risk. These respondents are less educated and more tolerant of ambiguity.
2. Factor 4 in the Don't Race group: belief that Carter does not have the skill to decide and that it has alternatives to racing. They are reluctant to make a decision.

Internal Consistency of Answers

The Survey was designed to evaluate the internal consistency of answers by including seven separate measures of risk propensity. These comprised the dependent variables, plus five questions measured on Likert scales:
1. To achieve something in life one has to take risks
2. I like to play it safe
3. In general I am less willing to take risks than my colleagues
4. In my personal life (e.g. hobbies, recreation, leisure pursuits), I tend to take a lot of physical risks
5. In relation to my personal finances (e.g. investments, superannuation and borrowing), I tend to take a lot of financial risks
6. In my business life, I tend to take a lot of financial risks on behalf of my employer or clients

Table 7.3 shows the correlations between these various measures.

Table 7.3. Correlation Coefficients of Survey Risk Measures

	Race?	% Race	Need to take risk	Like to play it safe	Less willing to take risk	Personal Risk Propensity	Personal Financial Risk Propensity	Business Risk Propensity
Race?	1	0.868(**)	0.163	-0.016	-0.073	0.105	-0.108	0.052
% Race	0.868(**)	1	0.229	-0.063	-0.037	0.064	-0.162	-0.005
Need to take risk	0.163	0.229	1	-0.410(**)	-0.317(**)	0.089	0.130	0.161
Like to play it safe	-0.016	-0.063	-0.410(**)	1	0.527(**)	-0.273	0.412(**)	0.411(**)
Less willing to take risk	0.073	-0.037	-0.317(**)	0.527(**)	1	-0.260	0.347(**)	0.342(**)
Personal Risk Propensity	0.105	0.064	0.089	-0.0273	-0.260	1	0.087	0.147
Personal Financial Risk Propensity	-0.108	-0.162	0.130	0.412(**)	0.347(**)	0.087	1	0.525(**)
Business Risk Propensity	0.052	-0.005	0.161	0.411(**)	0.342(**)	0.147	0.525(**)	1

** Correlation is significant at the 0.01 level (2-tailed) ($p < 0.01$).

The probability of racing proved a close match to the decision to race (R = 0.87), and hence is used as the principal dependent variable in the analysis.

Responses to questions on personal risk attitudes – risk is necessary for success, and subjects' preference for safety and relative risk propensity – are significantly ($p<0.01$) correlated and have the intuitively correct sign. Thus respondents who believe that risk is necessary for success do not like to play it safe and are more willing than their colleagues to take a risk.

Validity of responses gains further support from the statistically significant ($p < 0.01$) links between three of the four independent risk measures (the exception is personal risk propensity). Thus respondents who report themselves as more willing to take risks than their colleagues also report significantly ($p<0.01$) higher risk propensity in relation to their personal finances and business decisions. Moreover each relationship has the intuitively appropriate sign. Even so, an interesting pointer to the complexity of the analysis is that the decision to take a risky position in the case study (i.e. race) is not significantly related to any of the subjects' evaluations of their own risk propensity.

Another test of the data was to validate the representativeness of respondents. A total of 750 e-mails were sent out inviting participation; some 210 (28 percent) were returned as mis-addressed or otherwise rejected to give a net sample of 540; the 67 useable responses provided a 12.5 percent response rate.

Whilst the response rate was in the expected range for unsolicited e-mail contacts, it is desirable to test whether this might comprise a biased group of the sample population. The approach suggested by West and Berthon (1997) was employed to check for the possibility of bias from self-selection by respondents. This involved using a two-tailed t-test to compare the first quarter of responses with the last quarter. The methodological assumption is that the non-responding pool is closer in sentiment to the late respondents than it is to the early respondents. Thus the representativeness of the sample would be questionable if late respondents (who are close to non-respondents) differ significantly from early respondents.

The last quarter of respondents were slightly less likely to race (44 percent probability of racing versus 52 percent for the initial respondents), but the variation is not significantly different ($p>0.47$) to that of early respondents. This gives considerable comfort that the survey data are not likely to be biased.

A further test of consistency is that most of the questions which relate to respondents' psychology were drawn from published sources. This is qualitatively explored in table 7.4 which compares the answers collected in this study with those from the original studies. To interpret the table, the sign '+' means that risk prone decision makers agree that the phrase describes their behaviour or beliefs; a negative relationship is represented by the sign '-'; and the absence of any meaningful (p>0.2) relationship is shown by a '0'. The statistical significance of the relationships is shown by '*' where p<0.1, and by '**' where p<0.05.

Whilst it is recognised that asking similar questions in different contexts can produce different answers, there was a serendipitous level of agreement between the results of this study and those of previously published studies. Specifically, no statistically important relationship (p<0.2) found in this study contradicted the original relationship that was identified between personal attribute and risk propensity.

Although findings here were consistent with the literature, a number of previous findings were not confirmed. For instance, there was no evidence to support the conclusion of West and Berthon (1997: 30) that "successful risk-taking individuals are likely to believe that they can beat the odds, that nature is good to them, and that they have special abilities."

To isolate the influences of personality on risk taking, multi-linear regression was used to explain the dependent variable (i.e. probability of racing) in terms of the variables in table 7.4. The analysis showed that six variables were significant (p<0.1), and that personality features are able to explain 24.2 percent of the variance in the independent decision making variables. This is consistent with the recent literature reported in chapter four (table 4.1) that around 30 percent of variance in decision making is related to personality.

Table 7.4.   Personality Links to Risk Propensity

Author	Measure of Risk Propensity[1]	Sign of Relationship Original	Coleman[2]
Austin et al. (2001)	Successful people take risks	+	+
Budner (1962)	Tolerance of ambiguity: many important decisions are based on insufficient information	+	0
Casssidy and Lynn (1989)	I prefer to work in situations that require a high level of skill	+	0
Goldberg (1990)	My behaviour can be described as		
	Adaptable	+	+
	Modest		+ (**)
	Companionable		+
	Inhibited		+
Keinan (1984)	I would like to undertake an interesting experience, even if it is dangerous	+	0
Levenson (1974)	Locus of control:		
	My life is chiefly controlled by powerful others		0
	When I get what I want, it's usually because I'm lucky		+
Pennings (2002)	I like to play it safe	-	0
Robinson et al. (1991)	I am calm and relaxed when participating in group discussions	+	+ (**)
	I have gotten more of the breaks in life than most of the people I know	+	0
	In general I am very confident of my ability	+	+ (**)
	Everyone should have an equal chance and an equal say	+	0

Table 7.4.   (cont)

Rohrmann (1997)	I've not much sympathy for adventurous decisions	-	-
Williams and Narendran (1999)	Type A: my behaviour can be described as	+	
	Competitive		0
	Hard driving		0
	I regularly set deadlines for myself	+	+(**)
Zaleskiewicz (2001)	To achieve something in life, one has to take risks	+	+(*)
	If I play a game (e.g. cards) I prefer to play for money	+	0
Zuckerman and Kuhlman (2000)	Impulsivity: rapidly responds to cues and is not inhibited from risk-taking	+	0
	My behaviour can be described as		
	Aggressive	+	0
	Sociable		+
	Risk is higher when facing situations we do not understand	-	-(*)
	I am easily bored	+	0

[1] Positive correlations with probability of racing result from risk prone decision makers agreeing that the phrase describes their behaviour or beliefs.
[2] Relationships shown where $p<0.2$; * = $p<0.1$; ** = $p<0.05$ [0 implies no significant relationship]

Univariate Influences on Risk Propensity

The next step in the analysis was to examine univariate influences on managers' risk propensity, using the dependent variable Percentage Probability of Racing. When this was compared with the 69 independent variables, seven correlations were significant at the 99 percent level, and twelve were significant at the 95 percent level. These are shown in table 7.5.

To interpret the table: a positive value of R means that subjects choosing the risky option (that is to race) agree with the statement. In the case of income and investments, the negative sign for R indicates that a higher value of income or investments is associated with choice of the less risky option. Investors with a high exposure to overseas equities are more likely to select the risky option of racing.

There are a number of interesting conclusions to be drawn from the table. First is that the strongest pointers to respondents' intent to race, or confidence in their decision, comprise perceptions about the outcomes from racing and the available alternatives. Respondents who chose the risky course judged that Carter will not have another opportunity as good as this. They anticipate that the decision to race will prove successful, has a large potential for gain, and will meet Carter's strategic objectives. They also believe that Carter can tolerate large risks and has the skill to make the right decision. These attitudes share much in common with managers who display the longshot bias discussed in chapter five. An interesting pointer to risk-takers' confidence in the success of possibly high-risk activities is that they do not believe that the average person would take the same decision.

The table also shows that respondents who choose to race share several personal characteristics. In financial terms, they have lower incomes and lower value of investments, but allocate a higher portion of their investments to overseas equities. In terms of personality, they tend to set deadlines for themselves (a type-A personality trait), and believe that they are calm, confident and modest.

A third finding is that several variables which are intuitively important to risk judgements did not influence the decision. Specifically age had only weak explanatory power ($p > 0.4$), and there was no link ($p > 0.8$) between gender and risk taking.

Table 7.5. Correlation Coefficients with Percentage Probability of Racing[1]

Measure	R
99 percent Significance (p<0.01)	
If this opportunity is passed up, there will never be another as good	0.531
Carter Racing is likely to succeed tomorrow.	0.514
Carter Racing can tolerate large risks	0.510
The situation faced by Carter Racing has large potential for gain.	0.424
Carter's management have the skill to make their own decision	0.369
Success tomorrow will meet Carter's strategic objectives	0.319
The average person would make the same decision as me.	-0.318
95 percent Significance (p<0.05)	
Carter Racing is in a positive situation.	0.311
Please indicate the approximate allocation of your investments (excluding principal residence) to overseas equities	0.383
Carter has a record of making the right decisions	0.269
Indicate the extent to which the following statement fits your behaviour or beliefs:	
I regularly set deadlines for myself	0.293
What is the value of your investments (excluding principal residence)?	-0.311
What is your annual income before tax.	-0.319
Please indicate how well you think the following adjective fits your behaviour or beliefs: calm	0.261
Please indicate how well you think the following adjective fits your behaviour or beliefs: modest	0.273
I would make the same recommendation if I were driving the car.	0.241
Tomorrow's race is very risky	-0.263
The situation faced by Carter Racing is a significant threat	-0.241
Please indicate how well you think the following adjective fits your behaviour or beliefs: confident	0.263

[1] Percentage Probability of Racing is the principal dependent variable. As discussed in the text, it is obtained using a question "If you were the owner of Carter Racing, what is the probability that you would decide to race?" and is measured using a seven point Likert scale where 1=zero probability and 7=100 percent probability.

A conclusion from the univariate analysis which challenges normative models is that none of the `facts' of the case proved significant in respondents' decisions. The cases were internally manipulated to provide opposing yes-no values to four elements which seem essential to the decision: finishing position in the last ten races; number of blown engines in the last ten races; expert opinion on the cause of engine failure; and anticipated consequences of the wrong decision. The next table shows the four risk dimensions which were manipulated in the case and their raw correlations with probability of racing.

With the exception of the existence of an alternative to racing, none of the risk-related variables in the case study has a statistically meaningful link ($p>0.15$) with the subjects' decision. Even the fact that Carter Racing had limited alternatives (the case study reads: "tomorrow's race is particularly important to Carter … Success will see a new star in Grand Prix racing and bring additional sponsors. But without them Carter faces [either: almost certain bankruptcy, or some financial pressures]") has at best a weak ($p>0.12$) link with the decision. Taken together, the four risk dimensions explain a mere 6.2 percent of variability in the probability of racing.

Table 7.6. Links Between Decision and Risk Dimensions of Problem

Risk Dimension	Response Parameters	Correlation with Probability of Racing
Results: Number of top five finishes in the last ten Grand Prix races	One = 0 Five = 1	0.117
Risk probability: number of blown engines in the last ten races	One = 0 Five = 1	-0.048
Expert Opinion: technical explanation for cause of failure by an industry expert.	Temperature is cause = 0 Temperature is not cause = 1	-0.130
Alternative: result if Carter races and fails	Almost certain bankruptcy = 1 Some financial pressures = 0	0.177

Multiple Regression of Influences on Risk Taking

The next step in the analysis was to use multiple regression to explain the recommendation on whether or not to race. The aim was to derive an expression that is parsimonious (that is, one which has a small number of variables) and logical. It was also desirable to show the extent to which subjects' decision making matches, or fails to match, the processes in the hypothesised decision making model.

The result is shown in table 7.7 with details of the model's statistics (the layout follows Hair et al. (1998: 212)). The independent variable is 'Probability of Racing' which is expressed in a seven point Likert scale where 1=zero probability of racing and 7=100 percent probability; Investments refers to the value of investments excluding principal residence measured on a six point Likert scale where 0=less than \$25K and 5=\$1 million or more; Ignorance-risk refers to the expression 'Risk is higher when facing situations we do not understand' and is measured on a five point Likert scale; No Altern refers to the expression 'If this opportunity is passed up, there will never be another as good' and is measured on a five point Likert scale; Carter Succeed refers to the expression 'Carter Racing is likely to succeed tomorrow' and is measured on a five point Likert scale.

Thus the probability of racing is increased by agreement with the following statements:

- 'If this opportunity is passed up, there will never be another as good'
- 'Carter Racing is likely to succeed tomorrow'

And the probability of racing is decreased:

- in proportion to the value of investments; and
- by agreement with the statement: 'Risk is higher when facing situations we do not understand'.

Table 7.7. Statistics Associated with Probability of Racing

Summary of Model					
R squared	0.494	Standard Error of Estimate		1.344	
Adjusted R squared	0.462	Observations		67	
Variables in the equation					
Term	Coefficient	Standard Error	Standardised Regression Coefficient (beta)	t value	Significance
Intercept	8.125	0.766		10.61	0.00
Investments	-0.240	0.103	-0.214	-2.338	0.023
Ignorance-risk	-0.439	0.186	-0.219	-2.367	0.021
No Altern	0.492	0.149	0.328	3.309	0.002
Carter Succeed	0.687	0.175	0.387	3.926	0.000

These four variables relate to decision making attributes which can be recognised from the hypothesised model as, respectively: subjects' personal characteristics, their decision making style, evaluation of the decision frame, and their expectation of the decision's outcome.

Thus the solution in table 7.7 has identified mediating variables which determine a person's innate traits, propensity to select a risky alternative when making a decision, and their decision making style. These describe people who take risky decisions along four dimensions:

1. Personal attributes: the most important is low value of investments, which is correlated to lower income, fewer years of employment and younger age
2. A decision making style which believes that risk is not higher when facing decisions that we do not understand. These people describe themselves as 'controlled' and consider they have received more breaks in life than most
3. An assessment of the situation which concludes there is no alternative to taking the risk, and expectation it will bring substantial benefits. These people describe themselves as 'companionable'.
4. Judgement that risk will bring success. These people describe themselves as more willing to take risks than their colleagues and as 'confident'.

Discussion

This survey examined the reasons why people take risky decisions, and did not consider the effectiveness or results of these decisions. Even so, it raises a number of interesting conclusions:

1. Those who elect to take a risk or not fall into distinct groups which have different demographic and personality characteristics. Personality explains 24 percent of the variance in risk propensity which is a good match to previously published data (see table 4.1).
2. Just over half the managers surveyed proved willing to take a risk
3. A relatively parsimonious expression incorporating four independent variables is able to explain 49 percent of the variance.
4. The four principal variables relate to the subjects' characteristics, their decision making style, evaluation of the decision setting, and their expectation of the decision outcome. Subjects' beliefs and personal traits are mediated by these four variables.
5. In no case did any of the key factual elements of the case study have a significant impact on the decision. That is to say, there is no statistically meaningful link between the risk dimensions of the problem and the subjects' decisions on whether or not to take a risk.

6. The most important influence on risky decision making is judgement about the outcome rather than the facts of the situation.

The finding that a majority of managers will take a risky decision matches the results of other studies. For instance, Williams and Narendran (1999: 109) obtained survey responses from 285 Indian managers and found that "risky and safe responses were evenly distributed." MacCrimmon and Wehrung (1984: 378) compiled a sample of 464 senior North American managers which contained "significantly [p>0.001] more executives [who] were risk seeking than risk averse." Levy and Levy (2002) studied investment-type decisions by students, faculty and professionals and found that between 33 and 54 percent of their subjects were not risk averse.

The robust conclusion that only a minority of managers prefers a low risk alternative needs to be distinguished from the assumption in modern finance theory that investment decision makers are risk averse. The latter assumes that decision makers have diminishing marginal utility for money: thus a gain is of less utility than a loss of the same magnitude. As a result, decision makers are assumed to be risk averse, and their level of risk aversion is measured by the premium they require to prefer a risky choice rather than accept a guaranteed amount with the same expected value [Haugen (2001)]. Even so, CAPM and other finance theories allow for decision makers to select a risky alternative if the expected payout is sufficiently higher than that expected from a lower risk choice. Therefore the evidence that a majority of managers are willing to take a risky position does not of itself contradict modern finance theory.

Conversely there are studies involving managers that report lower levels of risk propensity with fewer than half of respondents prepared to take a risk. For instance Hartog et al. (2000) surveyed 3,000 Dutch chartered accountants and found that only 9 percent took a risky option, whilst 37 percent were risk neutral and 54 percent were risk averse. Mullins et al. (1999) surveyed hypothetical investment decisions of 164 part-time MBA students and found that 76 percent chose less risky alternatives.

Another important conclusion in table 7.7 is that almost half of the variation in respondents' willingness to take a risk is driven by just four factors. Save for a group of personal characteristics, the decision to take a risk is not driven directly by respondents' traits but is mediated by contextual and process variables. This confirms the finding from a similar study by Sitkin and Weingart (1995) that decision maker traits do not act directly on risk taking, but exert their influence through the way that decision makers perceive a risky decision. The finding here is also consistent with the observation by Kahneman (2003: 1469) that "the central characteristic of agents is ... that they often act intuitively. And the behavior of these agents is not guided by what they are able to compute, but by what they happen to see at a given moment."

The first variable that explains risk propensity is demographic, and the most important personal characteristic was the value of investments, excluding the principal residence: the more wealth, the lower the willingness to take risk. Because wealth rises with income, age and years of employment, these three factors were also associated with lower risk taking. It should be noted, though, that this does not imply that older managers do not take risks, only that they take fewer risks. Moreover the analysis was not able to discriminate between the quality of judgement, so the fewer risks taken by older managers may be better (or worse) judged than those of younger peers.

In this case study, gender was not a significant influence on whether or not people chose a risky alternative. This confirms other studies which have found that there are many situations in which women are as willing as men to take well-judged risks [Byrnes et al. (1999)].

The second determinant of risk taking is a mediating variable which can be thought of as decision making style, typified by expectation that risk is not higher when facing decisions we do not understand. This is driven by a variety of style features such as decision makers' belief that they have not received more of the breaks in life than others, and that the description 'controlled' does not match their behaviour.

This conclusion that managers have a distinctive decision making style which determines their risk propensity was also demonstrated in the factor analysis of respondents who preferred a risky alternative and those who did not. This showed that they form two distinct groups that are divided by demographic and personality characteristics.

Those subjects who take risky decisions can be described by four factors. The first is belief that the race was risky and that the Carter Team had an alternative; fewer years of employment experience; and perception by respondents that they are modest and not easily bored. A second group believed the outlook for Carter was positive; they had a lower education level and were more tolerant of ambiguity. The third group reported themselves as insecure, with low measures of personal risk propensity; they also believed that their life is controlled by powerful others. The fourth group believed that the situation was a threat to Carter, but that the team had a large potential for gain from the race; respondents reported that they could not be described as calm or controlled.

Factor analysis was repeated on the respondents who preferred the low risk alternative and chose not to race. The most powerful factor grouped subjects who felt risk was not necessary for success, did not want to be better than others, and believed that they were less willing to take risks than their colleagues and that they could not be described as confident or hard driving. A second group was not competitive, and did not set deadlines for themselves; they did not agree that decisions are often based on insufficient information. A third group was not easily bored and did not have much sympathy for adventurous decisions. The fourth group believed that Carter did not have the necessary skills to decide and had an alternative to racing.

These results from factor analysis classify risk takers as: inexperienced; less educated and more tolerant of ambiguity; fatalistic and insecure; and biased to longshots. Those respondents who did not take a risk are: risk averse; not of Type-A personality; not adventure seeking; and reluctant to make a decision. Significantly these findings are generally consistent with normative expectations about risk propensity, and they provide a useful means of classifying risk attitudes.

The third variable mediating risk propensity relates to evaluation of the alternatives to taking risk. Risk takers agreed that: "if this opportunity is passed up, there will never be another as good"; this variable was most strongly related to risk propensity (R=0.53). These respondents had concluded that a favourable outcome would provide a large gain, and reported that the description 'companionable' matched their behaviour.

The final mediating factor is decision makers' expectation about the outcome. Risk takers agree with the statement that: "Carter Racing is likely to succeed". This variable was the second most strongly related to risk propensity (R=0.51), and mediated respondents' confidence in Carter's decision making capability, and their self-report of higher risk propensity and personal confidence.

Overall nearly half the variance in decisions was about equally explained by the subjects' characteristics and decision making style, and their evaluation of the decision setting and expectation of the outcome. Other possible explanations include expected return, cognitive biases and noise.

Another important result is shown in table 7.6: none of the facts in the case study had a significant impact on the decision. Regression of the probability of racing on the facts was only able to explain a trivial portion of the variance ($R^2 = 0.06$), indicating that facts had no statistically meaningful link with subjects' decisions on whether to take a risk or not. Although this finding contradicts the normative assumption that decisions are principally determined by their facts, it is consistent with previous studies [e.g. Forlani (2002), and Mullins et al. (1999)] which found that a significant influence on risk propensity came from contextual factors such as a history of successful decision making and positive framing of the problem.

Another excellent example of the irrelevance of facts is given by Fair (2002) who tracked the United States S&P 500 futures contract between

1982 and 1999 to identify moves of greater than 0.75 percent within any five minutes (about seven standard deviations above average). He found 1,159 moves, and then searched newswires at that hour but found that 90 percent had no identifiable cause. Risk perception is clearly very ephemeral.

It is hard to resist the counter-intuitive conclusion that – in this study, at least – managers pay little heed to the content of a risky decision. Depending on their own unique perspective and the decision context, they look to the future, virtually independently of the stated risks, and make their decision.

An extension of the analysis above is to use its results to examine the real-world validity of Prospect Theory [Kahneman and Tversky (1979)] which is currently vying as a principal paradigm in decision theory. The discussion of Prospect Theory (PT) in chapter six suggests four hypotheses for the Carter Team case study where the probability of racing should be inversely related to:

H1   Recent performance

H2   Agreement with the statement: 'Carter Racing is in a positive situation'

H3   Value of respondents' investments

And, the probability of racing should be directly related to:

H4   Agreement with the statement: 'The situation faced by Carter is a significant threat'

Table 7.5 bears out hypotheses 3 and 4; in addition, hypothesis 1 has the correct sign, but not a significant relationship ($p > 0.4$). Importantly, though, this survey's results contradict hypothesis 2: managers who take the risky alterative and recommend racing do not believe that Carter Racing is in the domain of losses. This matches the conclusions of chapter six and provides further evidence that Prospect Theory has limited real-world explanatory power.

These findings have significant implications for management because risk-takers' beliefs and personal risk preferences are major drivers of their decisions. People who choose risky alternatives are confident after a record of successful risk-taking and receiving the benefits of luck. There are also indications that at least some risk-prone individuals believe they can use strategies such as planning to control the risks they face. Taken together, the insignificance of facts and confidence of success suggest that affect is a major decision driver. People decide to take a risky alternative because of their innate features, learned decision making style, and feeling about success.

The evidence also helps explain the prevalent longshot bias in managerial decision making. For instance, table 7.5 shows that two of the variables with strongest links to risk propensity ($p<0.01$) were belief that the situation has large potential for gain and confidence in a successful outcome. These factors, respectively, tempt managers to gamble in the hope of a big success, and encourage them to think that their skill can increase the probability of success.

These conclusions could prove particularly important in attempts to change risk-taking behaviours of (say) managers. If the facts of a risky decision are less important than personal attributes and the affect of risk-taking, then simply expanding on data and analysis will not change decisions. In a conclusion familiar to many students of organisational design, the people need to be changed not just the structure. Secondly, framing of the decision, especially its outcome, is important for its influence on affect. Thus managerial risk propensity can be encouraged by rewarding individuals' initiative and success, rather than forcing adherence to process [Pablo et al. (1996)]. Longer term, there is a suggestion that successful experience in risky decision making and education about the process will help modify behaviour.

This study's results point to several gaps in the management research agenda. The first is the need to examine decisions (and, by implication, other managerial practices) in a real-world context where subjects follow their natural decision styles, rather than conforming to norms imposed by experimental settings. The second implication is that managers and (if the agent-principal relationship holds true) their firms do not follow the logical decision making process assumed in strategy textbooks: collect the facts, weight them by probability, evaluate each outcome, and choose the highest value adding alternative [e.g. Dearlove (1998)]. Thus decision theory needs to specifically recognise affect and the concept of decision maker utility [Samson (1987)], even though it has waned in popularity in the last decade.

Given that risk propensity can explain half the variance in managerial decision making, a further area for research is the impact of risk on firm performance. Although there has been considerable effort using risk with its meaning of variance [see Nickel and Rodriguez (2002) for a useful review], less research has used risk in the way managers think of it. This is particularly important as existing strategy paradigms have proven unable to explain firm performance [Campbell-Hunt (2000)].

CHAPTER 8   How Companies Control Risks

This chapter reports results from a survey of senior executives that recorded their personal attributes and obtained a comprehensive assessment of their perception of the risk environment inside their organisations. The survey sought the name of each respondent's organisation to validate responses against observed crisis incidents, and to explain reported financial results. A wealth of information was obtained in the 137-question survey that was completed by over 170 executives.

The chapter first describes the survey data, and then reports the results which - for convenience – have been grouped into six sections: organisational risk strategies; executives' perception of the business environment; their attitudes towards risk; predictors of risk outcomes for organisations; influence of risk on financial results; and corporate risk propensity. The chapter concludes with a discussion on its principal findings.

Data and Respondents' Characteristics

A total of 172 subjects were recruited by e-mail. The largest response (N=132) was achieved through the support of the Australian Institute of Company Directors (AICD) whose Victorian Manager wrote to Institute members seeking their participation. A number of public companies were approached, and a senior executive in three agreed to secure participation by between five and ten colleagues. Additional subjects were recruited through e-mails to members of several professional groups, and from a small number of interested colleagues. Respondents logged anonymously onto a University of Melbourne website and completed a survey which took about 25 minutes; results were collated through the Perseus survey software.

The Survey contained 137 questions, largely requiring a single choice from a five-point scale. The questions related to the respondent's demography and work history (11 questions) and personality and risk attitudes (41); and to their organisation (76) and its industry (9). Responses (N=36) included 15 companies with publicly available statutory accounts (93 organisations were named, but – in keeping with the pattern of corporate Australia - many were small).

Respondents are: predominantly male (84 percent), tertiary qualified (97 percent), with considerable work experience (92 percent have 16 or more years in employment), and relatively high incomes (56 percent earn over $150,000 per year). 47 percent are a Director of their organisation; most of the balance are very senior executives.

Respondents covered a wide range of organisations in terms of industry and structure. Between 15 and 19 percent came from each of the manufacturing, finance and insurance, and services sectors. Just over a third of respondents came from private companies, with 17 percent from listed public companies, and others from not-for-profit organisations and statutory authorities. A further indicator of the diversity of backgrounds is the range of professional memberships: 63 percent are members of the Australian Institute of Company Directors; around 20 percent are members of either the Australian Institute of Management or the Society of CPAs; and others are members of the Institution of Engineers Australia, Finance and Treasury Association, and the Association of Risk and Insurance Managers of Australia.

Importantly for the generalisability of these results, the respondents share many of the characteristics of the (younger and lower paid) respondents in the Carter Racing survey reported in the previous chapter. In addition, respondents in this second survey were representative of the AICD Victorian membership. Statistics compiled by the Institute show that 83 percent of members are male (versus 84 percent in the sample in this section) and 59 percent are company directors (47 percent). Some 61 percent of members come from organisations with turnover under $100 million (68 percent), 13 percent from organisations in the finance sector (16 percent) and 9 percent from manufacturing (15 percent); 33 percent of members come from private companies (35 percent).

The close match between characteristics of respondents and those of AICD members gives considerable confidence that the survey responses are representative of a broad cross section of senior executives.

Factor analysis was used to check for any natural groupings of respondents and organisations, but in neither case could even a seven-factor solution explain half the variance (45.7 percent of respondents and 47.9 percent of organisations). Although several factors proved logical (e.g. defining companies by governance ability, interest in risk and growth rate), their low explanatory power limited applicability.

Organisational Risk Strategies

An intuitively important determinant of risk outcomes is an organisation's risk management strategy, and this was measured in the Survey using a variety of questions about practices and procedures of senior management and Boards.

Table 8.1 summarises key risk management (RM) practices which were reviewed in the survey and includes description of strategy, existence of a specialist RM group, formal training, documented Risk Policy, plans to recover from disaster and minimise reputation risk, and product quality monitoring. The most important conclusions are:

1. Half the organisations have a company-wide approach to risk management. This is particularly true of: large companies; those involved in finance and regulated industries; and statutory authorities. Organisations that are least likely to have a formal RM strategy tend to be smaller, private companies, or involved in manufacturing.
2. About a third of organisations have a specialist risk management group, and these are largely confined to statutory authorities and companies that are larger and involved in finance.
3. Two thirds of organisations provide RM training to their senior management
4. 57 percent of Boards have a Risk Management policy and almost as many have a comprehensive disaster recovery plan to cope with identified risks. These are most common in statutory authorities and large companies, finance companies and regulated industries. Typically the CEO has championed the roll out of risk management policies.
5. Boards are very active in risk management, and - rather than delegating it to a Board committee or staff - almost half retain this responsibility. A similar proportion of Boards identify risks at their meetings or through Board papers.
6. Almost 60 percent of Boards receive formal risk assessments with proposals for approval. These are most common with large and listed companies.
7. 56 percent of organisations have a comprehensive disaster recovery plan, with a lower frequency (33 percent) in firms with smaller turnover.
8. Over 60 percent of Boards monitor product quality. An interesting counter to larger companies' generally strong RM practices is that Boards which monitor product quality tend to be in smaller organisations and private companies in industries which are responsive to consumer needs. These organisations have the fewest crises. Con-

versely, only 57 percent of companies which have product defects as a major concern monitor product quality at Board level.

9. Board level strategy to minimise risk to brand and reputation is relatively uncommon and largely confined to companies which are larger, listed, or in the finance sector. Even companies which have identified reputation as a major concern at Board level are only slightly more likely to have a reputation strategy (51 percent versus 45 percent for all organisations).

Table 8.2 provides granularity to the results above by examining risk management (RM) practices in terms of company size, legal structure and industry, and by respondents' assessment of their organisations' risk climate. The most important conclusions are:

1. The proportion of companies which have instituted RM practices is related to turnover. Around 80 percent or more of companies with an annual turnover above $1 billion have what might be considered 'best practice' risk processes. An important exception is that less than half of them monitor product quality at Board level. In marked contrast, 'best practice' risk processes exist in fewer than one third of small organisations with turnover below $100 million.

2. Legal structure also influences the prevalence of risk practices as they are relatively less common in private or unlisted companies. Statutory Authorities are most likely to have RM programs in place, followed by listed public companies and not-for-profit bodies.

3. The industry leader in RM is finance and insurance, followed by manufacturing. Relatively few services organisations have extensive RM practices, and they are uncommon in Information Technology and telecoms organisations.

4. Just over 50 percent of organisations which report that product defects and reputation are risks of major concern have formal Board policies in place to manage them (56.8 and 50.7 percent, respectively).

5. Organisations which are most crisis prone (reporting three or more crises in the previous three years) are less likely to have a Board Risk Management Policy (44.4 percent of crisis prone companies vs. sample average of 57.4 percent) or a comprehensive disaster recovery plan (33.3 percent vs. 55.4 percent). They are also less likely to conduct risk assessments as part of new strategies, monitor product quality, or have formal risk policies and plans to manage threats to reputation.

6. Organisations which are least crisis prone (reporting no crises in the previous three years) are more likely to monitor product quality at Board level and to have formal brand protection strategies.

7. Industries where companies implement good RM practices are characterised as regulated and socially responsible; whereas companies in risky industries are least likely to implement good RM practices

8. Companies which are more likely to implement good RM practices tend to have an Enterprise Risk Management Policy in place, high quality standards, and a Board with an RM focus. Those least likely to have RM practices in place are profit oriented, reward risk-taking, have complex activities and sell finished goods or services.

Whilst discussion of these points must wait for the next section, an irresistible conclusion from the data is that best practice RM procedures are least apparent in those companies that most need them due to their structure or track record.

Table 8.1. Corporate Risk Management (RM) Practices

Practice	Attribute	Percent of Respondents
Best description of risk management strategy	Formal process across whole company	50.4
	Informal process covering strategy and operations	13.2
Group responsible for risk management	Specialist risk management group	36.0
	Senior managers	37.3
	Board	13.5
Firms with formal Risk Management training		66.1
Boards with documented Risk Management Policy		57.4
Champion of RM Policy roll out	CEO	42.9
	Senior manager	24.5
How Board identifies risk	Through Board meetings	30.8
	Advice from RM group	25.0
Board Committee responsible for RM	Whole Board	48.7
Boards receiving risk assessment with strategic proposals		59.2
Firms with comprehensive disaster recovery plans		55.4
Boards which monitor product quality		60.5
Boards with formal strategies to minimise risk to brand and reputation		45.2

Table 8.2. Risk Management Strategy by Organisation Characteristics

	RM is formal	RM Group	Board RM Policy	Disaster Plan	Strategic Risk Assessment	Monitor Quality	Brand strategy
All Companies	50.4	36.0	57.4	55.4	59.2	60.5	45.3
Turnover:							
< $100 million	25.7*	12.2*	31.4*	37.1	48.6	74.3	44.1
$100 - 1000 million	54.0	50.0	65.6	57.1	55.6	56.5	30.0
> $ 1 billion	100.0*	80.0*	80.0*	78.6*	92.9*	43.8	80.0*
Legal Structure							
Not for profit	63.6	72.7*	81.8*	63.6	62.5	40.0*	40.0
Private Company	32.6	22.2	36.4*	39.5	46.5	68.2	40.5
Public Listed Company	68.4*	52.6	73.7	78.9*	84.2*	44.4	68.4
Public Unlisted	50.0	25.0	62.5	56.3	60.0	46.7*	43.8
Statutory Authority	81.3*	68.8*	93.8*	75.0*	62.5	62.5	50.0
Industry							
Manufacturing	42.9	13.3*	57.1	50.0	57.1	71.4	28.6
Education and Prof Dev	50.0	33.3	50.0	50.0	66.7	66.7	33.3
IT and telecoms	14.3	0.0*	14.3*	14.3*	28.6	28.6	28.6
Finance & Insurance	66.7	60.0*	93.3*	80.0*	85.7*	71.4	71.4
Services	27.8*	15.8*	26.3*	47.4	57.0	84.2*	57.9
Major Risks of Concern							
Product defects	45.9	26.3	44.7	47.4	64.9	56.8	42.1
Reputation	53.4	39.2	63.5	61.6	58.9	63.4	50.7
Crises in last Three years							
Nil	45.8	33.3	58.3	55.9	56.9	66.1	50.0
1-2	54.2	38.8	58.3	58.3	56.3	56.5	39.1
> 2	55.6	50.0	44.4	33.3*	77.8*	55.6	37.5

Table 8.2. (cont)

Industry is **:							
Competitive	44.5	36.6	54.3	52.7	63.3	57.3	46.1
Responsive to consumers	51.1	35.2	58.2	54.4	56.2	64.4	41.4
Regulated	62.3	45.5	67.5	64.9	62.3	57.1	46.6
Risky	37.7	36.0	56.9	46.0	64.0	47.6	40.8
Socially responsible	59.1	40.4	65.2	63.6	63.2	65.9	47.6
Company **							
Profit oriented	43.2	35.5	49.3	66.7	60.3	61.6	49.3
Sells finished goods	46.7	30.0	50.0	53.3	53.3	60.0	46.4
Rewards risk-taking	41.5	24.4	46.3	46.3	68.2	65.9	42.5
Has complex activities	54.1	46.7	60.8	58.9	72.6	57.5	47.1
Board has RM focus	66.3	48.1	72.8	68.8	69.6	65.4	61.8
High quality standards	63.1	36.3	58.9	58.9	61.8	60.6	48.6
Has an ERM Policy in place	69.4*	50.7	80.6*	71.8	72.9	61.4	59.4

* p < 0.1: as a guide, result differs from the mean by more than 18 percent.

** percent of respondents who Agree or Strongly Agree

Organisational Risk Outlook

To extend the analysis of risk management strategies, questions probed executives' views on the types of risk they expected to face in future.

Respondents were provided with a list of 29 different risks and asked to indicate which ones were of 'major concern': the most frequent responses are listed in table 8.3. More than half the respondents (53 percent) reported computer breakdown as a major concern to make this the most significant risk for Australian organisations. Another common risk that was not intuitively obvious is government regulation which 39 percent identified as a major risk. Other risks of concern which were frequently mentioned include reputation (45 percent), operational processes and technologies (44 percent), competitor activity (42 percent), and occupational health (41 percent).

Those risks which have been the most frequent causes of corporate crises in Australia during the1990s [see Coleman (2004)] fell well down respondents' list of concerns: product defects (23 percent report as a major concern); industrial accidents (23 percent); and financial mismanagement (18 percent). Similarly terrorism and international exposures barely rated, even though the Survey was compiled in November 2003 when both were topical media issues.

Table 8.3.   Major Risks of Concern

Risk	Respondents Reporting (%)
Computer breakdowns	53.3
Reputation	44.8
Processes and technologies used in operations	43.6
Competitor activity	41.8
Occupational health	40.6
Government regulation	39.3
Organisational issues	35.8
Product defects, including recalls	23.0
Industrial accidents	23.0
White collar crime and other illegal activities	22.4
Environmental	21.8
Financing (derivatives, debt)	17.6
Discrimination, including sexual harassment	17.6
Credit	16.4

Respondents were asked to think in general about the intensity of risks facing their company, and then decide on the change that had taken place in the last three to five years and what they expected to occur in the next three to five years. Table 8.4 shows that over 73 percent reported that risk had risen in the past few years, and 69 percent expected that the trend would continue. Only 8.4 percent of executives had experienced a fall in risk, and fewer (5.3 percent) expected a fall in the next few years; each of these respondents came from a smaller organisation with annual turnover of less than $100 million.

Table 8.4.   Changes in Risk Facing Respondents' Organisation

	Last 3-5 years	Next 3-5 years
Increase in risk	73.3	68.7
Fall in risk	8.4	5.3
Risk stays the same	16.8	25.2
Don't know	1.5	0.8

These trends are important given judgements that risk plays a vital in decisions. Respondents were asked what proportion of decisions taken by the Board involve risk: the proportion was 49.3 percent (standard deviation 32.3); 21 percent put the proportion of decisions involving risk at 80 percent or greater, whilst 31 percent put it at 20 percent or less.

Executives' Perceptions of the Business Environment

Although it was not a specific purpose of this Survey to examine respondents' views of the business environment, a number of relevant questions were included as gauges of risk-related attitudes and perceptions. Table 8.5 summarises the most important responses.

Executives overwhelming see their industry as competitive (77 percent agree or strongly agree), responsive to customer needs (74 percent), socially responsible (70 percent); and regulated (66 percent). There is greater spread of opinions over profitability (only 56 percent agree or strongly agree that their industry is profitable). So, too, with risk where 44 percent believe that their industry is risky.

In terms of their own organisations, 93 percent of respondents agree or strongly agree that they have an ethical approach to business. Organisations seem to have a balanced focus on performance as respondents provide comparable support for statements that their organisation 'is very people oriented' (78 percent agree or strongly agree), 'has high standards for product quality' (86 percent), and 'imposes strong pressures for performance' (82 percent).

On the other hand, many organisations were weak in manager selection, intolerant of innovation, and did not provide incentives for risk taking. Only 69 percent of respondents agreed or strongly agreed that their organisation 'appoints the best candidates as managers'; just 41 percent believe that their organisation 'tolerates unpopular ideas'; and a low 29 percent 'reward entrepreneurial risk taking'.

Table 8.5. Perceptions of the Business Environment

	Agree or Strongly Agree	Disagree or Strongly Disagree
My company's industry is:		
very competitive	76.9	10.1
responsive to consumer needs	73.8	8.7
socially responsible	70.4	9.2
strongly regulated	65.8	23.6
profitable	56.2	14.8
risky	43.5	35.4
My company:		
has an ethical approach to business	92.5	3.7
has high standards for product quality	86.3	3.7
believes it can take well-judged risks	82.4	2.5
imposes strong pressures for performance	81.5	6.2
has good internal controls	78.1	9.1
is very people oriented	77.7	7.4
generally succeeds when implementing new strategies	76.5	10.5
respects diversity of opinion and style	73.5	10.5
Board and senior management have expertise covering all areas of operations	71.0	16.7
appoints the best candidates as managers	68.9	23.0
has implemented repeated cost-cutting programs in recent years	43.8	38.8
tolerates unpopular ideas	41.0	23.0
rewards entrepreneurial risk taking	29.4	32.6

Executives' Attitudes Towards Risk

Analysis of executives' risk attitudes lends itself to intensive survey methods [e.g. March and Shapira (1987)] and they were measured by questions which asked about decision making processes and respondents' gambling style 'the last time that I bet on the races'.

Answers to the questions on risky decision making style are summarised in table 8.6, and suggest an ambivalent attitude towards risk. It is clear that 85-90 percent of executives see risk as the *sine qua non* for success because they agree with statements such as 'to achieve something in life one has to take risks' (92 percent agree or strongly agree); and 'successful people take risks' (85 percent). In addition, 72 percent of the respondents disagree or strongly disagree with the statement 'I am less willing to take risks than my colleagues.' In marked contrast to this apparent support for, and commitment to, risk-taking, less than 30 percent agree that they 'tend to take a lot of risks' in any one of three key aspects of their lives (personal life, personal finances and business life).

Ambivalence also accompanies processes involved in risky decision making. On one hand 87 percent of respondents agree or strongly agree that 'risk is higher when facing situations we do not understand'; and almost half believe that 'many important decisions are based on insufficient information.' On the other hand, 96 percent of executives believe that 'risky situations can be made safer by planning ahead.'

These answers suggest that respondents are providing normative, textbook responses to generic questions about decision making; but they acknowledge their own decision making is personalised.

To further explore decision making style, respondents were asked to report on their actual behaviour in a real-world setting. The example chosen was the last time they went to the races. Questions probed decision strategy in the way that selections are chosen (favourites, value horses, longshots, or other) and type of bet that is placed (win or place; multiple bet as quinella, trifecta and double; or other)[62].

---

[62] Favourites have the lowest dividend: they are predicted by the wagering market as most likely to win. The Survey did not define longshots, but they are usually thought to have a lower probability of winning and are assumed here to have a dividend of more than $10 for a $1 bet (i.e. about nine percent probability of winning).

Table 8.6. Respondents' Attitudes Towards Risky Decision Making

Survey Question	Respondents (%) who:	
	Agree or Strongly Agree	Disagree or Strongly Disagree
Risky situations can be made safer by planning ahead.	96.3	0.6
To achieve something in life one has to take risks.	91.9	4.2
Risk is higher when facing situations we do not understand	86.9	8.1
Successful people take risks	85.1	3.1
Many important decisions are based on insufficient information	49.7	38.5
In my personal life, I tend to take a lot of physical risks	29.2	47.2
I like to play it safe.	25.4	42.3
In relation to my personal finances, I tend to take a lot of risks	24.2	50.9
I've not much sympathy for adventurous decisions	17.4	56.5
In my business life I tend to take a lot of financial risks on behalf of my company o r clients	17.3	57.4
In general, I am less willing to take risks than my colleagues.	9.9	71.5

Table 8.7 compares the stated allocation of respondents' bets with those of all bettors who placed their bets with the Victorian parimutuel operator, Tabcorp Limited, on Derby Day in Melbourne[63] (this is claimed to be the 'best day's racing of the year', and is a major occasion for corporate entertaining with the second highest racecourse attendance in Melbourne; the value of bets is about four times that of a normal Saturday meeting, although the distribution of bets is no different; and it occurred on the Saturday before most surveys were completed).

As shown in the table, respondents' type of bet (e.g. win or place) was very similar to that of the average bettor: for instance 41 percent of all wagers placed on Derby Day were win bets, whilst 70 out of 172 respondents (41 percent) reported that 'the largest dollar value' of their wagers went to win bets. A Chi-squared test showed that there was no statistically significant difference ($p < 0.1$) between the type of wager placed by respondents and by the average bettor.

Table 8.7. Allocation of Wagers (Percent by Value)

Type of bet	Respondents	TABCORP (Derby Day 2003)
Win	40.7	40.6
Place	25.7	22.3
Quinella	4.4	5.9
Trifecta	15.0	19.9
Double	0.9	4.8
Other	12.8	6.5
Favourite	9.7	24.0
Value Horses	67.2	46.9
Longshots (Dividend >$10)	9.7	29.1
Other	13.4	-

There is, however, a significant ($p<0.01$) difference between executives and the general public in their agreement with the wagering market's evaluation of the probability that a given horse will win. The general betting public places 24 percent of its wagers on favourites which – as discussed in chapter four - have the highest expected return; conversely only 9.7 percent of executives bet on favourites. Similarly executives bet far less on longshots than the general public (9.7 percent and 29.1 percent, re-

---

[63] Information was taken from TABCORP's website www.tabracing.com.au

spectively). Executives place 67 percent of their bets on 'value' horses, whereas only 47 percent of the public supports these runners.

These results suggest that the risk propensity of executives - as revealed by their preferences between racecourse bet types (e.g. win vs. place) - is little different to that of a much broader cross-section of the population. There is, however, a significant difference in the way that winning selections are chosen, or what might be called decision making process or strategy. A majority (53 percent) of the general public chooses to bet almost equally on favourites or longshots; conversely only 19 percent of respondents choose these most or least favoured runners[64].

Risk Outcomes for Organisations

An important objective was to identify the determinants of organisations' risk-related outcomes, particularly crises and financial results. In the Survey, a crisis was defined as 'an incident or issue which escalates uncontrollably and causes such serious damage to the assets, reputation and performance of an organisation that its viability is threatened.' Executives were asked to think about crises that had involved their organisation during the last three years, and then indicate the frequency. Table 8.8 breaks down the frequencies by organisation turnover and industry, and adherence to various risk management practices.

Half the organisations (47 percent) had not experienced a crisis in the previous three years, whilst 39 percent experienced one or two, and 15 percent had experienced three or more crises. Based on the survey data and assuming that crises are distributed randomly, any particular organisation would experience a crisis on average every 2.1 years. Although not tabulated here, another question asked about the frequency of serious incidents that could have become crises: they occurred on average every 1.5 years.

Not surprisingly, crises primarily affect larger companies: 57 percent of organisations with an annual turnover under $100 million had not experienced a crisis, whereas only 37 percent of larger organisations had been crisis free. Companies in the manufacturing sector were most likely to have experienced a crisis (60 percent compared to 52 for all other industries), whereas they are relatively rare in services organisations (26 percent experienced a crisis).

---

[64] Although not pursued here, this is not inconsistent with the counter-intuitive observation by Bradley (2003: 413) that "bettors may not have fundamentally different attitudes to risk than non-bettors."

Crises are also more common in industries which are not fast growing (64 percent experienced a crisis), and in industries which are strongly regulated (62 percent) and risky (59 percent). They are more likely to affect companies which have many complex activities (67 percent experienced a crisis), cut corners to get results (90 percent), imposed strong cost pressures (68 percent), and tolerate poor managers (85 percent).

Table 8.8.   Frequency of Crises in Previous Three Years

	None	1-2	3 or more
All Companies	46.5	38.9	14.6
Turnover:			
< $100 million	57.3	36.6	6.1
$100 - 1000 million	28.6	52.4	19.0
> $ 1 billion	50.0	50.0	0
Industry			
Manufacturing	40.0	46.7	13.3
Finance & Insurance	60.0	33.3	6.7
Services	73.6	21.1	5.3
Other Industries	44.9	46.4	8.7
Risk Management (RM) Practices			
RM is formal company-wide process	46.5	44.8	8.7
Have specialist RM group	46.5	44.2	9.3
Board has documented RM policy	52.2	41.8	6.0
Risk assessment accompanies strategic proposals	49.3	40.3	10.4
Has comprehensive disaster plan	51.6	43.8	4.6
Board monitors product quality	55.7	37.1	7.2
Strategy to protect brand	58.0	36.0	6.0
Industry and Organisation Characteristics			
Industry is not fast growing	36.1	42.6	21.3
Industry is strongly regulated	37.9	42.7	19.4
Industry is risky	40.9	40.9	18.2
Cuts corners to get results	10.5	47.4	42.1
Does not appoint best candidates as managers	15.4	30.8	53.8
Implemented repeated cost cuts	33.3	56.9	9.8
Has many rapid complex activities	32.7	46.9	20.4

Risk management (RM) practices have a mixed effect on crisis frequency. On one hand crisis prone companies are more likely to follow good practices as they tend to have specialist RM groups (54 percent of organisations with such a group experienced a crisis), provide risk assessments to accompany strategy proposals (51 percent), and treat RM as a formal process across the whole company (54 percent). On the other hand they are less likely to document risk policies (48 percent), develop comprehensive plans to respond to identified risks (48 percent), monitor product quality (44 percent), or have a formal strategy to minimise risk to brand and reputation (42 percent).

The analysis was then extended to incorporate three variables which measured the frequency of crises and serious incidents. Two came from questions in the survey which asked about the number of crises and the number of serious incidents that could have become crises that each organisation had experienced in the last three years. The third variable came from my event history analysis of crises experienced by Australian companies during the 1990s [Coleman (2004)]. There were 55 such incidents, and the data were used to create a dummy variable for 'crisis prone': companies which had been involved in one of these 55 public crises were coded with a '1', whilst those which had not been involved in one of the crises were coded '0'.

The most significant (p<0.01) correlations between each of the three measures of adverse risk outcomes and survey questions are shown in table 8.9 in decreasing order; a positive correlation implies that respondents who agree with the statement are describing an organisation which was likely to have experienced a crisis or serious incident.

An important feature of the table is that the relationships between survey questions are qualitatively consistent across the three measures of risk outcome. The table has 13 examples involving two or more of the dependent variables: in every case the signs are the same.

Results in table 8.9 suggest that companies with poor risk outcomes tend to be: operating in a regulated, uncompetitive, technologically advanced industry which is not responsive to consumer needs; internally competitive with many complex activities and a willingness to cut corners to get results; growing slowly, selling finished products and operating offshore and through part owned subsidiaries; and having carried out numerous cost-cutting programs, with a poor record of strategy implementation, and high turnover of executives. These companies are characterised by weak governance with a complacent Board that lacks expertise, particularly in finance, and low regard for ethics and product quality.

Table 8.9.   Correlation of Survey Responses with Risk Outcomes (p<0.01)

Survey Question	Value of R		
	Crisis Prone	Crises #	Potential Crises #
Crisis Prone	1.0	0.271	0.369
Crises - #	0.271	1.0	0.678
Potential Crises	0.369	0.678	1.0
Turnover	0.520		0.300
My company has direct investments offshore	0.397		0.234
My company produces finished consumer products	0.376		0.287
My company appoints the best candidates as managers	0.337	-0.341	-0.262
My company owns an interest in joint ventures or independent subsidiaries	0.336		
My company deals in commodities or derivatives	0.334		
My company has a high level of internal competition	0.328	0.298	0.322
My company has implemented repeated cost-cutting programs in recent years		0.318	0.225
My company cuts corners to get results	0.293	0.296	
My company has many rapid and complex activities	0.294		
My company's industry is strongly regulated		0.263	
My company has high standards for product quality		-0.293	-0.252
My company has an ethical approach to business		-0.280	-0.226
My company's industry is technologically advanced	0.268		
The Board and senior management have expertise covering all areas of operations		-0.239	-0.265
The Board and senior management understand the company's financial exposures		-0.257	-0.233

Table 8.9. (cont)

My company has high turnover of executives	-0.240	0.202	0.257
My company's industry is very competitive	0.238		
Board has a formal strategy to minimise brand risk			0.231
My company is resistant to sharing bad news	-0.227		
My company is expanding rapidly			-0.225
My company's industry is responsive to consumer needs	0.217		
I have gotten more of the breaks in life than most people I know		-0.210	
My company generally succeeds when implementing new strategies			
Thinking about my company … The Board and senior management operate inside their comfort zones			0.209

An interesting aspect is that - out of the 52 measures associated with respondents' personal characteristics – only one was significantly related to risk outcomes (life satisfaction: I have gotten more of the breaks in life than most people I know). Intuitively one would expect a correlation between personal attributes of senior executives and the risk outcomes of their organisations. Such a link would be formed as follows: personality and demography influence individuals' risk propensity; the risk propensity of organisations results from the decisions of its senior management; and risk attitudes and risk management practices of organisations determine their risk outcomes. However, less than 10 percent of the variance in reported risk outcomes is explained by executive traits. This matches a conclusion from the Carter Racing Survey in chapter seven that executives' attributes do not directly determine risk taking, but act through mediating variables which influence the way that decision makers perceive a risky situation

Also interesting is that there was only a weak statistical linkage between risk management practices and risk outcomes. RM policies seem to be virtually irrelevant to the frequency of crises and serious incidents which are determined by broader company strategies and practices.

The next step used multiple regression to derive parsimonious explanations for organisations' risk outcomes: the frequency of crises and serious incidents. Results are summarised in tables 8.10 and 8.11, and - not surprisingly – they bear out the stereotype of companies which are prone to poor risk outcomes.

Seven variables explained 35 percent of variance in crisis frequency. Four company-specific factors explained 31 percent of the variance: cutting corners to get results; not appointing the best candidates as managers; having complex activities; and producing finished goods. Two executive attributes ('I have always wanted to be better than others' and 'Compared to the average manager I give much more effort') explained seven percent of variance; and industry regulation explained a further six percent.

Table 8.10. Statistics Associated with Frequency of Crises

Summary of Model					
R squared	0.352	Standard Error of Estimate			0.693
Adjusted R squared	0.323	Observations			165
Variables in the equation					
Term	Coefficient	Standard Error	Standardised Coefficient	t value	Signifi- cance
Constant	2.857	.432		6.61	.000
43:4: Company appoints best candidates as managers	-.285	.072	.280	3.93	.000
44:8: Company has many complex activities	.222	.056	.263	3.98	.000
42:4: Industry is regulated	.105	.044	.160	2.39	.018
46:5: My company cuts corners to get results	.176	.065	.191	2.69	.008
23:8: I have always wanted to be better than others	-.179	.063	.196	2.84	.005
23:15: Compared to the average manager I give much more effort	.189	.078	.166	2.42	.017
43:11: My company produces finished consumer goods	.078	.038	.133	2.03	.044

A similar pattern emerged from regression of respondents' reports on the frequency of serious incidents that could have become crises. The most important variables were production of finished goods and weak company culture (lack of Board expertise, low quality standards, pressures on performance, and cost-cutting programs) which explained 28 percent of the variance; and an industry that is regulated and unresponsive to customers which explained nine percent of the variance.

These analyses suggest that crises and serious incidents are largely determined by a few attributes related to organisations' strategic choices, with less influence from industry factors, and virtually no direct contribution from the personal traits of directors and executives.

Table 8.11.   Statistics Associated with Frequency of Potential Crises

Summary of Model					
R squared	0.343	Standard Error of Estimate			0.838
Adjusted R squared	0.314	Observations			165

Variables in the equation					
Term	Coefficient	Standard Error	Standardised Regression Coefficient (beta)	t value	Significance
Constant	2.192	.339		6.46	.000
43:11: Company produces finished products	.214	.046	.306	4.63	.000
45:6: The Board has expertise covering all operations	-.282	.073	-.268	3.84	.000
42:3: Industry responds to customer needs	-.285	.085	-.225	3.34	.001
44:9: Company has implemented cost-cutting	.134	.064	.143	2.11	.036
46:4: Company has high standards for product quality	-.305	.096	-.231	3.19	.002
44:1: Company imposes pressures for performance	.287	.091	.229	3.14	.002
42:4: Industry is regulated	.125	.052	.159	2.38	.019

This was probed by assuming that crisis-related attributes of an organisation are dependent on the traits of its executives, and then examining the correlations between executive attributes and the principal variables which are associated with companies that experience crises and serious incidents. Table 8.12 shows the correlation co-efficients between six variables associated with crises and a number of executive attributes.

Table 8.12. Significant Correlations between Executive Traits and Determinants of Crises (p<0.10)

	Turnover	42:1 Industry is competitive	42:4 Industry is regulated	43:4 Company appoints best candidates	43:11 Company produces finished products	44:8 Company has many complex activities	45:6 Board has expertise covering all operations	46:4 Company has high standards for quality
Direction of relationship between crisis determinant and crisis frequency	+	+	+	-	+	+	-	-
Male		0.27		0.16	0.13			
Age				0.17	0.16		0.25	0.19
Years with current employer	0.34	0.20	0.20		0.29		0.19	
Many important decisions are based on insufficient information			-0.12	-0.25				-0.23
I set difficult goals for myself which I attempt to reach	-0.21			0.23				
I get what I want because I'm lucky	0.19		0.12				-0.26	-0.16
I regularly set deadlines for myself	-0.20			0.26				0.21
Risky situations can be made safer by planning ahead	-0.11		-0.17	0.28				0.15
I am very confident of my ability	-0.14		0.12	0.21		0.18		0.13
My life is chiefly controlled by powerful others				-0.25				
My behaviour is: hard driving	-0.18	0.15	-0.13	0.28		0.13		0.26
My behaviour is: controlled	0.11	0.12	-0.17		-0.21			
My behaviour is: insecure			-0.24	-0.25	0.15	-0.14		-0.13
In business I tend to take a lot of financial risks on behalf of my company or clients								

Executive attributes are strongly related to strategic factors that predispose companies to crises. Take turnover, for instance, which is the independent variable with the strongest single correlation with crises. Respondents who worked for organisations with higher turnover were long serving, fatalistic ('When I get what I want it's usually because I'm lucky'), not type-A personalities (e.g. they do not set deadlines or difficult goals), and insecure and not confident of their ability. Respondents in regulated industries have similar traits as they tend to be longer serving and fatalistic, but are more confident and secure.

By contrast the variable which is most strongly associated with low frequency of crises is to appoint the best candidates as managers. Employees in these organisations are hard driving, type-A personalities who are confident and self-sufficient and more likely to be male and older. Interestingly, respondents in companies which have high standards for product quality have virtually identical traits. A similar pattern is typical of companies in competitive industries where employees also tend to be male, longer serving and hard driving.

Further confirmation that executive traits impact through organisation parameters, rather than directly driving risk outcomes, is that they are able to explain high risk strategies such as rapid expansion, belief that the organisation can take well-judged risks, reward for entrepreneurial risk-taking, pride in innovative business models, and success in implementing new strategies. Regression showed that between 18 and 26 percent of these variables was explained by executive traits such as: being companionable and belief that outcomes are controllable and that planning can minimise risk (these factors also proved significant in the previous survey).

An extension of the analysis of crisis frequency was to evaluate their nature. Respondents were given a list of 13 incident types and asked to indicate which had characterised their organisation's crises or serious incidents. Table 8.13 shows the most common responses as the proportion of respondents who indicated each category (multiple choices were allowed). Significantly, reputation proved the most frequent catalyst for crisis. Also important were process failures, and product contaminations and defects. A surprise is that spectacular incidents such as plant fires, serious frauds and fatal accidents are relatively common (with one affecting around ten percent of organisations in any given year), but rarely escalate into crises.

Table 8.13.   Major Types of Crisis and Serious Incident

Description	Respondents Reporting (%)	
	Crisis	Serious Incident
Reputational issue	28.5	33.3
Process failure	21.2	29.1
Product contamination	7.9	9.1
Product recall	7.9	9.1
Labour disruption or major strike	7.9	11.5
Plant fire or explosion	5.5	7.9
Serious fraud	3.6	10.9
Fatal accident	0	12.7

To identify what might predispose an organisation to a particular crisis type, dummies were introduced for crises involving reputation and for crises which arise out of operations and involve process failure, plant fire or explosion or product contamination or recall (1 for organisations reporting the crisis type, 0 otherwise). This showed that reputational crises tend to be associated with corner cutting, rapid and complex activities, centralised decision making and a high level of internal competition. On the other hand, operational crises were associated with cost-cutting programs, low turnover of executives, directors who are not comfortable with RM processes, and a regulated industry.

Influence of Risk on Financial Results

Another important analytical goal was to identify the extent to which financial results are impacted by risk-related attributes of an organisation and by those of its employees and industry. To match comparable studies, the dependent variable was chosen as return on shareholders' funds; and - to remove biases from small organisations - responses were limited to organisations which are included in Australia's biggest 1000 enterprises [Kavanagh (2003)]. This gave a sample of 36 responses.

The next table shows significant univariate correlations between Survey measures and return on shareholder funds. Turnover was the most significant variable, with larger companies enjoying a higher return than smaller companies. The second most important variable was the frequency of crises as they significantly reduce returns. Lesser influences are offshore investments (which is strongly correlated with turnover: $R= 0.491$; $p < 0.01$) and a competitive attitude in executives.

Table 8.14. Correlations of Survey Responses with Return on Shareholders' Funds (p<0.05)

	R
Turnover	0.595
Q71: Frequency of crises in last three years	- 0.425
Q43:13: My company has direct investments offshore	0.375
Q35: The following describes my behaviour: competitive	0.357

Table 8.15 shows the results of regressing return on shareholder funds against survey variables: almost two thirds of the variation in returns was explained by turnover and the frequency of crises. Not surprisingly, risk outcomes have a significant direct impact on financial results: every crisis during a three-year period reduces returns to shareholders by almost two percent

Table 8.15. Statistics Associated with Return on Shareholders' Funds

Summary of Model			
R squared	0.635	Standard Error of Estimate	3.859
Adjusted R squared	0.554	Observations	36

Variables in the equation					
Term	Coefficient	Standard Error	Standardised Regression Coefficient (beta)	t value	Significance
Constant	10.142	2.995		3.39	0.008
Turnover	2.640	0.788	0.684	3.35	0.009
71: Number of crises	-3.601	1.366	-0.538	2.64	0.027

Although turnover was the most significant indicator of return, it acts as a proxy for important risk variables. As shown in table 8.12, turnover is strongly associated with a number of employee traits such as long service, fatalism, non-type A personality, insecurity and lack of confidence. In addition it is correlated with variables that directly contribute to crises, particularly strong competition, regulation, producing finished products, and incorporating complex activities: each of these variables is statistically significant (p<0.01).

Thus it seems that the risk-related influence of executive traits and company strategies on financial results operate through the mediating variables of turnover and crisis frequency.

Corporate Risk Propensity

A prompt for this study was a cover of *Business Review Weekly* which warned: 'Obsessed with corporate governance, company boards are afraid to take risks' [Way and Thomson (2003)]. Survey questions designed to quantify organisations' risk propensity took the form of problems which are representative of business decisions and each has four paired alternatives with different financial outcomes and risks (two outcomes x two risks). One of the values is left blank, and respondents are required to estimate it for their organisation. The value is then used to quantify the organisation's utility curve and risk propensity.

The following hypothetical business problems were used:

1. Consider your company is offered the opportunity to participate in a new investment. The project has a 50 percent probability of success which would pay your company $20 million; and the project has a 50 percent probability of failure in which case half the investment would be lost. How much would your company invest to participate in the project? [Howard (1988)]

2. If the payout from the project were $5 million, how much would your company invest to participate in the project?

3. Consider your company is suing a contractor for damages from alleged negligence caused a major accident during construction of a new facility. The best legal advice available to you is that the maximum damages the court would award is $20 million. The contractor has now offered to settle for $10 million. Your legal team is considering its advice and wants to know the company's attitude towards the risks of going to trial. What is the minimum probability of a favourable judgement from a trial for your company to reject the settlement and allow the case to go to trial? [Samson (1987)]

No further information was given. Risk neutral decision makers, though, would follow expected utility and give an answer equal to the expected value of the two alternatives. In the first case, an investment of $40 million has an equal probability of paying $20 million or losing $20 million. In the second case, a $10 million investment has equal probability of paying $5 million or losing $5 million. In the third case, a 50 percent probability of receiving the maximum payout is equal to the contractor's settlement offer. Thus a risk neutral executive would answer $40 million, $10 million and 50 percent, respectively. A risk-averse executive requires a positive expected return to take a risk and would give answers that are less than $40 million and $10 million and more than 50 percent, respectively. A risk-taking executive welcomes the chance of better returns and would give answers that are more than $40 million and $10 million and less than 50 percent, respectively.

A number of respondents (N=53) indicated that their organisation would not participate in any of the investment opportunities, or else gave a very low value suggestive of extreme risk aversion; conversely others (N=8) provided values that fell outside a sensible range (taken as above $60 and $7.5 million and below 21 percent, respectively) suggesting the questions had been misinterpreted or respondents were extremely risk loving. To provide meaningful analysis, extremes were eliminated and this left 52 useable responses.

Following chapter two, respondents were assumed to have an exponential utility function of the following form:

$$u(x) = x.e^{-x/\rho}$$

where u(x) is the utility to the decision maker of a sum $x and ρ is the decision maker's risk tolerance.

Thus responses enabled calculation of three values of ρ for each respondent[65]. The mean values calculated for ρ were $29.7 million, $28.3 million, and $29.9 million, respectively, and these proved statistically equivalent (p<0.01). Risk propensity as calculated from problems one and two was closely linked (R=0.56, p<0.001), but neither was correlated to results from problem three (p>0.7) [66].

---

[65] For investment $I in problems 1 and 2: U(I)=0.5*U(20) + 0.5*U(-0.5I). Using the utility function, this expands to: $I.e^{-I/\rho} = 0.5*20.e^{-20/\rho} - 0.5*0.5*I*e^{0.5I/\rho}$. In problem 3, if π is the probability of receiving $20 million at trial, U(10) = π*U(20) + (1-π).U(0), which expands to: $10*e^{-10/\rho} = \pi*20*e^{-20/\rho}$, and $\rho = 10/\ln(2\pi)$

[66] Although the different methods here yielded virtually identical values of ρ, Hershey et al. (1982) reported that different elicitation methods yield different values

Table 8.16. Correlations of Survey Measures with Corporate Risk Tolerance ($p<0.05$) [* = $p<0.01$]

Survey Measure	Value of R		
	Problem 1	Problem 2	Problem 3
Risk Tolerance from problem 1	1.0	0.557*	
Risk Tolerance from problem 2	0.557*	1.0	
Years of employment	-0.381*		
Years with current employer	-0.480		
Male gender	0.296		
Age in years	-0.399*		
Organisation Turnover (sales revenue)	0.322	0.304	0.323
23:9 I am calm and relaxed when participating in group discussions	-0.275		
23:12 When I get what I want, it's usually because I'm lucky	0.395		
23:21 In general I am less willing to take risks than my colleagues			0.313
29 My behaviour is companionable	-0.325		
38 In my business life I tend to take a lot of financial risks on behalf of my company or clients		0.287	
42:5 My company's industry is innovative	-0.281		
42:6 My company's industry is risky	0.275		0.245
43:4 My company appoints the best candidates as managers	-0.282		
43:5 My company has excellent human resource strategies		0.281	
43:6 My company is very profit oriented	-0.332		
43:7 My company tolerates unpopular ideas	-0.348		
43:8 My company has high turnover of executives	0.346		
43:11 My company produces finished consumer products		0.297	
44:1 My company imposes strong pressures for performance	-0.307		0.366*
44:5: My company is resistant to sharing bad news	0.527*	0.373*	

Table 8.16. (cont)

44:11: My company has decentralised decision making	0.301
45:6 The Board and senior management of my company have expertise covering all areas of operations	-0.385*
45:7 The Board and senior management of my company understand exposures in process operations	-0.373*
45:8 The Board and senior management of my company understand its environmental exposures	-0.313
45:9 The Board and senior management of my company understand its financial exposures	-0.412*
46:3 My company has an ethical approach to business	-0.387*
46:4 My company has high standards for product quality	-0.445*
46:5 My company cuts corners to get results	0.346
46:6 My company takes pride in innovative business models	-0.423*

The next step was to use ρ for each respondent as the dependent variable in univariate regressions against other data from the survey. The most significant (p<0.05) relationships are shown in table 8.16.

Risk tolerance tended to be higher for: males; younger and shorter-serving employees; respondents who believe in chance and feel they take risks in business; and for respondents who are neither companionable nor calm in group discussionsA higher level of risk tolerance was associated with: an industry that is risky and not innovative; higher sales revenue (which was true for each measure); companies whose Boards lack expertise in risks associated with operations, environment and finance; companies which are not profit oriented, cut corners to get results, do not have an ethical approach to business, do not have high standards for product quality and do not take pride in innovative business models; and organisations which resist sharing bad news, do not appoint the best candidates as managers, do not tolerate unpopular ideas and have high turnover of executives; and in companies which produce finished consumer goods, and have decentralised decision making and excellent human resource strategies.

Values of ρ as obtained from the survey were then analysed using multiple regression. Results are shown in tables 8.17 and 8.18.

Table 8.17. Statistics Associated with Corporate Risk Tolerance – Problem 1

Summary of Model					
R squared	0.900	Standard Error of Estimate			13.790
Adjusted R squared	0.8490	Observations			52
Variables in the equation					
Term	Coefficient	Standard Error	Standardised Regression Coefficient (beta)	t value	Significance
Constant	-60.13	27.54		-2.18	0.061
23:22 Everyone should have an equal chance and an equal say	26.58	4.794	0.645	5.54	0.001
46:6 My company takes pride in innovative business models	-28.00	-6.417	-0.520	-4.36	0.002
46:4 My company has high standards for product quality	-31.91	-8.213	-0.498	-3.89	0.005
42:2 My company's industry is fast growing	-14.857	-5.498	-0.335	-2.70	0.027

In two of the cases, a powerful parsimonious solution was obtained: four variables explained 85 percent of the variance in estimates of ρ from the first hypothetical problem, and 90 percent of the variance from the third problem.

Using responses to the first business problem, increased corporate risk tolerance is linked to employees with egalitarian views ('everyone should have an equal chance and an equal say'), companies in slow growing industries, and companies which have low quality standards and do not take pride in innovative business models.

Table 8.18. Statistics for Corporate Risk Tolerance – Problem 3

<u>**Summary of Model**</u>

R squared	0.936	Standard Error of Estimate	13.806
Adjusted R squared	0.904	Observations	52

<u>**Variables in the equation**</u>

Term	Coefficient	Standard Error	Standardised Regression Coefficient (beta)	t value	Significance
Constant	170.88	26.89		6.36	0.001
43:1 My company recruits high calibre employees	63.82	8.25	1.145	7.74	0.001
23:1 Many important decisions are based on insufficient information	37.04	5.68	0.728	6.53	0.001
22 Value of investments	22.32	4.32	0.703	5.17	0.001
46:8 My company has an Enterprise Risk Management policy	-11.67	4.33	-0.345	2.70	0.027

Responses to the third business problem show that increased corporate risk tolerance is linked to employees who accept ambiguity ('many important decisions are based on insufficient information') and have more investments; and to companies which recruit high calibre employees and do not have an Enterprise Risk Management policy. Analysis of responses to the second business problem showed that only one variable (weak industry regulation) was significant, and it explained 34 percent of the variance.

Another measure of risk propensity came in a question which told respondents that their organisation had received a windfall capital inflow equal to five percent of assets and asked what proportion of these funds would the organisation allocate to acquisition of existing business or plant. 37 percent of respondents said 20 percent or less; 26 percent chose between 21 and 40 percent; and 40 percent expected their organisation to allocate over 40 percent of the windfall to acquisition. There was no significant link ($p > 0.15$) between the preference for acquisition and measures of risk propensity calculated above. However, over 70 percent of the bias towards acquisition was explained by the respondents' agreement with the proposition that 'in my business life I tend to take a lot of financial risks on behalf of my company or clients.' Executives clearly see acquisition as a risky strategy.

Discussion

This Survey is the first of its type to comprehensively evaluate the risk management practices of companies and simultaneously examine the attitudes of executives towards risk. It aimed to quantify these practices and attributes, establish links between risk-taking and financial performance, and identify factors that determine organisations' risk outcomes. A large part of its success has come from the active support of the Australian Institute of Company Directors, which is one of the country's leading professional bodies.

The survey obtained responses from over 170 executives, 47 percent of them directors of their organisation. Comparison of the mean survey responses against the gender, industry and organisation size of AICD membership showed a close match, and suggested that respondents are a good cross-section of Australian senior executives and directors.

The most important finding is that each organisation can expect to be affected by a crisis, or by a serious incident with the potential for crisis, on average once every two years. Importantly they are not random events as half can be explained in terms of company practices and strategies.

A 'corporate crisis' can be defined as: a single incident or issue which escalates uncontrollably and causes such serious damage to the assets, reputation and performance of an organisation that its viability is threatened [Coleman (2004)]. The causes are sourced in: product defect, operational failure, finance, organisation, regulation and external threats. Thus crises arise because of the occurrence of the 'wrong' scenario following selection of a risky strategy [Porter (1985: 476)]; or through failures within linked systems.

An organisation's risk outcomes result from overlays imposed by societal constraints, industry regulation and competition, and the organisation's strategic decisions and processes. Factors which are typically thought to trigger crises and serious incidents – such as risk management practices and executives' attributes – have minimal direct influence: about half of all crises and serious incidents can be traced to structural exposures, pressure for results, and poor management practices.

Table 8.19 shows a 'Quick Risk Quiz' with eleven questions from the Survey which were most strongly linked to poor risk outcomes. Although a five-point scale was used, it is likely that respondents who agreed or disagreed with the question would answer yes and no, respectively, to the identical questions as posed in the quiz.

Table 8.19. Quick Risk Quiz

Think about whether your organisation:	
1. Is in a regulated industry	Yes/No
2. Has many complex activities	Yes/No
3. Has direct investments offshore	Yes/No
4. Produces finished consumer goods or services	Yes/No
5. Has a high level of internal competition	Yes/No
6. Has implemented repeated cost-cutting	Yes/No
7. Cuts corners to get results	Yes/No
8. Is expanding rapidly	Yes/No
9. Has a Board with expertise in all areas of operations	Yes/No
10. Has an ethical approach to business	Yes/No
11. Appoints best candidates as managers	Yes/No
Scoring Questions 1-7: 1 for 'Yes', 0 for 'No'; Questions 8-11: 0 for 'Yes', 1 for 'No'.	

Risk-prone companies are in industries which are regulated, uncompetitive, technologically advanced and not responsive to consumer needs. Companies which experience crises have activities which contain the seeds of major problems. They undertake many complex activities, and this sets them up for strategic failures from a wave of knock-on impacts through process systems. Crisis-prone companies produce finished products and so any failure means they face immediate customer impact. They also have offshore investments which are common sources of crises because of control and reporting difficulties.

Given the influence of company strategy and goals, it is not surprising that companies that are crisis-prone have Boards which lack expertise, and have weak management structures through not appointing the best candidates as managers. Apart from structural factors, companies create the potential for crises by promoting a pressure-cooker atmosphere with demands for results and repeated cost-cutting programs. This inevitably leads to instability; but it also induces a climate of corner cutting, and tolerance of low standards in product quality and performance.

Thus organisations experience crises because of their strategies and processes, rather than an absence of good risk management practices.

Companies which do not experience crises take practical steps to monitor problems through product quality reviews and attention to brand and reputation protection; and they are more likely to have appropriate policies and contingency plans in place. These thumbnail sketches enable development of simple measures of organisations' risk-propensity.

Table 8.20 shows that the quiz score is a powerful indicator of crisis frequency. Executives in 62 percent of companies which experienced a crisis either agreed or strongly agreed to at least four questions. Put another way, 72 percent of organisations with a quiz score of four or more had experienced a crisis in the previous three years. Thus the Quiz could be a useful way of quickly indicating whether an organisation has an elevated probability of experiencing a crisis.

Table 8.20. Quick Risk Quiz - Scores

Crises in last three years - #	Percent of Companies with Quiz Score	
	0-3	≥ 4
0	72.6	27.4
1-2	45.9	54.1
≥ 3	17.4	82.6
Memo: ≥ 1	38.1	61.9

When crises occur, they most commonly involve reputational issues; followed by process failures, and product defects. Although plant fires, fatal accidents and serious frauds are common (each causing a serious incident in ten percent of the organisations every three years), they rarely escalate to crises. This possibly reflects the ability of organisations to contain such issues and manage them using traditional public relations strategies. Criminal activities, including extortion, cause minimal impact and rarely lead to serious incident or crisis (affecting less than two percent of organisations).

Although various types of crises tend to be lumped together, they have different root causes. For instance, reputational crises occur in organisations with corner cutting, rapid complex activities, centralised decision making and a high level of internal competition. Operational crises occur in organisations with cost-cutting programs, low turnover of executives, directors who are not comfortable with RM processes, and a regulated industry. This suggests that reputational crises arise in the way an organisation is governed, whereas operational crises stem from inadequate resources and staid management.

A second important finding from the survey is that crises have significant financial impact on organisations. In fact, after turnover, the frequency of crises proved the most significant of all variables and explains 28 percent of the variation in return.

In rough terms, a crisis reduces the expected return on shareholder funds by about 1.5 percent. For a typical organisation with $200-500 million in shareholder funds, a crisis cuts profits by between three and ten million dollars a year for several years. This confirms anecdotal reports that crises cost between ten and fifty million dollars [Coleman (2004)].

Regression showed that only a few percent of variation in any of the risk outcomes is *directly* explained by executive attributes. These include tolerance for ambiguity ('risk is higher when facing situations we do not understand'), achievement orientation ('I have always wanted to be better than others') and a tendency to work hard ('compared to the average manager I give much more effort'). This finding was a surprise, but – as discussed in relation to the previous survey – could arise because executive traits do not act directly on risk taking but exert their influence through mediating variables such as company risk evaluation and risk propensity. Senior executives, in particular, could be expected to self-select their organisation, and their personal attributes would mould, or be moulded by, its attitudes. This explains the linkages between executive traits and attributes of their organisation which predispose it to crises. For instance, executives in slow growing companies are insecure and not aggressive; and those in companies which do not appoint the best managers are fatalistic (belief that others control their lives), not type A personalities (e.g. they do not set deadlines), and have a hierarchical view of the world.

Similarly executive traits and risk attitudes provided little direct explanation for variation in organisations' risk propensity. Executives' traits did explain a number of high-risk strategies including rapid expansion of the company, belief that it can take well-judged risks, reward for entrepreneurial risk-taking, pride in innovative business models, and success in implementing new strategies. Up to a quarter of these variables was explained by executive traits, particularly: being companionable; and belief that outcomes are controllable and that planning can minimise risk.

Thus it seems that executive traits impact on organisation parameters, rather than directly driving risk propensity and risk outcomes. This implies that organisation risk is a pooled outcome of executives' risk propensity: in other words, corporate risk propensity is an output of group dynamics.

This means that it must be measured using group responses or revealed corporate behaviour rather than (say) the average responses of a firm's senior executives.

These findings propose the model shown in figure 8.1: executive attributes are related to industry characteristics and company size, and feed into organisation strategies and practices; these in turn combine with industry features to determine the frequency of crises, and – along with turnover - have major impact on financial results. Return on Shareholder Funds (ROSH) is directly correlated with turnover and inversely correlated with crisis frequency. The influence of risk on financial performance is not surprising given that executives report that an average of 49 percent of decisions taken by their Board involve risk. The issue is likely to grow in importance as 73 percent of executives believe that the level of risk facing their organisation had risen in the last three years; and 69 percent expect a similar trend in the next three years.

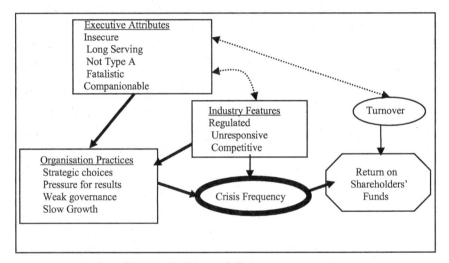

Fig. 8.1. Depiction of Risk's Sources and Consequences

The risks of greatest concern comprise computer breakdowns; external factors including reputation, competitor activities and government regulation; and internal factors including operating processes, occupational health and organisational issues.

It might be a surprise that computer breakdown was noted by 53 percent of respondents to make this issue the most common potential risk. However, modern organisations are exceedingly dependent upon technology, and it has proved a disappointment through under-performance of high cost projects and unreliability of many PC based systems. As just one recent example of an IT project failure, Hughes and Needham (2004: 1) reported that the National Australia Bank suffered "a cost blow-out of up to $600 million on a software project". The poor quality, performance and payout of current computer systems is similar to that of cars in the 1970s and early 1980s: the IT industry may be facing the same performance blowtorch which was felt by car manufacturers during the 1980s.

The second most common potential risk is reputation: this, too, is easily understood following high profile corporate crises - such as the collapse of Ansett Airlines in 2001 and the massive product recall by Pan Pharmaceuticals in 2003 – which have sensitised Boards to potential damage from operational failures. Almost half the responding organisations have a strategy in place to respond to threats to brand and reputation.

There are mixed messages in the report that 39 percent of executives see government regulation as a major source of risk. At one level, regulation is intrusive and a risk which ranks with traditional concerns such as occupational health and product defects. On the other hand, regulation is clearly having an impact, and – if properly designed – should be achieving its goals. This suggests a continuing need for government to ensure its regulation is appropriate; and - in times of activist governments - it behoves those being regulated to constructively work alongside governments to help develop regulations which meet policy objectives with least burden.

An interesting feature of the ranking of potential risks is that operational issues which have proven to be frequent causes of actual crises – such as strikes, fraud and industrial accidents - were well down the list of concerns. And those risks which have caused the worst corporate crises – environment and finance – rank even further down. This disengagement between actual events and perception is familiar to students of decision making: Lovallo and Kahneman (2003), for instance, document the tendency for managers to ignore population-based statistics in preference to their own personalised estimates.

Risk management (RM) practices by organisations vary considerably according to their size, industry and philosophy. Overall this shows that risk management is strongest in organisations in the finance and insurance sectors and weakest in manufacturing and services. Industries which are relatively weak on risk management practices are characterised as competitive, and - counter-intuitively - as risky; whilst those which display best RM practices tend to be described as regulated and endorsing the objectives of Corporate Social Responsibility.

A major determinant of RM practices is the Board: those organisations whose Board has risk as a major concern are more likely to develop an enterprise risk management policy and other appropriate polices. The same is true of larger organisations, public companies, and organisations which are in the finance sector and are profit oriented.

Just over half the organisations make risk management a formal process which covers the whole organisation, and two thirds have provided formal RM training. 57 percent of organisations have a Board Risk Management policy, and about the same proportion seeks to minimise risk through procedures including disaster plans to cope with identified risks, risk assessment of strategic proposals, and regular monitoring of product quality.

In most organisations responsibility for managing risks sits with either senior managers (37 percent of organisations) or in specialist risk management groups (36 percent). The latter are primarily in finance and insurance firms. Only 31 percent of organisations believe that the Board identifies risks itself, and most rely on the risk group, Board papers and less formal communications.

The Survey found that virtually all executives believe that taking risks is essential for success, but few are willing to actually do so: 85+ percent believe that risk is essential for success, but only 17 percent take a lot of financial risks in their business life. What are we to make of an intelligent group that recognises the need for risk, but is unwilling to embrace it? A pointer to the reason for this dichotomy came from gambling attitudes where executives' risk propensity is almost exactly the same as that of the general public. This suggests that their risk taking is socially conditioned: the risk propensity of any group is an outcome of its own dynamics and pressures from its context, rather than the average of its members.

Although any Survey involving risk will naturally focus on some negative issues, executives were generally very positive. Most judged their industry as competitive, responsive to customer needs and socially responsible; regulation is strong and profits only modest; whilst risk is low. Their companies are ethical, with a balanced focus on performance, profit and people; the Board and management are competent, and have high expectations in regards to quality and internal controls. This strong affirmation of positive organisation values is a powerful counter to those who criticise the ethics and stakeholder commitment of executives.

Another outcome of the survey was to calibrate corporate risk propensity, ρ, using executives' responses to hypothetical business decisions. This showed that risk tolerance is influenced by age (it is reduced by older, experienced executives); whilst it increases in companies with larger turnover, offshore investments and decentralised decision making.

The average value of ρ calculated from survey responses was $29.3 million, which is comparable to that derived in chapter two for US companies whose risk propensity fell in a range equivalent to $A (2003) 25-50 million. The US companies are significantly larger than the Australian sample (by at least a factor of ten in terms of turnover) and - given that risk taking rises with size - qualitatively different values would have been expected. Although risk propensity varies according to its context and compiling the data using different methodologies does not permit comprehensive comparisons, an intriguing possibility is that the risk propensity of Australian firms could be *higher* than that of their US peers.

This material also has implications for the way Boards might treat risk in the future. The first is that risk management (RM) is not well advanced in Australia. Only half the responding organisations have adopted good RM practices, and the take up appears lower amongst organisations that are most at risk.

Another gap is that organisations have not matched risk management practices to their identified risks. For instance, companies that sell finished consumer goods and are concerned at product defects are actually slightly less likely to formally monitor quality at Board level. In fact, almost half the companies do not have comprehensive plans in place to respond to identified risks.

A second implication is that risk outcomes are not significantly influenced by RM practices: industry factors and broader organisation strategy and policies are the main contributors to crisis frequency. These major risk factors can be neatly summarised into eleven Yes/No questions: organisations with a score of four or more are most at risk. This means that organisations can evaluate their relative risk profile, and then tailor specific strategic initiatives to tackle exposures.

A third implication (and strong justification for better risk management) is that poor risk outcomes significantly reduce returns: a crisis typically cuts return on shareholder funds by almost two percent for several years.

The characteristics of senior executives do not directly impact risk outcomes; rather they are shaped by industry norms and organisational mores, and in turn determine organisational strategy and thus affect risk. Firms which wish to increase their risk taking need to decentralise their decision making, and encourage greater participation in the process by younger, less experienced executives.

A fifth finding is that – although Australian executives appear risk averse – the risk propensity of their organisations is no lower than that of their US counterparts and may actually be higher. This inevitably impacts strategic decisions and financial performance.

CHAPTER 9   Summary and Discussion

This book started with two simple research questions: when individuals make decisions, what leads them to choose a risky alternative? And: what determines whether the decision proves correct?

Through the literature survey, analyses of published empirical data, and surveys of manager outlooks, answers to these questions come logically in two strands of thought: the influence of risk on natural, or real-world, decision making; and the links between risk and organisation performance. This chapter uses these two headings to discuss the book's principal findings.

Influence of Risk on Real-World Decision Making: An Update of *Applied Behavioural Economics*

In the 1960s and 1970s, research into individuals' decision making was focussed on personal factors such as the role of skill and the ability to influence the outcome (real and imagined). Decisions were acknowledged to have a probability basis, but people's methodology clearly did not meet statisticians' tests. In short, decision theory had a qualitative perspective and research was directed at determining the *process* of reaching a decision.

However, in the early 1980s the field of subjective, qualitative decision research was abandoned in favour of what McFadden (1999) called K-T Man (in contrast to the rational Chicago man). He acknowledged the achievements of psychologists-turned-cconomists Daniel Kahneman and Amos Tversky: in a decade of dazzling intellectual power, they used laboratory experiments to systematically expose the weaknesses in pre-1980s decision theory, and developed a replacement in Prospect Theory [Kahneman and Tversky (1979)]. The latter made objective risk the cornerstone of a quantitative model of decision making.

Although proponents of Prospect Theory and like models allowed that personal, qualitative considerations arose through framing and editing of decisions, these were generally dismissed as of interest only for the biases they might introduce. Similarly the context of risk received little consideration beyond acknowledging different treatments of decision types such as those involving losses and gains, or high and low probabilities. Moreover the models typically assumed a continuous distribution of decision makers between the extremes of risk aversion and risk embrace. Unfortunately – as pointed out in chapter six – such quantitative models are generally unable to explain decision making in the real world.

The poor applicability of normative decision models should not be a surprise as decision making has always been an all-too-fallible process. As far back as the 17th century, English philosopher Francis Bacon (1620: Book 1, aphorism 46) wrote:

"The human understanding when it has once adopted an opinion (either as being the received opinion or as being agreeable to itself) draws all things else to support and agree with it. And though there be a greater number and weight of instances to be found on the other side, yet these it either neglects and despises, or else by some distinction sets aside and rejects, in order that by this great and pernicious predetermination the authority of its former conclusions may remain inviolate."

Another indication of the wide rejection of normative decision theories is implicit in folklore and common wisdom because so much of it is designed to simplify everyday decision making: 'when you're on a good thing, stick to it'; 'a stitch in time saves nine'; 'look before you leap'; '*caveat emptor*'; and so on.

As noted in the comprehensive study of managerial behaviour by March and Shapira (1987), decision makers do not follow normative decision theory and do not manage risk with academic rigor. Decision makers are loss-averse, rather than risk-averse; and they alter risk preferences in light of how much they could lose relative to a reference level. Although experience tends to form relatively stable risk attitudes and decision processes, most decision makers are willing to alter their risk propensity in light of circumstances, including needs.

This willingness to alter risk propensity – which is termed 'risk-sensitive foraging' in animal studies [Smallwood (1996)] - is exhibited by animals, humans and organisations across a wide variety of settings and is probably the most striking aspect of decision making. The process incorporates a reference level which instinct anchors at survival: below this level, a decision maker faces demise and will prefer any alternative that can result in survival. Then, in a hierarchy reminiscent of Maslow (1954), better endowed decision makers target a satisficing level; whilst the wealthiest turn loss averse and husband their endowments. As March and Shapira (1987: 1409) found: "fewer risks should, and would, be taken when things are going well."

This risk sensitivity in decision making displays predictable patterns that are most easily thought of in terms of the source of the influences (either internal to the decision maker or not), and as the extent to which the decision influences are generalisable across risk types.

The principal source of received or external risk attitudes is genetic inheritance, largely personality and instinctive attitudes towards risk (which are often seen as cognitive biases). Received risk attitudes also come from a controlling institution (e.g. an employer); or can be imposed by the pressures and expectations of society. Internally sourced risk attitudes are shaped or elected by an individual decision maker. These include identification with the outcome; incorporation of a reference or target level in setting decision parameters; trade-offs between current and future costs and benefits; and – because few decisions are made in isolation - the portfolio of choices facing a decision maker.

These seven determinants of risk attitudes can be stable and used widely across different types of risky decision making; or they can be specific to one setting or risk type and apply to a single decision. Pressures from an institutional framework, for instance, tend to be confined to decisions that are specific to that institution. As an example, employees of a charitable trust may be very risk-averse at work, but this need not carry over into their personal lives. On the other hand, a decision maker will continually take into account the portfolio of decisions, both past and pending: thus the decision to change employment or make a significant investment will be influenced by recent vocational and financial choices, and will shape future decisions.

This approach broadens decision criteria to encompass the personal attributes of individual decision makers and the influences that come from their decision environment. This is consistent with the contemporary rediscovery of classical, positive theories of decision making under risk. The figure below classifies the seven major influences of risk on decision making according to risk source and decision generalisability, and then uses them as the headings for discussion in the remainder of this section.

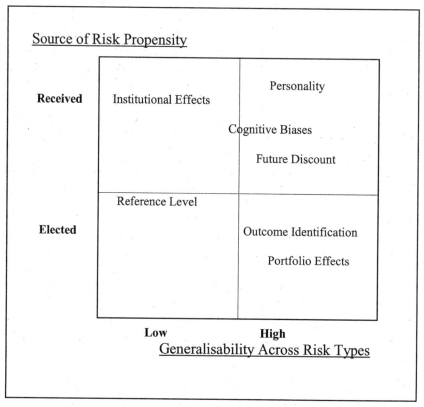

Fig. 9.1. Influences of Risk on Decision Making

Personality

Between a quarter and a third of the variation in risk propensity is explained by decision maker personality [Trimpop (1994); table 4.1 and chapter 7]. And, although people differ in their preferred degree of aversion to loss, probably only a quarter of the population can be described as naturally risk taking [Hartog et al. (2000) and Schneider and Lopes (1986)], although the proportion is close to half for managers [MacCrimmon and Wehrung (1984) and Williams and Narendran (1999)].

Risk takers are motivated by a desire for reward, whilst risk-averse people are motivated by a desire for security [Lopes (1987)]. Risk takers are more likely to be single with lower wealth levels; engage in several types of risk across work and leisure; and drink alcohol and smoke cigarettes [Balabanis (2001)]. Age and gender have an inconsistent effect on risk taking, although older people and women may be slightly more risk averse [Byrnes et al. (1999)].

The role of nationality is also unclear, but most studies suggest the following ranking from risk-averse to risk-embracing: Southern Europe (Greece, Portugal), Japan and Korea, Latin America, Middle East (Israel, Saudi Arabia) and West Asia (Turkey), Western Europe, Scandinavia, Australia, North America, and East Asia [Hofstede (1997) and Yates (1990)]. When overconfidence is measured as the decision makers' estimated probability of being correct minus their demonstrated accuracy, Asian decision makers tend to be more overconfident than those in Western nations.

Risk takers are psychologically flexible [Wally and Baum (1994)]. They are usually better educated, and have a history of successful risk-taking, tolerate ambiguity, seek novel experiences, and rapidly respond to stimuli. They are described as adaptable, adventurous, aggressive, informal, optimistic and sociable. Risk takers have a need to be better and faster, and agree with statements such as 'I set difficult goals for myself which I attempt to reach.' They are typical Type-A personalities. Risk taking can also be higher in people who prefer hierarchical organisation structures (with experts in control) because they have lower perceptions of risk from any given outcome [Slovic (2000)].

Risk-averse decision makers see higher risk in any action, allocate more effort to risk management, and so are more likely to succeed in entrepreneurial settings. Risk neutral decision makers give greatest weight to the facts of a decision, and they tend to place greatest value on expert input because it is related to decision facts [Eeckhoudt and Godfroid (2000)].

A mechanism that is useful in understanding this result is the proposal by Lopes (1987) that decision makers' risk propensity leads them to place different weights on the consequences of success or failure: risk takers look more to a decision's potential and so place greater weight on success; whereas risk-averse decision makers place greater weight on the costs of failure. Risk propensity leads decision makers to focus on different aspects of the same choice, and to weight them according to inherent attributes, rather than probability of occurrence.

Decisions are driven by the affect of a successful outcome, where 'affect' is used with its psychological meaning of the associated feeling or emotion. For instance, applicable skill is an important consideration in making choices: decision makers prefer a choice where they can add value by reducing the expected risks or costs of an event [Heath et al. (1999)].

Allocation of decision weights according to choice attributes is consistent with a number of physiological studies. Those using an MRI by Greene et al. (2001) found that different parts of the brain – and hence different decision criteria (e.g. emotion or logic) – are used when decision features vary. Miller et al. (2000) found a switch in the brain that gives decision makers a view of any decision that alternates from the optimistic, big picture to a cautious, detail focus.

This idea can be extended so that a variety of factors influence the relative weight that is placed on success and failure. These might include the affect of each outcome, and role of skill. Thus when decision makers face a distant outcome or one where their skill can control the risk, they focus on the benefit and its affect. Conversely when the outcome involves a near-term consequence or possibly large loss, decision makers focus on the risk involved.

Another possible explanation for the mechanism proposed above is that personality mediates motivation to drive subjective weighting of decision cues. This could operate as shown in the figure below that assumes a standard risk:reward trade-off: to the left of the diagram, the probability of success is low and the potential reward is high; whilst to the right, the probability of success is high, although reward is low. As risk-embracing decision makers concentrate on potential payout so their decision weights are highest at low probability of success; whereas risk-averters place greater weight on probability of success.

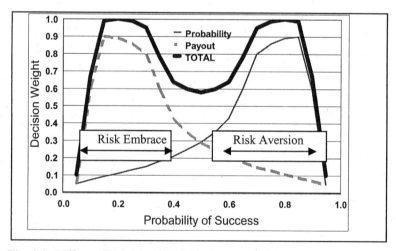

Fig. 9.2. Different Weights of Risk Embracers and Averters

A corollary of the assumption that decision makers' risk propensity leads them to focus on different decision parameters is that they do not have a continuous utility function as assumed in many standard decision models.

Heavy Discount for Future Costs

An important influence on decision weights is time until the outcome. This is because decision makers facing choices with a future outcome place a significantly greater weight on their benefits than they place on the costs of achieving the outcome, including risks of failure [Sagristano et al. (2002)]. That is, decision makers use a higher discount rate for future costs than for future benefits.

This led Das and Teng (2001) to develop a temporal framework to explain how attitudes towards risky decisions change depending on whether results are immediate or delayed. Given that the discounted value of any delayed payoff falls with the length of delay, the decision maker's current situation becomes less important as the outcome moves further into the future. Thus the decision maker's immediate situation and current endowment are most important to short-term decisions; whereas future choice is related more to the decision maker's innate risk attitudes, including their perception of planning horizons.

Panel data from US households compiled by Lawrance (1991) found that the household's discount rate (i.e. aversion to delay in receipt of income) is inversely related to its income: less wealthy households are less willing to accept delay, and will prefer to accept a risk to their income, rather than accept the possibility of postponing a possibly favourable result. This replicates the finding of Kacelnik and Bateson (1996) where animals are more willing to risk variability in outcome than they are to accept the risk of a delay in the outcome.

Another impact of time is that a shortage promotes risk aversion. More rapid decision making is required under time pressure, and Mano (1990) found that this simplifies decision techniques and leads to over-weighting of negative data.

This is consistent with ambiguity aversion: when decision makers do not have enough data, time or resources to adequately analyse a problem, the surrounding uncertainty and doubt open up the possibility of loss: decision makers adopt a risk averse position and prefer the safe choice. A related bias results from suspected information asymmetry, so that decision makers prefer a known outcome, rather than a possibly better, but unfamiliar, alternative: thus they retain assets that would never be bought. In terms proposed by Simon (1955), bounded decision makers are risk averse. Conversely their confidence rises markedly as they gain background information, even if it is not directly relevant to the decision [Yates (1990)].

Decision Making Biases

So many biases have been identified in human decision making that Kahneman (1991) suggests researchers' diligence may have uncovered too many! In any event, the biases are amenable to aggregation and – as discussed in chapter seven – can be grouped into seven sets of principal characteristics of decision making under risk.

These groups form decision rules that provide mental shortcuts (`heuristics') to simplify a potentially complicated process, much in the same way as making all hazard lights red simplifies warnings. These rules, however, can lead to oversimplification; they also make a poor fit with risk sensitivity and Nature's pressure to throw up opportunities for natural selection. The most important biases in managerial decision making are: overconfidence; framing; and representativeness.

Overconfidence has complex roots. People typically rank their skills in the top quartile [Svenson (1981)] and believe they can successfully shape outcomes [Langer (1975)]. Decision makers not only exaggerate their degree of control over events, but will seek outcomes which rely on their skill rather than on chance [Howell (1971)]. Although managers, in particular, do not like gambling, they will take greater risks when they have control over the execution of the decision. Inevitably when their skill is low or inadequate, the risk of failure is high. Gambling studies have shown that the most addictive games are those which require skill [Balabanis (2001)], and the skill required in many difficult business decisions probably explains the prevalence of high risk management strategies.

Overconfidence leads decision makers to minimise the prospect of negative or adverse outcomes. Competitor response, for instance, will be downplayed [Lovallo and Kahneman (2003)]; the high probability of failure of complex systems will be discounted; and flawless execution will be assumed for ambitious strategies. As a result, decision makers are overly optimistic in assessing any decision. They can also prove slow to modify their assessment, either ignoring new information or misinterpreting it as confirming the initial position. Overconfidence induces a number of biases in decision making which compound the probability of failure [Camerer and Lovallo (1999)].

Framing is evidenced by a change in decision preference when identical data are represented in a different format. The bias is stark in experiments that use the example of two drug trials which have either a 20 percent mortality rate or 80 percent survival rate, and find that decision makers are not neutral between these identical choices. Other experiments show that twice as many people prefer a risky alternative when it is described as an opportunity than when it is framed as a threat [Highhouse and Yüce (1996)]. One of the most graphic depictions of framing's effects came in a study by Frederick (2003) of intergenerational time preferences which compared lives saved today and those saved in the future. Seven different elicitation methods variously valued a life today as equal to between less than one and more than 45 lives in 100 years.

A number of features of organisation behaviour actively frame decisions. The first is a high level of internal competition – especially for resources such as staff and capital – which means that decision proponents have a vested interest in over-stating the positive aspects of their case. The second feature is an unwillingness to question consensus expectations as pessimism can be seen as being disloyal to the team [Lovallo and Kahneman (2003)].

Framing can also be internal in the way that decision makers perceive information, which Wang (2004) calls *self-framing*. This is the mechanism that gives rise to an inverse relationship between risk and reward: an event that is preferred is expected to have more benefits and greater probability of success. Thus low risk outcomes have high expected return; and high risk, less preferred outcomes have lower returns.

As noted above, risk-embracing decision makers tend to concentrate on the benefits of success and risk averse decision makers look to the costs of failure. Finucane et al. (2000) go further to suggest that decision makers refer to a mental database of images, and mentally tag the decision's attributes with positives and negatives. Thus low risk activities are seen as moral, beneficial, known and prestigious; and a decision that is preferred tends to have more perceived benefits, and to be judged as more probable.

Representativeness is the inclination to reach decisions based on a small, non-random sample (such as favourable recent outcomes, or personal experience) [Grether (1980)]. In part this is due to limits on decision makers' capacity to assemble and process large samples: Miller (1956), for instance, was only somewhat tongue in cheek in suggesting that human recall capacity was seven, as Caraco et al. (1990) found that birds choose with a sample of eight and Real (1991) estimated that bees have a sample of 15. But simple small samples are relatively efficient: the estimate from a sample of ten has a 70 percent probability of being within ±30 percent of a distribution's true mean.

Small samples have a cost, though. As suggested by Tversky and Kahneman (1971) they encourage overweighting of recent experiences and underweighting of population-based data. Small samples are also subject to self-framing: decision makers require a lower standard of proof, including smaller samples, for a preferred outcome than they do for an undesirable event.

There is strong evidence that many of these biases are not limited to humans, but apply in similar fashion to animals . For instance, animal studies have shown that bees and rats are risk averse [Battalio et al. (1985)]; and birds are risk sensitive [Smallwood and Carter (1996)]. Previous outcomes have a bearing on the decisions of gray jays [Waite (2001)] and starlings [Marsh and Kacelnik (2002)]. According to Bateson (2002), animals are driven by an over-arching need to ensure survival, rather than maximisation of utility: irrespective of the merits of choices, they are naturally risk averse, but will turn risk-prone when facing a threat to their survival.

Arguably analysts can have a lot more confidence in the validity and robustness of decision modes and attitudes towards risk when they prove true across different animal species, including humans.

Overconfidence, representativeness and framing combine with excessive optimism to foster a widespread distortion to managerial decisions: the longshot bias. Its operation is clearly shown in table 5.2 which summarises the outcomes of various complex strategies – R&D, IT projects, mineral exploration, M&As – and shows that an average of just 21 percent succeed. Simple math shows that only the top quartile of performers have a better than fifty percent chance of achieving a successful outcome when facing such risks. Thus it is no surprise to find that most people, including managers, put their skill level in the top quartile [Svenson (1981)], as this is the only way to explain the persistence of strategies which are unlikely to prove successful: each strategy proponent is confident they possess the capabilities to ensure success even though the majority of such challenging strategies fail.

What causes risk sensitivity and these decision making biases? A number of researchers [see Hodgson (1995)] have suggested they may have an evolutionary basis and be the result of natural selection which is designed to maximise survival. Although decision anomalies – such as the longshot bias and overconfidence – appear economically sub-optimum, they are actually Nature's way of promoting a diversity of outcomes that is the key to natural selection. Unless some decision makers prefer improbable outcomes, they will never be tested and there will be few discoveries; innovation will not occur; and economic growth cannot capture the Schumpeterian rent that comes from change.

Reference Level

A consequence of decision makers' limited computational capacity is that they rely on reference levels as a guide to the distribution of uncertain events. These include: expectations of others, such as experts or a decision's proponents; historical precedents, including market extremes and milestones (e.g. Dow 10,000); and the current value (e.g. use today's weather as a first approximation to tomorrow's weather). Although recent experience is important to reference levels, its relevance decreases as the decision outcome becomes more distant with less immediate impact.

Reference levels exert their importance through three features of decision making: anchoring and adjustment; assumption of mean reversion; and breakeven results.

The process of anchoring and adjustment is described by Lovallo and Kahneman (2003). The anchor comes from the starting point of any decision, which is typically some kind of sales pitch: it could be a manager seeking funds for a favoured project; a researcher with a brilliant insight; or a financial adviser with a new investment idea. In each case it is in the interests of the decision's proponent to have it go ahead, and so they naturally put a positive – if not necessarily exaggerated – spin on the probable result. Prudent decision makers recognise that the decision can be framed by the self-interest of the sponsor, and adjust the projected result. Inevitably, though, the adjustment is inadequate: the initial estimate acts as a proverbial anchor and provides an optimistic forecast.

Because initial estimates of enthusiastic sponsors are inadequately adjusted, they retain a favourable bias. This explains why new technology projects typically have a success rate of between 15 and 30 percent [Palmer and Wiseman (1999), Whiting (1998)]; and why initial estimates of the costs of pioneer projects are less than half the actual result [Davis (1985)]. Post audits of decisions that assume that normative processes were employed and ignore behavioural biases can be scathing in their criticism. For instance, Flyvbjerg et al. (2002: 279) reviewed cost estimates for over 200 major transportation projects and found a distortion – 90 percent of costs were underestimated by an average of 28 percent – which they felt was so strong that it "is best explained by ... lying".

A second application of reference levels arises because decision makers anticipate mean reversion unless there is reason to think otherwise [Heath et al. (1999)]. In betting studies, this is known as the gamblers' fallacy where decision makers believe that a trend of identical outcomes of independent events (e.g. a run of reds from successive spins of a balanced roulette wheel) will be reversed.

Mean reversion appears to be one of the most important (but largely unrecognised) influences on risky decision making. Although it can readily be shown that historical outcomes of independent events have no bearing on the future outcomes of identical events[67], many important sequential decisions involve events which are not independent. Examples include stockmarket moves, managed investment returns and doctors' diagnoses. As discussed in chapter four, many biases attributed to poor cognition can actually be explained as a product of assuming mean reversion. This is a common decision tool, even for statistically unrelated events.

Another application of reference levels is to establish the breakeven point which distinguishes gains from losses. In general, decision makers are loss averse: they feel a greater decline in utility from any loss than the increase in utility from an equal gain. Their loss aversion grows with the magnitude of loss, which is why poorly performing firms can make decisions which accelerate their decline [Singh (1986)].

Reference levels relate not just to money, but also to other aspects of personal endowment. As a rule, decision makers with greater endowment have a higher reference level. For instance when job risks are measured using accident frequency rates, the cut-off level for a `dangerous job' is lower for better educated workers [Gaba and Viscusi (1998)]. The implication is that higher education brings greater lifetime earnings capability: those with a higher level of occupational endowment are less willing to take risks. Another example comes with illness which reflects a lower level of health endowment: when compared to sick people, healthy subjects are prepared to accept a greater hypothetical shortening of life to remain in good health rather than live longer in ill health [Treadwell and Lenert (1999)]. This arises because healthy people see any hypothetical ill state as more of a loss than would sick people, and hence further below their reference level.

Identification with Outcome

An important aspect of individuals' decision making is that they identify strongly with the preferred outcome. This comes in two guises. The first is

---

[67] Assume a decision maker is facing a series of independent events, say three tosses of a fair coin; and that the results are somehow pre-ordained by a cosmic plan. If the decision maker believes in mean reversion, after two identical outcomes (e.g. both tails), she is likely to predict the opposite on the next throw (i.e. heads). But in three throws of a coin, there are only two possible combinations that will deliver two tails in the first two throws: T-T-T and T-T-H. Thus there remains a 50:50 chance of a head on the third throw, irrespective of the outcomes of the first two throws.

the tendency for decision makers to project the unfolding of decision consequences in light of their own active involvement. Managers have multiple opportunities to optimise the outcome of their decisions through the time from first consideration until execution. At the early stages they negotiate changes, explore alternatives or prevaricate. Later they use expenditure, bargaining and influence to enhance the outcome [Wehrung et al. (1989)].

When decision makers take into account the potential for them to guide decision outcomes, they tend to see the process as unique and hence pay little heed paid to others' experience in comparable situations. Given that most decision makers put their skill in the top quartile of their peers, this renders their expectations of outcomes as far too optimistic.

Identification with decision outcomes also produces overly pessimistic projections of rival alternatives. This is partly strident advocacy and partly the mirror image of hubris or overconfidence in the preferred choice. It also reflects the psychological affect of the tendency to see worse consequences, including greater risks, from unwanted actions.

There are many examples of experts predicting that disaster will follow an unwanted action[68]. One is the statement by the Chairman of the US Securities and Exchange Commission that – because institutions had lifted their share of trading volume on the New York Stock Exchange from 39 percent in 1961 to 68 percent in 1971: "...we are already starting to witness a decline in the unique ability of this country's capital market system to raise capital for many thousands of corporations throughout the country" [Lease et al. (1974: 414)].

As part of their personalisation of decisions, people will endow them with a positive hedonic tone [Antonides et al. (1997)]. Thus low risk activities are judged to be moral, beneficial and prestigious, as well as more rewarding; and they are generally familiar to the decision maker.

Decisions have a large personal component: this involves not just the decision maker's personality, but also their expectation and even aspirations. This explains why results from the Carter Racing survey reported in chapter seven showed that decision makers pay little heed to decision facts; and that about half the variance in decision making was explained by personality, decision style, and expectations.

---

[68] Typical is *"Apres moi, le deluge"* which has famously accompanied Gallic shrugs by President de Gaulle and Louis XV, amongst others

Portfolio Effects

Decision makers do not act in isolation, nor are decisions made in isolation. Most obviously, decisions are path dependent, and are affected by decision makers' prior and prospective choices. This can be partly Bayesian where previous outcomes are factored into decision assessments; and it can be a recognition of the need to diversify outcomes and avoid a series of compounding risks.

One example of decisions' path dependency was provided by Heath et al. (1999) in relation to exercise of employee stock options. The rate of option exercise is sensitive to historical extremes and increases when stock prices rebound from a fall and rise above peaks recorded during the preceding few years. In another setting, Odean (1998) found that investors are more willing to sell assets such as stocks and houses which have risen in price since they were purchased than they are to sell identical assets which have fallen in price.

As noted above, decision makers assume mean reversion unless they have reason to think otherwise. This can encourage managers to persist with a strategy that has proven unsuccessful on the basis that outcomes are about to revert to the mean. This, for instance, might explain results from Odean (1998), and the finding of Baucus and Near (1991) that firms are more likely to break the law if they have a prior conviction. When the causes of failure are systemic, chronic failures can set in: this is why some firms and industries are plagued by recurring crises.

To ensure that the outcomes of serious risks cannot compound, decision makers will diversify their exposures so that risks are minimally correlated and their total exposure (value at risk) is not excessive. Unfortunately this is not always easy to achieve, especially as historical correlations (whether high or low) do not always persist, particularly when systems become stressed. For instance a rapid fall in a major equity market can spill over to affect other markets, even those which are normally minimally correlated. The same can apply to a firm which suffers a crisis, possibly in a narrow operational area, but finds that it suddenly has problems on a broad front because of concerns at its viability from creditors, suppliers, bankers, customers and so on.

An extension of the portfolio effect is the existence of a central decision making style which is applied across different choices [Wehrung et al. (1989)]. This is developed over time and so becomes more pronounced with experience. It is also affected by occupation. For instance lawyers think in terms of longtitudinal cause-and-effect chains of events; whilst psychologists look for historical associations between outcome variables [Amsel et al. (1991)]. Engineers think in systems terms and remember techniques that can be used to solve a problem; whereas doctors think of facts and remember the solutions to problems.

Institutional Framework and Socialisation Effects

Just as personality has a strong influence on individuals' choices under risk, so do organisations' unique attributes determine their risk propensity[69]. Similarly decisions may be made by individuals, but this rarely occurs in isolation from socialising influences around them.

Organisations' policies and norms are lenses through which managers examine decisions; they remove uncertainty by setting objectives and defining acceptable methods to achieve them. But organisations are also social, with complex motivations. Their discretionary (if not always democratic) decision processes leave room for individuals to sway outcomes: self-interest by managers, for instance, may promote loss aversion rather than profit maximisation; similarly the ego of Boards may increase risk propensity. Thus managers' decisions are socialised by those around them, and by the norms and expectations of their organisation and its institutional setting. This is apparent in the findings that facts have little influence on executives' decisions, and that executives' personal traits have little direct influence on their organisation's risk propensity.

An organisation's risk culture has a significant influence on its managers' risk propensity, particularly the way they frame alternatives. Some studies suggest that this can explain as much as half the variance in risky decision making [Bozeman and Kingsley (1998)]. In particular risk taking is promoted when managers trust their subordinates, and when goals are clear; conversely risk is reduced by red tape and insistence on following rules and procedures. Managers can also take advantage of institutional factors to modify a risky choice through negotiation, expenditure or exploring other options to promote a better outcome, and by delay.

The risk culture of organisations is impacted, too, by the composition of management teams. According to Sitkin and Pablo (1992), homogeneity in an organisation's senior management reduces the quality of decision analysis, and can lead to groupthink with extreme perceptions of risk.

Evans (1997) found that individuals' anomalous behaviours are reduced in market settings where diverse decisions smooth outcomes or rational participants exert pressures to correct errors (however, they are not always

---

[69] Hofstede (1997) might argue that nationality shapes the risk-propensity of both corporations and individuals; the direction of cause-and-effect, though, is not germane to this discussion.

eliminated, and need to be recognised in order to explain anomalies [De Bondt and Thaler (1990)]).

The attributes of an organisation and its executives can lead to development of a powerful guiding paradigm (with the meaning intended by Kuhn (1970, 2nd edition)) or framework within which decisions are evaluated. When paradigms constitute patterns of thought, they lead to near reflexive decisions, even with new problems. Their ability to affect whole industries explains the waves of common strategies – diversification, mergers, aggressive downsizing, overinvestment in new markets – that frequently emerge to sweep up many companies simultaneously.

Brogan (1996) provided a good example of the power that paradigms have to sway decisions in his analysis of the presidency of John Kennedy. He contrasts Kennedy's decisiveness over the Berlin blockade, Cuban Missile Crisis and civil rights with his prevarication over the gradual breakdown of Vietnam under the incompetence of President Diem. The explanation (pages 182-183) was the `Cold War paradigm' where Communism was seen as the greatest foe and source of all threats; thus "the peace and prosperity of the United States depended on an active assumption of international responsibility, even to the point of going to war ..." The turmoil in Vietnam was perceived reflexively as an important element in the advance of the Sino-Soviet bloc across Asia and thence to Europe and the world; it was evaluated solely in terms of American prestige and interests. Kennedy and others were blind to the revolutionary nationalism that swept Third World colonies which began to assert their independence from Britain, France, Holland and Portugal in the wake of Japan's eviction from south-east Asia in 1945. Brogan (1996: 182) concluded: "it seems almost incredible that the intellectual foundations of the American commitment should have been so fragile."

Paradigms are seen in organisations, too. Consider the CIA and FBI which are two of the world's pre-eminent decision makers under risk. Kessler (2003) described how CIA Director John Deutch

"diminished its effectiveness by creating a risk-averse atmosphere ... Deutch imposed a rule requiring special approval before a CIA officer could recruit a spy who was not an upstanding citizen ... The extra hassle of obtaining approval meant many CIA officers simply avoided anyone with a history of problems ..."

Similar examination of FBI processes found that Director Louis Freeh was averse to technology and his refusal to have a personal computer sent a powerful anti-technology message to the organisation. Thus as the war against terrorism grew more fierce, the CIA was short of appropriate agents; and the FBI had inadequate technologies.

This experience is frequently seen in corporations, too. For instance, Sykes (1994) describes the driving paradigms and analytical weaknesses that led to a wave of corporate collapses in Australia in the late 1980s and early 1990s. Burrough and Helyar (1990) provide a similar explanation for the near simultaneous US experience.

In conclusion, decision making is not mathematically precise: the ideal normative process of research, analysis and optimisation is simply not consistent with incorporating individual attributes such as personality, nor with comprehending environmental influences such as reference levels and portfolio effects. Moreover decision makers do not develop continuous distributions of probability, nor use monetary values when comparing alternatives; in many cases they do not pay much heed to the facts of a decision. At best they use general cues, and subjectively weight certain aspects of decisions based on internal attributes such as personality and external guides such as paradigms. Not surprisingly, decision theories which are blind to decision makers and their context struggle to explain real-world evidence.

The Links Between Risk and Organisation Performance

This section summarises materials presented earlier in relation to the impact that risk-taking has on organisation performance.

Measures of Organisational Risk

It is not possible to directly measure an organisation's 'risk', and thus a variety of approaches have emerged. These determine risk *ex ante* or *ex post* using either extensive or intensive techniques, and take the form of objectively qualified measures or subjective responses. The typical assumption (and indeed an initial hypothesis in my own research) is that these measures are not related. March and Shapira (1987), for instance, found that managers believe risk is related to negative outcomes, not variance.

There is consistent evidence, though, that many measures of risk are in fact linked: more often than not, the correlations are statistically significant. For instance Miller and Reuer (1996) tested 13 different measures of risk - analysts' forecasts, credit default risk, earnings volatility, and CAPM beta – and found that most were significantly correlated ($p<0.10$). Miller and Bromiley (1990) used factor analysis to form three nine measures of risk: income stream variation; stock returns variation; and strategic risks such as debt to equity and capital intensity. Each was significantly ($p<0.05$) linked.

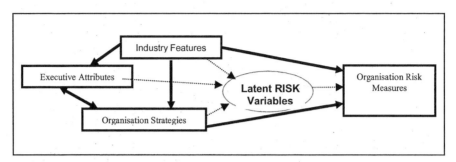

Fig. 9.3. Sources and Measures of Organisation Risk

This suggests that seemingly unrelated measures of risk are actually reflecting common underlying risk attributes that are related to an organisation's characteristics and strategies. This is consistent with results reported in chapters seven and eight, and suggests figure 9.3. Given that most senior executives probably self-select their employment, their attributes are related both to the strategies and practices of their employer, and to principal characteristics of their industry (such as regulation, innovation and risk). Consistent with the Porter (1980) model, the nature of an industry drives organisation strategy, and its decisions are also shaped by executives' attributes. The organisation's strategy and decisions determine its underlying risk. The last is a latent variable that is not directly measurable, but is common to the numerous observable measures of organisation risk. The relationships shown in solid lines in the diagram have been confirmed in the body of this book, and in turn linked to organisational risk outcomes and financial performance.

This mechanism is consistent with the suggestion by Baird and Thomas (1985) that risk is an endogenous variable and impacts firm performance in a two stage process:

> Risk $= fn$ [Strategy, Industry Characteristics]
> Firm Performance $= fn$ [Industry Characteristics, Strategy, Risk]

Thus firms select their risk exposures based on a combination of industry characteristics (such as technology, markets, competition, substitutes, inputs) and internal strategy (organisation, governance, resource allocation, marketing).

Organisational Risk Attractors

According to Chaos Theory, some systems do not approach equilibrium nor decay to instability but remain within a region that is defined by an attractor. Although the system moves unpredictably within the region, it respects its boundaries and in doing so can trace an exquisite geometrical pattern known as a fractal [Gleick (1987)].

Dolan et al. (ca. 2000) propose that organisations are chaotic, and their inherent characteristics act as attractors that confine behavioural results to a particular space. Thus the risk-related performance of any organisation is constrained, although it is unpredictable within these constraints. It is easy to envisage this arising in the way that organisations socialise the risk propensity of their decision makers and form a unique risk culture that establishes a framework that determines risk outcomes. At its most obvious level, this renders some industries and firms as chronically risk prone, whilst others operate successfully without incident.

The risk survey reported in chapter eight pointed to determinants of the organisational risk attractor, or how likely a firm is to occupy a risk-prone behavioural space. For instance, risk propensity is higher in organisations with decentralised decision making and those with greater participation in decision making by younger and less experienced executives.

Companies which are crisis prone (defined as a report by their executives that they have suffered three or more crises in the previous three years) are less likely than crisis-free companies to conduct risk assessments as part of new strategies, or monitor product quality. They are also less likely to have plans to cope with disaster or manage threats to reputation. Companies which are crisis-prone tend to be in regulated industries, larger, with many complex activities and are involved in manufacturing. Executives in crisis-prone companies report that they impose strong cost pressures, cut corners to get results, and tolerate poor managers.

The analysis in chapter eight concluded that about half of all crises and serious incidents can be traced to structural exposures, pressure for results and poor management practices. Through their strategic decisions on industry, process and market, organisations establish operating exposures and create the potential for bad risk outcomes. They compound potential risks by promoting a pressure cooker atmosphere through demands for results and repeated cost-cutting programs. Thus it seems that corporate strategies and practices are the major influences on risk outcomes, rather than risk management practices such as policies and procedures.

Very little of the variation in crisis frequency is directly related to executive attributes. This counter-intuitive finding is consistent with evidence that the influence of executive traits is exerted through mediating variables such as company strategies, risk evaluation and risk propensity. For instance, companies which are crisis-prone tend to be large and in regulated industries; executives in those sectors share attributes such as long service, fatalism ('when I get what I want it's usually because I'm lucky'), and non type-A personalities. Conversely companies which are relatively crisis-free tend to be in competitive industries, appoint the best candidates as managers and have high product quality standards; their executives are hard driving, type-A personalities who are confident and self-sufficient.

Another influence on organisation risk comes from framing. Kessler (2003) provides graphic examples of how imposition of a few relatively simple rules by the directors of the CIA and FBI were able to significantly reshape their organisations' decision making, including risk propensity. Pablo et al. (1996) take this further and suggest that framing can be used to establish organisational risk levels by modifying the attitudes of executives who are involved in planning and implementing major decisions. They propose that measuring performance against outcomes and rewarding success will increase risk taking; whilst forcing adherence to process (which occurred in the CIA) promotes risk aversion.

Organisational climate is affected by entrepreneurial attitudes. Skaperdas and Gan (1995) found that risk-averse decision makers are more fearful of loss than risk seekers and so will expend more effort on risk management as a form of insurance. This explains another counter-intuitive finding that risk-averse managers can be more successful in risky environments than entrepreneurs. Busenitz and Barney (1997) concluded that the main differences between entrepreneurs and managers in large organisations are in their thinking, rather than risk propensity: entrepreneurs are more overconfident and more inclined to decide on instinct than through detailed analysis.

Moreover the way an issue is presented (threat or opportunity; possible loss or probable gain) influences the decision: stylising a decision as low-risk will gain more broad based support, especially from risk intolerant executives; whereas focussing on its upper bound is more attractive to risk seeking executives [Lopes (1987)].

Other studies have confirmed that organisation parameters have a strong influence on risk taking. The speed of decision making is higher in more centralised firms [Pablo et al. (1996)], and quicker strategic decisions lead to superior financial results [Wally and Baum (1994)]. Risk taking is promoted in organisations where managers trust their subordinates, and those with less red tape and less insistence on following rules and procedures [Bozeman and Kingsley (1998)].

Firms from different industries use different strategies to reach the same objective: Brouthers et al. (2002), for instance, studied the preferred mode of international market entry and found that services firms used wholly-owned subsidiaries, whereas manufacturing firms use less integrated approaches. A similar dichotomy was apparent from analysis of the frequency of Caesarean surgery in California hospitals by Goodrick and Salancik (1996): at low levels of risk to baby and mother, empirical evidence of the best treatment is equivocal and doctors use their discretion to the institution's advantage with a high Caesarean rate in for-profit hospitals.

Organisational Performance

There are many measures of an organisation's performance ranging from outcomes against a single yardstick through to the value added for each of many stakeholder groups. Similarly there are many measures of an organisation's risk. This book has concentrated on two measures of risk-related performance: financial results, particularly return on shareholders' funds which allows ready comparison of different sized organisations; and the frequency of crises which are the ultimate risks of any decision.

Discussion above suggests a concave link between risk and financial results as shown in figure 9.4: organisations that take few risks or many risks have a worse financial record than firms with a median risk profile. The worst decision makers are either timid or gamblers: this is true no matter what measure of risk chosen, and at both the firm level and market level.

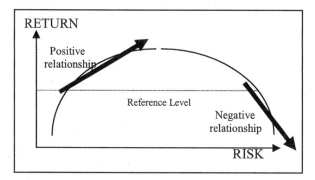

Fig. 9.4. Concave Return:Risk Links

Harvey (1995), for instance, provided data on the performance of more than 800 listed stocks in 20 countries: this showed a concave relationship between return and volatility in stock price. My own analysis of racecourse wagering markets [Coleman (2004)] showed a concave relationship between return and risk as measured by the probability of a win. Fiegenbaum and Thomas (1988) made a detailed study of 47 US industries between 1960 and 1979 and provided data that is also consistent with a concave risk-return relationship. Walls and Dyer (1996) found a concave relationship between US oil explorers' returns and their risk. And numerous studies have identified a negative relationship between return and risk [e.g. Amit and Wernerfelt (1990), Bowman (1980), and Miller and Bromiley (1990)].

The idea of a concave risk-reward relationship is not new, and dates to at least early last century [Higgs (1926)]. The rationale is most obvious at company level. At low levels of risk, it is difficult to achieve the diversification and exposures that produce reasonable returns. As increasing risk is accepted, financial results improve to give a roughly constant risk-weighted return. Eventually, though, the implicit and explicit costs of higher risk start to rise faster than income: the rate of return begins to decline. The implicit costs include management time and resources that become less productive when they are increasingly diverted towards resolving risk-related problems. Explicit costs include higher interest rates because creditors require a premium to support risky companies [Amit and Wernerfelt (1990)]. In addition, risk brings uncertainty to the firm's income stream and so investors use a higher discount rate that reduces the share price of risky companies relative to the prices of less risky companies.

Alternatively the concave relationship may be sourced in two decision maker populations. The first has a higher level of endowment, is risk averse, and – by demanding higher return from higher risk – has a positive expected return. The second group has less wealth and seeks risk for the small probability it offers to make a large return. The decision processes followed by these groups have important differences because they, respectively, expect: a positive risk-reward relationship and mean reversion of successive outcomes; and a negative risk-reward relationship and trends that persist.

Within this broad concave risk-return relationship, it is possible to discern the influence that organisation-specific risks have on returns. At a macro level, Aaker and Jacobson (1987) found that return on investment is linked to unsystematic risk, or the diversifiable component of a firm's risk: thus financial results are significantly related to the risk consequences of managers' decisions and strategies.

More specifically, studies by Reuer and Leiblein (2000) of US manufacturing companies and by Walls and Dyer (1996) of oil explorers showed that larger firms have a lower risk propensity than smaller firms. Singh (1986) found that poor financial results promote risk taking which – in conformance to a concave risk-return relationship – accelerate the decline in performance.

The empirical results presented in chapter eight confirm the findings of other studies which indicate that risk has a major impact on organisational performance, including financial return and risk outcomes such as crises. Importantly returns and crisis frequency are strongly linked: occurrence of a crisis reduces return on shareholder funds by about 1.5 percent a year for several years. This adds validity to the relationships shown in figure 9.3 as the measures of risk outcomes are linked to latent risk variables.

Conclusion

This chapter draws together the key points that have been identified in the literature survey and empirical studies. The result is to show the pattern of influences of risk on decision making, and how these flow through to organisational performance.

CHAPTER 10   Risk Budget Theory

This chapter describes a principal contribution of the book and begins by using the literature survey and empirical analyses to provide a fully sourced summary of the key elements of decision making under risk; the next sections develop an explanatory model called Risk Budget Theory (RBT) and validate it using real-world data; a discussion concludes.

Key Elements of Decision Making Under Risk

It is a daunting task to meaningfully distil the many influences of risk on decision making. Even so, the previous discussion suggests that the key elements of risk's role in decision making correspond to individuals' risk-taking dimensions as identified in chapters seven and eight as: personal characteristics of a decision maker, their decision making style, they way they evaluate decisions, and their expectation of the results.

This section proposes to use these categories to examine the key risk-related factors influencing decision making using three headings:
1. Personality and perception
2. Risk sensitive foraging and reference levels
3. Mental accounting and longshot bias.

Decision Maker Personality and Perception

Trimpop (1994) proposed that up to a quarter of the variance in individuals' risk-taking is explained by personality factors, and this has been confirmed in a variety of studies of real-world decision making [e.g. Austin et al. (2001), Smith and Friedland (1998), Williams and Narendran (1999), and Zuckerman and Kuhlman (2000)]. It also matches results from the Carter Racing Survey reported in chapter seven which showed that just over 24 percent of the variation in decision making was explained by subjects' demographic and personality attributes.

The most likely explanation of *how* this link might arise is the proposal by Lopes (1987: 275-276) that

"Risk-averse people appear to be motivated by a desire for security, whereas risk-seeking people appear to be motivated by a desire for potential. The former motive values safety and the latter, opportunity … Risk-averse people look more at the downside and risk seekers more at the upside."

An important corollary of this proposal is that people structure decisions as a choice between two alternative outcomes (broadly `success' and `cost'), and then place more emphasis on one or the other. A risk-averse decision maker will place a high weight on the possible cost of a risky alternative, whereas risk seekers will place a higher weight on the benefits from a successful outcome.

This `lumpy' approach rejects the assumption that decision makers' utility functions can be described by a continuous distribution. Although conflicting with normative assumptions, lumpy decisions follow Keynes who argued that: "under uncertainty, rational decision making could not be represented by any algorithm" Munier (1988: 3). Continuous distributions are psychologically irrelevant (Lopes, 1984) because people use intuition which tends to trigger spontaneous decisions (Kahneman, 2003). This matches an extensive literature that indicates decision makers think largely of two alternative outcomes.

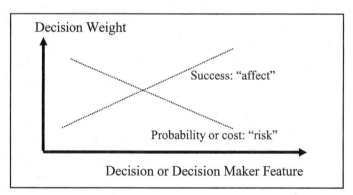

Fig. 10.1. Decision Maker Weightings

Figure 10.1 operationalises this for decision features by assigning different weights to each principal outcome. Assume, for instance, that the horizontal axis measures the decision maker's risk propensity: risk-seekers lie to the right of the figure and place relatively greater weight on the results of success; whereas risk-averse decision makers lie to the left of the figure and place more weight on the risks of a decision.

In similar fashion is the way that a decision is framed and perceived by the decision maker. This can arise in the way that decisions are styled, with a positive frame (i.e. projecting gains) inducing a greater weighting for a successful outcome [Kühberger (1988)]. Decision makers also place their own frame on a decision by instinctive perception of the costs and benefits of each outcome [Finucane et al. (2000)], and through self framing[Wang (2004)] which is the process underpinning the observation by Pablo et al. (1996: 728) that "perceived risk depends upon the type of information to which the decision maker attends."

The literature indicates that decision makers weight the two principal outcomes according to four other features of the decision.

The first is time until the outcome is expected. Sagristano et al. (2002) showed that the more distant the outcome the greater is the weight given to its benefits or success. A second influence on decision weighting is the ability of the decision maker to use his or her own skill to advantage in making a decision, or in shaping the outcome. People place greater weight on success when they have a competence through relevant skill or knowledge [Heath and Tversky (1991)], or when they are able to exercise some control over the outcome [Slovic (2000)].

The third driver of weights is the extent to which the decision maker is bounded by constraints such as limits on data, analytical resources, and time to make the decision. Decision makers become more risk averse as limits are placed on them [Mano (1990)], and so tend to increase the weighting on risk. Similarly they do not like ambiguity [Ellsberg (1961)], and so will avoid outcomes which have unknown probabilities.

Other cognitive biases are built into the weighting of alternative outcomes. As discussed in chapter three, when facing decisions involving an object (or event), people place greatest weight on those of its characteristic(s) which are most closely related to the terms of the response [Tversky et al. (1990)]. For example, in a decision involving payoffs, price is most important; whilst a decision involving risks sees over-weighting of probabilities. Decision makers also mentally tag objects and events with positive or negative feelings, and thus create an inverse relationship between risk and benefit [Antonides et al. (1997)].

In summary, people think in terms of win-lose outcomes and will tend to place greater weight on the risk of an outcome (i.e. its probability or the cost of failure) relative to the psychic value of success (its affect) when: the outcome is near term; the decision maker does not have relevant skills; decision making capability is constrained; and the decision's outcomes are ambiguous. This means that figure 10.1 can be used to describe six decision features: personality-driven risk propensity; decision frame; time to decision outcome; applicability of decision maker's skill; extent of data and analytical resources; and certainty of outcome.

Risk Sensitive Foraging and Reference Levels

Arguably the most striking of all decision behaviours is risk sensitivity. Although personality, training and experience incline decision makers to be instinctively risk averse or risk seeking and give them a unique perspective on alternative choices, this is not immutable and can alter in light of needs and domain (e.g. recreation and retirement savings). Also – as discussed in the following sections – people (as well as animals and organisations) are risk sensitive in response to circumstances. In keeping with risk-sensitive foraging [Bateson (2002)], risk preference changes around the decision maker's satisficing level, or endowment which meets expectations or requirements at the time When endowment is below the satisficing level, decision makers *tend* to be loss averse and take more risks, while they tend to be less risk prone above the satisficing level. This is why, for instance, the Carter Survey found that respondents' risk propensity was not significantly related to evaluations' of their risk propensity, and assessments of the latter were not significantly correlated across decision domains (i.e. personal risk, personal financial risk and business risk).

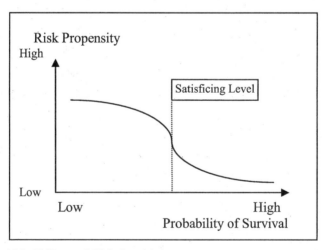

Fig. 10.2. Utility and Risk Sensitivity

As shown in the diagram above, when endowment is inadequate to sustain the decision maker, risk propensity is high: animals and humans will take greater risks when their survival is threatened. When endowment is above the satisficing level, survival is probable and so a lower risk strategy is adopted. In terms of figure 10.1, when decision makers' endowment is below the satisficing level they tend to over-weight success; and they over-weight risk above the satisficing level.

An important element of risk-sensitivity is loss aversion. Typically a loss is valued more than a corresponding gain, and the utility of any loss relative to an equal gain increases with the size of the loss. In words, the pain of any loss relative to an equivalent gain is directly proportional to the amount, and inversely proportional to risk propensity. This is most obvious in laboratory studies where decision makers are offered a variety of choices [e.g. Schneider and Lopes (1986)]: as the size of the potential loss increases, people increasingly prefer a low risk outcome. As discussed in chapter two, this behaviour is consistent with an exponential utility curve of the type proposed by Pratt (1964): $u(x) = x.e^{-x/\rho}$ where $u(x)$ is the utility to the decision maker of $\$x$ and ρ is a measure of the decision maker's risk propensity or willingness to accept risk. The higher the value of ρ the greater a person's risk propensity.

The shapes of various utility functions are shown in the figure below. A positive value of ρ produces a concave ∩-shaped curve typical of risk aversion; whilst a negative value of ρ produces a convex U-shaped curve that points to risk embrace. As the size of ρ increases, the curves become flatter which means, for instance, that risk averse decision makers become less loss averse, and are more willing to accept decisions with larger risk.

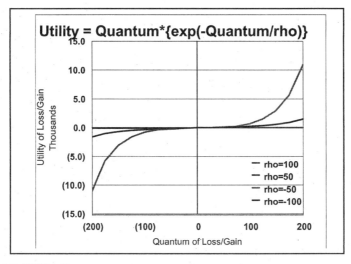

Fig. 10.3. Utility Curves.

Thus risk sensitivity becomes linked to reference levels and guides decision makers in applying appropriate weightings to decision outcomes.

Mental Accounting and Longshot Bias

A third important influence on decision makers is recent experience because it provides a personalised sampling of outcomes and changes their endowment relative to satisficing levels. This process is a form of mental accounting [Thaler (1985)[70]] and means that sequential outcomes have synergetic impacts on risk propensity and decisions. In terms of figure 10.2, for instance, a gain will lift a decision maker's endowment and tend to make them less risk prone. Decision makers can operationalise this process by continually aggregating their net endowment, and then altering risk propensity (the value of ρ in figure 10.3 above).

Mental accounting also leads to what Tversky and Kahneman (1971) called the law of small numbers. Because it is too demanding to collect and process a statistically robust sample, decision makers overgeneralise from small samples and tend to overweight personal experience and striking observations (e.g. crises, highly publicised incidents, freakish calamities). Moreover the influence of recent experience is more salient than population-based distributions, and – because of framing by the decision makers - is especially likely to be over-weighted when it supports a preferred outcome [Zackay (1984)].

Selective analysis can induce a level of overconfidence in decision makers that borders on hubris [Roll (1986)], or excessive optimism [Smith (1776, reprinted 1937)]. This explains the common longshot bias, or willingness of decision makers to prefer low probability outcomes that cannot be justified by their statistical record. Chapter five discusses evidence of the longshot bias in management which appears as over-reliance on high-risk strategies such as mergers and acquisitions, research and development, and mineral exploration.

Mental accounting can make people slow to adjust their decision when new information comes to hand. This is almost a loss averse process, where acknowledging the need for change implies an initial error. Thus decision makers can reject new information, or edit out conflicting data:

---

[70] Thaler (1985) suggested that non-linearity in the shape of utility curves means that consumers place greater value on multiple separate changes in endowment rather than an equivalent single change. This explains the ubiquitous marketing strategies of segregating benefits (as multiple benefits have greater cumulative value than their aggregate) and quoting prices as list less a discount (because the benefit of the discount is greater than the value of the higher cost).

this can give the counter-intuitive result where a flow of largely contradictory data can be winnowed to support an increasingly incorrect position.

One of the most important aspects of mental accounting is the considerable volume of evidence which indicates that decision makers assume mean reversion will apply unless there is reason to believe otherwise [Heath et al. (1999)]. Examples include studies by Camerer et al. (1997), Heath et al. (1999), and Odean (1998); further support comes from evidence of the gamblers' fallacy in Morrison and Ordeshook (1975) and Terrell (1997). This assumption of mean reversion exerts Bayesian influences so that successful decision makers expect a run of wins to be followed by losses, and – in the absence of overconfidence - will tend to become less risk prone; whilst unsuccessful decision makers expect a turn for the better and can become more risk prone (note, though, that it is also common to see risk embrace after gains and loss aversion after losses [e.g. Thaler and Johnson (1990)]).

Outline of Risk Budget Theory

The previous section drew on earlier material - particularly table 7.1 - to list the principal characteristics of decision making under risk. This section proposes an explanation termed Risk Budget Theory.

Risk Budget Theory

Risk Budget Theory (RBT) relies on five attributes of decision making:
1. Risk is the possibility and quantum of loss. This is the dictionary meaning of risk and is how managers think of it [March and Shapira (1987)]
2. Although decision makers are instinctively *loss averse* (because natural selection has yielded an over-arching goal of survival), they have personalised levels of risk propensity that constitute an initial response. Thus personality determines between a quarter and a third of risk propensity [Trimpop (1994) and table 4.1].
3. Decision makers are risk sensitive and will alter their risk propensity between decision contexts and as circumstances shift. This involves mentally accounting for changes in endowment relative to a reference level. MacCrimmon and Wehrung (1984) showed that managers have a preferred decision style, but this proved flexible in their study and those by Pablo et al. (1996) and Wally and Baum (1994).

4. People facing decisions with risk think of two alternative outcomes: the desired or target result, and the risk or consequence of failure. Decision makers evaluate the two principal outcomes separately. As discussed in detail in the previous section, supporting evidence is widespread in psychology studies: Lopes (1984), for instance, concluded that continuous distributions of decision variables were unsuitable for the way people make decisions.

5. The carriers of decision preferences are risks in the short term, and in decisions with large potential costs or where skill and control are irrelevant. The carriers are aspirational goals or gains in the long term and in decisions where skill is applicable. This is supported by Heath and Tversky (1991), Sagristano et al. (2002) and Slovic (2000).

Under Risk Budget Theory, the quantum of risk that decision makers are prepared to accept is path-dependent and related to the probability of survival that is offered by alternative choices. Prior to choosing between alternative outcomes, decision makers compare the possible losses against their current endowment. Decision makers then overlay this evaluation on a core risk propensity based on demography, personality and experience. They consider the decision domain, and then personalise the risks in terms of their knowledge, level of control and personal aspirations. The final step is to calculate the size of possible loss, and compare it to the risk budget or level of acceptable risk.

This approach sees most decisions as a comparison between two discrete outcomes of target gain and potential downside loss. Individuals tend to make Yes-No decisions: does a prospective heart transplant candidate consider the population-based 60 percent probability of its success? or does (s)he worry only about the personalised outcome? These decision makers – whether managers contemplating acquisitions or sick people evaluating treatment options – do not treat risky decisions as laboratory gambles, but shape their outcomes by altering their execution (e.g. retaining a good adviser or surgeon) and understanding their nature.

Decision makers pay relatively little heed to the probabilities of various alternatives because most are highly uncertain. Thus they capture complex distributions using small, recent samples and simple heuristics such as mean reversion, pattern recognition, milestones, realistic extremes and recent changes. The net result is that people place more emphasis on the consequences of decision outcomes than on their probabilities. Thus decisions involving risk turn on expectations of how the alternative outcomes will impact endowment, rather than on the probabilities of the outcomes. This explains why a number of studies [e.g. Carter Racing in chapter seven] find that the facts of a decision are frequently ignored.

Risk Budget Theory of Decision Making (RBT) can be expressed in core assumptions:

1. Decision makers assign a value to any outcome that is exponentially related to its quantum. Thus u(x), the utility of any outcome x, is proportionate to $x.e^{-x/\rho}$ (Pratt, 1964).

2. Here ρ is the *Risk Budget* and measures risk propensity or the amount of endowment or wealth that the decision maker is prepared to lose. ρ is determined by intrinsic risk preferences, decision domain and current endowment relative to a reference level. It is comparable to the Arrow-Pratt risk aversion coefficient.

3. The value of ρ is positive, indicating loss aversion, when current endowment is above a satisficing reference level and survival is not threatened. Conversely the value ρ is negative, indicating risk embrace, when current endowment is below the reference level (as discussed below, ρ can also be negative when current endowment is so far above a satisficing level that no amount of risk can endanger survival).

4. In addition, ρ will vary with difficult-to-quantify factors including the decision maker's unique personal traits. For instance, the value of ρ falls with wealth, and - less certainly - with female gender and marriage (typical population-average values of ρ are calculated in the appendix).

5. The value of ρ may be different in the domains of losses and gains (although it has been simplified in the following discussion so that ρ has the same value in both domains)

6. Decision makers apply weights to the principal outcomes (target result, and downside risk in the event of failure) that are determined by the content and clarity of decision stimuli, and the available time and cognitive resources to make the decision. A decision maker will tend to place greater weight on the risk of an outcome (i.e. its probability or cost of `failure) relative to the psychic value of success (its affect) when: the outcome is near term; the decision is negatively framed; the decision outcome is uncertain; limits are imposed on the decision maker's knowledge or analytical ability; and the decision maker does not have relevant skills.

7. Decision makers have only a vague understanding of the objective distributions of many events. They place minimal reliance upon probability calculations, use simple heuristics, and - when facing uncertain outcomes – will typically assume mean reversion (although they may assign outcomes equal probability, or give a high probability to the more desired outcome).

Under RBT, individual decision makers choose an alternative that maximises the value of the following expression:

$$
\begin{aligned}
\text{Utility} \; &= \; w_G \cdot \pi_G \cdot u(Q_G) \; + \; w_L \cdot \pi_L \cdot u(Q_L) \\
&= \; w_G \cdot \pi_G \cdot Q_G \cdot e^{-Qg/\rho} \; + \; w_L \cdot \pi_L \cdot Q_L \cdot e^{-Ql/\rho}
\end{aligned}
$$

where: the decision is simplified to have only two outcomes of Gain or Loss; Q_G and Q_L are the quanta of gains and losses, respectively; w refers to their weightings; and π_G and π_L are respective probabilities of occurrence.

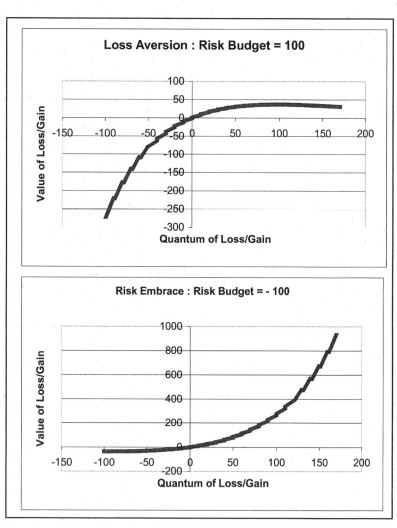

Fig. 10.4. Risk Budget Theory

The sign of ρ is set by whether the decision maker is risk averse (positive value), risk neutral (ρ = 0), or risk-embracing (negative value of ρ). As shown in figure 10.4, a positive value of the Risk Budget, ρ, gives a concave shaped curve where losses are valued more than equivalent gains; and a negative value of ρ gives a convex shaped utility curve where gains are valued more than equivalent losses.

The value of the Risk Budget, ρ, has four main determinants: the risk propensity of the decision maker; their personal attributes; the decision setting; and the outcomes of previous decisions. These combine as shown in figure 10.5 to derive the value of ρ for any particular decision.

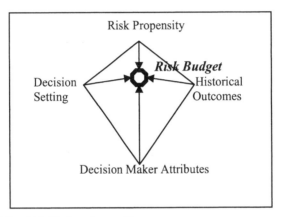

Fig. 10.5. The Risk Budget Pyramid

The other important variable in the equation above is the weighting of decision alternatives (represented by w_G and w_L) that are assigned, respectively, to the decision's best and worst outcomes and operate as shown in figure 10.1. w_G increases relative to w_L (i.e. greater weight is placed on the value of success than on the risk) when: the decision is positively framed; the outcome is distant; the decision maker has relevant skills; decision making capability is unconstrained; and the decision's outcomes are clear.

The various pressures that shape the values of w and ρ mean that different decision makers facing identical datasets will make their own unique judgements about the meaning and prospects of each alternative, and so choose differently. Victims of a hotel fire, for instance, can variously choose to flee down the stairs, jump from a window in desperation, or - like deer trapped in headlights - huddle beneath wet sheets until help arrives.

How might RBT play out in practice? Think of a decision and assume that conventional analysis has derived Q, π and w for the principal gain and loss outcomes. The first step is to establish the value(s) of ρ, and this largely depends on the context of the decision. For instance, it may be a fixed budget, as is the case of a recreational gambler who puts $100 in their pocket before going to the casino: when the $100 is gone, decisions (i.e. risk taking) stop. Alternatively the value of ρ may be set by reference to income: a person relying on investments for their income may allocate a portion of wealth to high risk returns such as start-up biotechnology or mineral exploration companies.

The next step is to compare the values of Q_G and Q_L against ρ. If ρ is very much bigger than possible gains or losses, then the exponential form of the utility function means that the choice is made largely on expected values. The decision maker looks to weightings and probabilities; when weightings of losses and gains are similar (such as in the case of near term outcomes where data are adequate and skill is not relevant), probability rules the decision. This is typically when mean reversion is assumed.

Consider the example of a gambler who can bet on a coin toss. Designating heads by capital letters and tails by lower case, and assuming that ρ is much greater than the possible gain or loss, the decision maker must choose the higher of:

$$[w_G . \pi_G . Q_G + w_L . \pi_L . Q_L] \quad \text{and} \quad [w_g . \pi_g . Q_g + w_l . \pi_l . Q_l]$$

The values of Q and w are identical, and the only uncertainty for the gambler relates to π. A common basis for probability estimates in sequential (even statistically unrelated) decisions is the assumption of mean reversion [Heath et al. (1999)]. Where gamblers assume mean reversion, they place a higher weight on previously losing outcomes than on winning outcomes. This leads to the gamblers' fallacy which suggests, for example, that in a coin toss a tail has a greater than 50 percent probability after two heads are thrown.

A different set of forces come into play when possible gains and losses are large relative to ρ. This can arise following reduction of ρ, such as might occur to the gambler with $100 who consistently loses. Alternatively it could be a decision with important potential impact on endowment or projected income: change of job, large investment, or marriage. Here all but extreme probabilities become irrelevant as they are dwarfed by the exponential influence of gains and losses, and the most important factor is the sign of ρ: a positive, risk-averse value overweights losses and leads to loss aversion; whilst a negative ρ leads to risk embrace. Again context is important because the gambler looking for a get-out bet on the last race will be risk-embracing (and also overweight w_G), whilst a retiring employee may be risk averse in investing termination payments.

Decisions under risk, then, are a function of stable personal traits and aspirations, and changing parameters such as evaluation of the decision features, the relevance of skill, and level of current endowment. RBT acknowledges this by specifically incorporating individual differences such as personality and skill as well as personal situation and decision domain.

Discussion

The essence of Risk Budget Theory is that when any decision maker faces a decision, they reduce it to two probable outcomes – expected Gain and risk of Loss - with respective values Q_G and Q_L and respective probabilities π_G and π_L; assign weights w_G and w_L; and mentally revise their risk budget, ρ. The last will differ between decision makers who have different risk propensities. The final decision step is to maximise the value of:

$$\text{Utility} \quad = \quad w_G \cdot \pi_G \cdot Q_G \cdot e^{-Qg/\rho} \quad + \quad w_L \cdot \pi_L \cdot Q_L \cdot e^{-Ql/\rho}$$

Decision makers are generally loss-averse, rather than risk-averse; their risk preferences are set by a Risk Budget, ρ, which is a measure of the amount they are prepared to lose relative to a reference level and is related to the wealth being managed in the decision domain. The Risk Budget is mentally adjusted as decisions unfold, and can be shaped by expectation; it can differ in the domains of gains and losses. Thus a decision maker with a relevant skill will reduce the anticipated probability of loss, and – for a given reference level – will have a higher risk propensity than less skilful peers.

Risk Budget Theory (RBT) unashamedly draws upon concepts from multiple disciplines. Behavioural economics contributed mental accounting [Thaler (1985)], framing [Kühberger (1988)], ambiguity aversion [Ellsberg (1961) and Fox and Tversky (1995)], and aggregation of possible outcomes into either a gain or loss [Lopes (1987), Starmer (2000) and Weber et al. (2002)]; economics pointed to bounded rationality [Simon (1955)]; management science provides utility theory [Pratt (1964)] and the everyday meaning of risk [March and Shapira (1987)]; finance adds the concept of value-at-risk [Simons (1996)].

Away from economics, physiology pointed to engagement of different parts of the brain for different decision types [Greene et al. (2001)], and switching between left and right brain perception [Miller et al. (2000)];

studies of animal behaviour propose risk sensitive foraging [Bateson (2002)], and the energy budget rule [Caraco et al. (1980)]. Psychology shows that a shortage of resources simplifies decision making strategies and overweights losses [Mano (1990)]. It also suggests the importance of loss aversion [Lopes (1994)], and that personality plays a major role in risk propensity [Trimpop (1994)].

Numerous studies have shown that decision makers will evaluate probabilities on the assumption of mean reversion [Heath et al. (1999)]. Whilst the instinctive preference for most decision makers is to target survival rather than maximise value [figure 3.3], many managers will preferentially pursue high risk strategies [table 5.2].

In addition, the empirical studies reported in chapters seven and eight provided a number of important new findings and confirmation of other results, particularly: decision makers pay little heed to the facts of a decision [table 8.6 and Fair (2002)], including probabilities [see data in table 3.1]; and personality is important to decision making, although it acts on the way decision makers perceive problems rather than directly on their decision [Sitkin and Pablo (1992)].

Moreover, RBT is rooted in principles of natural selection, rather than those of normative economics; thus decision makers can increase their risk propensity when survival is threatened [Highhouse and Yüce (1996) and Singh (1986)]. RBT makes room for individuals' personality, skill and experience so that different decision makers in identical circumstances reach different decisions (chapter seven found about half the managers took a risky choice which confirms results in Levy and Levy (2002) and Williams and Narendran (1999)).

Superficially RBT is similar to many existing models: probabilities, weightings and utility are set by the decision maker's risk attitude in relation to the specific decision and combine to shape the relative attractiveness of alternative decision outcomes. However, RBT differs from Expected Utility and other models in a number of significant details.

The most important innovation by RBT is to disaggregate win and lose outcomes. This enables loss aversion to be taken into account because the exponential shape of the utility curve makes losses more significant than gains. Disaggregation also allows the win/lose alternatives to have different weightings and even different values of ρ: it better encapsulates the influences of parameters such as timing, framing, skill, and decision constraints.

A second innovation in RBT is the flexible nature of ρ. Individuals have a unique ρ for various decision domains (e.g. recreational gambling, investment, and life insurance) that is based on their personality and other attributes. As few decisions are taken in isolation, it is unrealistic to expect that they are made using fixed parameters (and incremental outcomes). Decision makers experience Bayesian pressures because their risk propensity is altered when successive outcomes change their endowment relative to a satisficing level (where endowment above a satisficing level implies 'survival' and fosters risk aversion). Thus allowing ρ to vary builds risk sensitivity into decision making, and adjusts risk propensity in light of the outcomes of multiple decisions.

Consider a person who makes sequential decisions and experiences a run of favourable outcomes. This will improve their endowment relative to a satisficing level, but they will expect reversion to the mean. These changes will lead, respectively, to increases in ρ and w_L, the weighting of possible risks. As a result, decision makers whose endowment is above their satisficing level and so projects a high probability of survival will adopt a risk neutral stance. If their endowment is below the satisficing level, in order to survive they may have little choice but to embrace risk. Those with very high endowments can take risks without threatening their survival. Conversely, a person who has experienced a run of unfavourable outcomes will see a reduction in endowment relative to a satisficing level, and thus a decrease in ρ, but – on the expectation of mean reversion – an increase in w_G.

This shows that a run of poor outcomes makes the risk budget negative, renders a loss virtually certain, and can induce high-risk gambles. Similarly a run of good outcomes makes the value of the risk budget so high that it can induce risk embrace even in naturally risk-averse decision makers.

To clarify the difference between Risk Budget Theory and Prospect Theory (PT), consider the example in table 10.1 using data provided by Payne et al. (1984). This is typical of the evidence from standard gambles that is used to support and quantify PT. The experiment involves two separate decisions, case 1 and case 2, given to a group of managers. Each case provides two choices, A and B, which have three possible outcomes of varying probability. The outcomes can be gains or losses, and are $60K higher in case 2 than in case 1. Although the probability weighted expected values of each choice are the same, the proportion of managers selecting them differs significantly, and is reversed between cases 1 and 2 (the shaded lines are the preferred choices). According to the authors, adding the $60K moves the gambles from below the managers' reference level to above their reference level. Thus case 1 implies risk seeking in the domain of losses, whilst case 2 implies risk aversion in the domain of gains.

Table 10.1. Managers' Preferences in Gambling Experiment

Case	Choice	Outcome 1		Outcome 2		Outcome 3		Expected Value - $ K	Percent Choosing
		$ K	Prob	$ K	Prob	$ K	Prob		
1	A	14	.5	-30	.1	-85	.4	-30	67
	B	-20	.3	-30	.5	-45	.2	-30	33
2	A	74	.5	30	.1	-25	.4	30	17
	B	40	.3	30	.5	15	.2	30	83

An alternative explanation is that managers are loss averse and consistently prefer the choice which minimises their risk, or possibility of loss: they refuse choice B in case 1 as this would mean a loss is certain; and they prefer choice B in case 2 as this means no possibility of loss. RBT offers an explanation in which the domain is irrelevant.

To further illustrate the operation of Risk Budget Theory, consider four decision choices, each with two possible outcomes that produce respective payments of $100 and between $0 and -$60. If the win and lose outcomes are equally weighted with equal probability of occurrence, the utilities of the various decisions are shown in the table below as a function of the risk budget, ρ. In the top row, for instance, the value of ρ is 50 and – as the quantum of possible loss rises from 0 to –60 – the utility of the outcome falls from 14 to –182.

Table 10.2. Utilities of Different Decision Choices

	Choice 1	Choice 2	Choice 3	Choice 4
Win	100	100	100	100
Loss	0	-20	-40	-60
Rho	Utility as a function of ρ			
50	14	-8	-73	-182
75	26	12	-32	-104
100	37	26	-7	-61
-100	272	283	315	370
-75	379	394	437	510
-50	739	760	826	934

The table above shows that the properties of Risk Budget Theory are such that:

- For loss averse decision makers with a positive risk budget, an increase in ρ lifts the utility of any choice pair: a higher risk budget accelerates decision making, which is consistent with real-world behaviour [Wally and Baum (1994)]

- For risk-seekers, as the risk budget becomes increasingly negative, the utility of any choice pair falls so that a more negative risk budget slows decision making. Again this matches real-world evidence that risk averse decision makers seek to delay the process [Wehrung et al. (1989)]
- For any given positive risk budget, the disutility of a loss grows with the loss: thus risk-averse decision makers are loss averse, and the loss aversion grows as risk budget falls
- For any given negative risk budget, the utility of a loss grows with the quantum of loss: thus risk-embracing decision makers prefer exposure to losses, but their loss preference declines as the risk budget becomes more negative.

The significance of the Theory is that decision makers maximise their prospects of long-term survival, rather than select a course that offers the most valuable short-term outcome. Because the existence today of any sentient being implies that its future outlook is positive, survival is probable and so there is no need to take any action that offers the possibility of risk or loss. Thus loss aversion is the normal preference, and decision makers do not only optimise incremental opportunities.

Validation of Risk Budget Theory

The explicit goal of this section is to validate Risk Budget Theory using real-world evidence. The first approach is to examine how well RBT explains typical financial decisions – insurance, investment and wagering – that have proven beyond the explanatory capability of other models. The second approach is to test the real-world applicability of RBT's conclusions in a process similar to that used in chapter six.

RBT's Explanation of Financial Decisions

This section examines the applicability of RBT using published data. This is to demonstrate its effectiveness in real-world decision environments, particularly those which have proven bothersome to decision theorists, such as simultaneous purchase of insurance and gambling [Neilson and Stowe (2002)].

The approach here is a little different to that in previous discussions as – rather than examining individuals' choices – it takes population-based data that aggregate many individual decisions. The population is assumed to choose between a high risk or a low risk outcome, and so divide itself into two groups: one is risk embracing with a high (or possibly negative) value of ρ; and the other is risk averse with a lower value of ρ. The respective populations with different risk propensities are designated risk-embracing, RE, and risk-averse, RA.

The decisions comprise pairs of alternative outcomes with known probabilities; and it is assumed that relative utilities are revealed by decision maker support for each of the outcomes. The utilities of the respective populations are given by:

$$W_{RE} \cdot \pi_{RE} \cdot Q_{RE} \cdot e^{-Q_{RE}/\rho_{RE}} \quad \text{and} \quad W_{RA} \cdot \pi_{RA} \cdot Q_{RA} \cdot e^{-Q_{RA}/\rho_{RA}}$$

where: RE and RA designate risk-embracers and risk-averters; Q designates the expected outcome for each group; w refers to the weights, and π refers to the probabilities.

This analysis will show that RBT is able to provide a solution in typical real-world situations by providing population risk budgets of risk embracers and risk averters, ρ_{RE} and ρ_{RA}, respectively. The aim is twofold. Most importantly to show that representative data from real-world financial decisions can be incorporated into RBT to provide an explanation of decision making under risk. The second aim is to show a methodology for analysis of decisions using RBT. Whilst care has been taken in this study to derive accurate data, there are many other datasets available[71], and it is expected that clear demonstration of RBT's application will promote its use.

Three decision domains are considered: purchase of life insurance, race-track wagering, and investments. Each case incorporates high and low risk decision makers, which are respectively taken to be: those who do not purchase life insurance and those who purchase life insurance; people who back longshots and favourites; and people who invest in equities and bonds.

Published data are used to insert actual values in the two expressions above. The only unknowns, then, are the values of ρ for risk-takers and risk-averters, and these were derived by calculating paired values of ρ_{RE} and ρ_{RA} that solve for the population data. The calculations are provided in Appendix 10.A.

Table 10.3 summarises core results. The first column in the table shows the risk budget for the risk averse section of the population: those who

---

[71] For instance, Thaler and Johnson (1990) report the outcomes of a series of gambles by undergraduates in a classroom setting; and Donkers et al. (2001) provide risk attitudes of Dutch adults. See also Harless and Camerer (1994). In addition data from chapter five on mineral exploration have been analysed using RBT and derived an intuitively sound solution.

purchase insurance, back favourites and invest in bonds. The other columns show the equivalent risk budget for risk embracing portions of the population.

Table 10.3. Risk Budgets for Risk Averters and Risk Embracers

Risk Averse	Risk Embracing		
			Investing
	Insurance	Betting	
5,000	5,684	5,027	19,242
10,000	12,490	10,110	34,800
50,000	300,000	53,200	191,000
100,000	-155,000	141,900	500,000

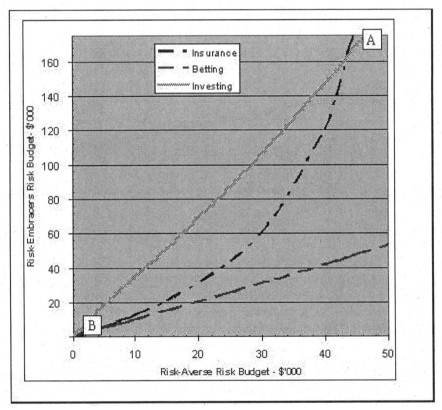

Fig 10.6. Risk Budgets for Financial Decisions

Figure 10.6 graphs the results. The vertical axis shows the risk budget of risk prone decision makers, ρ_{RE}, who prefer: no life insurance, betting on longshots and investing in equities. The horizontal axis shows the risk budget of decision makers who prefer lower risk alternatives, ρ_{RA}: purchase of life insurance, betting on favourites, and investing in bonds. The three lines show the loci of risk budgets for risk embracers and risk averters that match population-based data in each financial market. Point A is at the intersection of lines that solve for decision makers involved in insurance and investing, and point B provides a simultaneous solution for bettors and insurers.

The important result from this figure is that RBT provides simultaneous solutions for three quite different sets of financial decisions. Certainly the curves do not intersect at a single point, but that would only be expected if decision makers came from the same population (which does not apply here as the curves involve 35-44 year old males, racetrack bettors, and US investors).

Overall, this analysis shows that equilibrium solutions can be simultaneously derived across individuals' disparate financial decisions by assuming two populations of decision makers. The first is a higher risk propensity group whose average risk budget is in the range -$10,000 to $150,000. The second group has lower risk propensity and its risk budget is in the range $5,000 to $40,000.

These results indicate that decision makers with risk budgets across a wide range will follow the observed behaviours. In summary this section showed that Risk Budget Theory can explain behaviours in quite different risk domains, including those that have proven beyond the explanatory capability of other theories.

Conclusion Testing

This section first restates the conclusions of Risk Budget Theory, and then tests their applicability against representative real-world data from the papers that were used to evaluate Prospect Theory in chapter six.

The discussion so far in this chapter points to 16 conclusions that form the core of RBT, and suggest that decision makers:

C1   Aggregate the range of possible outcomes so that they evaluate only two (or at most a few) alternative outcomes

C2   Have different risk propensity depending on unique personal traits

C3   Pay minimal heed to probabilities

Decision makers are usually loss averse. This means that they will avoid a choice that has an ambiguous outcome, such as missing data. A second implication is that they will have a decreasing preference for choices where the worst outcome becomes increasingly unfavourable. This suggests decision makers:

C4   Will prefer a choice with a known, rather than ambiguous, out-come

C5   Usually prefer the alternative with the least unfavourable outcome

C6   Rank alternatives from best to worst on the basis of increasing possible loss

The over-riding objective of decision makers is to ensure their long-term survival, and this can offset the normative assumption that they seek short-term financial optimisation of incremental decisions. Thus decision makers:

C7   Can select alternatives that are financially sub-optimum

C8   Do not necessarily revise choices when made aware they are financially sub-optimum

C9   Aspire to achieve stretch long-term goals with limited regard to short-term issues

The willingness of decision makers to accept a risk or the possibility of loss is forward looking and sensitive to changes in their prospects of survival. Decision makers:

C10 Expect mean reversion with successive choices

C11 Have stable risk propensity during the time when survival prospects are favourable

C12 Become more risk prone as survival prospects diminish

C13 Are loss averse in an unviable position and so can become risk prone

Decision makers mentally account for changes in their level of endowment relative to some specific aspiration level, which may be an historical reference point or a future target. Their risk propensity is path-dependent so that decision makers adjust their willingness to accept losses in response to the current difference between their endowment and reference level, and in response to the direction and magnitude of changes in the difference. Thus decision makers:

C14 Become more loss-averse as losses mount

C15 Eventually become risk prone as gains increase

A corollary of conclusions 12 and 15 is that decision makers facing sequential decisions will tend to start out as loss averse; if the outcomes are consistently unfavourable they will become more loss-averse, until losses are so ruinous as to threaten survival and the decision makers turn risk-embracing. If, however, the outcomes are consistently favourable, they eventually move so far above the reference levels as to induce risk embrace. Thus decision makers are risk prone when their survival is threatened, and when their endowment is well above satisficing levels. This leads to a convex relationship between risk and changes in endowment as shown in the accompanying figure. Thus:

C16 Risk or loss propensity has a convex relationship with the cumulative outcome of successive decisions

These 16 conclusions are set out in table 10.4. The far right column uses the papers listed in table 6.2 (plus others discussed in the literature survey of chapters three and four) as representative tests of whether or not the conclusions of RBT satisfactorily explain real-world evidence.

Almost without exception, real-world evidence of decision making under risk or uncertainty supports the key conclusions of Risk Budget Theory. And even the conclusion which is partially contradicted – conclusion 12: Decision makers become more risk prone as survival prospects diminish – is not immutable, but varies by situation.

Conclusion

This chapter proposes a new way of understanding decision making under risk or uncertainty. It is a parsimonious solution that reconciles a number of anomalies that have plagued students of behavioural economics.

RBT overcomes the deficiencies of other decision theories that were identified in chapter six because it: specifically incorporates decision maker personality; softens the central role of reference levels; and rejects a continuous probability weighting function.

Although RBT may appear similar to many existing models, it has important points of difference. The first is to separately consider gains and losses. The second is to set ρ as the value of decision makers' *risk budget*, which is a measure of the amount they are prepared to lose at any point in time. The budget is a unique function of the decision maker's personality, endowment and context. For instance, if decisions proceed through a sequence, decision makers accumulate their net change in endowment, and – when further decisions are offered – deduct potential losses from the accumulated position, and revise the risk budget. The theory is applicable to all forms of endowment ranging from wealth to health and prestige.

In summary, RBT explains well-recognised decision making anomalies such as framing and time preference, and commonplace economic puzzles such as the longshot bias, the house money effect, and catastrophe insurance. Moreover the Theory is robust to numerous real-world tests using empirical data derived from representative decision making situations. That is not to say that RBT resolves every behavioural anomaly. But it is a significant enhancement to our understanding of decision making.

Table 10.4. Risk Budget Theory Conclusions and Real-world Tests

Hypothesis		Reference	Implication for Risk Budget Theory
C1	Decision makers evaluate only two (or at most a few) alternative outcomes	March and Shapira (1987)	Supported
C2	Decision makers have different risk propensity depending on unique personal traits	Kahneman and Tversky (1982)	Supported
C3	Decision makers pay minimal heed to probabilities	Lovallo and Kahneman (2003) Schneider and Lopes (1986)	Supported Supported
C4	Decision makers will prefer a choice with a known, rather than ambiguous, outcome	Ellsberg (1961)	Supported
C5	Decision makers usually prefer the alternative with the least unfavourable outcome	Schneider and Lopes (1986)	Supported
C6	Decision makers rank alternatives from best to worst on the basis of increasing possible loss	Walls et al. (1995)	Supported
C7	Decision makers select alternatives which are financially sub-optimum	Rabin (1998)	Supported
C8	Decision makers do not necessarily revise choices when made aware they are financially sub-optimum	Rabin and Schrag (1999)	Supported
C9	Decision makers aspire to stretch long-term goals with limited regard to short-term issues	Sagristano et al. (2002)	Supported

Table 10.4.   (cont)

C10	Decision makers expect mean reversion with successive choices	Camerer et al. (1997)	Supported
		Heath et al. (1999)	Supported
C11	Decision makers have stable risk propensity whilst survival prospects are favourable		Supported
C12	Decision makers become more risk prone as survival prospects diminish	Hollenbeck et al. (1994)	Supported
		Laughhunn et al. (1980)	Contradicted
		Metzger (1985)	Supported
C13	Decision makers are loss averse in an unviable position and become risk prone	D'Aveni (1989)	Supported
		McGlothin (1956)	Supported
C14	Decision makers become more loss-averse as losses mount	Barberis et al. (2001)	Supported
		Willman et al. (2002)	Supported
C15	Decision makers eventually become risk prone as gains increase	Mullins et al. (1999)	Supported
		Thaler and Johnson (1990)	Supported
C16	Risk or loss propensity has a concave relationship with the cumulative outcome of successive decisions	Jullien and Salanié (2000)	Supported

Appendix 10.A – Mathematical Solution of RBT Examples

This Appendix provides details of the calculations used to derive figure 10.6. The explicit goal is to validate Risk Budget Theory using real-world evidence, and to examine how well RBT explains a number of decisions that have proven beyond the capabilities of other models.

In the following sections, three typical decision situations – insurance, investment and wagering – are created and tested using RBT. Each comprises a pair of alternative outcomes where population-based data are available to calculate expected outcomes and probabilities. There are two populations of different risk propensities, one designated risk-embracing, RE, and the other risk-averse, RA; and - for simplicity - relative utilities are assumed to be given by decision maker support for each of the outcomes. The aim of this analysis is to solve for the population risk budgets of the risk embracers and risk averters, ρ_{RE} and ρ_{RA}, respectively. The value of each decision is set at \$80,000, which is the salary of a senior lecturer at an Australian university.

As an aside, it is recognised that the various numbers used in the examples are open to considerable debate. In one example, for instance, the \$80,000 is an annual income, whilst in others it is a lump sum. The impact of taxes, too, is ignored. And published data used to derive utilities are the means of many different utilities, risk propensities, strength of conviction and so on. However, it is not the role of this analysis to provide comprehensive evaluations of ρ, but to demonstrate the ability of RBT to solve some real-world problems. Moreover sensitivity analysis showed that this approach can provide solutions even with significant change to the assumptions.

The first decision category is purchase of life insurance. Consider an Australian male aged 35-44: he has a statistical mortality rate (probability of death in any year) of 0.0017 (i.e. 1.7 deaths per 1,000 population) [ABS (2002)] and can purchase life insurance for an annual premium of \$470 per \$100,000 in cover [Diners Club, personal communication, 21 January 2004]. Assume he has an average annual income of \$80,000, and purchases cover of \$700,000 which is the net present value of future earnings using a discount rate of ten percent and expected working life of 15 years. Assume that the relative utility of the risk-averse and risk-embracing choices is given by the ratio of the number of people taking life insurance to the number not taking insurance, which is equal to 0.27 [Fitzgerald (2003)].

For both insurers and non insurers, consider that living is a 'gain' and dying is a 'loss'. Given the lack of bias in timing, limited role of skill, and clarity of the decision, make the weightings, w_G and w_L, equal. Thus the only unknowns are ρ_{RE} and ρ_{RA}.

The utilities of the decision alternatives of taking insurance and not taking insurance in any single year are as follows:

Utility of taking insurance (i.e. the risk-averse decision)

= utility of living + utility of insurance payout on death

= u(earnings − insurance premium) + u(insurance payout)

= $0.9983*(80000\text{-}3290)*e^{-(80000\text{-}3290)/\rho RA}$
+ $0.0017*(700000\text{-}3290).e^{-(700000\text{-}3290)/\rho RA}$

Utility of not taking insurance (i.e. the risk-embracing decision)

= utility of living without paying an insurance premium + utility of death

= $0.9983*(80000)*e^{-80000/\rho RE} + 0.0017*0*e^{0/\rho RE}$

From the equation above:

$$\frac{0.9983*(80000\text{-}3290)*e^{-(80000\text{-}3290)/\rho RA} + 0.0017*(700000\text{-}3290).e^{-(700000\text{-}3290)/\rho RA}}{0.9983*(80000)*e^{-80000/\rho RE}}$$

= 0.27

Table 4 shows the average risk budgets of the proportions of the population that takes up life insurance and does not take up life insurance. The data provide solutions across relatively wide risk budgets, but at all meaningful levels, people buying insurance are risk-averse with a positive risk budget; and those not buying life insurance have a greater risk propensity as evidenced by a markedly higher value of ρ_{RE} (which becomes negative for aggressive risk embracers).

Table 10.5. Risk Budgets for Life Insurance

Insurers' Risk Budget ρ_{RA}	Non Insurers' Risk Budget ρ_{RE}
46,000	200,000
53,000	500,000
57,000	1,000,000
75,000	-300,000
100,000	-155,000
200,000	-90,000
300,000	-78,000
1,000,000	-66,000

In Australia the working population is covered by compulsory occupational superannuation which typically includes a life insurance component. Thus most life insurance policies are "top ups" and this can make the risk-reward trade-offs hard to evaluate. Even so, the RBT approach provides a working explanation for the different decisions.

The second decision category is racetrack wagering markets and data are drawn from Coleman (2004). Consider for simplicity that bettors have a choice between backing a favourite (average dividend \$2.3 and probability of winning of 0.46) and a longshot (\$10.1 and 0.08). In each case a win is the 'gain' result which provides a net profit of the winnings (dividend x wager) less the wager; and a loss equal to the wager is a 'loss'. Assume that the relative utility of backing favourites and backing longshots is 0.64 (this value comes from the respective proportions of the pool bet on favourites and longshots of 0.39 and 0.61).

Assuming equal weights, the utilities of the decision choices of backing favourites and longshots for \$80,000 are as follows:

Utility of backing favourites

$$= \quad u(win) + u(loss)$$
$$= \quad 0.46*(1.3*80,000)*e^{-(1.3*80000)/\rho RA} \; + \; 0.54*-80000.e^{80000/\rho RA}$$

Utility of backing longshots

$$= \quad 0.08*(9.1*80000)*e^{-(9.1*80000)/\rho RE} + 0.92*-80000*e^{80000/\rho RE}$$

Thus:

$$\frac{0.46*(1.3*80,000)*e^{-(1.3*80000)/\rho RA} + \quad 0.54*-80000.e^{80000/\rho RA}}{0.64}$$
$$= 0.08*(9.1*80000)*e^{-(9.1*80000)/\rho RE} + 0.92*-80000*e^{80000/\rho RE}$$

The table below shows the average risk budget, ρ, of the proportions of the wagering population that back favourites and longshots. Again the data provide solutions across relatively wide ranges of ρ. But at all meaningful levels, people backing favourites are risk-averse with a positive risk budget; and those backing longshots have a much greater risk propensity

Table 10.6. Risk Budgets for Racetrack Bettors

Back Favourites ρ_{RA}	Back Longshots ρ_{Re}
25,000	25,700
100,000	152,300
150,000	430,000
194,000	790,000

The third decision domain is investor preference between bonds and equities, and relevant US data from Ibbotson Associates (1996) are summarized in the table below.

Table 10.7. US Investment Returns from 1926 to 1995: percent per year

	Large Company Stocks	Long Term Government Bonds
Annual Total Return		
Arithmetic mean	12.5	5.5
Standard deviation	20.4	9.2
Years with Negative Return		
Proportion (%)	28.6	27.1
Average return (%)	-12.3	-3.2
Years with Negative Return		
Annual return (%)	22.4	8.7

A typical portfolio mix of 70 percent equities and 30 percent bonds suggests that the relative utility of investing in equities is around 2.3 times that of investing in bonds. Define a `win' in any year as receiving the expected return and a `loss' as a negative return, and consider an investor with $80,000:

Utility of investing in equities (i.e. risk embracing choice)

$$= u(\text{positive return}) + u(\text{negative return})$$
$$= 0.714*(0.224*80000)*e^{-(0.224*80000)/\rho RE} + 0.286*-(0.123*80000).e^{(0.123*80000)/\rho RE}$$

Utility of investing in bonds

$$= 0.729*(0.087*80000)*e^{-(0.087*80000)/\rho RA}$$
$$+ 0.271*-(0.032*80000)*e^{(0.032*80000)/\rho RA}$$

Table 10.8 shows the ranges of risk budgets for a typical investment of $80,000.

Table 10.8. Risk Budgets for Investors in US Markets

Bond Investors	Equity Investors
10,000	34,500
25,000	85,000
50,000	180,000
200,000	1,300,000

Again RBT explains different decision maker preferences and shows that equity investors are markedly higher risk takers than bond investors

CHAPTER 11   Conclusions

"The essence of ultimate decision remains impenetrable to the observer - often, indeed, to the decider himself ... There will always be the dark and tangled stretches in the decision making process - mysterious even to those who may be most intimately involved."
President John F. Kennedy Allison (1971: vi)

This final chapter summarises the book's resolution of its research questions, and draws conclusions for practicing managers into what might be termed *Enterprise Level Risk Strategy*.

Answers to the Research Questions

This book had two research questions: when managers make decisions, what leads them to choose a risky alternative? And: what determines whether the decision proves correct? This section provides answers in the form of conclusions from the book's research.

What Leads Managers to Choose a Risky Alternative?

The two surveys in this book separately examined individuals' decision making in isolation, and in the context of their organisations' influence. Without the overlay of their organisation, people choose a risky alternative because of their personality, circumstances and expectations. Their risk propensity is a mixture of relatively stable personal traits such as risk attitudes and decision style; more fluid determinants such as current endowment and other risks being faced; and transient factors such as the decision attributes, especially the most likely outcome. Contrary to normative decision models, the `facts' of a decision have minimal influence on decision makers' choices.

In terms of decisions made for organisations, the principal-agent assumption would suggest that organisational risk propensity should be driven by factors similar to those above. This proved only partly true because the attributes of executives are mediated by industry factors and by corporate strategies and practices. In particular, companies that have higher risk propensity are larger, in less dynamic industries, and tend to have low standards and weak management practices.

Looking at managers' decisions outside an organisational context, the first variable that explains risk propensity is demographic, and the most important personal characteristic was the value of investments, excluding the principal residence: the more wealth, the lower the willingness to take risk. Because wealth rises with income, age and years of employment, these three factors were also associated with lower risk taking. It should be noted, though, that this does not imply that older managers do not take risks, only that they take fewer risks. Moreover the analysis was not able to discriminate between the quality of judgement, so the fewer risks taken by older managers may be better (or worse) judged than those of younger peers.

Gender was not a significant influence on whether or not people chose a risky alternative. This confirms other studies which have found that there are many situations in which women are as willing as men to take well-judged risks [Byrnes et al. (1999)].

The second determinant of risk taking is a mediating variable which can be thought of as decision making style, typified by expectation that risk is not higher when facing decisions we do not understand. This is driven by a variety of style features such as decision makers' belief that they have not received more of the breaks in life than others and belief that the description 'controlled' does not match their behaviour.

Factor analysis classifies risk takers as: inexperienced; less educated and more tolerant of ambiguity; fatalistic and insecure; and biased to longshots. Those respondents who did not take a risk are: risk averse; not Type-A personality; not adventure seeking; and reluctant to make a decision. Significantly this is generally consistent with normative expectations about risk propensity, and they provide a useful means of classifying risk attitudes.

These findings have significant implications for management: risk-takers' beliefs and personal risk preferences are major drivers of their decisions. People who choose risky alternatives are confident after a record of successful risk-taking and receiving the benefits of luck. There are also indications that at least some risk-prone individuals believe they can use strategies such as planning to control the risks they face. Taken together, the insignificance of facts and confidence of success suggest that the affect of an outcome is a major decision driver. People decide to take a risky alternative because of their innate features, learned decision making style, and feeling about success.

The evidence also helps explain the prevalent longshot bias in managerial decision making. For instance, table 8.7 shows that two variables with the strongest links to risk propensity (p<0.01) were belief that the situation has large potential for gain and confidence in a successful outcome. Managers who take risky decisions with low probability of success believe that they can succeed.

The second survey links managers' decisions to their organisation, and showed that risk propensity was shaped by societal constraints, industry regulation and competition, and the organisation's strategic decisions and processes. Risk tolerance tended to be higher for: males; younger and shorter-serving employees; respondents who believe in chance and feel they take risks in business; and for respondents who are neither companionable nor calm in group discussions.

Respondents indicated that a higher level of risk tolerance in their organisations was associated with: an industry that is risky and not innovative; higher sales revenue; companies whose Boards lack expertise in risks associated with operations, environment and finance; companies which are not profit oriented, cut corners to get results, do not have an ethical approach to business, do not have high standards for product quality and do not take pride in innovative business models; and organisations which resist sharing bad news, do not appoint the best candidates as managers, do not tolerate unpopular ideas and have high turnover of executives; and companies which produce finished consumer goods, and have decentralised decision making and excellent human resource strategies.

What Determines Whether Risky Choices Prove Correct?

The second research question is what determines whether a risky choice proves successful or not. As the *process* of decision making was not examined in the book, no conclusion can be reached about decision quality. The book's empirical research showed that companies which have poor risk outcomes and suffer crises are in industries which are slow growing, regulated, risky, uncompetitive, technologically advanced and not responsive to consumer needs.

Companies which are most likely to encounter crises and serious incidents share several common traits which contain the seeds of major problems. In terms of their operations, they produce finished products, have many complex activities, grow slowly, and hold offshore investments. Their staffing practices are weak as they do not appoint the best candidates as managers. These risky organisations impose strong pressures for results with a record of repeated cost-cutting programs. They tolerate poor management practices such as cutting corners to get results, and low quality standards.

This sets them up for strategic failures from a wave of knock-on impacts through process systems. When failure does occur, a company which produces finished goods faces immediate customer impact. Control and reporting difficulties mean that offshore investments are also common sources of crises. Not surprisingly, crises primarily affect larger companies: 57 percent of organisations with an annual turnover under $100 million had not experienced a crisis, whereas only 37 percent of larger organisations had been crisis free. Companies in the manufacturing sector were most likely to have experienced a crisis (60 percent experienced a crisis, compared to 52 percent of companies in other sectors), whereas they are relatively rare in services organisations (26 percent experienced a crisis).

Conversely, factors which are typically thought to trigger crises and serious incidents – such as risk management practices and executives' attributes – have minimal *direct* influence: about half of all crises and serous incidents can be traced to structural exposures, pressure for results, and poor management practices.

Given the influence of company strategy and goals, it is not surprising that companies which are crisis-prone have Boards which lack expertise, and have weak management. Further support for the conclusion that organisations largely cause their own crises is that companies impacted by crises tend to have slightly weaker risk management practices (although this is not significant in crisis frequency).

Apart from structural factors, companies create the potential for crises by promoting a pressure-cooker atmosphere with demands for results and repeated cost-cutting programs. This inevitably leads to instability; but it also induces a climate of corner cutting, and tolerance of low standards in product quality and performance.

Thus organisations experience crises because of their strategies and processes, rather than an absence of good risk management practices.

Although different types of crises tend to be lumped together, they have different root causes. For instance, reputational crises occur in organisations with corner cutting, rapid complex activities, centralised decision making and a high level of internal competition. Operational crises occur in organisations with cost-cutting programs, low turnover of executives, directors who are not comfortable with risk management processes, and a regulated industry. This suggests that reputational crises arise in the way an organisation is governed, whereas operational crises stem from inadequate resources and staid management.

Enterprise Level Risk Strategy

The discussion and empirical data from earlier chapters show that risk has significant strategic implications for the decision making processes of firms. Logically then, enterprise-level decisions should specifically incorporate risk. This section draws on material in the book to detail processes whereby enterprise-level strategic decisions can specifically incorporate measures of risk. This answers the question: how can a manager dial up the right level of risk?

As discussed in chapter two, the topic of corporate risk strategy promoted a vibrant literature during the 1970s and 1980s, but lacked real-world validity and fell into abeyance. Despite this past lack of success, the growth of interest in strategic risk management points to a pressing need to develop practical guidance on how to incorporate risk into corporate strategy. For instance, Baird and Thomas (1985: 231) found "that because of the nature of strategy, risk is embedded in most long-range decisions. Yet risk may be ignored or misunderstood by strategists who have received little systematic help in understanding risk from the field of business policy." Aaker and Jacobson (1987: 277) were similarly clear: "failures to account for risk adequately will unquestionably lead to inappropriate decisions."

This section seeks to fill a gap in the literature by providing guidance on how to specifically incorporate risk into corporate decisions. It updates a useful management tool by examining the need for an enterprise-level risk strategy, and developing its key elements by extending conclusions drawn from the book. The aim is to establish risk strategy as a core managerial competence.

The Case for Enterprise Level Risk Strategy

Risk management is usually seen as a desirable goal in itself because it reduces costs and improves organisational quality. In addition it is an imperative of corporate governance given the exposures of directors and executives to legislation and community outrage. Unfortunately risk strategy in corporates has been reduced to either elimination of workplace hazards or detailed documentation to support a defence against accusations of irresponsible decision making. This ignores the obvious fact that Board due diligence is ineffectual unless the organisation culture is right.

A strong case can be made for a more sophisticated approach that promotes risk strategy at the enterprise level as a technique to benefit: shareholders, managers and employees, and customers and community. Let us consider each in turn.

First shareholders. According to the assumptions of modern capital markets theory, shareholders are able to diversify away firm-specific risks; thus they derive no benefit from a reduction in firm risk, and may in fact incur a penalty if risk management diverts managers from other duties, or if risk is directly related to return. There is, however, considerable theoretical argument and empirical evidence to dispute these normative assumptions.

As discussed in chapter five, a number of studies have explained a significant portion of the variance in accounting returns using firm parameters that encompass risk. Aaker and Jacobson (1987) found a highly significant ($p<0.01$) link between unsystematic risk and Return on Investment, which suggests that return is influenced by the risk consequences of strategy and managerial decisions. Amit and Wernerfelt (1990) found a strong inverse relationship ($p<0.001$) between return and business risk, and concluded it arose because lower risk improved operational efficiency and increased cash flows. A similar conclusion emerged in work by Miller and Bromiley (1990) who identified a factor called strategic risk which was related to higher ratios of debt to equity and capital to sales, and a lower ratio of R&D spending to sales. Strategic risk had a strong inverse relationship ($p<0.001$) with return on equity and return on assets, and they concluded that achieving the right level of business or strategic risk is critical to firms' financial performance.

Given the need for firms to simultaneously meet competing objectives and allocate scarce resources, it is not surprising that risk is important: in the case of cash flow, for example, shareholders always want a greater quantum (on the assumption that this increases the value of their equity), and the firms' decision makers rarely have enough cash to satisfy the competing demands for dividends, investment, capital expenditure, and debt servicing. Risk is the common factor in increasing cash flow and optimising its allocation.

The second group with an interest in a firm's risk strategy are its managers and other employees. In addition to changes in wealth through employee options and shares, they seek to preserve their jobs and promote their career through association with organisational success. Thus employees – especially senior executives – must avoid risks that could damage the firm. But they must also accept well-judged risks to demonstrate skill. Managers, then, need to be able to evaluate alternatives and accept appropriate risks.

The third group with an interest in risk strategy are a firm's customers and community who rely upon quality performance to minimise their own exposure to inadequate input goods and services and dangerous practices.

There is an opportunity cost to all stakeholders when firms do not optimise their performance.

The clear linkages between risk and stakeholder value provide strong motivation for better calibration of enterprise risk taking. The benefits of risk strategy are so broad and deep that CEOs should take on the role of making it a key part of corporate vision and mission; and risk strategy should be specifically incorporated in managers' goals. Without senior support, initiatives can be dismissed as another fad, and ignored whenever resources dry up. Further, unless the benefits of a new culture of risk strategy are demonstrated by senior management (and its successes rewarded), the organisation will not take it on.

People Selection

Because risk taking responds to institutional influences, the first critical step in corporate risk strategy relates to the Board as it sets the firm's goals, objectives and standards. The risk propensity and expertise of individual directors is important. The Board's composition is important, too, as groups have different risk propensities to those of their individual members. Group interaction – which lifts risk propensity [Stone (1968)] - is promoted by age differences (a decade or more), familiarity between members which facilitates mutual understanding, and distinct roles [Gummer (1998)]. Moreover, the way the Board is tasked (i.e. framed) shapes its effectiveness and the quality of its decisions: a group which is confident of success will choose an alternative which offers a high payout; one in a pessimistic frame of mind will contemplate disaster.

Once the Board composition is right, it selects the level of risk which is appropriate to stakeholders. Because implementing enterprise level risk strategy will be an integral part of manager decision making and managers have different levels of risk propensity depending on the personal traits and experience, the next step is to fill key decision making positions with individuals who have the appropriate risk credentials. This second step starts with the recognition that "the CEO is the single most important factor in a company's stock price" [Jackofsky et al. (1988)]. Also, as noted above, the CEO is particularly critical in setting a risk vision and implementing its elements. Thus the risk attributes of the CEO are important to firm risk strategy. So, too, with managers whose risk competencies are an essential prerequisite for implementing an enterprise level risk strategy. That is because the attitude of managers towards a decision's risks influences their evaluation of the available alternatives and their expectation of the outcomes, and will shape their behaviours and the success of the decision [Pablo et al. (1996)].

Managers' risk propensity is determined by their personal traits and decision making styles. Managers who are more likely to take risks are characterised as younger and comfortable with ambiguity; describe themselves as being companionable and confident; and have gained confidence from a history of successful risk-taking. They expect their risk taking to be successful.

Also important amongst these credentials are managers' tacit knowledge which Brockmann and Anthony (2002: 436) defined as:

"the work-related practical knowledge learned informally through experience on the job. It is an intellectual and cognitive process that is neither expressed nor declared openly but rather implied or simply understood. It is intimately related to action such that it reflects knowing how as contrasted with knowing what."

A consequence of selecting managers for their risk propensity is to make the organisation more diverse. The introduction of new ideas and viewpoints should improve the quality of decision making, and the diversification of culture has been shown to enhance revenues [Gilbert and Ivancevich (2000)]. A further consequence of specifically incorporating risk into decision making is to alter the way that scarce resources are allocated.

In summary the framework and setting of an institution shape the decision style and conclusions of its managers and hence the organisation's risk taking. These factors can be structural such as Board composition and financial objectives; or they can be more fluid and arise in setting goals, response to uncertainty and willingness to accept change.

Framing Corporate Risk Philosophy

The way that decisions are presented and comprehended is an important factor in risk taking. When decisions are framed positively by their proponents, risk propensity is high; so, too, with self-framing of the decision.

Framing impacts on risk propensity through structural factors from previous decisions so that the institutional setting of an organisation – in terms of its industry, environment and resources – exerts considerable influence on decision making processes. These include norms, expectations and policies which determine the information available to managers, their goals and objectives, and analytical processes: together these determine the way a firm identifies, evaluates and progresses strategies [Goodrick and Salancik (1996)]. Thus organisations not only reflect the views of their human constituents, but have decision attributes which are analogous to human traits of personality, decision making style, risk tolerance and aspirations.

A major contributor to an organisation's risk is uncertainty in the processes which it uses to calibrate risks and reach decisions, including selection of risk parameters. Thus in developing appropriate strategy there can be conflict over the level of risks that will be tolerated in order to strive for a particular goal. An important element of enterprise level risk strategy is to provide comprehensive education in the technique, including its justification and methodology. This will promote employee acceptance and buy-in.

Given that enterprise level risk is important to stakeholders, it should be operationalised in decision making. Achieving this requires resolution of possible conflicts between each stakeholder group's perception of the appropriate measure of risk and the desirable quantum. Without a sensible plan and set of goals, risk strategy will lack direction and operate inefficiently, if at all.

For these reasons organisation structure is very important. A decentralised organisational structure tends to promote risk taking. Organisational practices that discourage risk-taking include extensive procedures and complicated approvals processes. Organisations that reward success and measure results against outcomes promote risk taking. Conversely risk aversion comes in the absence of individual rewards [Pablo et al. (1996)]. As pointed out by Sitkin and Pablo (1992), framing can establish unseen organisational guidelines which act almost automatically to drive risk propensity.

Because firms with superior financial performance make quicker strategic decisions [Wally and Baum (1994)], it is desirable to accelerate the pace of decision making. One approach is to select managers with higher intelligence, greater tolerance for risk, and a strong propensity to act because they make decisions more quickly (as opposed to managers who are loss-averse and can complicate the decision making process to minimise possibility of failure). Risk taking is also promoted when managers trust their subordinates, and when goals are clear [Bozeman and Kingsley (1998)].

The pace of decision making will also respond to organisation structure. For instance, risk propensity is reduced by red tape and insistence on following rules and procedures [Bozeman and Kingsley (1998)]. Similarly the pace of decision making may be faster in more centralised firms [Pablo et al. (1996)], which – less certainly – leads to higher risk propensity.

Organisations do not simply reflect a single viewpoint, but operate organically to synthesise disparate information and to reach a consensus decision amidst conflict over goals and uncertain outcomes. In terms of risk propensity, this can lead groups to be more risk prone than the average of their members. A second implication arises if there are unclear processes followed in reaching decisions under risk: it can be hard to distinguish between the risks associated with a particular decision, and the attitudes of decision makers towards the risks [Spetzler (1968)].

Framing is a powerful tool in risk management and is also important to any firm's risk propensity. Risk is `sticky' as evidence shows it is related to historical risk [Bromiley (1991)], and so framing (and other structural influences on risk) establishes a lasting pattern of risk behaviours.

Evaluating Decision Risk

The first step in evaluating decision risk is to establish corporate risk propensity in a two-stage process. This evaluates the individual propensity of senior executives, then uses a group to decide the corporate measure. The two stages are essential as corporate risk taking is driven by group strategy, and is not directly related to individuals' attitudes. Thus simply taking an average of the values for senior executives may not reflect reality. Once corporate risk propensity, ρ, has been evaluated, it can be applied to project evaluation using Risk Budget Theory.

Even if an enterprise correctly titrates its risk appetite and puts in place the right structure and managers, it still faces unknown exposures if the risks associated with individual decisions are not correctly determined. In particular, if managers over-estimate the probability of success from any decision, the risk is increased. This can arise, for instance, in organisations with industry average skills whose managers project outcomes on the basis that the organisation's skills are top quartile.

Unrecognised enterprise risk can also come from over-estimating the probability of success of a complex strategy. Consider a system with n individual elements, each with an individual probability of failure of $Pr(F_x)$; and assume that success for the system relies upon every element operating correctly. The probability of failure of the system is equal to:

$$1 - [(1 - Pr(F_1)) * (1 - Pr(F_2)) * ... * (1 - Pr(F_n))]$$

The maximum probability of success for the system is equal to the probability of success of the least reliable component (the weakest link). The next table shows that multiple inter-relationships can give an objective probability of failure which is relatively high[72]: for a strategy with more than about 20 elements to have a greater than 50 percent probability of success, each element needs to be 95+ percent reliable. Failure to acknowledge these inter-relationships explains consistent overestimation of

---

[72] Over and above that, of course, is a layer of complexity and uncertainty involved in chaotic or non-linear dynamic systems whose course is determined by their unknowable initial conditions.

the probability of complex events. It also explains why tightly coupled systems can experience catastrophic failure.

Table 11.1. Equal Probability of System Success or Failure

Number of Elements, n	Probability of any Single Element's Failure (%)
5	13
10	7
20	3.5
50	1.4

Significantly most studies of decision making by managers show that they "do not trust, do not understand, or simply do not use probability estimates" [March and Shapira (1987: 1411)]. This reflects the difficulty in making probability estimates, which itself is an excellent justification for the steps discussed above. But of greater significance is the possibility that lack of interest in probabilities may also reflect the compatibility principle where managers see decisions as optimising income, and so place most weight on financial measures. The net effect is to induce systematic underweighting of the negatives of a decision, including its probability of failure (which is: 1 – probability of success).

There are several key steps to ensuring that decision risks are correctly evaluated, most of them built around the hard-nosed realism of legendary investor Paul Cabot: "first you've got to get the facts. Then you've got to face the facts" [Yogg (2003: 35)]. One step in avoiding outcome myopia is to prepare a population-based estimate using historical data from comparable strategies executed by the enterprise, by its peers in the same industry, and by firms in other sectors. The second is to frame problems broadly, specifically by preparing three scenarios in which the decision is executed badly, as it would be by a competitor, and flawlessly. A third step is to independently review the decision and implementation plans – ideally this should involve disinterested third parties with appropriate experience.

The sole objective of these steps is to ensure consistent application of the enterprise's risk strategy.

Managing Implementation Risk

There are few risky decisions that implement themselves, never need monitoring, and cannot offer lessons from a post-audit. Each of these is an important component of enterprise level risk strategy.

Once a decision has been made, a key managerial competence is to successfully shape its outcomes. As part of this, managers seek to preserve optionality in decisions because this flexibility permits incremental optimisation of outcomes as they unfold. This is an act-then-learn strategy. On the other hand, if every aspect of a decision is locked in, then there is no scope to make improvements as experience and understanding are gained. Good managers also allocate surplus resources to match the risks associated with a decision: this is risk management at its best mitigates exposure from high-risk actions.

Another important component of a practical risk strategy is to meaningfully post-audit risky strategic decisions to publicise the learnings on risk evaluation and decision making. All too often firms do not learn from their mistakes as they do not study them and do not share their lessons.

All of this sets up a neat tension between strategic options. Consider a company that wishes to grow. It can decide on an acquisition with a 25 percent probability of adding shareholder value. Or it can decide to grow organically with R&D projects that are rarely profitable, major capital projects that massively over-run their budgets, and very long lead times from new products. Is it more risky to grow organically or abruptly?

Risk strategy is clearly more art than science, so continuous application will enable firms to develop appropriate competencies in their managers. This, for instance, would include definition of strategic initiatives, evaluation of potential risk sources, and implementation management. The consequences of the converse position are so serious that Chatterjee et al. (2003: 69) warn: "*ad hoc* risk-taking threatens firm survival."

Reporting Corporate Risk Strategy

A significant potential risk from corporate risk strategy is that it can be misinterpreted when viewed in hindsight or isolation. In a provocative analysis, Viscusi (2000: 586) suggests that product liability suits where juries awarded the highest penalties involved defendants which had conducted risk evaluations and cost-benefit analyses, but decided not to eliminate a known (usually small) risk associated with use of their products. He pointed out: "This result is the opposite of what would occur if the legal system fostered better corporate risk behavior."

Viscusi (2000: 548) asks whether "a corporation is being irresponsible if it undertakes a risk analysis and chooses not to make an unbounded cost commitment to safety." Although it might be desirable for companies to think systematically about risk and to sensibly balance safety with stakeholders' willingness to pay for it, doing so in a logical manner can be misconstrued as putting a price on safety.

The same misinterpretation risk applies to post-implementation audits and analyses of incidents or crises. Viscusi (2000: 567) provides a sober warning to risk strategists:

"The analysis [following a serious product failure] should highlight shortcomings that can be fixed to prevent future tragedies. The effect of such a frank assessment, however, could be to increase the company's liability... Companies face a complex Catch 22 situation. If they [do not undertake a] post-accident risk evaluation, they might be found irresponsible for failing to address the risks that caused the accident ... But a frank post-accident report that is shared with the plaintiffs could affect the company's liability for the accident if the report finds fault with the company practices that led to the accident."

Moreover, if the company fails to produce the report or destroys it, then juries could potentially draw an adverse inference and presume that the report would have been unfavourable.

In summary, implementing an enterprise-level risk strategy has numerous elements. Given that the facts of a risky decision are less important than personal attributes and the affect of risk-taking, then simply expanding on data and analysis will not change decisions. In a conclusion familiar to many students of organisational design, the people need to be changed, not just the structure. Sitkin and Pablo (1992), for instance, hypothesise that homogeneity in an organisation's senior management reduces the quality of decision analysis, and can lead to groupthink with extreme perceptions of risk. Moreover the cultural norms, including risk values, of an organisation will shape managers' decisions, particularly the way they frame alternatives. Thus framing of the decision, especially its outcome, is important for its influence on affect. Managerial risk propensity can be promoted by rewarding individuals' initiative and success, rather than forcing adherence to process [Pablo et al. (1996)]. Longer term, there is a suggestion that successful experience in risky decision making and education about the process will help modify behaviour.

Endnote

The final point follows President Kennedy's epigram at the opening of this chapter. No matter how much researchers would like to claim a definitive conceptual framework for decision making under risk, it remains an enigmatic process. No matter how much managers would like to assert control of their decisions, their ability to do so is sorely constrained. The study of decision making under risk remains a fertile field of study.

Appendix: Copy of Survey Materials

The following pages contain copies of the two Surveys used in this study.

Carter Racing Case Study

- Letter to potential respondents
- Description of the case
- Survey Questionnaire

Survey on Corporate Risk Management

- Survey Questionnaire

Letter to Potential Respondents

Re: Invitation to Participate in Melbourne University Survey on Risk and Decisionmaking

This note is to invite you to take part in a web-based survey which examines strategies followed by experienced decision makers. The work is the field research component of my PhD thesis entitled "The Influence of Risk on Decision-making"; it is being conducted in the University of Melbourne's Department of Management under the supervision of Professor Danny Samson. The project has been approved by the University's Human Research Ethics Committee.

If you elect to participate, you will need to read the attached case study and then follow a link onto the University of Melbourne's website to complete a questionnaire. The process is designed to be similar to that involved in an everyday business decision; it should take no more than about 20 minutes to complete, and has no associated risks.

Your participation is completely voluntary and you may withdraw at any time, including return of any data supplied. Participation is anonymous; all materials will be kept strictly confidential and not used for any purposes other than this study.

It is anticipated that the results will be available later this year – you will be advised then and a summary made available electronically. If you are interested, I would also be delighted to send you a copy of the full results and welcome feedback.

If you have any questions please do not hesitate to e-mail me (p.coleman1@pgrad.unimelb.edu.au) or call on 0413 901085. Alternatively, if you have any concerns regarding the conduct of this research project you can contact the Executive Officer, Human Research Ethics, the University of Melbourne, Victoria 3010, ph: (03) 8344 7507; fax: (03) 9347 6739.

Regards,

Les Coleman

International Race Engineering Limited

Re: Carter Racing – Should They Start Tomorrow?

We have been asked to advise Carter Racing Team on whether they should race their car in tomorrow's Formula One Grand Prix.

You will recall that this is Carter's critical first year in Grand Prix racing and it has been [not very/very] successful with [one/five] top five finishes in ten races [RESULTS]. Their performance has been due to use of a unique engine head which was designed to produce more power while maintaining modest fuel consumption. Casting the head in a high-strength aircraft alloy saved almost 20 kilograms of weight, but the alloy is not as temperature sensitive as the material in the engine block. However, an appropriate head gasket handles the different expansion rates.

Unfortunately, the Carter team has suffered [mild/chronic] engine problems with [one/five] blown engines in their ten outings [RISKPROB]. The loss is high given $50,000 per engine and wasted racing costs. The cause of the problem is unknown.

One possibility is that engine failure is related to ambient air temperature: when the weather is cold the different expansion rates for the head and block damage the head gasket and cause engine failure (see chart).

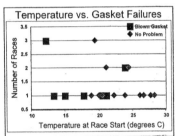

Temperature vs. Gasket Failures

Carter Racing has spent considerable money and effort in trying to resolve the problem. Its engineering expert is a qualified mechanical engineer and industry expert with a master's degree. He believes that ambient temperature [is/is not] the cause of the engine failures [EXPERTQUAL].

The temperature tomorrow is forecast to be 15°C, which is in the 'danger zone' if ambient temperatures cause the engine failures.

It is clear to all of us that luck is important in racing. Teams like Carter push the limits of what is known and cannot expect to have everything under control. We all know that winning involves risks: the drivers have their lives on the line, we contractors have careers hanging on results, and owners have got every dollar tied up in the business.

Even so, tomorrow's race is particularly important to Carter given the prize money and TV exposure and the critical need to cement their position. Goodstone Tyre has finally decided on a big sponsorship deal worth $400,000 per year plus bonuses if Carter Racing finishes in the top five in its next race. But if they race and lose another engine, Goodstone will want this year's money ($150,000) back. Even worse, Carter may lose $250,000 in oil sponsorship: no company wants a national TV audience to see a smoker dragged off the track with their name plastered all over it.

So another success will see a new star in Grand Prix racing and bring additional sponsors. But without them Carter faces [almost certain bankruptcy/some financial pressures] [ALTERN].

*   *   *   *   *

Please think about whether you recommend that Carter Race tomorrow or not. Then click on the link below to go to a questionnaire which records your answer and associated information

http://tintin.ecom.unimelb.edu.au/carter01CL/

Web Survey

SHOULD CARTER COMPETE?

1. Should Carter compete in the race tomorrow? Please advise your recommendation by ticking one of the boxes.

- ○ Race
- ○ Do not race

Thank you for your answer. To help us understand the influences on decisions, please complete the balance of this survey. It should take you about 15 minutes. Although questions are voluntary, please answer as many as possible because incomplete results limit the value of the data you provide. Each question requires you to indicate one response that best represents your view. There are no right and wrong answers. Do not spend too much time on any question, but try to answer each one frankly and thoughtfully. To ensure absolute confidentiality, the surveys are anonymous, and no individual results will be reported.

THANK YOU FOR YOUR PARTICIPATION

ABOUT YOUR DECISION ON CARTER RACING

Think about the decision you made on whether Carter Racing should compete.

2. If you were the owner of Carter Racing, what is the probability that you would decide to race (where 0%=Definitely not race, and 100%=Definitely race)?

- ○ 0 %
- ○ 1-20%
- ○ 21-40%
- ○ 41-60%
- ○ 61-80 %
- ○ 81-99 %
- ○ 100 %

The statements below relate to the Case Study you have just read. Please indicate how much you *__agree__* or *__disagree__* with each statement.

3. Tomorrow's race is very risky

- ○ Strongly Agree
- ○ Agree
- ○ Neutral
- ○ Disagree
- ○ Strongly Disagree

4. Carter Racing can exert control over the situation.

- ○ Strongly Agree
- ○ Agree
- ○ Neutral
- ○ Disagree
- ○ Strongly Disagree

5. Carter's management have the skill to make their own decision

- ○ Strongly Agree
- ○ Agree
- ○ Neutral
- ○ Disagree
- ○ Strongly Disagree

6. The situation faced by Carter is a significant threat.

- ○ Strongly Agree
- ○ Agree
- ○ Neutral
- ○ Disagree
- ○ Strongly Disagree

7. If this opportunity is passed up, there will never be another as good.

- ○ Strongly Agree
- ○ Agree
- ○ Neutral
- ○ Disagree
- ○ Strongly Disagree

8. The situation faced by Carter Racing has large potential for gain.

- ○ Strongly Agree
- ○ Agree
- ○ Neutral
- ○ Disagree
- ○ Strongly Disagree

9. The opinion of Carter's engineering expert was influential in my recommendation.

- ○ Strongly Agree
- ○ Agree
- ○ Neutral
- ○ Disagree
- ○ Strongly Disagree

10. I would make the same recommendation if I were driving the racing car.

- ○ Strongly Agree

○ Agree
○ Neutral
○ Disagree
○ Strongly Disagree

11. Carter Racing can tolerate large risks.

○ Strongly Agree
○ Agree
○ Neutral
○ Disagree
○ Strongly Disagree

12. Carter Racing will probably follow the recommendation of International Race Engineering.

○ Strongly Agree
○ Agree
○ Neutral
○ Disagree
○ Strongly Disagree

13. The choice was difficult for me to make.

○ Strongly Agree
○ Agree
○ Neutral
○ Disagree
○ Strongly Disagree

14. Carter Racing is in a positive situation.

○ Strongly Agree
○ Agree
○ Neutral
○ Disagree
○ Strongly Disagree

15. Carter has a record of making the right decisions.

○ Strongly Agree
○ Agree
○ Neutral
○ Disagree
○ Strongly Disagree

16. Success tomorrow will meet Carter's strategic objectives.

○ Strongly Agree
○ Agree
○ Neutral
○ Disagree

○ Strongly Disagree

17. The outcome is very important to Carter Racing.

- ○ Strongly Agree
- ○ Agree
- ○ Neutral
- ○ Disagree
- ○ Strongly Disagree

18. Although Grand Prix is risky, Carter Racing can expect safe operation.

- ○ Strongly Agree
- ○ Agree
- ○ Neutral
- ○ Disagree
- ○ Strongly Disagree

19. The average person would make the same decision as me.

- ○ Strongly Agree
- ○ Agree
- ○ Neutral
- ○ Disagree
- ○ Strongly Disagree

20. Carter Racing is likely to succeed tomorrow.

- ○ Strongly Agree
- ○ Agree
- ○ Neutral
- ○ Disagree
- ○ Strongly Disagree

ABOUT YOU

Before proceeding further, please be sure you have read the instructions and description of the survey: please tick the item below as confirmation
Consent.

○ I have read the survey and agree to participate

Please help us to understand your decision by providing some information about yourself.

21. What is your gender.

- ○ Male
- ○ Female

22. What is your age in years.

- ○ 25 or less
- ○ 26-35
- ○ 36-45
- ○ 46-55
- ○ 55-65
- ○ 66 or older

23. What is your marital status.

- ○ Never married
- ○ Married
- ○ Separated
- ○ Divorced
- ○ Widowed

24. What is your nationality.

- ○ Asian
- ○ American
- ○ Australian
- ○ European

25. What is the highest education level you have completed.

- ○ Year 11 or 12
- ○ Apprenticeship or TAFE
- ○ Diploma
- ○ Bachelor Degree
- ○ Postgraduate Degree

26. How many years in total have you been in paid employment.

- ○ Less than 5
- ○ 5-10
- ○ 11-15
- ○ 16-20
- ○ 21 or more

27. Please indicate if you are a member of any of the following organisations

- ○ Association of Risk and Insurance Managers of Australasia
- ○ Australian Institute of Company Directors
- ○ Australian Institute of Management
- ○ CPA Australia

○ Finance and Treasury Association
○ Taxation Institute of Australia

28. Are you currently employed

○ Yes
○ No

29. If yes, are you employed.

○ Full time
○ Part time

30. What industry best describes that of your current job or most recent job.

○ Manufacturing
○ Wholesale or Retail Trade
○ Agriculture or Resources
○ Finance
○ Services
○ Government

31. What is the best description of your current or most recent job function.

○ Clerical
○ Craftsman
○ Professional
○ Executive
○ Student

32. How large is your current or most recent employer.

○ Less than 25 employees
○ 26 - 99 employees
○ 100 - 499 employees
○ 500 - 999 employees
○ 1000 - 10, 000 employees
○ Over 10,000 employees

33. What is your annual income before tax.

○ Less than $25,000
○ $25,000-50,000
○ $50,001-75,000
○ $75,001-100,000
○ $100,001-150,000
○ Over $150,000

34. What is the value of your investments (excluding principal residence)?

○ Less than $25,000

○ $25,000-100,000
○ $100,001-250,000
○ $250,001-500,000
○ $500,001-999,000
○ $1 million or more

35. Please indicate the approximate allocation of your investments (excluding principal residence)? (Each category is a percentage, and the total needs to add to 100%)

Australian equites or shares (%)	
Overseas equites or shares (%)	
Fixed interest or bonds (%)	
Investment property (%)	
Cash (%)	
Other (%)	

Think about each of the following statements. Please indicate how well you think that they fit *your* behaviour or beliefs.

36. Many important decisions are based on insufficient information.

○ Strongly Agree
○ Agree
○ Neutral
○ Disagree
○ Strongly Disagree

37. I would like to undertake an interesting experience even if it is dangerous.

○ Strongly Agree
○ Agree
○ Neutral
○ Disagree
○ Strongly Disagree

38. To achieve something in life one has to take risks.

○ Strongly Agree
○ Agree
○ Neutral
○ Disagree
○ Strongly Disagree

39. Risk is higher when facing situations we do not understand.

○ Strongly Agree
○ Agree
○ Neutral
○ Disagree
○ Strongly Disagree

40. I've not much sympathy for adventurous decisions.

○ Strongly Agree
○ Agree
○ Neutral
○ Disagree
○ Strongly Disagree

41. I become bored easily.

○ Strongly Agree
○ Agree
○ Neutral
○ Disagree
○ Strongly Disagree

42. I have always wanted to be better than others.

○ Strongly Agree
○ Agree
○ Neutral
○ Disagree
○ Strongly Disagree

43. I am calm and relaxed when participating in group discussions.

○ Strongly Agree
○ Agree
○ Neutral
○ Disagree
○ Strongly Disagree

44. Successful people take risks.

○ Strongly Agree
○ Agree
○ Neutral
○ Disagree
○ Strongly Disagree

45. I prefer to work in situations that require a high level of skill.

○ Strongly Agree
○ Agree
○ Neutral

○ Disagree
○ Strongly Disagree

46. When I get what I want it's usually because I'm lucky.

○ Strongly Agree
○ Agree
○ Neutral
○ Disagree
○ Strongly Disagree

47. I regularly set deadlines for myself.

○ Strongly Agree
○ Agree
○ Neutral
○ Disagree
○ Strongly Disagree

48. Risky situations can be made safer by planning ahead.

○ Strongly Agree
○ Agree
○ Neutral
○ Disagree
○ Strongly Disagree

49. If I play a game (eg. cards) I prefer to play for money.

○ Strongly Agree
○ Agree
○ Neutral
○ Disagree
○ Strongly Disagree

50. I have gotten more of the breaks in life than most of the people I know.

○ Strongly Agree
○ Agree
○ Neutral
○ Disagree
○ Strongly Disagree

51. I like to play it safe.

○ Strongly Agree
○ Agree
○ Neutral
○ Disagree
○ Strongly Disagree

52. In general I am very confident of my ability.

- ○ Strongly Agree
- ○ Agree
- ○ Neutral
- ○ Disagree
- ○ Strongly Disagree

53. My life is chiefly controlled by powerful others.

- ○ Strongly Agree
- ○ Agree
- ○ Neutral
- ○ Disagree
- ○ Strongly Disagree

54. In general, I am less willing to take risks than my colleagues.

- ○ Strongly Agree
- ○ Agree
- ○ Neutral
- ○ Disagree
- ○ Strongly Disagree

55. Everyone should have an equal chance and an equal say.

- ○ Strongly Agree
- ○ Agree
- ○ Neutral
- ○ Disagree
- ○ Strongly Disagree

Think about each of the following adjectives. Please indicate how well you think they fit *your* behaviour or beliefs.

56. Adaptable.

- ○ Strongly Agree
- ○ Agree
- ○ Neutral
- ○ Disagree
- ○ Strongly Disagree

57. Temperamental.

- ○ Strongly Agree
- ○ Agree
- ○ Neutral
- ○ Disagree

○ Strongly Disagree

58. Hard driving.

○ Strongly Agree
○ Agree
○ Neutral
○ Disagree
○ Strongly Disagree

59. Modest.

○ Strongly Agree
○ Agree
○ Neutral
○ Disagree
○ Strongly Disagree

60. Impulsive.

○ Strongly Agree
○ Agree
○ Neutral
○ Disagree
○ Strongly Disagree

61. Companionable.

○ Strongly Agree
○ Agree
○ Neutral
○ Disagree
○ Strongly Disagree

62. Controlled.

○ Strongly Agree
○ Agree
○ Neutral
○ Disagree
○ Strongly Disagree

63. Unconventional.

○ Strongly Agree
○ Agree
○ Neutral
○ Disagree
○ Strongly Disagree

64. Independent.

- O Strongly Agree
- O Agree
- O Neutral
- O Disagree
- O Strongly Disagree

65. Insecure.

- O Strongly Agree
- O Agree
- O Neutral
- O Disagree
- O Strongly Disagree

66. Inhibited.

- O Strongly Agree
- O Agree
- O Neutral
- O Disagree
- O Strongly Disagree

67. Aggressive.

- O Strongly Agree
- O Agree
- O Neutral
- O Disagree
- O Strongly Disagree

68. Competitive.

- O Strongly Agree
- O Agree
- O Neutral
- O Disagree
- O Strongly Disagree

Please think about your own attitude towards risk in different aspects of your life, and consider which of the following best fit *your* behaviour or beliefs.

69. In my personal life (eg. hobbies, recreation, leisure pursuits), I tend to take a lot of physical risks.

- O Strongly Agree
- O Agree
- O Neutral
- O Disagree
- O Strongly Disagree

70. In relation to my personal finances (eg. investments, superannuation and borrowing) I tend to take a lot of financial risks.

- O Strongly Agree
- O Agree
- O Neutral
- O Disagree
- O Strongly Disagree

71. In my business life I tend to take a lot of financial risks on behalf of my employer or clients.

- O Strongly Agree
- O Agree
- O Neutral
- O Disagree
- O Strongly Disagree

Submit Survey

Powered by SurveySolutions XP survey software

Web Survey

2003 AICD-Melbourne University Survey on Corporate Risk Management

Thank you for agreeing to take part in this survey which is designed to understand the risk environment inside Australian companies and the techniques followed by experienced directors and managers when facing risky decisions. The Survey is a joint project between the Australian Institute of Company Directors and the Department of Management at Melbourne University. Responses will be used by AICD to provide information to members on current approaches to risk management; and will allow Boards and Directors to review their management of risk and reduce exposures.

The work also forms the field research component of a PhD thesis entitled "The Influence of Risk on Decisionmaking" which is being conducted in the University of Melbourne's Department of Management by Les Coleman and supervised by Professor Danny Samson. The project has been approved by the University's Human Research Ethics Committee.

The Survey should take you about 15 minutes. Although questions are voluntary, please answer as many as possible because incomplete results limit the value of the data you provide. Most questions require you to indicate one response that best represents your view. There are no right and wrong answers. Do not spend too much time on any question, but try to answer each one frankly and thoughtfully. To ensure absolute confidentiality, the surveys are anonymous. Responses will be analysed by University of Melbourne researchers, and no individual results will be reported.

The process is designed to be similar to that involved in an everyday business task; and has no associated risks. Participation is completely voluntary and you may withdraw at any time, including return of any unprocessed data supplied. The identity of participants is anonymous to the researchers; all materials will be kept confidential within the limitations of the law and will not used for any purposes other than this study. It is anticipated that the results will be available in early December, and a summary distributed electronically through AICD's website.

If you have any questions regarding the study please do not hesitate to e-mail Les Coleman (p.coleman1@pgrad.unimelb.edu.au) or call him on 0413 901085. If you have any concerns regarding the conduct of this research project you can contact the Executive Officer, Human Research Ethics, the University of Melbourne, Victoria 3010, ph: (03) 8344 7507; fax: (03) 9347 6739

THANK YOU FOR YOUR PARTICIPATION

Before proceeding further, please be sure you have read the instructions and description of the survey, and tick the item below as confirmation

1. Consent

     ○ I have read the survey and agree to participate

ABOUT YOU

lease help us understand your decisionmaking processes by providing some information about yourself.

2. What is your gender.

     ○ Male
     ○ Female

3. What is your age in years.

- ○ 25 or less
- ○ 26-35
- ○ 36-45
- ○ 46-55
- ○ 55-65
- ○ 66 or older

4. In which region is your home country.

- ○ Asia
- ○ Australasia
- ○ Europe
- ○ North America
- ○ South America

5. What is the highest education level you have completed.

- ○ Year 11 or 12
- ○ Apprenticeship or TAFE
- ○ Diploma
- ○ Bachelor Degree
- ○ Master's Degree
- ○ Doctorate

6. How many years in total have you been in paid employment.

- ○ Less than 5
- ○ 5-15
- ○ 16-25
- ○ 26-35
- ○ 36 or more

7. Please indicate if you are a member of any of the following organizations (choose as many as applicable)

- ☐ Association of Risk and Insurance Managers of Australasia
- ☐ Australian Institute of Company Directors
- ☐ Australian Institute of Management
- ☐ CPA Australia
- ☐ Economic Society of Australia
- ☐ Finance and Treasury Association
- ☐ Institution of Engineers
- ☐ Taxation Institute of Australia

8. Please indicate the nature of your affiliation with AICD

- ☐ Honorary Member of AICD
- ☐ Fellow of AICD
- ☐ Member of AICD
- ☐ Graduate Member of AICD

☐ Affiliate Member of AICD
☐ Alumni of Company Directors' Course
☐ Colleague of one of the above
☐ No affiliation with AICD

If your principal occupation is (or most recently was) as a Director, please answer questions 9 to 14. Otherwise go to question 15.

9. What industry best describes that of your current or most recent company?

○ Accounting
○ Accounting - Architecture, Engineering & Building
○ Agriculture - Forestry & Fishing
○ Architecture, Engineering, Building
○ Banking - Finance, Investment, Consulting
○ Communication Services
○ Cultural & Recreational Services
○ Design - Marketing
○ eBusiness
○ Education/Professional Devpt.
○ Finance & Insurance
○ Food & Beverage, Tobacco
○ Government
○ Health services
○ Health & Community Services
○ Human Resources
○ Import/Export
○ Information Technology
○ Insurance
○ Legal
○ Libraries/museums/arts
○ Management Consulting
○ Manufacturing
○ Marketing/media/PR/Advertising
○ Mining/Oil/Gas Extraction
○ Motor Vehicle
○ N/A
○ Other
○ Printing/Publishing
○ Professional Services
○ Property Services/Real Estate
○ Retail
○ Retail/Wholesale
○ Science & Research
○ Sport & Recreation
○ Telecommunications
○ Textile/clothing & Footware

○ Tourism, Hospitality
○ Tourism and Storage
○ Unknown
○ Utilities
○ Welfare/Charity/Religious

10. What best describes your company's legal structure?

○ Co-operative
○ Incorporated Association
○ Not-for-Profit
○ Partnership
○ Private
○ Public Listed
○ Public Unlisted
○ Statutory Authority
○ Trust
○ Other
○ Unknown

11. What is the best description of your current or most recent Director role.

○ Non Executive Chair
○ Non Executive Director
○ Executive Chair
○ Executive Director

12. If you are an executive director, please indicate the main functional line of your responsibilities

○ Research and development
○ Manufacturing
○ Operations
○ Marketing
○ Finance
○ Legal
○ Human Relations
○ Other

13. What is the annual turnover of your company.

○ Less than $10 million
○ $10 million to $100 million
○ $100 million to $500 million
○ $500 million to $1 billion
○ $1 billion to $5 billion
○ Greater than $5 billion

14. How many years have you been a director or employee of your current company?

○ Less than one year

- O 1 - 3 years
- O 4 - 9 years
- O 10 - 15 years
- O Over 15 years

Now please go to question 21 and complete the remainder of the survey.

If your principal occupation is (or most recently was) as an employee (other than as an executive director), please answer questions 15 to 20. Otherwise go to question 21.

15. What industry best describes that of your current or most recent company?

- O Accounting
- O Accounting - Architecture, Engineering & Building
- O Agriculture - Forestry & Fishing
- O Architecture, Engineering, Building
- O Banking - Finance, Investment, Consulting
- O Communication Services
- O Cultural & Recreational Services
- O Design - Marketing
- O eBusiness
- O Education/Professional Devpt.
- O Finance & Insurance
- O Food & Beverage, Tobacco
- O Government
- O Health services
- O Health & Community Services
- O Human Resources
- O Import/Export
- O Information Technology
- O Insurance
- O Legal
- O Libraries/museums/arts
- O Management Consulting
- O Manufacturing
- O Marketing/media/PR/Advertising
- O Mining/Oil/Gas Extraction
- O Motor Vehicle
- O N/A
- O Other
- O Printing/Publishing
- O Professional Services
- O Property Services/Real Estate
- O Retail
- O Retail/Wholesale
- O Science & Research
- O Sport & Recreation
- O Telecommunications
- O Textile/clothing & Footware

○ Tourism, Hospitality
○ Tourism and Storage
○ Unknown
○ Utilities
○ Welfare/Charity/Religious

16. What best describes your company's legal structure?

○ Co-operative
○ Incorporated Association
○ Not-for-Profit
○ Partnership
○ Private
○ Public Listed
○ Public Unlisted
○ Statutory Authority
○ Trust
○ Other
○ Unknown

17. What is the best decsription of your current or most recent role?

○ Academic
○ Barrister/Solicitor
○ Chairman - Executive
○ Chief Executive Officer
○ Chief Financial Officer
○ Company Chair - Executive
○ Director - Executive
○ Manager
○ Managing Director
○ Partner
○ Senior Executive
○ Other

18. Please indicate the main functional line of your responsibilities

○ Research and development
○ Manufacturing
○ Operations
○ Marketing
○ Finance
○ Legal
○ Human Relations
○ Other

19. What is the annual turnover of your company.

○ Less than $10 million
○ $10 million to $100 million

○ $100 million to $500 million
○ $500 million to $1 billion
○ $1 billion to $5 billion
○ Greater than $5 billion

20. How many years have you been with your current company?

○ Less than one year
○ 1 - 3 years
○ 4 - 9 years
○ 10 - 15 years
○ Over 15 years

21. What is your annual income before tax.

○ $25,000-50,000
○ $50,001-75,000
○ $75,001-100,000
○ $100,001-150,000
○ $150,000 - $300,000
○ Over $300,000

22. What is the value of your investments (excluding principal residence)?

○ $25,000-100,000
○ $100,001-250,000
○ $250,001-500,000
○ $500,001-999,000
○ $1 million to $3 million
○ Over $3 million

Think about each of the following statements. Please indicate how well you think that they fit *your* behaviour or beliefs.

23. Influences on Your Decisionmaking

	Strongly Agree	Agree	Neutral	Disagree
Many important decisions are based on insufficient information.	○	○	○	○
I set difficult goals for myself which I attempt to reach	○	○	○	○
I would like to undertake an interesting experience even if it is dangerous.	○	○	○	○
To achieve something in life one has to take risks.	○	○	○	○
Risk is higher when facing situations we do not understand	○	○	○	○

I've not much sympathy for adventurous decisions.	O	O	O	O
I become bored easily.	O	O	O	O
I have always wanted to be better than others.	O	O	O	O
I am calm and relaxed when participating in group discussions.	O	O	O	O
Successful people take risks.	O	O	O	O
I prefer to work in situations that require a high level of skill	O	O	O	O
When I get what I want it's usually because I'm lucky.	O	O	O	O
I regularly set deadlines for myself.	O	O	O	O
Risky situations can be made safer by planning ahead.	O	O	O	O
Compared to the average manager, I give much more effort	O	O	O	O
If I play a game (eg. cards) I prefer to play for money.	O	O	O	O
I have gotten more of the breaks in life than most of the people I know.	O	O	O	O
I like to play it safe.	O	O	O	O
In general I am very confident of my ability.	O	O	O	O
My life is chiefly controlled by powerful others.	O	O	O	O
In general, I am less willing to take risks than my colleagues.	O	O	O	O
Everyone should have an equal chance and an equal say.	O	O	O	O

Think about each of the following adjectives. Please indicate how well you think they fit *your* behaviour or beliefs.

24. Adaptable.

    O Strongly Agree
    O Agree
    O Neutral
    O Disagree
    O Strongly Disagree

25. Temperamental.

    O Strongly Agree
    O Agree
    O Neutral
    O Disagree
    O Strongly Disagree

26. Hard driving.

    O Strongly Agree
    O Agree
    O Neutral
    O Disagree
    O Strongly Disagree

27. Modest.

- ○ Strongly Agree
- ○ Agree
- ○ Neutral
- ○ Disagree
- ○ Strongly Disagree

28. Impulsive.

- ○ Strongly Agree
- ○ Agree
- ○ Neutral
- ○ Disagree
- ○ Strongly Disagree

29. Companionable.

- ○ Strongly Agree
- ○ Agree
- ○ Neutral
- ○ Disagree
- ○ Strongly Disagree

30. Controlled.

- ○ Strongly Agree
- ○ Agree
- ○ Neutral
- ○ Disagree
- ○ Strongly Disagree

31. Unconventional.

- ○ Strongly Agree
- ○ Agree
- ○ Neutral
- ○ Disagree
- ○ Strongly Disagree

32. Independent.

- ○ Strongly Agree
- ○ Agree
- ○ Neutral
- ○ Disagree
- ○ Strongly Disagree

33. Insecure.

- ○ Strongly Agree

○ Agree
○ Neutral
○ Disagree
○ Strongly Disagree

34. Aggressive.

○ Strongly Agree
○ Agree
○ Neutral
○ Disagree
○ Strongly Disagree

35. Competitive.

○ Strongly Agree
○ Agree
○ Neutral
○ Disagree
○ Strongly Disagree

To help us understand your attitudes towards risk in different aspects of your life, please think about which of the following best fit *your* behaviour or beliefs.

36. In my personal life (eg. hobbies, recreation, leisure pursuits), I tend to take a lot of physical risks

○ Strongly Agree
○ Agree
○ Neutral
○ Disagree
○ Strongly Disagree

37. In relation to my personal finances (eg. investments, superannuation and borrowing) I tend to take a lot of financial risks.

○ Strongly Agree
○ Agree
○ Neutral
○ Disagree
○ Strongly Disagree

38. In my business life I tend to take a lot of financial risks on behalf of my company or clients

○ Strongly Agree
○ Agree
○ Neutral
○ Disagree
○ Strongly Disagree

39. The last time that I bet on the races, the largest dollar value of my bets went to (tick one):

- ○ Favourites
- ○ Value horses
- ○ Longshots
- ○ Other

40. The last time that I bet on the races, the largest dollar value of my bets went to (tick one):

- ○ Win bets
- ○ Place bets
- ○ Quinella bets
- ○ Trifecta bets
- ○ Doubles
- ○ Other

ABOUT YOUR COMPANY

In strictest confidence, the researchers wish to match your description of your company with information contained in the company's Annual Report. To enable this, please provide brief details of your company.

41. What is the name and street address of your company

Please think about your company's industry, and indicate how well each of the following describe the environment of your company's <u>industry.</u>

42. My company's industry is

	Strongly Agree	Agree	Neutral	Disagree	Strongly Disagree
Very competitive	○	○	○	○	○
Fast growing	○	○	○	○	○
Responsive to consumer needs	○	○	○	○	○
Strongly regulated	○	○	○	○	○
Innovative	○	○	○	○	○
Risky	○	○	○	○	○
Technologically advanced	○	○	○	○	○
Socially responsible	○	○	○	○	○

	Strongly Agree	Agree	Neutral	Disagree	Strongly Disagree
Profitable	○	○	○	○	○

Please think about the management and performance of your company. Indicate how well each of the following statements describe your company.

43. My company

	Strongly Agree	Agree	Neutral	Disagree	Strongly Disagree
Recruits high calibre employees	○	○	○	○	○
Provides good training and development	○	○	○	○	○
Respects diversity of opinion and style	○	○	○	○	○
Appoints the best candidates as managers	○	○	○	○	○
has excellent human resource strategies	○	○	○	○	○
Is very profit oriented	○	○	○	○	○
Tolerates unpopular ideas	○	○	○	○	○
Has high turnover of executives	○	○	○	○	○
Generally succeeds when implementing new strategies	○	○	○	○	○
Deals in commodities or derivatives	○	○	○	○	○
Produces finished consumer products	○	○	○	○	○
Owns an interest in joint ventures or independent subsidiaries	○	○	○	○	○
Has direct investments offshore	○	○	○	○	○

Please think about the changes and strategies of your company. Indicate how well each of the following statements describe your company.

44. My company

	Strongly Agree	Agree	Neutral	Disagree	Strongly Disagree
Imposes strong pressures for performance	○	○	○	○	○
Is expanding rapidly	○	○	○	○	○
Has inexperienced employees in key positions	○	○	○	○	○
Rewards entrepreneurial risk taking	○	○	○	○	○
Is resistant to sharing bad news	○	○	○	○	○
Is very people oriented	○	○	○	○	○
Has a high level of internal competition	○	○	○	○	○
Has many rapid and complex activities	○	○	○	○	○
Has implemented repeated cost-cutting programs in recent years	○	○	○	○	○
Has good performance measures for all key activities	○	○	○	○	○

Has decentralised decisionmaking	O	O	O	O	O
Insists on following rules and procedures	O	O	O	O	O

Please think about the environment created inside your company by the attitudes and values of the Board and senior management. Indicate how well each of the following statements describe *your* judgement of the company.

45. Thinking about my company

	Strongly Agree	Agree
Best practice is expected in all tasks	O	O
The Board has risk management as a major concern	O	O
The Board and senior management communicate their expectations on risk	O	O
Senior management is complacent about risks and weaknesses	O	O
The Board and senior management operate inside their comfort zones	O	O
The Board and senior management have expertise covering all areas of operations	O	O
The Board and senior management understand exposures in the company's process operations	O	O
The Board and senior management understand the company's environmental exposures	O	O
The Board and senior management understand the company's financial exposures	O	O
There is an independent risk reporting channel to the Board	O	O
Directors are comfortable with risk management processes	O	O

RISK MANAGEMENT PRACTICES

Please think about the risk management practices of your company, and indicate how well each of the following statements describe the environment of your company.

46. My company

	Strongly Agree	Agree	Neutral	Disagree	Strongly Disagree
Has well documented practices and procedures	O	O	O	O	O
Has good internal controls	O	O	O	O	O

Has an ethical approach to business	O	O	O	O	O
Has high standards for product quality	O	O	O	O	O
Cuts corners to get results	O	O	O	O	O
Takes pride in innovative business models	O	O	O	O	O
Believes it can take well-judged risks	O	O	O	O	O
Has an enterprise risk management policy	O	O	O	O	O
Endorses the objectives of Corporate Social Responsibility	O	O	O	O	O
Includes risk management in evaluating managers' performance	O	O	O	O	O

Please think about the approach taken <u>specifically by the Board</u> to managing risk in your company, and indicate applicable items in the following questions.

47. What is the best description of your company's risk management strategy?

    O Is principally managed through insurance
    O Mainly involves financial issues
    O Mainly involves occuptaional health and safety
    O Informal process covering strategy and operations
    O Formal process across the whole company
    O Does not have a developed strategy

48. Does your company have a specialised risk management group?

    ☐ Yes
    ☐ No
    ☐ Don't know

49. In which functional line does the group reside (eg. Audit, Treasury, Legal, Operations)?

50. If there is no risk management group, who manages risks in your company?

    O Audit department
    O Senior managers
    O Board
    O Company secretary
    O Consultants
    O Other

○ No formal process exists

51. Have any of the following been trained in Risk Management practices?

○ Audit department
○ Senior managers
○ Board
○ Company secretary
○ Consultants
○ Other

52. Approximately how many days training was involved for each trainee?

Days: [   ]

53. Does the Board have a documented Risk Management Policy?

○ Yes
○ No
○ Don't know

54. Who has been the champion in rolling the Risk Management Policy through the company?

○ CEO
○ Another Director
○ Senior manahger
○ Mid-level manager
○ Consultant
○ No champion
○ There is no Risk Management Policy

55. How does the Board identify risks?

○ Advice from Audit
○ Advice from Risk Management group
○ From Board papers
○ Through Board meetings
○ Advice from consultants
○ Other

56. Which Board Committee is responsible for Risk Management?

○ Audit
○ Risk Management
○ Whole Board
○ Other

57. What are the Major Risks of Concern to your company (tick as many as relevant)?

- [ ] Processes and technologies used in operations
- [ ] Product defects, including recalls
- [ ] Industrial accidents
- [ ] Sabotage
- [ ] On-site tampering
- [ ] Computer breakdowns
- [ ] Organisational issues
- [ ] Discrimination, including sexual harassment
- [ ] Workplace violence
- [ ] Occupational health
- [ ] White collar crime and other illegal activities
- [ ] Executive dismissal
- [ ] Financing (derivatives, debt)
- [ ] Credit
- [ ] Bankruptcy
- [ ] Environmental
- [ ] Natural disasters
- [ ] Competitor activity
- [ ] Hostile takeover
- [ ] Government regulation
- [ ] Shareholder activism
- [ ] Strikes
- [ ] Reputation
- [ ] Consumer action, including boycotts
- [ ] Class actions
- [ ] Supplier product quality
- [ ] International exposures
- [ ] Terrorism
- [ ] Executive kidnapping

58. Please list any other risks of concern

59. Does your company have a comprehensive disaster recovery plan to cope with identified risks?

- O Yes
- O No
- O Don't know

60. When strategic proposals are submitted to the Board for approval, are they accompanied by a risk assessment (eg. worst, best, most likely scenarios)?

- O Yes
- O No
- O Don't know

61. Does the Board formally monitor product quality?

○ Yes
○ No
○ Don't know

62. Does the Board has a formal strategy to minimise risk to brand and reputation?

○ Yes
○ No
○ Don't know

To help us quantify the attitude towards risk inside your company, please project its response to several hypothetical scenarios.

63. Consider your firm had a windfall capital inflow equal to about five percent of its asset base, and is considering how to allocate the money between organic growth (building new facilities, developing products in-house) and buying assets (acquisition of existing businesses and plants). What proportion of the windfall would you recommend allocating to acquisition of <u>existing</u> business or plants?

○ 0-20 percent
○ 21-40 percent
○ 41-60 percent
○ 61-80 percent
○ 81-100 percent

Consider your company is offered the opportunity to participate in a new investment. The project has a 50 percent probability of success which would pay your company $20 million; and the project has a 50 percent probability of failure in which case half the investment would be lost.

64. How much would your company invest to participate in the project?

$ [   ]

65. If the payout from the project were $5 million, how much would your company invest to participate in the project?

$ [   ]

66. Consider your company is suing one of its contractors for damages after the contractor's alleged negligence caused a major accident during construction of a new facility. The best legal advice available to you is that the maximum damages the court would award is $20 million. The contractor has now offered to settle for $10 million. Your legal team is considering its advice and wants to know the company's attitude towards the risks of going to trial. What is the minimum probability of a favorable judgement from a trial for your company to reject the settlement and allow the case to go to trial? (tick one)

○ 0-20 percent
○ 21-40 percent
○ 41-60 percent

○ 61-80 percent
○ 81-100 percent

67. Consider your company can invest in a new venture which has equal probability of doubling the investment or losing half the investment (eg. there is a 50:50 chance that $100 would become $200 or $50). How much would you invest?

$ [   ]

68. What percentage of decisions taken by the Board of your company involve risk?

% [   ]

69. Think about risks facing your company today and over the next three to five years. Relative to the level today, what do you expect to happen to risk in the medium term?

○ Risk will rise in the next 3-5 years
○ Risk wil fall
○ Risk will stay about the same
○ Don't know

70. What has happened to the level of risk facing your company in the last three to five years?

○ Level of risk has risen in recent years
○ Level of risk has fallen
○ Risk has stayed about the same
○ Don't know

A crisis is often described as an incident or issue which escalates uncontrollably and causes such serious damage to the assets, reputation and performance of an organization that its viability is threatened. Please think about crises that might have involved your company during the last three years.

71. In the last three years, my company has experienced.

○ No crises
○ One or two crises
○ Between three and five crises
○ Between six and ten crises
○ More than ten crises

72. Please indicate the type of crisis that occurred (choose as many as applicable)

☐ Fatal accident
☐ Process failure
☐ Plant fire or explosion

- ☐ Product contamination
- ☐ Product recall
- ☐ Threat or extortion
- ☐ Kidnapping
- ☐ Labour disruption or major strike
- ☐ Hostile takeover
- ☐ Fraud in excess of $100,000
- ☐ Suspended from ASX trading
- ☐ Reputational issue
- ☐ Criminal prosecution

Incidents with potentially serious consequences do not always become crises. Please think about serious incidents that might have involved your company.

73. In the last three years, my company has experienced.

- ○ No serious incidents that could have become crises
- ○ One or two such incidents
- ○ Between three and five such incidents
- ○ Between six and ten such incidents
- ○ More than ten such incidents

74. Please indicate the type of incident(s) that occurred (choose as many as applicable)

- ☐ Fatal accident
- ☐ Process failure
- ☐ Plant fire or explosion
- ☐ Product contamination
- ☐ Product recall
- ☐ Threat or extortion
- ☐ Kidnapping
- ☐ Labour disruption or major strike
- ☐ Hostile takeover
- ☐ Fraud
- ☐ Suspended from ASX trading
- ☐ Reputational issue
- ☐ Criminal prosecution

Many thanks for your help. To provide added depth to the responses, we would be grateful if you could invite several colleagues from different managerial levels in your company to complete the Survey.

Submit Survey

Powered by SurveySolutions XP: Conduct your own customer satisfaction surveys

References

Aaker DA and Jacobson R (1987) The role of risk in explaining differences in profitability. Academy of Management Journal 30: 277-296.

Abdellaoui M (2000) Parameter-Free Elicitation of Utility and Probability Weighting Functions. Management Science 46: 1497-1512.

ABS (2002). Deaths, Australia. Catalogue 3302.0. Australian Bureau of Statistics, Canberra.

Alchian AA (1950) Uncertainty, Evolution, and Economic Theory. The Journal of Political Economy 58: 211-221.

Ali MM (1977) Probability and utility estimates for racetrack bettors. Journal of Political Economy 85: 803-816.

Allais M (1988). The general theory of random choices in relation to the invariant cardinal utility function and the specific probability function. Published in BR Munier (ed). Risk, decision, and rationality. Dordrecht, Holland.

Allison GT (1971). Essence of Decision: Explaining the Cuban Missile Crisis. Harper Collins, New York.

Amit R and Wernerfelt W (1990) Why Do Firms Reduce Business Risk? Academy of Management Journal 33: 520-533.

Amsel E, Langer R and Loutzenhiser L (1991). Do Lawyers Reason Differently from Psychologists? Published in RJ Sternberg and PA Frensch (ed). Complex Problem Solving. Lawrence Erlbaum Associates, Hillsdale NJ.

Antonides G, Tyszka T, Farago K and Ranyard R (1997). Perceptions of Economic Activities: A cross-country comparison. Published in G Antonides, WF van Raaij and S Maital (ed). Advances in Economic Psychology. John Wiley & Sons, Chichester.

Arrow KJ (1971). Essays in the Theory of Risk-Bearing. Markham, Chicago.

Arrow KJ (1982) Risk Perception in Psychology and Economics. Economic Inquiry 20: 1-9.

Asch P, Malkiel BG and Quandt RE (1984) Market Efficiency in Racetrack Betting. Journal of Business 57: 165-175.

Asch P and Quandt RE (1987) Efficiency and Profitability in Exotic Bets. Economica 54: 289-298.

Augier M and March JG (2002). Chapter 1: Introduction - Richard M Cyert: the work and the legacy. Published in M Augier and JG March (ed). The Economics of Choice, Change and Organization. Edward Elgar, Cheltenham.

Austin EJ, Deary IJ and Willock J (2001) Personality and Intelligence as Predictors of Economic Behavior in Scottish Farmers. European Journal of Personality 15: S123-S137.

Bacon F (1620). *Novum Organum*. Accessed: 1 June 2004. www.constitution.org.

Baird IS and Thomas H (1985) Toward a Contingency Model of Strategic Risk Taking. Academy of Management Review 10: 230-243.

Balabanis G (2001). The Relationship between Lottery Ticket and Scratch-Card Buying Behaviour, Personality and other Compulsive Behaviours.

Baldwin W (1992). The crazy things people say to justify stock prices. Forbes. 27 April 1992

Band RE (1989). Contrary Investing for the '90s. St Martin's Press, New York.

Barberis N and Huang M (2001) Mental Accounting, Loss Aversion and Individual Stock Returns. The Journal of Finance 56: 1247-1293.

Barberis N, Huang M and Santos T (2001) Prospect Theory and Asset Prices. The Quarterly Journal of Economics 116: 1-53.

Barberis N and Thaler R (2002). A Survey of Behavioral Finance. Working Paper. National Bureau of Economic Research, Cambridge, MA.

Barrett C and Fiddick L (1999) Evolution and Risky Decisions. Trends in Cognitive Sciences 4: 251-252.

Bateson M (2002) Recent advances in our understanding of risk-sensitive foraging preferences. Proceedings of the Nutrition Society 61: 1-8.

Battalio RC, Kagel JH and MacDonald DN (1985) Animals' choices over uncertain outcomes: Some initial experimental evidence. American Economic Review 75: 597-613.

Baucus MS and Near JP (1991) Can Illegal Corporate Behavior be Predicted: An event history analysis. Academy of Management Journal 34: 9-36.

Bauer T and Rotte R (1997). Prospect Theory Goes to War: Loss-aversion and the duration of military conflict. Accessed: 9 September 2003. http://citeseer.nj.nec.com/bauer97prospect.html.

Beach LR (1997). The Psychology of Decision Making. Sage Publications, Thousand Oaks CA.

Beck U (1992). Risk Society, Towards a New Modernity. Sage Publications, London.

Benartzi S and Thaler RH (1995) Myopic Loss Aversion and the Equity Risk Puzzle. Quarterly Journal of Economics 110: 73-92.

Benartzi S and Thaler RH (1999) Risk Aversion or Myopia? Choices in repeated gambles and retirement investments. Management Science 45: 364-381.

Berg N (2003) Normative Behavioral Economics. Journal of Socio-Economics 32: 411-427.

Bernasconi M (1998) Tax Evasion and Orders of Risk Aversion. Journal of Public Economics 67: 123-134.

Bernoulli D (1738, translated 1954) Exposition of a New Theory on the Measurement of Risk. Econometrica 22: 23-26.

Bewley T (2002) Interviews as a valid empirical tool in economics. Journal of Socio-Economics 31: 343-353.

Biggadike R (1979) The Risky Business of Diversification. Harvard Business Review 57: 103-111.

Bird R, McCrae M and Beggs J (1987) Are gamblers really risk takers? Australian Economic Papers 26: 237-253.

Birnbaum MH (2004) First Stochastic Dominance and Cumulative Prospect Theory: Comment on Levy and Levy (2002) and Wakker (2003). In Press.

Bleichrodt H (2001) Probability Weighting in Choice under Risk: An empirical test. The Journal of Risk and Uncertainty 23: 185-198.

Blondel S (2002) Testing Theories of Choice under Risk: Estimation of individual functionals. The Journal of Risk and Uncertainty 24: 251-265.

Bodie Z, Kane A and Marcus AJ (2005). Investments (6th Edition). McGraw Hill, New York.

Bowman EH (1980) A Risk-Return Paradox for Strategic Management. Sloan Management Review 21: 17-33.

Bowman EH (1982) Risk Seeking by Troubled Firms. Sloan Management Review 23: 33-42.

Bozeman B and Kingsley G (1998) Risk culture in public and private organizations. Public Administration Review 58: 109-119.

Bradley I (2003) The representative bettor, bet size and prospect theory. Economics Letters 78: 409-413.

Brailsford TJ, Easton SA, Gray PK and Gray SF (1995) The Efficiency of Australian Football Betting Markets. Australian Journal of Management 20: 167-195.

Brehmer B (1992) Dynamic decisionmaking: human control of complex systems. Acta Psychologia 81: 211-241.

Brickman P, Coates D and Janoff-Bulman R (1978) Lottery Winners and Accident Victims. Journal of Personality and Social Psychology 36: 917-927.

Brockmann EN and Anthony WP (2002) Tacit Knowledge and Strategic Decision Making. Group and Organization Management 27: 436-455.

Brogan H (1996). Kennedy. Longman, London.

Bromiley P (1991) Testing a causal model of corporate risk taking and performance. Academy of Management Journal 34: 37-59.

Brouthers KD, Brouthers LE and Werner S (2002) Industrial sector, perceived environmental uncertainty and entry mode strategy. Journal of Business Research 55: 495-507.

Budner S (1962) Intolerance of ambiguity as a personality variable. Journal of Personality 30. 29-50.

Burns PC and Wilde GJS (1995) Risk-taking in Male Taxi Drivers: Relationships among personality, observational data and driver records. Personality and Individual Differences 18: 267-278.

Burrell G and Morgan G (1985). Sociological Paradigms and Organisational Analysis. Gower, Aldershot.

Burrough B and Helyar J (1990). Barbarians at the Gate: the fall of RJR Nabisco. Harper & Row, New York.

Busche K and Walls WD (2000) Decision Costs and Betting Market Efficiency. Rationality and Society 12: 477-492.

Busenitz LW and Barney JB (1997) Differences between Entrepreneurs and Managers in Large Organizations: Biases and heuristics in strategic decision-making. Journal of Business Venturing 12: 9-30.

Byrnes JP, Miller DC and Schafer WD (1999) Gender Differences in Risk Taking: A meta-analysis. Psychological Bulletin 125: 367-383.

Camerer C (1990). Behavioural Game Theory. Published in RM Hogarth (ed). Insights in Decision Making. The University of Chicago Press, Chicago.

Camerer C (1995). Chapter 8 - Individual Decision Making. Published in JH Kagel and AE Roth (ed). The Handbook of Experimental Economics. Princeton University Press, Princeton.

Camerer C (1998). Prospect Theory in the Wild. Working Paper. California Institute of Technology, Division of the Humanities and Social Sciences,

Camerer C (1999) Behavioural economics: reunifying psychology and economics. Proceedings of the National Academy of Sciences 96: 10575-10577.

Camerer C, Babcock L, Loewenstein GF and Thaler R (1997) Labor Supply of New York City Cab Drivers: One day at a time. Quarterly Journal of Economics 112: 407-441.

Camerer C and Lovallo D (1999) Overconfidence and Excess Entry: An Experimental Approach. American Economic Review 89: 306-318.

Camerer CF and Loewenstein GF, Eds. (2004). Advances in Behavioral Economics. Princeton University Press, Princeton NJ.

Campbell-Hunt C (2000) What Have We Learned About Generic Competitive Strategy? A meta-analysis. Strategic Management Journal 21: 127-154.

Capen EC, Clapp RV and Campbell WM (1971) Competitive Bidding in High Risk Situations. Journal of Petroleum Technology 23: 641-653.

Caraco T, Blanckenhorn W, Gregory G, Newman J, Recer G and Zwicker S (1990) Risk-sensitivity: ambient temperature affects foraging choice. Animal Behaviour 39: 338-345.

Caraco T, Martindale S and Whittam TS (1980) An empirical demonstration of risk-sensitive foraging preferences. Animal Behaviour 28: 820-830.

Casssidy T and Lynn R (1989) A multifactorial approach to achievement motivation: The development of a comprehensive measure. Journal of Occupational Psychology 62: 301-312.

Charreton R and Bourdaire JM (1988). Industrial Practice of Decision Theory. Published in BR Munier (ed). Risk, Decision and Rationality. D. Reidel Publishing Company, Dordrecht.

Chatterjee S, Wiseman RM, Fiegenbaum A and Devers CE (2003) Integrating Behavioural and Economic Concepts of Risk into Strategic Management: the twain shall meet. Long Range Planning 36: 61-79.

Claessens S, Djankov S and Nenova T (2000). Corporate Risk Around the World. 2271. World Bank Policy Research Working Paper, Washington DC.

Clemen RT and Reilly T (2001). Making Hard Decisions. Thomson Learning, Pacific Grove CA.

Clotfeller CT and Cook PJ (1993) The Gamblers Fallacy in Lottery Play. Management Science 12: 1521-5.

Clyman DR, Walls MR and Dyer JS (1999) Too Much of a Good Thing? Operations Research 47: 957-965.

Cochrane JH (1999). New Facts in Finance. Working Paper. Working Paper. National Bureau of Economic Research, Washington DC.

Coleman L (1984). The Economics of Uranium Exploration in Australia. The Australasian Institute of Mining and Metallurgy Annual Conference, Darwin.

Coleman L (2004) The Frequency and Cost of Corporate Crises. Journal of Contingencies and Crisis Management 12: 2-13.

Coleman L (2004) New Light on the Longshot Bias. Applied Economics 36: 315-326.

Coleman L (2005) Why Explore for Oil When it is Cheaper to Buy? Applied Economics Letters 12: 493-497.

Cooper RG and Kleinschmidt EJ (2000) New Product Performance: What distinguishes the star products. Australian Journal of Management 25: 17-45.

Corner JL and Corner PD (1995) Characteristics of decisions in decision analysis practice. Journal of the Operational Research Society 46: 304-314.

Croson R and Buchan N (1999) Gender and Culture: International experimental evidence from trust games. American Economic Review 89: 386-391.

Cubitt RP and Sugden R (2001) Dynamic Decisionmaking under Uncertainty. Journal of Risk and Uncertainty 22: 103-128.

D'Aveni RA (1989) Dependability and Organizational Bankruptcy: An application of agency and prospect theory. Management Science 35: 1120-1138.

Dahlbäck O (1990) Personality and Risk-Taking. Personality and Individual Differences 11: 1235-1242.

Damasio A (1994). Descartes' Error: Emotion, Reason and the Human Brain. Avon Books, New York.

Das TK and Teng B-S (2001) Strategic Risk Behavior and its Temporalities: Between risk propensity and the decision context. Journal of Management Studies 38: 515-534.

Davis D (1985) New Projects: Beware of false economies. Harvard Business Review 63: 95-101.

de Blaeij AT and van Vuuren DJ (2003) Risk perception of traffic participants. Accident Analysis and Prevention 35: 167-175.

De Bondt WFM and Thaler RH (1990) Do Security Analysts Overreact? American Economic Review 80: 52-57.

Dearlove D (1998). Key Management Decisions. Financial Times, London.

Deloach J (2000). Enterprise-wide Risk Management: Strategies for linking risk and opportunity. Arthur Andersen, Houston.

Dess GG and Beard DW (1984) Dimensions of Organizational Task Environments. Administrative Science Quarterly 29: 52-73.

Di Mauro C and Maffioletti A (2001) The Valuation of Insurance Under Uncertainty. The Geneva Papers on Risk and Insurance Theory 26: 195-224.

Dillman DA, Phelps G, Tortora R, Swift K, Kohrell J and Berck J (2001). Response Rate and Measurement Differences in Mixed Mode Surveys Using Mail, Telephone, Interactive Voice Response and the Internet. Accessed:13 February 2004. http://survey.sesrc.wsu.edu/dillman/papers

Dolan SL, Garcia S, Diegoli S and Auerbach A (ca. 2000). Organisational Values as `Attractors of Chaos'. Accessed: 1 March 2004. www.econ.upf.es

Donkers B, Melenberg B and van Soest A (2001) Estimating Risk Attitudes using Lotteries: A large sample approach. The Journal of Risk and Uncertainty 22: 165-195.

Dostoevsky F (1914). The Gambler and Other Stories. William Heinemann Ltd, Melbourne.

Drucker P (1992). Management. Butterworth-Heineman Ltd, Oxford.

Edwards KE (1996) Prospect Theory: A literature review. International Review of Financial Analysis 5: 19-38.

Edwards W (1954) Theory of Decisionmaking. Psychological Bulletin 51: 380-417.

Eeckhoudt L and Godfroid P (2000) Risk Aversion and the Value of Information. Journal of Economic Education 31: 382-388.

Ellsberg D (1961) Risk, Ambiguity, and the Savage Axioms. The Quarterly Journal of Economics 75: 643-669.

Evans DA (1997) The role of markets in reducing expected utility violations. Journal of Political Economy 105: 622-636.

Fair RC (2002) Events that Shook the Market. Journal of Business 75: 713-731.

Fama EF and French KR (1992) The cross-section of expected stock returns. Journal of Finance 67: 427-465.

Fama EF and French KR (2003). New Lists: Fundamentals and Survival Rates. Working Paper No. 03-15. Amos Tuck School of Business at Dartmouth College, Hanover, NH.

Fiegenbaum A and Thomas H (1988) Attitudes Toward Risk and the Risk-return Paradox: Prospect Theory explanations. Academy of Management Journal 31: 85-106.

Finucane ML, Alhakami A, Slovic P and Johnson SM (2000). The Affect Heuristic in Judgements of Risks and Benefits. Published in P Slovic (ed). The Perception of Risk. Earthscan, London.

Fitzgerald B (2003). Insurance on the decline despite high risks. Commonwealth Bank, Sydney.

Flyvbjerg B, Holm MS and Buhl S (2002) Underestimating costs in public works projects: error or lie? Journal of the American Planning Association 68: 279-295.

Forlani D (2002) Risk and Rationality: The influence of decision domain and perceived outcome control on managers' high-risk decisions. Journal of Behavioral Decision Making 15: 125-140.

Forlani D and Mullins JW (2000) Perceived Risks and Choices in Entrepreneurs' New Venture Decisions. Journal of Business Venturing 15: 305-322.

Foster RN and Kaplan S (2001). Creative Destruction. Financial Times, London.

Fox CR and Tversky A (1995) Ambiguity Aversion and Comparative Ignorance. Quarterly Journal of Economics 110: 585-603.

Fox CR and Tversky A (1998) A Belief-based Account of Decision Under Uncertainty. Management Science 44: 879-895.

Frederick S (2003) Measuring Intergenerational Time Preference: Are future lives valued less? The Journal of Risk and Uncertainty 26: 39-53.

French KR and Poterba JM (1991) Investor diversification and international equity markets. American Economic Review 81: 222-226.

Friedman M (1953). Essays in Positive Economics. University of Chicago Press, Chicago.

Friedman M and Savage LJ (1948) The Utility Analysis of Choices Involving Risk. Journal of Political Economy 56: 279-304.

Gaba A and Viscusi WK (1998) Differences in Subjective Risk Thresholds: Worker groups as an example. Management Science 44: 801-811.

Gasser M, Kaiser M, Berrigan D and Stearns SC (2000) Life history correlates of evolution under high and low adult mortality. Evolution 54: 1260-1272.

Gigerenzer G (2002). Reckoning with Risk. Allen Lane, London.

Gilad B, Kaish S and Loeb PD (1984) From Economic Behavior to Behavioral Economics: the behavioral uprising in economics. Journal of Behavioral Economics 13: 1-22.

Gilbert JA and Ivancevich JM (2000) Valuing Diversity: A tale of two organizations. Academy of Management Executive 14: 93-105.

Gill RWT (1979) The in-tray exercise as a measure of management potential. Journal of Occupational Psychology 52: 185-197.

Gleick J (1987). Chaos - Making a new science. Penguin Group, New York.

Goldberg LR (1990) An Alternative 'Description of Personality': The Big-Five Structure. Journal of Personality and Social Psychology 59: 1216-1229.

Golec J and Tamarkin M (1998) Bettors Love Skewness, Not Risk, at the Horse Track. Journal of Political Economy 106: 205-225.

Goodrick E and Salancik GR (1996) Organizational Discretion in Responding to Institutional Practices: Hospitals and Cesarean births. Administrative Science Quarterly 41: 1-28.

Grable JE (2000) Financial Risk Tolerance and Additional Factors that Affect Risk Taking in Everyday Money matters. Journal of Business and Psychology 14: 625-630.

Gray V and Lowery D (1998) To lobby alone or in a flock: foraging behaviour among organized interests. American Politics Quarterly 26: 5-34.

Greene JD, Sommerville RB, Nystrom LE, Darley JM and Cohen JD (2001) An fMRI Investigation of Emotional Engagement in Moral Judgment. Science 293: 2105-2108.

Grether DM (1980) Bayes Rule as a Descriptive Model: The Representativeness Heuristic. Quarterly Journal of Economics, 95: 537-557.

Griffin-Pierson S (1990) The Competitiveness Questionnaire: A measure of two components of competitiveness. Measurement and Evaluation in Counselling and Development 23: 108-115.

Griffith RM (1949) Odds adjustment by American horse race bettors. American Journal of Psychology 62: 290-294.

Gummer B (1998) Decision Making under Conditions of Risk, Ambiguity and Uncertainty: Recent perspectives. Administration in Social Work 22: 75-93.

Guthrie C, Rachlinski JJ and Wistrich AJ (2001) Inside the judicial mind (study of the decision-making processes of federal magistrate judges). Cornell Law Review 86: 777-830.

Haas ML (2001) Prospect Theory and the Cuban Missile Crisis. International Studies Quarterly 45: 241-270.

Hair JEJ, Anderson RE, Tatham RL and Black WC (1998). Multivariate Data Analysis. Prentice Hall, Upper Saddle River NJ.

Halek M and Eisenhauer JG (2001) Demography of Risk Aversion. Journal of Risk and Insurance 68: 1-24.

Hamer D and Copeland P (1998). Living with our Genes. Doubleday, New York.

Hammond JS, Keeney RL and Raiffa H (1998) The hidden traps in decision making. Harvard Business Review 76: 47-55.

Harless DW and Camerer C (1994) The Predictive Utility of Generalized Expecetd Utility Theories. Econometrica 62: 1251-1289.

Harries C, Evans JSBT and Dennis I (2000) Measuring Doctors' Self-Insight into their Treatment Decisions. Applied Cognitive Psychology 14: 455-477.

Hartog J, Ferrer-i-Carbonell A and Jonker N (2000). On a Simple Measure of Individual Risk Aversion. Rotterdam.

Harvey CR (1995) Predictable Risk and Returns in Emerging Markets. The Review of Financial Studies 8: 773-816.

Haugen RA (2001). Modern Investment Theory. Prentice Hall, London.

Heath C, Huddart S and Lang M (1999) Psychological Factors and Stock Option Exercise. The Quarterly Journal of Economics 114: 601-627.

Heath C and Tversky A (1991) Preference and belief: Ambiguity and competence in choice under uncertainty. Journal of Risk and Uncertainty 4: 5-28.

Henkel J (2003). The Risk-return Paradox for Strategic Management: Disentangling true and spurious effects. Academy of Management Meeting 2003, Seattle.

Henrich J and Gil-White FJ (2001) The Evolution of Prestige: Freely conferred deference as a mechanism for enhancing the benefits of cultural transmission. Evolution and Human Behavior 22: 165-196.

Herschey JC, Kunreuther HC and Schoemaker PJH (1982) Sources of Bias in Assessment Procedures for Utility Functions. Management Science 29: 936-954.

Hershey JC, Kunreuther HC and Schoemaker PJH (1982) Sources of Bias in Assessment Procedures for Utility Functions. Management Science 28: 936-954.

Hey JD and Orme C (1994) Investigating Generalizations of Expected Utility Theory Using Experimental Data. Econometrica 62: 1291-1326.

Higgs H, Ed. (1926). Palgrave's Dictionary of Political Economy. Macmillan and Co, London.

Highhouse S and Yüce P (1996) Perspectives, Perceptions and Risk-Taking Behavior. Organizational Behavior and Human Decision Processes 65: 159-167.

Hodgson GM (1995). Economics and Biology. Edward Elgar Publishing, Cheltenham UK.

Hofstede G (1997). Cultures and Organisations: Software of the Mind. McGraw Hill, London.

Hollenbeck JR, Ilgen DR, Phillips J and Hedlund J (1994) Decision risk in dynamic contexts: Beyond the status quo. Journal of Applied Psychology 79: 592-8.

Holloway CA (1979). Decision Making Under Uncertainty: Models and choices. Prentice- Hall Inc, Englewood Cliffs NJ.

Houston AI and McNamara JM (1982) A sequential approach to risk taking. Animal Behaviour 30: 1260-1261.

Howard RA (1988) Decision Analysis: Practice and promise. Management Science 34: 679-695.

Howard RA and Matheson JE, Eds. (ca 1989). Readings on the principles and applications of decision analysis. Strategic Decisions Group, Menlo Park CA.

Howell W (1971) Uncertainty from internal and external sources. Journal of Experimental Psychology 89: 240-243.

Hsee CK and Weber EU (1999) Cross-National Differences in Risk Preference and Lay Predictions. Journal of Behavioral Decision Making 12: 165-179.

Huber O and Kühberger A (1996) Decision Processes and Decision Trees in Gambles and More Natural Decision Tasks. The Journal of Psychology 130: 329-339.

Hughes A and Needham K (2004). Analyst lists NAB's 14 evil sins. The Age. Melbourne. 15 January 2004.

Humphrey SJ (2001) Are Event Splitting Effects Actually Boundary Effects? Journal of Risk and Uncertainty 22: 79-93.

Hvide HK (2002) Pragmatic beliefs and overconfidence. Journal of Economic Behavior and Organization 48: 15-28.

Ibbotson Associates (1996). Stocks, Bonds, Bills and Inflation - 1996 Yearbook. Ibbotson Associates, Chicago IL.

Intech (2002). Sector Funds Performance Survey. Melbourne.

Isaac RM and James D (2000) Just Who are You Calling Risk Averse? The Journal of Risk and Uncertainty 20: 177-187.

Jackofsky EF, Slocum JWJ and McQuaid SJ (1988) Cultural Values and the CEO: Alluring companions? Academy of Management Executive 2: 39-49.

Jarvik R (2003). Management Quote. AIM News. October 2003

Jullien B and Salanié B (2000) Estimating Preferences under Risk: The case of racetrack bettors. Journal of Political Economy 108: 503-530.

Kacelnik A and Bateson M (1996) Risky Theories: The effects of variance on foraging decisions. American Zoologist 36: 402-434.

Kahneman D (1991) Judgement and Decision Making: A personal view., Psychological Science 2: 142-145.

Kahneman D (2003) Maps of Bounded Rationality: Psychology for Behavioral Economics. The American Economic Review 93: 1449-1475.

Kahneman D and Lovallo D (1993) Timid Choices and Bold Forecasts: A cognitive perspective on risk taking. Management Science 39: 17-31.

Kahneman D, Slovic P and Tversky A (1982). Judgement Under Uncertainty: heuristics and biases. Cambridge University Press, Cambridge.

Kahneman D and Tversky A (1979) Prospect Theory: An analysis of decision under risk. Econometrica 47: 263-291.

Kahneman D and Tversky A (1982) Variants of Uncertainty. Cognition 11: 143-157.

Kamil AC and Roitblat HL (1985) The Ecology of Foraging Behaviour: Implications for animal learning and memory. Annual Review of Psychology 36: 141-169.

Kavanagh J (2003). The BRW 1000. Business Review Weekly. 20 November 2003

Keinan G (1984) Measurement of Risk Takers' Personality. Psychological Reports 55: 163-167.

Kessler R (2003). The CIA at War. St. Martin's Press, New York.

Khatri N and Ng HA (2000) The Role of Intuition in Strategic Decision Making. Human Relations 53: 57-86.

Kilka M and Weber M (2001) What Determines the Shape of the Probability Weighting Function Under Uncertainty? Management Science 47: 12-26.

Kirkwood CW (2002). Approximating Risk Aversion in Decision Analysis Applications. Accessed: 21 October 2003. www.public.asu.edu

Klein GA, Orasanu J, Calderwood R and Zsambok CE (1993). Decision Making in Action: Models and Methods. Ablex Publishing, Norwood NJ.

Knight F (1921). Risk, Uncertainty and Profit. Houghton-Mifflin, Boston.

Kogan N and Wallach MA (1964). Risk taking, A study in cognition and personality. Holt, Rinehart, and Winston, New York.

Kouradi J (1999). Decisionmaking. Orion, London.

KPMG (1999). Unlocking shareholder value: the keys to success [Mergers and Acquisitions: Global Research Report 1999]. London. Accessed: 12 September 2002. www.kpmg.fi/attachment.asp?Section=176&Item=352.

Krebs JR and Davies NB (1984). Behavioural Ecology. Blackwell, Oxford.

Kuhberger A (1988) The influence of framing on risky decisions: A meta-analysis. Organizational Behavior and Human Decision Processes 75: 23-55.

Kühberger A (1988) The influence of framing on risky decisions: A meta-analysis. Organizational Behavior and Human Decision Processes 75: 23-55.

Kuhn TS (1970, 2nd edition). The Structure of Scientific Revolutions. University of Chicago Press, Chicago.

Laibson DI and Zeckhauser R (1998) Amos Tversky and the Ascent of Behavioral Economics. Journal of Risk and Uncertainty 16: 7-47.

Langer EJ (1975) The Illusion of Control. Journal of Personality and Social Psychology 32: 311-328.

Laughhunn DJ, Payne JW and Crum RL (1980) Managerial Risk Preferences for Below-target Returns. Management Science 26: 1238-1249.

Lawrance EC (1991) Poverty and the rate of time preference: evidence from panel data. Journal of Political Economy 99: 54-77.

Lease RC, Lewellen WG and Schlarbaum GC (1974) The Individual Investor: Attributes and attitudes. The Journal of Finance 29: 413-433.

Lee K-H, Tse DK, Vertinsky I and Wehrung DA (1994). Responsible Business Behaviour: A comparison of managers' perceptions in the People's Republic of China, Hong Kong and Canada. Published in WM Hoffman, JB Kamm, RE Frederick and ESP Petry (ed). Emerging Global Business Ethics. Quorum Books, Westport CT.

Levenson H (1974) Activism and Powerful Others. Journal of Personality Assessment 38: 377-383.

Levinthal DA and March JG (1993) The myopia of learning. Strategic Management Journal 14: 95-112.

Levy H and Levy M (2002) Arrow-Pratt Risk Aversion, Risk Premium and Decision Weights. Journal of Risk and Uncertainty 25: 265-290.

Livingstone C (2002). Managing Risks in Innovation. "Living with Risk in Our Society" Conference, Sydney, Australian Academy of Technological Sciences and Engineering. NSW Division.

Lo AW (1999) The three Ps of total risk management. Financial Analysts Journal 55: 13-26.

Loewenstein GF and Adler D (1995) A Bias in the Prediction of Tastes. Economic Journal 105: 929-937.

Lopes LL (1984) Risk and Distributional Inequality. Journal of Experimental Psychology: Human Perception and Performance 10: 465-485.

Lopes LL (1987). Between Hope and Fear: The psychology of risk. Published in L Berkowitz (ed). Experimental Social Psychology. Academic Press, San Diego. 20.

Lopes LL (1994) Psychology and Economics: Perspectives on risk, cooperation and the marketplace. Annual Review of Psychology 45: 197-227.

Lovallo D and Kahneman D (2003) Delusions of Success: How optimism undermines executives' decisions. Harvard Business Review 81: 56-63.

MacCrimmon KR and Wehrung DA (1984) The Risk In-Basket. Journal of Business 57: 367-387.

MacCrimmon KR and Wehrung DA (1990) Characteristics of Risk Taking Executives. Management Science 36: 422-435.

Machina MJ (1987) Choice Under Uncertainty. Journal of Economic Perspectives 1: 121-154.

Machlup F (1978). Methodology of Economics and Other Social Sciences. Academic Press, New York.

Mackenzie BW (1981) Looking for the improbable needle in the haystack: The economics of base metal exploration in Canada. CIM Bulletin 74: 115-123.

Mackenzie BW and Doggett MD (1992). Economics of Mineral Exploration in Australia. Australian Mineral Foundation, Glenelg SA.

Maital S (1988). Applied Behavioral Economics. Wheatsheaf, New York.

Malli H, Kuhn-Nentwig L, Imboden H and Nentwig W (1999) Effects of Size, Motility and Paralysation Time of Prey on the Quantity of Venom Injected by the Hunting Spider *Cupiennius Salei*. The Journal of Experimental Biology 202: 2083-2089.

Malthus TR (1798, reprinted 1973). An essay on the principle of population. J M Dent, London.

Mano H (1990). Anticipated Deadline Penalties: Effects on goal levels and task performance. Published in RM Hogarth (ed). Insights in Decision Making. The University of Chicago Press, Chicago.

March JG and Shapira Z (1987) Managerial Perspectives on Risk and Risk Taking. Management Science 33: 1404-1418.

March JG and Shapira Z (1992) Variable risk preferences and the focus of attention. Psychological Review 99: 172-183.

Markowitz HM (1952) The Utility of Wealth. Journal of Political Economy 60: 151-6.

Marsh B and Kacelnik A (2002) Framing effects and risky decisions in starlings. Proceedings of the National Academy of Sciences 99: 3352-3355.

Maslow AH (1954). Motivation and personality. Harper, New York.

Mayo E (1933). The human problems of an industrial civilization. Macmillan, New York.

McCarthy MP and Flynn TP (2004). Risk from the CEO and Board Perspective. McGraw-Hill, New York.

McClelland DC (1961). The Achieving Society. The Free Press, New York.

McDermott R (2002) Experimental Methods in Political Science. Annual Review of Political Science 5: 31-61.

McFadden D (1999) Rationality for Economists? Journal of Risk and Uncertainty 19: 73-105.

McGlothin WH (1956) Stability of Choices among Uncertain Alternatives. American Journal of Psychology 69: 604-615.

McNamara G and Bromiley P (1997) Decision Making in an Organizational Setting: Cognitive and organizational influences on risk assessment in commercial lending. Academy of Management Journal 40: 1063-1088.

Mehra R and Prescott EC (1985) The Equity Premium: A Puzzle. Journal of Monetary Economics 15: 145-161.

Meso P, Troutt M and Rudnicka J (2002) A Review of Naturalistic Decision Making Research with Some Implications for Knowledge Management. Journal of Knowledge Management 6: 63-73.

Metzger RS (1985) Biases in betting: an application of laboratory findings. Psychological Reports 56: 883-888.

Miller GA (1956) The Magical Number Seven. Psychological Review 63: 81-97.

Miller KD and Bromiley P (1990) Strategic Risk and Corporate Performance. Academy of Management Journal 33: 756-779.

Miller KD and Reuer JJ (1996) Measuring organizational downside risk. Strategic Management Journal 17: 671-691.

Miller SM, Liu GB, Ngo TT, Hooper G, Riek S, Carson RG and Pettigrew JD (2000) Interhemispheric switching mediates perceptual rivalry. Current Biology 10: 383-392.

Monk P (2003). War and the Lying Machine. Australian Financial Review. Sydney. 14 February 2003. 1-9.

Morris R (2001). 2000 Operating Trends and Finding Cost Study. Salomon-SmithBarney, New York.

Morrison RS and Ordeshook P (1975) Rational Choice, Light Guessing and the Gambler's Fallacy. Public Choice 22: 79-89.

Mullainathan S and Thaler RH (2000). Behavioural Economics. 7948. National Bureau of Economic Research, Cambridge, MA.

Mullins JW, Forlani D and Walker OC (1999) Effects of organizational and decision-maker factors on new product risk taking. Journal of Product Innovation Management 16: 282-294.

Munier BR (1988). A Guide to Decision-making Under Uncertainty. Published in BR Munier (ed). Risk, Decision and Rationality. D. Reidel Publishing Co, Dordrecht.

Neilson W and Stowe J (2002) A Further Examination of Cumulative Prospect Theory Parameterizations. The Journal of Risk and Uncertainty 24: 31-46.

Nelson R and Winter S (1982). An Evolutionary Theory of Economic Change. Cambridge University Press, Cambridge.

Nickel MN and Rodriguez MC (2002) A Review of Research on the Negative Accounting Relationship Between Risk and Return: Bowman's Paradox. Omega 30: 1-18.

Nutt PC (1999) Surprising but True: Half the decisions in organizations fail. Academy of Management Executive 13: 75-90.

Odean T (1998) Are Investors Reluctant to Realize Their Losses? The Journal of Finance 53: 1775-1798.

Ohmae K (1990). The Borderless World. William Collins, London.

Oldman D (1974) Chance and Skill: A study of roulette. Journal of the British Sociological Association 8: 407-426.

Osborn RN and Jackson DH (1988) Leaders, riverboat gamblers, or purposeful unintended consequences in the management of complex, dangerous technologies. Academy of Management Journal 31: 924-948.

Ozzens JG (1942). The Just and the Unjust. HBJ, New York.

Pablo AL (1994) Determinants of Acquisition Integration Level. A decision making perspective. Academy of Management Journal 37: 803-836.

Pablo AL, Sitkin SB and Jemison DB (1996) Acquisition decision-making processes: the central role of risk. Journal of Management 22: 723-746.

Palmer T and Wiseman RM (1999) Decoupling risk taking from income stream uncertainty: A holistic approach. Strategic Management Journal 20: 1037-1062.

Pålsson A-M (1996) Does the degree of relative risk aversion vary with household characteristics? Journal of Economic Psychology 17: 771-787.

Park SH and Ungson GR (1997) The Effect of National Culture, Organizational Complementarity and Economic Motivation on Joint Venture Dissolution. Academy of Management Journal 40: 279-307.

Parsons AG (2001) The Association Between Daily Weather and Daily Shopping Patterns. Australasian Marketing Journal 9: 78-84.

Payne JW, Laughhunn DJ and Crum R (1980) Translation of gambles and aspiration level effects in risky choice behaviour. Management Science 26: 1039-1060.

Payne JW, Laughhunn DJ and Crum R (1984) Multiattribute Risky Choice Behavior: The editing of complex prospects. Management Science 30: 1350-1361.

Peirson G, Brown R, Easton S and Howard P (2002). Business Finance (8th Edition). McGraw-Hill Irwin, Sydney.

Pennings JME (2002) Pulling the trigger or not: Factors affecting behavior of initiating a position in derivatives markets. Journal of Economic Psychology 23: 263-278.

Perez SM and Waddington KD (1996) Carpenter Bee Risk Indifference and Review of Nectarivore Risk-Sensitivity Studies. American Zoologist 36: 435-446.

Perlow LA, Okhuysen GA and Repenning NP (2002) The Speed Trap: Exploring the relationship between decisionmaking and temporal context. Academy of Management Journal 45: 931-955.

Pesaran MH (1990) An Econometric Analysis of Exploration and Extraction of Oil in the U.K. Continental Shelf. Economic Journal 100: 367-390.

Pickering D (1999). The Cassell Dictionary of Folklore. Cassell, London.

Pietras CJ and Hackenberg TD (2001) Risk-Sensitive Choice in Humans as a Function of an Earnings Budget. Journal of the Experimental Analysis of Behaviour 76: 1-19.

Pilcher J (1984) The cocaine trial: could he be acquitted? People Weekly 21: 103-105.

Porter ME (1980). Competitive Strategy: Techniques for analysing industries and competitors. Free Press, New York.

Porter ME (1985). Competitive Advantage. Free Press, New York.

Potters J and van Winden F (2000) Professionals and Students in a Lobbying Experiment: Professional rules of conduct and subject surrogacy. Journal of Economic Behavior and Organization 43: 499-522.

Potters J and Wit J (1995). Bets and bids: favorite-longshot bias and winner's curse. Amsterdam.

Pratt JW (1964) Risk Aversion in the Small and the Large. Econometrica 32: 122-135.

Preston MG and Baratta P (1948) The auction value of an uncertain outcome. American Journal of Psychology 41: 183-193.

Qualls WJ and Puto CP (1989) Organizational Climate and Decision Framing. Journal of Marketing Research 26: 179-192.

Quandt RE (1986) Betting and Equilibrium. Quarterly Journal of Economics 49: 201-207.

Quiggin J (1982) A Theory of Anticipated Utility. Journal of Economic Behaviour and Organization 3: 323-343.

Rabin M (1996). Psychology and Economics. Accessed: 4 May 2003. http://elsa.berkeley.edu/~rabin/peboth7.pdf.

Rabin M (1998) Psychology and Economics. Journal of Economic Literature 36: 11-46.

Rabin M and Schrag JL (1999) First Impressions matter: A model of confirmatory bias. Quarterly Journal of Economics 114: 37-82.

Raiffa H (1961) Risk, Ambiguity and the Savage Axioms: Comment. The Quarterly Journal of Economics 75: 690-694.

Raiffa H (1968). Decision Analysis - Introductory lectures on choices under uncertainty. Addison-Wesley, Reading MA.

Rau PR and Vermaelen T (1998) Glamour, Value and the Post-Acquisition Performance of Acquiring Firms. Journal of Financial Economics 49: 223-253.

Real L (1991) Animal choice behaviour and the evolution of cognitive architecture. Science 253: 980-986.

Reuer JJ and Leiblein MJ (2000) Downside Risk Implications of Multinationality and International Joint Ventures. Academy of Management Journal 43: 203-214.

Robinson JP and Shaver PR (1973). Measures of Social Psychological Attitudes. Institute for Social Research, Ann Arbor.

Robinson JP, Shaver PR and Wrightsman L (1991). Measures of personality and social psychological attitudes. Academic Press, San Diego.

Rohrmann B (1997). Risk Orientation Questionnaire: Attitudes towards risk decisions. University of Melbourne, Melbourne.

Rohrmann B (1999). Risk Perception Research - review and documentation. Accessed: 6 May 2003. www.fz-juelich.de/mut/hefte/heft_69.pdf.

Roll R (1986) The Hubris Hypothesis of Corporate Takeovers. Journal of Business 59: 197-216.

Roth AE, Prasnikar MO-F and Zamir S (1991) Bargaining and market behaviour in Jerusalem, Ljubijana, Pittsburgh and Tokyo. American Economic Review 81: 1068-1095.

Rothman M (2000) Personality Differences among Managers from Different Ethnic Groups in the United States. International Journal of Management 17: 379-385.

Ruefli TW, Collins JM and Lacugna JR (1999) Risk Measures in Strategic Management Research: Auld lang syne? Strategic Management Journal 20: 167-194.

Rumelt RP (1991) How Much Does Industry Matter? Strategic Management Journal 12: 167-185.

Sackett DL and Torrance GW (1978) The utility of different health states as perceived by the general public. Journal of Chronic Diseases 31: 697-704.

Sagristano MD, Trope Y and Liberman N (2002) Time-Dependent Gambling: Odds now, money later. Journal of Experimental Psychology 131: 364-371.

Samson DA (1987) Corporate risk philosophy for improved risk management. Journal of Business Research 15: 107-122.

Samson DA (1988). Managerial decision analysis. Irwin, Homewood, IL.

Sarin RK and Weber M (1993) Risk-Value Models. European Journal of Operational Research 70: 135-149.

Schneider SL and Lopes LL (1986) Reflection in Preferences Under Risk: Who and when may suggest why. Journal of Experimental Psychology: Human Perception and Performance 12: 535-548.

Schnytzer A, Shilony Y and Thorne R (2002). On the marginal impact of information and arbitrage. Published in L Vaughan Williams (ed). The Economics of Gambling. Routledge, London.

Schoemaker PJH (1982) The Expected Utility Model: its variants, purposes, evidence and limitations. Journal of Economic Literature 20: 529-559.

Schoemaker PJH (1993) Determinants of Risk-Taking: Behavioral and economic views. Journal of Risk and Uncertainty 6: 49-73.

Schoemaker PJH and Kunreuther HC (1979) An Experimental Study of Insurance Decisions. The Journal of Risk and Uncertainty 46: 603-618.

Schubert R, Brown M, Gysler M and Brachinger HW (1999) Financial Decision-making: Are women really more risk-averse? American Economic Review 89: 381-385.

Schumpeter JA (1939). Business cycles: a theoretical, historical, and statistical analysis of the capitalist process. McGraw-Hill, New York.

Shapira Z and Venezia I (2001) Patterns of behavior of professionally managed and independent investors. Journal of Banking and Finance 25: 1573-1587.

Simon HA (1955) A behavioural model of rational choice. Quarterly Journal of Economics 69: 99-118.

Simon HA (1959) Theories of decision-making in economics and behavioural science. American Economic Review 49: 253-283.

Simons K (1996) Value at risk: new approaches to risk management. New England Economic Review 2: 3-13.

Simons R (1999) How Risky is Your Company? Harvard Business Review 77: 85-94.

Simpson J, Ed. (2000). Dictionary of English Folklore. Oxford University Press, Oxford.

Singh JV (1986) Performance, Slack, and Risk taking in Organisational Decision Making. Academy of Management Journal 29: 526-585.

Sitkin SB and Pablo AL (1992) Reconceptualising the Determinants of Risk Behaviour. Academy of Management Review 17: 9-38.

Sitkin SB and Weingart LR (1995) Determinants of risky decisionmaking behavior. Academy of Management Journal 38: 1573-1592.

Skaperdas S and Gan L (1995) Risk Aversion in Contests. Economic Journal 105: 951-962.

Slattery JP and Ganster DC (2002) Determinants of risk taking in a dynamic uncertain context. Journal of Management 28: 89-106.

Slovic P (2000). The Perception of Risk. Earthscan Publications, London.

Smallwood PD (1996) An Introduction to Risk Sensitivity. American Zoologist 36: 392-401.

Smallwood PD and Carter RV (1996) Risk Sensitivity in Behavioural Ecology. American Zoologist 36: 389-391.

Smee A and Brennan M (2000). Electronic Surveys: A Comparison of E-mail, Web and Mail. ANZMAC 2000 Visionary Marketing for the 21 st Century: Facing the Challenge, Gold Coast.

Smith A (1776, reprinted 1937). The Wealth of Nations. The Modern Library, New York.

Smith SL and Friedland DS (1998) The Influence of Education and Personality on Risk Propensity in Nurse Managers. Journal of Nursing Administration 28: 22-27.

Soros G (1994). The Theory of Reflexivity. Speech to the MIT Department of Economics World Economy Laboratory Conference, Washington DC. Accessed: 12 November 2003. www.soros.org/textfiles/speeches

Spetzler CS (1968) The Development of a Corporate Risk Policy for Capital Investment Decisions. IEEE Transactions on Systems Science and Cybernetics SSC-4: 667-688.

Sprent P (1988). Taking Risks: The science of uncertainty. Penguin, London.

Stanton ML, Roy BA and Thiede DA (2000) Evolution in Stressful Environments. Evolution 54: 93-111.

Starbuck WH and Milliken FJ (1988) Challenger: Fine-tuning the odds until something breaks. Journal of Management Studies 25: 319-339.

Starmer C (2000) Developments in non-expected utility theory: the hunt for a descriptive theory of choice under risk. Journal of Economic Literature 38: 332-382.

Staw BM, Sandelands LE and Dutton JE (1981) Threat-rigidity effects in organizational behavior: A multi-level analysis. Administrative Science Quarterly 26: 378-397.

Stephens DW (1981) The logic of risk-sensitive foraging preferences. Animal Behaviour 29: 628-9.

Stoner JAF (1968) Risky and Cautious Shifts in Group Decisions: The influence of widely held values. Journal of Experimental Social Psychology 4: 442-459.

Studdert J (2004). Under the influence of a sober workplace. The Australian. Sydney. 8 March 2004. 7.

Sullivan A (1999). London Fog. The New Republic. 14 June 1999

Sunstein CR (2003). Moral Heuristics. Chicago. Accessed: 22 February 2004. www.law.uchicago.edu/Lawecon/WkngPprs_176-200/180.crs.moral.pdf.

Svenson O (1981) Are we all less risky and more skillful than our fellow drivers? Acta Psychologica 47: 143-148.

Svenson O (1996) Decision-making and the search for fundamental psychological regularities. Organisational Behavior and Human Decision Processes 65: 252-267.

Sykes T (1994). The Bold Riders: Behind Australia's corporate collapses. Allen & Unwin, Sydney.

Taylor FW (1967). The principles of scientific management. Norton, New York.

Terrell D (1997). Biases in Assessments of probabilities: Evidence from greyhound races. Accessed: 8 November 2002. http://citeseer.nj.nec.com

Thaler R (1985) Mental Accounting and Consumer Choice. Marketing Science 4: 199-214.

Thaler RH and Johnson EV (1990) Gambling with the house money and trying to break even: The effects of prior outcomes on risky choice. Management Science 36: 643-660.

Thaler RH and Ziemba WT (1988) Parimutuel Betting Markets: Racetracks and Lotteries. Journal of Economic Perspectives 2: 161-174.

The Standish Group (1995).Chaos. Accessed: 6 July 2002. www.scs.carleton.ca.

The Thomson Corporation (2003). Australian M&A Hits a Snag. The Thomson Corporation Hong Kong Limited, Sydney.

Treadwell J and Lenert LA (1999) Health Values and Prospect Theory. Medical Decision Making 19: 344-352.

Trimpop RM (1994). The Psychology of Risk Taking Behavior. Elsevier Science, Amsterdam.

Tsevat J, Cook EF, Green ML, Matchar DB, Dawson NV, Broste SK, Wu AW, Phillips RS, Oye RK and Goldman L (1995) Health Values of the Seriously Ill. Annals of Internal Medicine 122: 514-520.

Tversky A and Fox C (1994) Weighting Risk and Uncertainty. Psychological Review 102: 269-283.

Tversky A and Kahneman D (1971) Belief in the law of small numbers. Psychological Bulletin 76: 105-110.

Tversky A and Kahneman D (1992) Advances in Prospect Theory. Journal of Risk and Uncertainty 5: 297-323.

Tversky A and Simonson I (1993) Context dependent preferences. Management Science 39: 1179-1189.

Tversky A, Slovic P and Kahneman D (1990) Causes of Preference Reversals. American Economic Review 80: 204-217.

Tversky A and Wakker PP (1995) Risk Attitudes and Decision Weights. Econometrica 63: 1255-1280.

Twain M (1894, reprinted 1996). The Tragedy of Pudd'nhead Wilson. Oxford University Press, New York.

Vauclair J (1996). Animal Cognition. Harvard University Press, Cambridge MA.

Vaughan Williams L (1999) Information Efficiency in Betting Markets: A survey. Bulletin of Economic Research 51: 1-30.

Viscusi WK (2000) Corporate Risk Analysis: A reckless act? Stanford Law Review 52: 547-597.

Von Neuman J and Morgenstern O (1953). Theory of Games and Economic Behavior. Princeton University Press, Princeton.

Waite TA (2001) Background context and decision making in hoarding gray jays. Behavioral Ecology 12: 318-324.

Walls DW and Busche K (2002). Broken Odds and the Favourite-Longshot Bias in Parimutuel Betting: A Direct Test. Accessed: 26 August 2002. pareto.ucalgary.ca/%7Ewdwalls/papers/brokenodds.pdf.

Walls MR and Dyer JS (1996) Risk Propensity and Firm Performance: A study of the petroleum exploration industry. Management Science 42: 1004-1021.

Walls MR, Morahan GT and Dyer JS (1995) Decision Analysis of Exploration Opportunities in the Onshore US at Phillips Petroleum Company. Interfaces 25: 39-56.

Wally S and Baum JR (1994) Personal and structural determinants of the pace of strategic decision making. Academy of Management Journal 37: 932-956.

Wang XT (2004) Self-framing of Risky Choice. Journal of Behavioral Decision Making 17: 1-16.

Watman K, Wilkening D, Arquilla J and Nichiporuk B (1995). US Regional Deterrence Strategies. RAND Corporation.

Way N and Thomson J (2003). The Myth of Governance. Business Review Weekly. 17 April 2003

Weber EU, Blais A-R and Betz N (2002) A Domain-specific Risk-attitude Scale: Measuring risk perceptions and risk behaviors. Journal of Behavioral Decision Making 15: 263-290.

Weber EU and Hsee CK (1998) Cross-cultural Differences in Risk Perception, but Cross-cultural Similarities in Attitudes Towards Perceived Risk. Management Science 44: 1205-1214.

Wehrung DA, Lee KH, Tse DK and Vertinsky IB (1989) Adjusting risky situations. Journal of Risk and Uncertainty 2: 189-212.

West D and Berthon P (1997) Antecedents of risk-taking behavior by advertisers: Empirical evidence and management implications. Journal of Advertising Research 37: 27-40.

Whiting R (1998) Development in Disarray. Software Magazine 18: 20.

Williams S and Narendran S (1999) Determinants of Managerial Risk: Exploring personality and cultural influences. The Journal of Social Psychology 139: 102-125.

Willman P, Fenton-O'Creevy M, Nicholson N and Soane E (2002) Traders, managers and loss aversion in investment banking: a field study. Accounting Organizations and Society 27: 85-98.

Wilson EO (1975). Sociobiology. Harvard University Press, Cambridge MA.

Winterhalder B and Smith EA (2000) Analyzing Adaptive Strategies: Human behavioural ecology at twenty-five. Evolutionary Anthropology 9: 51-72.

Yates JF (1990). Judgement and Decision Making. Prentice Hall, New Jersey.

Yogg MR (2003). Vita Paul Cabot. Harvard Magazine. January 2003 34-35.

Zackay D (1984) The influence of perceived event's controllability on its subjective occurrence probability. Psychological Record 34: 233-240.

Zaleskiewicz T (2001) Beyond Risk Seeking and Risk Aversion: personality and the dual nature of economic risk taking. European Journal of Personality 46: S105-S122.

Zuckerman M and Kuhlman DM (2000) Personality and Risk taking: Common biosocial factors. Journal of Personality 68: 999-1029

Index